History Education and the Construction of National Identities

A Volume in:
International Review of History Education

Series Editors:
Peter Lee
Rosalyn Ashby
Stuart J. Foster
University of London

International Review of History Education
Series Editors:
Peter Lee
Rosalyn Ashby
Stuart J. Foster
University of London

History Education and the Construction of National Identities

Edited by

Mario Carretero
Mikel Asensio
María Rodríguez-Moneo
Universidad Autónoma de Madrid

INFORMATION AGE PUBLISHING, INC.
Charlotte, NC • www.infoagepub.com

Library of Congress Cataloging-in-Publication Data

History education and the construction of national identities / edited by
Mario Carretero, Mikel Asensio, Marma Rodrmguez-Moneo.
   p. cm. – (International review of history education)
  Includes bibliographical references.
  ISBN 978-1-61735-935-4 (pbk.) – ISBN 978-1-61735-936-1 (hardcover) –
ISBN 978-1-61735-937-8 (ebook) 1. History–Study and teaching. 2.
Nationalism and historiography. 3. National characteristics. 4.
Historicism. I. Carretero, Mario. II. Asensio, Mikel. III. Rodrmguez Moneo,
Marma.
  D16.2.H56 2012
  907.1–dc23

                 2012023958

Printed in the United States of America

CONTENTS

v

SECTION 2

PURPOSES OF HISTORY EDUCATION

SECTION 3

STUDENTS IDEAS AND IDENTITIES

SECTION 4

MUSEUMS AND IDENTITIES

SECTION 5

COLLECTIVE MEMORIES AND
REPRESENTATIONS OF PAST AND FUTURE

SERIES INTRODUCTION

Peter Lee

This book is the third volume of the *International Review of History Education* to be published by Information Age (and the seventh volume since the inception of the series). The *International Review of History Education* is designed to allow the editors of particular volumes to address salient questions in history education. Volumes two and five were, like this one, constructed from papers given at major international conferences. Others, like volume six, comprised papers specially written round a common theme. As well as the research papers which tend to form the backbone of any coherent collection, however, where appropriate, volumes can accommodate brief reports of debates on changes in curriculum, teaching approaches, and the place of history education in different political and social environments. In this way, while each issue emphasizes a particular theme, the series will continue to offer considerable flexibility to editors, and help to keep an international audience informed about developments from around the globe.

This current volume focuses on questions concerning history education and the construction of identities. The authors approach history education in a wide range of ways, but it is not the task of a series editor's introduction to comment on contributions, so the best we can try to do is to tentatively raise one or two questions that might prove relevant to future discussion.

History Education and the Construction of National Identities, pages ix–xiv
Copyright © 2012 by Information Age Publishing

A central issue here is the tendency of history education to pursue national narratives of one kind or another. In practice these are often linked to educational goals that emphasize social cohesion and the construction of specific identities. But it is not clear that national narratives *have to be* designed to produce certain kinds of citizens with circumscribed or shared identities. If we imagine a history curriculum designed to operate at different scales, we might envisage (among an indefinite range of possibilities) one that offered students the opportunity to construct (i) a big-picture account of the human past, (ii) an intermediate scale narrative at the national level, and (iii) numerous depth studies nesting in these bigger scale accounts. None of these accounts would be fixed, or "given." The point of each higher resolution study—(i) and (ii)—would be to test and complicate the bigger picture at the next scale up, but the grander scale studies would make possible discussion of the historical significance of the depth studies. The "national" study would allow students to consider aspects of a particular society that seemed appropriate at that level (often because political institutions themselves worked at that level). *But none of this need entail that the aim would be to construct a political or even a civic identity of any particular kind,* and *a fortiori* not a "nationalistic" one.

The reason for this is that connections between the scales (and attendant content) chosen for a history curriculum, and the construction of particular identities, are ultimately provided by assumptions about the nature of history and the purposes such assumptions generate for history education. The big issues for history education always turn on the ideas we bring about what history is, and what counts as a history education. The prevalence of national histories and misguided pleas for canonical content (or their nemesis in local and "community" claims for rival stories) derive from a disjunction between conceptions of the nature of history and the social purposes of education, in which history gives way to other forms of historical consciousness. This is a simplification, of course, but it enables us to focus on the assumptions of political and civic agendas (by no means all "national") that wish to minimize connections between "academic" history and the collective memories held to be essential for social, political or religious security and coherence.

History as it exists is a hard-won achievement. It makes higher demands on validity and truth than "memory," not because its individual practitioners are superior to anyone else, but because it is a public form of knowledge. The "disciplines" that have slowly emerged in the past centuries in certain parts of the world are not monoliths, but more like communities with family resemblances and overlapping characteristics and values. Some, like natural science and mathematics, are more closely knit than others. But even these cannot be defined on the basis of some unitary "method." "Disciplines" tend to have their own conceptual apparatus, their own forms of representation and expression, and their own explanatory ideals, all embodied to some degree in institutions carrying forward what amount to metacognitive traditions. They are subject to change and fragmentation, and can split into hostile rival camps, but these (*pace* Kuhn) generally continue talking with (or at least to) one another.

This is not the place to give any proper account of "disciplines" (public forms of knowledge), but if we allow that it is appropriate even to admit their existence, we can comment on the relationships that might exist between history and other forms of historical consciousness. People are rightly cautious about any attempt to privilege one narrative of the past over another. It is a commonplace to point out the connections between claims on the past and power relations or hegemonic intent, and that one community's stories must have equal rights with those of another. "Memory" is portrayed as wider and somehow more profound and richer than the narrow workings of "academic" history. So indigenous peoples can assert their own versions not only of the past, but of their relationship with it, and hence what counts as knowledge.

The mistake here is not that people are wrong to tell their stories, or even to claim their special relationship with the past. The mistake is to think that such stories or claims all have to be treated as if they compete with *historical* stories within history as a public form of knowledge. Stories people "own" are not historical stories, because the metacognitive traditions that are built into history do not treat knowledge in that way. This does not mean that the stories history produces are "better" *tout court* than other forms of historical consciousness, but that they are based on the idea that there are standards of validity and relationships to evidence that *anyone* can work with. (Hence history must sometimes have to "face up" to "memories" it had hitherto found inconvenient: the traffic between history and other forms of historical consciousness is not just one way.) While some stories are quite properly constructed to create or protect identities, they are not *history* stories. They are none the worse for that: but they are different in nature (fit into different domains of discourse) and serve different functions from the stories at stake in history.

The relationship between "history" and "memory" is important for history education. If history is just another form of "memory," then what goes on in schools cannot be based on the "discipline," because it cannot be enough to induct students into a *historical* way of seeing the world. Again, it is not possible to chase this line of argument down here, so two linked points will have to suffice. History is a very peculiar form of memory. To see this, we might compare the place forgetting plays in memory (collective or personal) and in history. Forgetting is essential to memory: it allows us to make memories perform the multitude of functions they perform in our lives. We *need* to forget some things, and constantly talk of "forgetting and moving on." But there is no praise to be won in history for forgetting. Selection for any particular historical work involves ruling some things as relevant and others thereby irrelevant (as does answering any question whatsoever), but history is not the same as single stories, nor is it the property of any person or group, and what is marginal to one question is central to another. Indeed the shifts of explanatory ideals that are sometimes mistakenly used to deny the existence of a discipline of history are often driven precisely by the demand *not* to forget (whether it be a class, a gender, a people or a local community). The claim that history is just one among many forms of memory is a misleading half-truth.

This kind of mistake, coupled with the noble motive of shunning anything that privileges particular stories about the past, is sometimes accompanied by arguments that the purpose of history education cannot be "merely" a matter of handing on a public form of knowledge. The aim of teaching students about the past, on this view, must ultimately be to make them better in some other way — frequently as democrats, but sometimes as patriots, or members of a religious faith. Such claims tend to problematize history but fail to problematize democracy (or the other identities at stake). The "discipline" of history is held to be, at best, just another form of "memory." Democracy, on the other hand, is often taken as a given, and a narrowly political and temporally restricted one at that. This is an ahistorical move.

If teaching *history* is the goal, then we cannot promise that success will produce democrats, patriots, or anything else. If we teach history *as* history, we will be handing on cognitive ethics (respect for evidence, respect for persons as sources of arguments and so on) which are closely related to democratic values. But this does not mean that a study of history will ensure that students will believe that democracy (and especially any particular current version of representative liberal democracy) is the only, or even the best way in which societies should be organized. Were we to take seriously the claim that the overriding aim for history education is to produce liberal democrats, we would have to "fix" any version of the past that failed to deliver that goal. That would mean abandoning the commitment to history. We cannot simultaneously guarantee both the history and the liberal democratic commitment (even if, to the extent that history shares important values with democracy, we may be justified in *hoping* for both).

All this suggests that questions about history education and the construction of identities depend for their answers on conceptions of history. But they also depend on the kind of identity at stake. Like constructions of the past, identities in turn may be constructed to fit into different social relations and serve different functions. My identity as a citizen or member of an ethnic group may mean that I am patriotic or wish for social cohesion, but my identity as someone committed to a historical understanding of the past may mean that in some circumstances I am prepared to overrule or set aside certain consequences of my citizen identity. History is often (correctly) said to be multi-perspectival, but identities are complex and multi-stranded too, and there seems no reason to suppose that internal tensions between different strands is necessarily problematic for either individuals or societies—especially if the societies claim to be "open" and democratic. In any case, we need far more empirical work (and perhaps conceptual clarity) before we can be sure how far stories of the past determine identities, rather than the other way about.

Education undoubtedly plays a legitimate role in the construction of identities, and among them may be some that give students a sense of belonging, and others that carry the opportunities and obligations that go with being a citizen. For *history* education, however, the key goal must be to help students acquire whatever is deemed to be an active, usable, knowledge and understanding of history as a way of seeing the world. It is a cognitive enterprise, but it would be a mistake to imagine that this rules out affective components. Historical understanding requires "rational passions" like a concern for truth and respect for persons. Students who care nothing for the scope or power of an explanation, omit to ask if another account is equally valid, or are happy to ignore evidence, have simply not begun to grasp the discipline of history. Acquiring all this is acquiring a different *kind* of identity from those demanded of particular community members or citizens of particular states. It therefore remains an open question what the relationship between these identities should be in education, but it is at least arguable that they should not be confused, and perhaps that we should not expect them to be taught together. The knowledge that helps in the construction of what might be called a "historically literate" identity is not inert, and never fixed or given. It transforms how people can see themselves and their world in time, and joins them to a metacognitive tradition (itself in time and never fixed) that cares about intersubjective agreement and accountability. This is an identity unlikely to be acquired outside school, and hence ought to be a central part of education.

We can always plunder the past: it can be used in any way we wish. We may construct stories that we can use to justify oppression, maintain policies and traditions, redress wrongs or mend wounds, encourage revolutions and rebellions, and to do much else besides. Education can employ these stories in attempts to construct or undermine any identities whatsoever. But so long as history education remains normative and we compel children to learn about the past in schools, we had better take care that what we offer them has some claim to knowledge that goes beyond harnessing the past to suit immediate social and political ends — however noble they may be. We cannot imagine what social and political forms may exist in the future, because we cannot predict future knowledge, but it is difficult to imagine a future in which people would not *want* knowledge of the past. And if we admit that knowledge claims must meet criteria which go beyond their convenience for any particular society, we must anticipate that something like history will continue to exist: that is, a public form of knowledge, not the property of any individual, local region, ethnic group, gender, or religion. History may be flawed, its practitioners divided and its explanatory ideals always up for grabs. But it is something different from memory and other forms of historical consciousness because it seeks knowledge of the past that constrains what we can assert, however inconvenient or unpalatable such knowledge may be. Stories produced by history are not designed to do the same job as community or national or sectarian stories. We cannot tell what identities our children will need in the future, but we can be sure they will want knowledge of the past that goes beyond special pleading or private ownership, and it would be odd to deny them the opportunity to acquire the kind of identity that encompasses subscription to historical understanding.

ACKNOWLEDGEMENTS

This book collects the papers presented at the International Seminar "Understanding history and the construction of identities in a global world: Denationalizing history teaching?" held from the 28th until the 30th of October 2010 at las Navas de Marqués, organized by the Universidad Autónoma de Madrid, Spain and funded by this University and by the Action SEJ2007-30887-E, from the Ministry of Education. Minor funding was provided by Department of Basic Psychology, the Faculty of Psychology, the IUCE of the mentioned university and also by FLACSO (Argentina).

The Seminar was related to the Project EDU2010-17725, funded by the Ministry of Education of Spain, about *History teaching and nation conceptions in Spanish and Latin American students*, coordinated by the first author. Both projects supported greatly the work of Chapter 1, 10, 11, and 23.

The organization of the Seminar was possible mainly to the careful and devoted work of Cesar López, Ph.D. assistant researcher on the mentioned project, who made a wonderful contribution to this activity since the very first day.

The Seminar took place at Palacio de Magalia (http://magalia.mcu.es), a Renaissance building administered by the Ministry of Culture, Spain. For certain, its magnificent and highly functional facilities provided a very in-spiring milieu for such an activity.

Concerning the preparation and editing of the book, Floor van Alphen, also Ph.D. assistant researcher on the mentioned project, made a very valu-able contribution working with the different versions of the chapters and taking care of numerous editing details.

For the preparation of this book the first editor received the FSI-Bliss Carnochan Fellowship of the Stanford Humanities Centre from December 2011 to March, 2012, where his work at this endeavor was greatly facilitated.

We would like to thank very much all the mentioned institutions and specific persons for their contribution to both the Seminar and the book.

Mario Carretero, Mikel Asensio and Maria Rodríguez-Moneo
Buenos Aires—Madrid, February 23rd 2012

CHAPTER 1

HISTORY EDUCATION AND THE CONSTRUCTION OF A NATIONAL IDENTITY

Mario Carretero, Maria Rodríguez-Moneo, and Mikel Asensio

HISTORY EDUCATION AND NATIONAL IDENTITY

The past decades have witnessed a profound controversy regarding the function of history teaching in educational systems and its contribution to civic education (Foster & Crawford, 2006; Grever & Stuurman, 2007; Nakou & Barca, 2010). Underlying this ongoing debate is the tension between two predominant theoretical perspectives that have influenced the organization of educational systems since the nineteenth century: the critical rationality of the enlightenment period and the emotionally based individualism of romanticism (Carretero, 2011; Carretero & Bermudez, 2012). Currently, despite transformations in school curricula and historical content in many countries, the teaching of history is still intimately related to the construction of individual identity and the transmission of collective memory.

Citizens of today's societies have experienced dramatic worldwide structural changes over the last decades, including the collapse of the former So-

History Education and the Construction of National Identities, pages 1–14
Copyright © 2012 by Information Age Publishing

1

viet Union, increased globalization, the rise of new world powers, and the widespread use of new digital tools for communication and knowledge creation. In this context, what has been termed the "collapse of great stories" has revealed the relevance of individual historical identities, new nationalisms, and the emergence of historical accounts that oppose the official narratives of the nation-state. In different cultures and societies, new identities have emerged seeking a historical basis for their claims.

Communities have adapted in different ways to the challenges raised by a globalization process that constantly creates cultural, social, economic, and political connections between various geographic areas throughout the world.

From this perspective, identifying the purpose of history education revives the tension between the enlightenment and romantic objectives and the issue of whether history teaching should produce educated citizens of the world or patriotic nationalists (Carretero & Kriger, 2011). This important question requires further research into the cognitive as well as educational, cultural, and historiographical aspects of the teaching of history. A multifaceted approach is essential for identifying the conditions needed to develop more critical, empathetic, and dynamic history education that both addresses the construction of the "self" and "we" in historical terms and analyzes diverse perspectives to transform the approach that *externalizes* the "other" to a view that *includes* the "other".

The philosopher Edgar Morin claimed that "the teaching of history is indispensable for the establishment of national identity" (Morin, 2000), and this claim may extend more generally to cultural identities. Research in cultural psychology (Wertsch, 2002) has noted that the teaching of history provides a basis for identity formation because it establishes a framework for social and cultural concepts. In the past, official school programs in many countries presented historical content that was explicitly intended to create a specific national or cultural identity. Researchers currently investigating the teaching of social sciences and history may not always appreciate this aspect of historical content because today its presence is often more implicit. The historical content that is closely linked to the construction of a national identity tends to positively value the predominant social group, to explain the features of the national identity in essentialist rather than historical terms, to reject sources that conflict with a socially acceptable account of events, to positively assess political developments in the country, to uncritically employ certain emblematic historical figures (often based on a "heroes and villains" dichotomy), and to create continuity and permanent links between the facts and characters of the past and the present circumstances of the national group. In addition, as discussed in this book, the relationship between history education and the construction of a national identity is not only mediated by the cognitive aspects of historical content but is also strongly based on its affective and emotional features. For example, the patriotic rituals of many countries demonstrate the importance of an emotional understanding of history (Carretero, 2011). The study of history education in schools provides a great deal of information regarding identity formation in contemporary societies.

We propose that the historical framework provided by this "return to the past" in contemporary societies reveals the importance of the historical content presented in the classroom. Changes in political and cultural systems have occurred over the past few decades, which have made future prospects uncertain and have replaced expectations of progress with fear of the future. Rather than adopting classical modernism, which promises communities a future filled with continual progress, communities now look to the past for sources of identity that enable them to understand the present and envisage the immediate future. People delve into the past, seeking certainties that the future does not offer. Fundamentalists look to the religious past, new nationalists look to the community's past, and societies that have suffered traumatic experiences look to the recent past. In general, these are mythicized pasts, which communities regard as stable bulwarks against a present that threatens fundamental values. As we will see, this understanding of the past is based on the conditions of a particular historical present as well as the expectations and conjectures that represent a society's vision of the future.

The reappropriation of a shared past does not occur without conflict—quite the contrary. Disagreements over specific historical content have led to "cultural wars" over the teaching of history in schools (Carretero, 2011; Taylor & Guyver, 2011; Zimmerman, 2005). Despite prophets of doom proclaiming the "end of history"—which triumphant capitalism has interpreted as the "end of ideologies"—conflicts regarding the management of the past in history education have arisen in different countries. This subject has sparked discussions that have extended beyond the educational sphere into the realms of politics and public opinion, because when discussing which past should be taught and how the task should be undertaken, what is at stake is nothing less than the values and identity of a community. Similarly, the inevitable tension that results is due to the nature of social life. The interweaving of various historical narratives abruptly transforms *common* history into *controversial* history. A discussion and analysis of the relationship between history in the classroom and the construction of cultural identity—particularly national identity—are also presented in this book.

PRODUCING PATRIOTIC NATIONALISTS OR EDUCATED CITIZENS OF THE WORLD? THEORETICAL ISSUES

The teaching of history plays an important role in constructing national identity. However, as Carretero, Lopez, & Rodríguez-Moneo note in this volume, there are various approaches to this topic. We can identify at least three perspectives with regard to the role of history in constructing national identity. The "romantic approach" of the mid-nineteenth century promotes national identity and social cohesion within a world that is organized into nation-states (Barton, 2001). In contrast, the "empirical approach" developed in the 1970s views the teaching of history as the transmission of historical knowledge (Lee, 2005). Finally, the recent "civic approach" focuses on the role of history in developing students' civic competence. Despite the emergence of new models, the traditional romantic view is still prevalent in history education.

The first section of this volume addresses this issue. As Alberto Rosa notes in Chapter 5, this section discusses the traditional role of history education as well as possible alternatives. In Chapter 3, for instance, which describes an attempt to construct a common European identity, Stefan Berger identifies the tension that exists in history education between a nationalist approach that acknowledges the critical role of the nation-state in political, economic, cultural, and social development and a transnational approach that acknowledges the flaws and reductionism of a nationalist approach.

In Chapter 2 of the same section, Jonathan Hansen provides a theoretical explication of a new perspective that "denationalizes history" (Grever & Stuurman 2007; Symcox & Wilschut, 2009), which is essential in an increasingly globalized world. Although many authors adopt international and community perspectives, disagreement exists with regard to the meaning of the various concepts. Hansen's proposed taxonomy of cosmopolitanism delineates the novel concepts involved in the "denationalization of history".

The section ends with Stuart Foster's analysis of the explicitly nationalist nature and narrative style of history textbooks in Chapter 4. These two prominent features of history textbooks contribute to their use as propaganda that ideologically reinforces a particular national identity. Moreover, because this type of textbook encourages students to adopt an uncritical perspective, which hampers their understanding of the world in which they live, a new approach to history textbooks is required.

All of the studies in this section provide a perspective on history education that contrasts with a process of indoctrination in a particular national identity. However, in Chapter 5, Rosa notes that the teaching of history is closely linked to national identity because learning about the past enables us to understand who we are now. Rosa also argues that it is difficult to separate history from national identity due to the functionality of a shared identity for the general population.

SELECTING THE CONTENTS OF SCHOOL PROGRAMS

The above chapters primarily consider issues in history education from a theoretical point of view. However, education is also a concrete process, which raises specific problems, such as the issues involved in deciding what content to teach in history classes and how to select the content of history programs. Resolving this issue requires an analysis of the existing content that considers both explicit and implicit meanings and appreciates how both types of meaning contribute to the construction of a national identity. As many studies have noted (e.g., Carretero, Jacott, & Lopez Manjon, 2002; Hammack, 2011), the textbooks and courses found in different countries frequently address a single theme in different and often contradictory ways.

These and related issues are discussed in the second section of this volume.

In Chapter 6, Maria Grever presents an analysis of the compatibility of the common history of a community and pluralistic history. Based on a study conducted in 12 secondary schools in the United Kingdom, France, and the Netherlands, she identifies the diverse identities found in the classroom and the meaning that history holds for students. Students appeared to favor a common history, despite the plurality of identities and histories that were present in a single classroom due to the presence of students from different countries and second-generation students with immigrant parents, among others. The students regarded history as knowledge that is shared with other people. These findings raise the possibility that students share a common history despite differences in their heritage and backgrounds because they reinterpret the past based on their common vision of the future. To achieve this goal in the practice of history education and to apply historical reasoning, certain skills must be acquired, which include the ability to identify cause and effect, the ability to distinguish between facts and opinions, and the ability to understand the differences between continuity and change, as well as the difference between the intentional and unintentional effects of people's actions. In addition, Grever argues that it is important to teach national history from the perspective of a nation that includes citizens from different backgrounds and to coordinate national history with both community and world history.

In Chapter 7, Keith Barton analyzes the contents of school history programs in the United States, Ireland, and New Zealand and identifies three approaches to history education and identity formation. The first approach considers history education as providing students with an identity that is deeply rooted in nationalist tenets. The second approach to history education incorporates students' ethnic, religious, and cultural identities. The third approach regards history education as being distinct from national identity. In this chapter, Barton also discusses the need to clarify the concept of identity.

In Chapter 8, Nicole Tutiaux-Guillon describes the paradoxical features of history education in France, particularly in regard to secondary education. For programs at the primary level, the main goal of history education is to construct a national identity, in contrast to the universalistic education provided at the secondary level, which defends civic values. This phenomenon is explained as an effect of the difficulty of adopting pluralistic educational practices that account for the considerable ethnic diversity present in French schools. In the everyday educational reality of the French classroom, promoting a shared and cohesive narrative is simpler than acknowledging that various previous cultures or identities adopt different perspectives and interpret the past in different ways. The author notes that although the latter approach is preferable, it is more difficult to implement.

Finally, in Chapter 9 of this section, Peter Seixas also raises the issue of the relation between history education and ethnic minorities and addresses the specific case of Canadian aboriginals. Although Canada has been regarded as a multinational state since the middle of the nineteenth century and the population of European immigrants in the society has been fully integrated into the narratives of the Canadian state, this has not been the case for Canadian aboriginals. Seixas analyzes this topic in terms of the requirements of a historical conscience (Seixas, 2004) and the discrepancy between indigenous ways of understanding the past and the understanding of the past in Western culture and Western historiography. His contribution is essential for appreciating the dynamics between appropriation and the resistance to official national narratives displayed by the narratives of minority ethnic groups, which are equally important in constructing a nation's identity. Moreover, as Lopez and Carretero note in Chapter 10, the issues described by Seixas with regard to Canada are similar to those faced by other countries such as the United States and Argentina (Carretero & Kriger, 2011), in which the history of indigenous groups has only recently been incorporated into school history programs in a limited way.

STUDENTS' HISTORICAL KNOWLEDGE

As noted above and further discussed in Section 2, the content of school history programs is important due to its influence on the historical representations that individuals acquire during their education. However, students do not learn everything that is taught in school. Several authors have highlighted this difference and have distinguished between the production and consumption of cultural symbols (Valsiner, Chapter 22 of this volume; Wertsch, 2002). The extensive and complex constructive process that links the creation of cultural symbols to their use requires detailed analyses of students' representations, which are not simply copies of the content presented at school. Section 3 of this book focuses on these issues. In Chapter 15, Alan Stoskopf discusses these concerns in detail and analyzes the contributions of other related sections.

In the context of everyday history, students form intuitive notions about history, which generally occurs before historical concepts are presented in the classroom. Intuitive ideas about history exhibit similarities and differences with intuitive notions in other fields (Carretero, Castorina, & Levinas, in press; Rodríguez-Moneo & Carretero, 2012). One similarity is functionality. Thus, intuitive ideas about historical contexts are functional because they are based on the need to explore and act on the past social environment. They are also functional because they often provide a practical way for an individual to relate to the past. Because many of these ideas are implicit and displayed in everyday actions, individuals tend to think that they are appropriate. Functionality also explains why these notions are resistant to change. Because these ideas seem to be appropriate and are typically supported by the social environment, people are reluctant to change them in favor of the more accurate historical information taught in school (Rodríguez-Moneo, Aparicio, & Carretero, 2012). In Chapter 11, for example, Carretero, Lopez, and Rodriguez-Moneo describe a study of university students that reveals that these students maintained an intuitive understanding of the concept of nationhood despite their history classes in school.

Two distinctive features of intuitive ideas in the domain of history are the way in which they are inculcated in an individual and the functionality that they provide due to an individual's need to belong to a group (Rodríguez-Moneo, & Carretero, 2012).

Regarding the way in which intuitive ideas are acquired, these historical concepts are typically generated through interactions with others, such as family, friends, and schoolmates. Other group members not only produce the need for a particular idea but also model it based on the rules of behavior, norms, and values of the group.

From the perspective of an individual's need to belong to a group, intuitive ideas satisfy two types of needs. From a cognitive standpoint, the individual's membership in a social group enables him or her to socially reference and organize or categorize the social environment into different types of groups. From a motivational and affective point of view, belonging to a group satisfies the needs for protection, security, and affiliation and provides a basis for further development.

Group membership is intimately connected with identity, and students who belong to a group progressively internalize the behavioral patterns, norms, and values that characterize the group. However, they also progressively internalize group biases that exhibit not only an understanding of the present but also an interpretation of the past that includes subjective and biased ideas.

Everyday history tends to consolidate the intuitive notions of the members of the community and, therefore, makes it more difficult to teach history in school. In Chapter 15 of this book, Stoskopf highlights the need for collaboration between researchers and educators to foster the teaching of history in a transnational world and suggests that the central issues discussed in six of the chapters in the present volume should be analyzed in terms of a transnational perspective. He also argues that it is necessary to identify educational tools that will improve history education and enable students to more rigorously and critically analyze the past and more accurately represent the future.

Section 3 of the text presents a number of studies that highlight the issues involved in the biased nature of present interpretations of the past, such as the study of the concept of the Spanish nation that Carretero, Lopez and Rodríguez-Moneo present in Chapter 11. Their study examined Spanish university students' conceptions of their own nation to determine whether these concepts continued to be traditional, romantic conceptions or whether the concepts changed as a result of school education.

In Chapter 12, Avishag Reisman and Sam Wineburg propose an educational intervention to enable students to develop the heuristic skills that historical experts employ when reading and interpreting texts, which would enable them to evaluate and reconcile the different perspectives that are presented and researched (Wineburg, 2001). Reisman and Wineburg note that these skills not only improve students' understanding of history but also provide a solid base for democratic participation because they enable students to become aware of their own historical subjectivity and to acquire a better understanding of other people.

In Chapter 13, Michelle Bellino and Robert Selman analyze the effects of emotion and ethical and moral reflection on historical reasoning and history education. The authors identify what is lost when adolescents are taught in strictly empirical terms without considering ethical and moral issues, which are naturally relevant to student development and provide an additional dimension to history education. They note that the inclusion of ethical and moral issues that are relevant to adolescents does not prevent history education from being empirical or accurate.

In Chapter 14, Angela Bermúdez discusses the few studies that have investigated the role of emotions and values in history education. She argues that research related to history education has primarily focused on analyzing the individual thinking skills involved in historical thinking and on the social production and consumption of historical narratives. Bermúdez believes that it is also necessary to analyze the effects of values and emotions on history education. This approach was adopted in a study she performed in which 120 students in the United States were assigned an emotionally charged case that involved value issues.

THE ROLE OF CULTURAL HERITAGE AND MUSEUMS IN HISTORY EDUCATION

In the complex process of constructing individuals' historical knowledge described above, schools are not the only influential socializing agent. Many publications have identified cultural heritage as a crucial factor in providing a framework for historical knowledge (Asensio, 2012), and Section 4 is devoted to this topic. Traditionally, national museums have always reflected history and provided a shared social reference (Knell et al., 2011). Most national history museums have adopted a traditional and romantic approach with an epistemological focus on classification and description (Caldera, Asensio, & Pol, 2010). In constructing historical knowledge, museums have benefited from material culture, which is often monumental and is generally a fundamental reference of most historical discourses and narratives. In recent years, national museums have presented historical knowledge in increasingly diverse ways. For example, spaces such as Colonial Williamsburg in Virginia provide a living history through personal experience; the "Haus der Geschichte" in Bonn presents a dual discourse that explicitly addresses the two Germanies. Exhibitions such as "Ibers" of the Fundació La Caixa have transformed how we view an entire culture and historical period. The new, more participatory museums also present ethical issues such as peace or democracy (Asensio & Pol, 2012). Museums and spaces that present a cultural heritage provide an interpretation of material culture that is based on informal learning, which contrasts with the formal learning provided in the classroom (Asensio, Asenjo, & Rodriguez, 2011).

The three chapters in Section 4 of this book discuss two central aspects of the relationship between museums and national identity in history education. On the one hand, museums—including the great national history museums—have considerably expanded and broadened their base to assume new roles and increasingly ambitious activities to transmit historical knowledge. On the other hand, new and participatory history museums combine civic and ethical narratives. These approaches address effective governance, which is based on universal human rights and focuses on values and the recognition of sociocultural diversity.

In Chapter 16, Marisa González de Oleaga discusses opposing national and civic narratives through an analysis of the messages conveyed by various Spanish and Latin-American museums.

In Chapter 17, Mikel Asensio and Elena Pol discuss the recent transformation in an approach that encourages visitor participation and narratives that incorporate local identities and the history of ideas. This chapter reviews the features of this new approach based on several recent history museum projects designed by this research team. The transformation of museums into environments that promote the development of historical knowledge is a task that already has a particular tradition (MacRaney & Russick, 2010). However, to make this experience effective, museums and cultural heritage must be modified to make it easier to understand, participate in, and reflect on historical knowledge. Museums, like text or audiovisual formats, are powerful weapons for revising history and creating mechanisms that manipulate collective memory. The challenge for societies is to precisely control the process of transmission to ensure that it is rigorous.

Finally, in Chapter 18, Veronica Boix Mansilla analyzes how museums link everyday history with academic history, illustrate the multiple functions of the messages transmitted by exhibitions, and document the many available mechanisms for eliciting visitors' attention, behavior, understanding, and emotion. As the design and ambiance of modern exhibitions become increasingly attractive, participative, and emotionally engaging, they can provide authentic experiences that convey historical knowledge more effectively.

COLLECTIVE MEMORY AND VISIONS OF THE PAST AND THE FUTURE

In addition to museums, monuments, and cultural heritage, there are other influences that decisively contribute to the construction of cultural and national identity, which are discussed in Section 5 of this book.

A shared cultural or national identity possesses considerable social and psychological functionality. From the social perspective, a cohesive group identity makes the group stronger and enhances its influence, which allows it to focus on obtaining political and economic advantages. Group membership, moreover, favors the sharing of a common perspective, which is generally based on identification with a particular nation-state (Barton, 2001). From the viewpoint of an individual, group membership confers certain cognitive and emotional benefits (Rodríguez-Moneo & Carretero, 2012). Therefore, it is no coincidence that a shared community identity strengthens the national identity.

A national identity is established through three types of history, as identified by Carretero (2011): history as an academic discipline, history taught in the classroom, and everyday history. Academic history, which consists of established empirical knowledge, sometimes exhibits biases that strengthen the national identity. The history taught in the classroom is historical knowledge that primarily tends to create a national identity, which often provides a biased interpretation of the past. Finally, everyday history or collective memory (Halbwachs, 1925), which consists of socially shared interpretations of the past, is a primary constituent of a community's identity because the past is frequently used to justify the present circumstances of a community or social group.

Section 5 of this volume consists of a series of studies that analyze collective memory and the process of constructing social representations that allow one to interpret the past and envisage the future. Van Alphen and Asensio comment on this section in Chapter 23.

In Chapter 19, Sabine Moller discusses a specific aspect of everyday history: the role of the family in interpreting the past. Although history can be constructed and influenced by various social agents, such as friends, school, or communication media, family memory plays a fundamental role in the interpretation of the past. This issue demands further research due to the critical role of generational transmission in the construction of collective memory.

In Chapter 20, Kyoko Murakami describes her work with veterans of World War II, which identified relationships between national history, collective memory, and people's individual experiences. She proposes that history is a dynamic process produced by the mutual interaction of national history and collective memory. In other words, national history produces a group's interpretation of the reality that was experienced, and in turn, the group interpretation produces the history of the nation.

As Orwell noted, the interpretation of the past interacts with the understanding of the present and future (Carretero & Solcoff, 2012). For this reason, investigating young people's ideas about the future is essential for understanding their knowledge of history. In Chapter 21 of this section, Helen Haste and Amy Hogan present data from a large-scale study of young people in Great Britain who were asked to describe their vision of the future. The results of this study illustrate how history education contributes to the construction of identity in a world where an individual's competence will be increasingly global.

Finally, in Chapter 22, Jaan Valsiner presents a theoretical analysis of the sociocultural processes that underlie not only the issues discussed in this section but many of the issues addressed in other sections of the book.

THE TRANSFORMATION OF HISTORICAL CONCEPTS AS A CHALLENGE FOR FUTURE EDUCATION

Everyday history tends to establish identity and strengthen the maintenance of individuals' intuitive conceptions of nationhood. These ideas develop in a day-to-day context and are consistent with other everyday representations. However, students acquire further historical information in the classroom when they attend school. As previously indicated, school history has the dual educational objectives of transmitting historical knowledge and creating a shared national identity (Carretero, 2011). Although these two objectives can be addressed simultaneously, one might dominate the other to the point that only one objective is effectively pursued. To understand the type of history education that students receive, the features of these two objectives must be analyzed (Rodríguez-Moneo & Carretero, 2012).

With regard to the objective of teaching history, the goal is to provide students with basic conceptual knowledge that will enable them to understand the relationships between past events and the connection of past events with the present and future.

Thus, to fulfill this objective, students must acquire knowledge that will enable them to distance themselves from their reference group and acquire a more critical understanding of the social, political, economic, and historical world. This "empirical objective" links classroom history to history as an academic discipline.

With regard to the objective of forming and consolidating a shared national or social identity, students are provided with information about the positive aspects of the group to which the students belong as well as the norms and values of the community. This "romantic objective" links classroom history to everyday history.

The empirical objective involves a process of conceptual change that restructures students' intuitive ideas, such as the evolution of the idea of a "nation" from a romantic ideal to a more empirically grounded concept (Lopez, Carretero, & Rodríguez-Moneo, 2012). However, the teaching of history may not foster conceptual change among students because they lack the skills needed to understand new historical content, because the instructor lacks expertise in the subject, because the students fail to grasp historical contents, or because of emotional factors.

However, the romantic, identity-producing objective of history education does not include the goal of restructuring the intuitive notions of history based on everyday history. Rather, this type of history education uses intuitive notions as the basis for constructing a shared identity. Students do not experience conceptual change because producing conceptual change is not a feature of this educational objective.

As we have noted here and in the other chapters of this volume, two changes in the past few years have profoundly affected the traditional teaching of history. On the one hand, global economic and political conditions have changed, and we no longer live in a world dominated by the individual interests of nation-states. The economic, political, and cultural union of countries has become established due to increasing globalization. A concomitant change has also occurred in the teaching of history. The students who study history can no longer be regarded as homogenous but often exhibit distinct national, ethnic, social, religious, and other identities. Nevertheless, the teaching of history does not appear to reflect these changes, and transnational and pluralist educational proposals have yet been fully adopted. History education still focuses on the nation-state. We hope that the research and analysis presented in this volume will provide an explanation for this state of affairs.

REFERENCES

Aparicio, J. J., & Rodríguez-Moneo, M. (2005). Constructivism, the so-called semantic learning theories, and situated cognition versus the psychological learning theories. *The Spanish Journal of Psychology, 8,* 180–198.

Asensio, M. (2012). Ruby Glass Boxes: How to develop a sciences and Arts wine museum. In S. Celestino & J. Blánquez (Eds.) *Vine and wine cultural heritage.* Almendralejo: Ayuntamiento de Almendralejo.

Asensio, M., Asenjo, E., & Rodríguez, M. (2011). El marco teórico del aprendizaje Informal [The theoretical framework for informal learning]. In M. Asensio & E. Asenjo (Eds.) *Lazos de Luz Azul. Museos y Tecnologías 1, 2 y 3.0 [Connections of blue light: Museums and technologies 1, 2, and 3.0]* (pp. 49–78). Barcelona: Editorial Universitat Oberta de Catalunya.

Asensio, M., & Pol, E. (2012). Nuevas tendencias en museología: Museos de Identidad y Museos de Mentalidad [New tendencies in museology: Museums of Identity and Museums of Mentality]. In J. Blánquez, S. Celestino, P. Bermedo & O. Sanfuentes (Eds.) *Patrimonio cultural y desarrollo sostenible en España y Chile. [Cultural patrimony and sustainable development in Spain and Chile].* Santiago de Chile: Universidad Católica de Chile.

Barton, K. C. (2001). A sociocultural perspective on children's understanding of historical change: Comparative findings from Northern Ireland & the United States. *American Educational Research Journal, 38,* 881–913.

Caldera, P., Asensio, M., & Pol, E. (2010). De los Museos de Identidad a los Museos de Mentalidad: bases teóricas de la recuperación de la memoria de los Modernos Museos de Extremadura. [From identity museums to mentality museums: theoretical bases for the recuperation of memory of the modern museums of Extremadura.] *Museo, Revista de la Asociación Profesional de Museológos de España (APME), 15,* 49–82.

Carretero, M. (2011). *Constructing patriotism. Teaching of history and historical memory in globalized world.* Charlotte, NC: Information Age Publishing.

Carretero, M. & Bermudez, A. (2012). Constructing histories. In J. Valsiner (Ed.), *Oxford handbook of culture and psychology* (pp. 625–646). Oxford: Oxford University Press.

Carretero, M., Castorina, J .A., & Levinas, L. (in press). Conceptual change of the historical knowledge about the nation. In S. Vosniadou (Ed.) *International handbook of research on conceptual change.* New York: Routledge.

Carretero, M., Jacott, L., & Lopez Manjon, A. (2002). Learning history through textbooks: are Mexican and Spanish students taught the same story? *Learning and Instruction, 12*(6), 651–665

Carretero, M., & Kriger, M. (2011). Historical representations and the conflicts about indigenous people as national identities. *Culture & Psychology, 17*(2), 177–195.

Carretero, M., & Solcoff, K. (2012). Past, present and future as metephor of memory. *Culture & Psychology, 18*(1), 14–22.

Carretero, M., & Voss, J.F. (Eds.) (1994). *Cognitive and instructional processes in History and the Social Science.* Hillsdale: LEA.

Foster, S. J., & Crawford, K. A. (Eds.) (2006). *What shall we tell the children? International perspectives on school history textbooks.* Greenwich, CT: Information Age Publishing.

Grever, M., & Stuurman, S. (Eds.) (2007). *Beyond the canon. History for the twenty–first century.* Basingstoke: Palgrave Macmillan.

Hammack, P. (2011). *Narrative and the politics of identity: The cultural psychology of Israeli and Palestinian youth.* New York: Oxford University Press.

Halbwachs, M. (1925). *Les Cadres Sociaux de la Mémoire.* París: Alcan. Edición París: Albin Michel, 1994. Collective memory.

Ibáñez, A., Asensio, M., Vivent, N., & Cuenca, J. M. (2012). Mobile devices: A tool for Tourism and Learning at archaeological sites. *International Journal of Web Based Communities (IJWBC), 8*(1), 57–72.

Knell, S. J., Aronsson, P., Amundsen, A. B., Barnes, A. J., Burch, S., Carter, J., Gosselin, V., Hughes, S.A., & Kirwan, A. (Eds.). (2011). *National Museums, new studies from around the world.* New York: Routledge.

Lee, P. (2005). Putting principles into practics: Understanding history. In M. S. Donovan & J. D. Bransford (Eds.), *How students learn: History, mathematics and sciences in the classroom.* Washington: National Academies Press.

Lopez, C., Carretero, M., & Rodríguez-Moneo, M. (2012). "In essence it is Spanish": College students' conceptions on their nation. In preparation.

McRainey, L., & Russick, J. (Eds.). (2010). *Connecting kids to history with museum exhibitions.* Walnut Creek, CA: Left Coast Press.

Morin, E. (2000). *Los siete saberes necesarios a la educación del futuro.* [The seven necessary lessons for education in the future.] Caracas: IESALC, FACES-UCV, CIPOST.

Nakou, I., & Barca, I. (Eds.). (2010). *Contemporary public debates over history education.* Charlotte NC: Information Age.

Rodríguez-Moneo, M., Aparicio, J. J., & Carretero, M. (2012). Conceptual change and the use of knowledge in different contexts. Manuscript in preparation.

Rodríguez-Moneo, M., & Carretero, M. (2012). Conceptual change in history. Piagetian influences and present approaches. In J.A. García Madruga, R. Kohen, C. Del Barrio, & I. Enesco y J. Linaza (Eds.) *Constructing minds. Essays in honor of Juan Delval.* Madrid: Editorial UNED.

Seixas, P. (2004). Introduction. In P. Seixas (Ed.). *Theorizing historical consciousness* (pp. 3–20). Toronto: University of Toronto Press.

Symcox, L,. & Wilschut, A. (Eds.). (2009). *National history standards: The problem of the canon and the future of teaching history.* Charlotte, NC: Information Age.

Taylor, T., & Guyver, R. (2011). *History Wars and the Classroom—Global Perspectives.* Charlotte, NC: Information Age Publishing.

Wertsch, J. (1998). *Minds as action.* New York: Oxford University Press

Wertsch, J. (2002). *Voices of collective remembering.* New York: Cambridge University Press.

Wineburg, S. (2001). *Historical thinking and other unnatural acts: Charting the future of teaching the past.* Philadelphia: Temple University Press.

Zimmerman, J. (2005). *Whose America?: Culture wars in the public schools.* Cambridge: Harvard University Press.

SECTION 1

THEORETICAL ISSUES

CHAPTER 2

DE-NATIONALIZE HISTORY AND WHAT HAVE WE DONE?

Ontology, Essentialism, and the Search for a Cosmopolitan Alternative

Jonathan M. Hansen

Ours is not the first generation of teachers and scholars to seek to transcend nationalist ontology and essentialism in historical textbooks and primary and secondary school education. In 1898, as Americans celebrated the United States' triumphant entry onto the global stage in the so-called "Spanish-American War," Jane Addams, the Chicago-based educator and social critic, cast about for an ideal of solidarity "strong enough to move masses of men out of their narrow national considerations and cautions into new reaches of human effort and affection." (1907, p. 236). Contact with young immigrant children in neighborhoods around Chicago made Addams impatient with the "abstract" and "institutionalized" patriotism taught in US public schools—so "remote from actual living." Among children, patriotic indoctrination spawned juvenile contests of one-upmanship;

History Education and the Construction of National Identities, pages 17–31
Copyright © 2012 by Information Age Publishing
All rights of reproduction in any form reserved.

among grownups, it promoted jingoism and inevitably led to war. Addams acknowledged that patriotism provided individuals a necessary "outlet for their beliefs," as well as a "sense of being in the sweep of the world's activities." But surely there were ways of meeting those needs more consistent with democracy and more in tune with the globalizing times (quoted in Hansen, 2003, pp. 154–5).

After years of searching Addams settled on an ideal she labeled "cosmic patriotism" (notwithstanding what she called the seeming "absurdity" of that). Combining a commitment to universal human rights with a passionate sense of belonging, the term captured Addams' conviction that in order to compete with nationalism for people's affection cosmopolitanism would have to be built on a local foundation. Internationalists could not ignore mankind's need for passionate engagement. Nor could they afford to give up on the heart. Addams would anchor cosmic patriotism in the social maelstrom of "the cosmopolitan city." In cities like her own Chicago, practicality overwhelmed Old-World jealousies, as neighbor reached out to neighbor to meet everyday problems. Mutual dependence, in turn, bred an irrepressible "power of association" at odds with "the old negative bonds of discipline and coercion" (Hansen, 2003, pp. 145–6). This dialectical clash between "tribal law" and "inter-tribal law" yielded a new synthesis, Addams claimed, "a higher moral line."(Hansen, 2003, p. 11).

Was Addams naïve in expecting peace to emanate from "the "quarrelsome mob" turned into the kindly citizens of the world through the pressure of the cosmopolitan neighborhood?" Addams harbored no illusions that peace was foremost in the minds of her urban neighbors. On the contrary, she conceded, if city folk clamored for anything, it was for war. But peace they unconsciously promoted by "attaining cosmopolitan relations through daily experience." No doubt her constituents would "believe for a long time that war is noble and necessary both to engender and cherish patriotism," Addams observed; "and yet all of the time, below their shouting, they are living in the kingdom of kindness. They are laying the simple and inevitable foundations for an international order." (Hansen, 2003, p. 11).

Addams' *international order* disintegrated amid the jingoistic frenzy unloosed by World War I. Over the course of the succeeding century her cosmopolitan ideal has been largely forgotten. But in an era when cosmopolitanism is back on the scholarly agenda, Addams' attempt to construct cosmic patriotism on the bedrock of local social and economic problem-solving offers a useful corrective to cosmopolitan projects that however elegant theoretically are often no less "abstract" and "institutionalized" than the patriotism Addams decried. Ontology and essentialism, the recent history of cosmopolitanism suggests, are not the province of nationalists alone. Can we describe a model of cosmopolitanism that does not fall prey to ontological and essentialist traps?

I think we can, one rooted in the early twentieth-century thought of American pragmatist thinkers Jane Addams, John Dewey, William James, and W. E. B. Du Bois, among others. Moving beyond what we have come to call identity politics, these thinkers came to see the world not in terms of identity, but in terms of problems—social, cultural, economic—that called on multi-various levels and degrees of solidarity for solution. They adumbrated what historian David Hollinger (2006) has called a "political economy of solidarity." To understand solidarity in terms of political economy is to ask how this precious commodity is distributed and fought over. To regard cosmopolitanism as a matter of the political economy of solidarity is to witness individuals struggling to reconcile real world, public and private, local, regional, national, and global commitments. To teach cosmopolitanism in this light means to pay close attention to context, to show individuals engaged across a range of solidarities that include, say, the nation state, while emphasizing that citizens of nation states is only part of whom we are.

My aim in this essay is to promote clarity about what we mean when we speak of "de-nationalizing history." Teachers and scholars who engage this challenge typically fall back on communitarian and cosmopolitan alternatives (though there is much disagreement about what these *terms* mean). Given this volume's interest in the construction of identities *in a global world* I will direct my attention to cosmopolitanism, providing both a brief taxonomy of cosmopolitanism and a case study of Jane Addams's attempt to transcend the ontology and essentialism that pervades much cosmopolitan thought. What is at stake in our campaign to de-nationalize history, what sort of cosmopolitanism do we envision, what are the primary impediments to bringing that vision about?

Historically, cosmopolitanism has unfolded along moral, legal, economic, political, and cultural lines.[1] Moral cosmopolitanism is thought to have originated in Cynic and Stoic thought dating back to the third and fourth centuries BCE. The cardinal tenet of moral cosmopolitanism is that human beings are worthy of equal treatment irrespective of the accidents of birth—race, gender, status, citizenship, etc. Accordingly, individuals have no justification for elevating the rights of members of particular political communities over the rights of strangers. As philosopher Martha Nussbaum has put it, moral cosmopolitans act not out of love for country or cultural group but out of commitment to Right. To pledge one's primary allegiance to one's nation or cultural group undermines "the values that hold a nation together, because it substitutes a colorful idol for the substantive values of justice and right"; to privilege one's national citizenship above one's membership in humanity is to define oneself "by a morally irrelevant characteristic." By

---

[1] For a useful taxonomy of cosmopolitanism and its critics, see "Cosmopolitanism," *Stanford Encyclopedia of Philosophy*, at http://plato.stanford.edu/entries/cosmopolitanism/.

contrast, to pledge allegiance to "what is morally good—and that which, being good, [we] can commend as such to all human beings," is to chip away at the artificial divisions that ignite conflict around the world (Nussbaum, 2002, pp. 6–10).

In order to promote this end, Nussbaum advances an ideal of "cosmopolitan education" designed to counter the emphasis on national education found in public school curricula throughout the world. Of course, schools will continue to give "special attention to the history and current situation of their own nation," she allows. But students should "learn a good deal more than is frequently the case about the rest of the world in which they live, about India and Bolivia," for instance, about "Nigeria and Norway and their histories, problems, and comparative successes." This is not a matter simply of making claims about Indians' equal human rights, Nussbaum cautions; students must learn "about the problems of hunger and pollution in India, and the implications of these problems for larger problems of global hunger and global ecology." Most important, students should be taught that they are members of a global community of human beings who just happen to be born in their native country.

I imagine that few readers would object to Nussbaum's call for in-depth study of other cultures and nations. But I don't think there is much to be gained—indeed, I think there's a lot to be lost—by Nussbaum's hierarchy of affiliations. Who's to say that we should affiliate *above all*—her emphasis—with this community rather than with that? To be fair, both Nussbaum and her classical predecessors acknowledge that individuals inhabit local communities as well as the globe. The Stoics, Nussbaum tells us, thought of affiliations in terms of a series of concentric circles: "the first one is drawn around the self; the next takes in one's immediate family; then follows the extended family," then neighbors, nation, world, and so on. The Roman thinker Seneca believed that individuals inhabit two communities—the community of their birth, and a universal community of human discourse and letters. Nussbaum maintains that it is morally arbitrary to expect individuals to value their nation over humankind. But is it any less arbitrary to insist that we value mankind over one or other of our concentric circles?

In appealing to Seneca's observation that humans comprise *two* kinds of communities—national and universal—Nussbaum inadvertently recapitulates one of the most troubling assumptions of the Westphalian nation-state paradigm, namely, the Manichean notion that human subjectivity can be reduced to *two* kinds of identity. Says who? How different is Seneca from the journalist who once asked writer Richard Wright. "Mr. Wright, are you a Negro or an American?" Not sure how to respond, Wright abandoned the United States for France, where he encountered slightly different but no less stifling assumptions about who individuals are.

It is hard to disentangle legal, economic, and political cosmopolitanism. Legal cosmopolitanism received its fullest early account in the work of Immanuel Kant, whose essay "Perpetual Peace," published in 1795, provided a blue print for the international legal order, including the idea of a league of nations. Like the Cynics and Stoics, Kant believed that human beings comprise a single moral community based on their rational capacity and governed by universal law. Kant also believed that individuals realize their human potential under republican governments ruled by civil laws that they themselves have authorized. Like individuals, individual republics could best promote their (citizens') interests by combining in a federation that would recognize both state sovereignty and individual rights. In this way, Kant's system combined civil rights with universal human rights—the rights of citizenship with the so-called rights of strangers. Kant's federation was more a realm of recognition of human universality than an instrument of enforcement. Kant hesitated to give the federation coercive powers lest it erode the sovereignty of individual republics, which he knew to be the sine qua non of liberty itself.

Kant's legal cosmopolitanism emerged in the context of—and hence is inseparable from—European commercial expansion. Still, one can differentiate Kant's emphasis on legal rights from Adam Smith's arguments on behalf of commercial freedom. Smith's thought also owed much to Stoic philosophy. Smith recognized no conflict between national citizenship and the global community of producers and merchants. Rightly conceived, state governments could promote their own and their citizens' interests at the same time that they contributed to humanity as a whole by ensuring the fair and efficient circulation of food and produce. With trade barriers down, different nations of the world would contribute to the market what each did best, providing their subjects the income necessary to purchase from abroad what could not be produced efficiently at home. Smith's market was reciprocal and elastic, ruled by the ancient *lex mercatoria* (merchant law), which had constrained commerce between East and West for centuries and which might be considered cosmopolitanism's first practical expression.

It is a long way from *lex mercatoria* to the contemporary world of global finance, commerce, and industry, with its lack of transparency, its migrating capital and labor, and its social and cultural upheaval. Some observers praise the economic and legal institutions sprung up around global capitalism for transforming human affiliations in a new cosmopolitan age.[2] Many others, however, follow Marx and Engels in regarding economic cosmopolitanism as merely an ideological reflection of capitalism blinding proponents to exploitation and alienation on a whole new scale. If the test of

---

[2] On Waldron and Habermas, see Garrett Wallace Brown, *Grounding Cosmopolitanism: From Kant to the Idea of a Cosmopolitan Constitution* (Edinburgh: Edinburgh University Press, 2009), pp. 204–5, 210–11.

cosmopolitanism is the accountability of global institutions to democratic governance and the rule of law, then the institutions of global capitalism don't look all that cosmopolitan.

Indeed, by almost any measure, legal institutions have not kept pace with the growing interdependence of richer and poorer nations. Witness the case of the United States and Mexico, for example, which neither together nor alone seem able to respond appropriately to the challenge of interdependence. If ever there were a need for transnational institutions, this would seem to be the time, and yet notice the United States falling back on increasingly nationalistic and atavistic responses to the unfolding economic and demographic crisis: it is building a thousand-mile fence.

The philosopher Anthony Appiah defines cosmopolitanism as engagement with cultural "others," thus bringing us nearly full circle to the moral cosmopolitanism with which this taxonomy began. To Appiah, cosmopolitanism implies sensitivity to the "the oneness of humanity" in all its *differentiated* glory. Appiah's cosmopolitanism celebrates what he calls "habits of coexistence." His cosmopolitan is a conversationalist, who seeks out the association of those different from her. Cosmopolitanism itself is "an adventure and an ideal," Appiah tells us; it is the fulfillment of the "Golden Rule" to take other people's interests seriously; it is a willingness to "walk a while in their moccasins" (Appiah, 2006, pp. xiv–xx, 63).

Like Nussbaum, Appiah has been accused of ignoring the structural inequality that characterizes the modern world and thwarts the cultural and intellectual reciprocity he champions.[3] Still, Appiah is useful in banishing widespread misconceptions about cosmopolitanism, foremost, perhaps, that it will promote agreement or even sympathy. Not so, Appiah cautions. Familiarity with other individuals and cultures is as apt to lead to alienation as to sympathy. The more we learn about someone, the more we may come to dislike him or her. In short, toleration is very different from agreement. Furthermore, we must be prepared for other cultures to dismiss our cosmopolitanism with all its vaunted curiosity, toleration, and fallibilism. They often have good reason for doing so. For, as Appiah concedes, ethical liberalism is no less imperialistic than economic liberalism. "When we seek to embody our concern for strangers in human rights law," Appiah observes, "and when we urge our government to enforce it, we are seeking to change the world of law in every nation on the planet." Such changes are as disruptive as capitalist incursion itself; indeed, the two often go together. Cosmopolitanism promises to "change the balance of power between men and women in everyday life"; it's bound to meet resistance (2006, pp. 82–3).

---

[3] See the critique of David Harvey, *Cosmopolitanism and the Geographies of Freedom* (New York: Columbia University Press, 2009), pp. 115–7.

But resistance need not deter the cosmopolitan, according to Appiah. Culture is change, after all, and the cultural contact cosmopolitanism promotes is inevitable, and has been the way of the world since time immemorial. To be sure, Appiah does not condone Western imperialism. But he insists that traditional cultures are not helpless in the face of cosmopolitan incursion; rather, they turn outside impositions in new cultural directions, with often surprising, sometime happy results. Appiah insists that we be clear on what it is cosmopolitanism threatens. Cosmopolitanism does not threaten cultural patrimony, for instance. Indeed, Appiah questions the very claims of cultural patrimony put forward by states whose supposed cultural artifacts pre-date the formation of the states themselves. To Appiah, art—indeed, the human mind—is inherently individualistic and transnational. The notion of the cosmos may be imaginary, but tribal and local identities are no less so. Local and tribal affiliations are meaningful and valuable to be people, but they are no more or not less sacred or imagined than cosmopolitanism (2006, pp. 111, 119, 126–35).

Well, what do we learn from all this? Let me conclude this taxonomy by briefly suggesting what I think are the strengths and weaknesses of these different perspectives for the project before us. Moral cosmopolitanism, with its exhortation to treat everybody equally and to open the curriculum to foreign cultures is noble in its inclusiveness but constraining in its understanding of who people are. It shares many of the presuppositions of the liberal state, namely, that individuals are first and foremost just that: individual rights bearers making their way in an atomized world. In this way, moral cosmopolitanism seems to displace rather than transcend nationalist ontology and essentialism.

Legal cosmopolitanism seems to be on the march at the turn of the 21st century, as more and more of the world is covered by layers of sovereign rights and laws, civil and universal. Still, there is resistance from powerful countries like the United States, whose refusal to abide by the dictates of the International Criminal Court highlights the weakness of enforcement mechanisms at an international level. Surely the test of both legal and political cosmopolitanism will be their ability to make global institutions accountable to democratic governance and the rule of law. The old nation state, with its representative institutions, will have a role in this. But just as the challenges of globalization transcend national borders, so too must the solution, suggesting the necessity of programs to ensure accountability at the local, national, regional, and global level simultaneously.

Like Nussbaum's "cosmopolitan education," Appiah's cultural cosmopolitanism—with its emphasis on openness and understanding—will be indispensible in this larger project. Responding to the challenges of globalization will require not only openness and understanding but recognition that you can't change the world without changing your neighborhood, and that work done in the neighborhood is no more or less authentic or fundamentally human than work done at the UN. Work must be done at all levels. Common work promotes common understanding (if not, as Appiah cautions, always agreement). Work is the condition of cosmopolitanism.

Which brings us back to Jane Addams and a cohort of early 20th century US intellectuals and social critics who shared Addams' conviction that cosmopolitanism begins at home. This cohort propounded its ideas amid a crisis of affiliation in American society. The influx of southern and eastern European immigrants at the end of the nineteenth century unsettled the Anglo-Saxon foundation of American citizenship, just as innovation in the retail and communications industries thrust individuals into a national marketplace, eroding traditional forms of local, voluntary, and religious affiliation. Along with women's suffrage and African-American civil rights agitation, these developments bred anxiety about the dissolution of an "American" consensus and engendered discussion about the nature, scope, and locus of national loyalty. To many politicians and cultural critics, America appeared a veritable Babel—its cacophony of voices and accents seemed to inhibit much-needed political reform.

This crisis of affiliation occurred amid seismic economic change. The foreign and domestic immigrants inundating American cities in the second half of the nineteenth century hoped to capitalize on an expanding industrial economy and steadily rising wages and living standards. There was cause for optimism in the nation's technological and industrial development, but there was ground for consternation too, as those advance spawned innovations in the management of labor and capital that alienated industrial workers and exposed the economy to prolonged episodes of depression. Although America prided itself on being a refuge for victims of political and religious persecution and economic upheaval, immigrants hailing from the autocratic regimes of eastern and southern Europe made dubious republicans, from the perspective of many old-stock Americans, and appeared prime targets for corrupt politicians and demagogues.

At a crossroads culturally and politically, America confronted troublesome political questions at century's end, to which Frederick Jackson Turner's pronouncement of the "closing" of the American frontier added urgency: could a burgeoning, increasingly disparate population perpetuate democratic virtues? Where would America's growing economy find markets and natural resources? What was America's proper role in an increasingly connected world? Alongside the insurgencies of industrial and agricultural workers, women suffragists, and civil rights agitators, these questions demanded immediate responses. Debate over these questions recalled the dispute between Federalists and Democratic Republicans about the meaning of American liberalism a century before. Corporate elites justified inequality in the language of social Darwinism: a capitalist economy needed resources, labor, and markets, and was it not appropriate that the fittest should survive and rule? Meanwhile, middle-class entrepreneurs decried the structural inequality inhibiting economic opportunity and social mobility for laborers, African Americans, immigrants, and women. Designed to strike the fetters of government tyranny, laissez-faire liberalism had come by the mid nineteenth century to impose severe economic restrictions of its own.

As long as labor remained unorganized, workers' dependence could pass unnoticed in a nation nurtured on the Protestant work ethnic and buoyed by a misreading of Darwin. But over the course of the late nineteenth century, labor conditions worsened, workers organized, and the public tranquility shattered. The dislocations of unbridled economic development clashed with the humanitarian principles at the heart of the American republic, pushing liberalism toward a critical reckoning. National politics provided a reckoning of sorts. In a spirit of North-South sectional reconciliation, Democrats conceded to Republicans the policies of tariff, deflation, and empire in exchange for Republican acquiescence in the South's disenfranchisement and segregation of African Americans. As the federal government turned legislation designed to curb business monopolies on striking workers, the representatives of labor, immigrants, and African Americans looked on with increasing alarm as a once-hallowed commitment to liberal individuality appeared to seep from American liberalism.

This, then, was the backdrop to Addams's cosmopolitanism. Along with John Dewey, William James, W. E. B. Du Bois, and Randolph Bourne, among others, Addams equated America not with some Anglo-Saxon inheritance, but with self-government. Where the so-called cultural pluralists of her day viewed the private, or cultural, realm as the route to self-realization, Addams insisted that self-expression was a function of public engagement—of political, social, and cultural exchange. Addams regarded self-discipline as one component of self-government; but, from her perspective, self-government demanded more than the "negative" ability to keep one's ego in check: it required a "positive" commitment among the citizenry to promote universal self-expression. Addams saw the debates about immigration restriction and military drill in schools not as a momentary aberration but as an inevitable consequence of Americans' failure to adjust the nation's democratic institutions to a century of demographic and economic change. In *Newer Ideals of Peace*, Addams evinced no surprise that a government unconcerned about the lives of ordinary people soon found itself alienated from its constituents and searching vainly for some mechanism by which to inculcate popular loyalty. A self-described "patriot," Addams confessed to being "jealous" of the American labor movement for receiving immigrants' "comradeship and fine *esprit de corps*," when it ought to have accrued to government. But it had been the union and the government, she regretted, that "had concerned itself with real life, shelter, a chance to work, and bread for [immigrant] children"; it had been the union and not the government that had approached immigrants "in a language they could understand"; it had been the union and not the government that had given immigrants their "first chance to express themselves through a democratic vote, to register by a ballot their real opinion upon a very important matter" (Addams, 1904, p. 443).

Resolved to make America's democratic institutions reflect the diversity of her age, Addams struck out in search of a "national ideality"—a "method by which to discover men, to spiritualize, to understand, to hold intercourse with aliens and to receive of what they bring." Although she admired the Socialist Party's determination to make politics bear on industry, she recoiled instinctively from its divide and conquer strategy. Addams viewed group morality as the product of reciprocal group relations; unless means jibed with ends, there would be no end to social resentment and economic oppression. Significantly, Addams accused Socialists of reinscribing the conservatives' "imperialism of virtue." Erecting "two substitutes for human nature"—proletariat and capitalist—Socialists ignored humankind's "imperfect" and "incalculable" character, thereby inadvertently throttling self-expression, and, ultimately, self-government. There had been a time when individuals had met in local public council to address the problems of industry, Addams observed. She urged the so-called advance men of her own era to investigate "those early organizations of village communities, folk motes, and mirs, those primary cells of both industrial and political organizations, where the people knew no difference between the two, but, quite simply, met to consider in common discussion all that concerned their common life" (1907a, p. 443).

Thus in *Newer Ideals of Peace*, Addams turned the conservative argument on its head, insisting that, far from constituting a grave threat to the American republic, the urban working class possessed the moral and cultural resources necessary to realize the ideal of self-government for the first time. Among isolated communities, Addams explained, ethics typically divided along lines of private compassion and public morality. But the proximity of life in a "cosmopolitan city," as she put it, demolished the private/public dichotomy, yielding a synthesis—"a higher moral line." In short, political, material, and cultural rights would never be secure until they were distributed universally, notwithstanding the challenge of that. They insisted that local rights have regional, national, and international repercussions that are both imprudent and immoral to ignore (1907a, p. 15).

In *Democracy and Social Ethics*, Addams provided an account of the interplay between local politics and universal sympathy while simultaneously describing how cosmopolitanism is born. This book recounted the challenge of trying to unseat a corrupt Chicago alderman in a ward comprising "fifty thousand people, representing a score of nationalities" having "little in common save the basic experiences which come to men in all countries and under all conditions." How might this mass of people, "so heterogeneous in nationality, religion, and customs," converge on a course of action? The solution, Addams discovered, lay in appealing to the "universal" self-interest of individual ward members. Such was the wisdom of urban bosses, who recognized the futility of invoking abstract "civic virtue" in an urban environment characterized by social and political alienation. Unlike the urban bosses, Addams did not renounce the goal of cultivating civic virtue. She recognized that civic virtue would have to be reconstituted from scratch. This entailed building on the "foundation" of machine politics: civic virtue was self-interest "socialized and enlarged." "If we believe the individual struggle for life may widen into a struggle for the lives of all," she wrote, "surely the demand of an individual for decency and comfort, for a chance to work and obtain the fullness of life may be widened until it gradually embraces all the members of the community, and rises into a sense of the common weal" (Addams, 1907, pp. 268–9).

Once embarked on a search for a moral foundation for peace, Addams did not have to venture far. The basis of peace, like the bulwark of virtue, lay at the heart of the cosmopolitan city. With people having come from all over the world, America's urban cauldrons constituted what Addams labeled an "American tribunal," in which inhabitants' practical concerns overwhelmed Old-World jealousies. In the modern metropolis, exigency demanded that neighbors regard one another sympathetically; mutual dependence, in turn, bred an irrepressible "power of association" at odds with "the old and negative bonds of discipline and coercion." Was Addams naïve in expecting peace to emanate from "the "quarrelsome mob" turned into kindly citizens of the world through the pressure of the cosmopolitan neighborhood? She harbored on illusions that peace was foremost in the minds of urban denizens. But peace they inadvertently promoted by "attaining cosmopolitan relations through daily experience." Indeed, she observed, immigrants "will probably believe for a long time that war is noble and necessary both to engender and cherish patriotism; and yet all of the time, below their shouting, they are living in the kingdom of human kindness. They are laying the simple and inevitable foundations for an international order" (Addams, 1907, p. 18).

To erect an edifice of peace on the foundation of cosmopolitanism, Addams summoned "philosophers"—men and women capable of integrating "the spiritual efforts of the common man into the internationalism of good will." Like St. Francis, these architects of peace would reveal "hitherto unsuspected . . . possibilities of the human soul"; like the "Gothic cathedrals," this edifice would be "glorious beyond the dreams of artists," notwithstanding that it was constructed "by unknown men, or rather by so many men that it was a matter of indifference to record their names." Addams believed that the fate of democracy and peace movement rested on the philosophers' ability to elevate industrial amelioration to the level of national defense. This, in turn, required exposing "those forms of governmental machinery and social organization which are the historic outgrowth of conquest and repression." Only then might Americans recognize the "subordination of sensation to sentiment in [the] hundreds of careers that are not military"; only then might they appreciate the "bodily pain and peril" endured by American workers as a moral equivalent of war (1907, pp. 218–9).

The way to vanquish jingoism, Addams argued, was not to replace one abstraction (patriotism!) with another (cosmopolitanism!). Fed up with the "abstract" and "institutionalized" patriotism taught in public schools ("so remote from actual living"), Addams was no fonder of the "made-up phi-lanthropy" with which the idealists sought to replace it. Both dispossessed schoolchildren of their appreciation for "the natural democratic relation." Viewing patriotism as a "great leveler and promoter of right relations," Addams hoped that it could be kept "normal and vital." Toward this end, she suggested that students be held accountable for the condition of their schools and playgrounds—a burden that would inculcate in them a more general sense of responsibility "in regard to the public streets and commu-nity duties" (Addams, 1898, p. 309).

Three years later, as her "normal" patriotism receded before the clamor for empire, Addams challenged the members of Chicago's Sunset Club to account for war's remarkable allure. Where Debs viewed America's jingo-ism as a symptom of materialism, Addams attributed it to a spiritual crisis emanating from a breakdown in the institutions of self-government. The uproar over expansion provided Americans with a necessary "outlet for their beliefs," Addams observed; it gave them "a consciousness of national-ity, the sense of being in the sweep of the world's activities." By contrast, the reform movement tapped none of the citizenry's latent altruism or craving for belonging. Orchestrated from on high, reform movements presuppose that the people are "paralyzed morally and have no share in pushing for-ward social reforms for themselves" (Addams, 1901, pp. 339–40).

Addams was tempted to cede patriotism to jingoists, so rabid had it be-come by the turn of the twentieth century. Her ambivalence is captured in a speech titled "Newer Ideals of Peace," from which her later book would get its title. A new peace required "a new type of patriotism," Addams an-nounced, though, with its disregard for national boundaries, her new ideal was hardly patriotism at all. This she seemed to recognize, imagining "the time when the feeling shall grow perhaps not into international patriotism but a certain sense of duty which shall soak up the old one of national patri-otism." Here Addams missed the truth that she would later champion—that patriotism and international fair play were not only compatible, but were indistinguishable; that, however well-meaning, it was fatuous to insist that American citizens were equally beholden to "an Italian living in the United States [and] one living in Italy" (Addams, 1902, p. 6).[4]

Nations *had* a role to play in promoting universal justice. The point was not to obliterate nations, she later recognized, but to impress upon national communities that their own rights and privileges could never be secure if they came at the expense of others. Could not American patriotism both "...hold up a standard of life for its people" and demand "that [the nation] shall compete on the highest possible planes." This Addams believed, is what patriotism had meant to America's Founding Fathers. This was a "wise patriotism" useful at home and abroad, capable of enacting and enforcing laws to resolve the era's social problems, aware "that if the meanest man in the republic is deprived of his rights, then every man in the republic is deprived of his rights." This, Addams insisted, was "the only patriotism by which public-spirited men and women, with a thoroughly aroused conscience, can worthily serve this republic" (Addams, 1902, p. 7; Addams, 1903, pp. 6–9).

Any ambivalence Addams harbored about patriotism vanished with *Newer Ideals of Peace.* A compilation of essays written over the course of a decade, this book provided the fullest statement of Addams's cosmopolitan patriotism. World peace, Addams believed, depended on the outward extension of cosmopolitanism from urban neighborhoods to municipal, state, and national governments, and ultimately to the institutions of international commerce and law. Addams's cosmopolitan patriotism consisted above all of sympathy, the compassion derived from common political and social activities. By personalizing the public, sympathy eradicated outworn stereotypes and age-old animosities. By contrast, official or state patriotism spawned an indoctrination campaign inimical to the social and cultural institutions of women and cultural minorities and incompatible with democratic principles. Addams lamented not only that educators treated pupils as empty receptacles of nationalist pabulum, but, in the case of immigrant children, tried to banish the cultural traditions that accompanied immigrants to the New World. Such policy alienated pupils, bred resentment, and thwarted the "natural foundations of patriotism"—"genuine sacrifice for the nation's laws." The result was a juvenile contest of one-upmanship, as common among adults as among children. Let me tell you about my ancestors, Addams overheard a young boy say to a friend. Let me tell you about mine, the friend replied. "Mine could beat yours out" (Addams, 1907, p. 77).

Let me conclude this essay by underscoring what I take to be most significant theoretically in Addams' "cosmopolitan patriotism." By adopting the adjective cosmopolitan to describe her cohort of patriots, I want to

---

[4] See Michael Walzer, *Thick and Thin: Moral Argument at Home and Abroad* (Notre Dame: Notre Dame Press, 1994), introduction.

highlight their perspective on social and political affiliations. Liberals of Addams's day are thought to have divided into two groups regarding the role of ethnoracial affiliation in people's lives. Universalists viewed ethnoracial allegiances as parochial and divisive, the source of untold misery the world over; cultural pluralists celebrated ethnoracial allegiances as wholesome and inviolable, the sine qua non of individual and collective agency. The cosmopolitan patriots recognized partial truth in both accounts. They shared the universalists' commitment to individual self-realization but insisted that individuals realize themselves in local, national, and global communities. They acknowledged that communities and nations have historically inhibited individuality at home and abroad but argued that this need not be so. A nation genuinely committed to liberal individuality, they maintained, would view affiliation as a product of choice rather than a consequence of stultifying ascription.[5]

Oliver Wendell Holmes, Jr. described cosmopolitanism as "a rootless self-seeking search for a place where the most enjoyment may be had at the least cost." Addams was neither parasitical nor theoretically naïve. She recognized that affiliations change with context. The unvarnished claims of either universalism or cultural pluralism are plausible only in a political or moral vacuum. In real life, individuals maintain overlapping, often competing, allegiances. Most people do not or cannot strive for theoretical cohesion in their workaday lives. Rather, individuals maintain dynamic equilibrium between their private and public, local and national, national and international affiliations—precisely the pragmatic response I associated with cosmopolitan patriotism. Which is not to say that sustaining such equilibrium is easy or pretty or perhaps even possible. But such is nevertheless what most individuals attempt to do.[6]

REFERENCES

Addams, J. (1898). Christmas fellowship. *Unity, 42* (December 22),

Addams, J, (1901). What is the greatest menace to twentieth-century progress? *The Sunset Club, one hundred eight meeting, Palmer House, Chicago* (February 14).

Addams, J. (1902). The newer ideals of peace, 2. *Chautauqua Assembly Herald, 27* (July 10), 6.

Adams, J. (1903). Address of Miss Jane Addams. *Union League Club, Chicago, Exercise in commemoration of the birthday of Washington* (February 23). Chicago: Metcalf Stationary Co.

---

[5] In appropriating the term "cosmopolitan" in this way I am once more trading on the work of David Hollinger, *Postethnic America: Beyond multiculturalism* (pp. 84–6). (New York: Basic, 2000).

[6] See the responses of Robert Pinsky and others to Nussbaum (2002), as well as Timothy Brennan, *At home in the world: Cosmopolitanism now* (Cambridge: Harvard University Press, 1997); and Eric Lott, The new cosmopolitanism: Whose America? *Transition, 72*(Fall 1996), 108–35.

Addams, J. (1906). Problems of municipal administration. *Congress of Arts and Science, Universal Exposition* (Vol. 1, p. 434). St. Louis, 1904, Boston: Houghton Mifflin.

Addams, J. (1907). *Newer ideals of peace.* New York: The MacMillan Company.

Appiah, K. A. (2006). *Cosmopolitanism: Ethics in a world of strangers.* New York: Norton.

Hansen, J. M. (2003). *The lost promise of patriotism: Debating American identity, 1890–1920.* Chicago: University of Chicago Press.

Hollinger, A. (2006). From identity to solidarity, *Daedalus,* (Fall 2006), 23–31.

Nussbaum, M. (2002). Patriotism and cosmopolitanism. In M. Nussbaum & J. Cohen (Eds.), *For love of country* (pp. 6–10). Boston: Beacon.

CHAPTER 3

DE-NATIONALIZING HISTORY TEACHING AND NATIONALIZING IT DIFFERENTLY!

Some Reflections On How to Defuse the Negative Potential of National(ist) History Teaching

Stefan Berger

INTRODUCTION

National history as a Western political concept is both "indispensable and inadequate."[1] On the one hand, given the historical importance of the nation state as a frame for political, economic, social and cultural developments, it is impossible to dispense with national history if we want to give

[1] I am taking the famous notion of "inadequate and indispensable" from Chakrabarty, 2000.

History Education and the Construction of National Identities, pages 33–47
Copyright © 2012 by Information Age Publishing
33

meaningful explanations of historical developments. On the other hand, historians have increasingly demonstrated that many aspects of historical development cannot be restricted to the national framework. Hence the profession has moved to more transnational and comparative forms of history writing since the 1980s (Berger, 2011; Haupt & Kocka, 2009; Iriye & Saunier, 2009). There is an analytical tension between the need for the national and the simultaneous imperative to transcend it. This has been exacerbated by a normative tension between those arguing that national history is necessary to underpin national identities that in turn underpin solidarities within the state, and those insisting on breaking the link between national history and national identity formation, because they hold this link responsible for some of the worst excesses of nationalism. The Janus-faced character of nationalism between emancipation and oppression has divided historians into liberal nationalists, for whom strong national identity is necessary in forging collective identities that sustain solidarity within communities and states (Neem, 2011; Roshwald, 2006; Tamir, 1993), and cosmopolitan universalists who have argued that strong national master narratives need to be problematized and undermined, because they ultimately feed xenophobia and intolerance and have been historically responsible for violence, war, ethnic cleansing and genocide (Berger, 2007; Iriye, 1996; McNeill, 1986). Liberal nationalists such as Avriel Roshwald, have been looking for a "responsible politics of nationalism," which "helps fulfil primordial human needs for a sense of connection and belonging in the context of impersonal structures of territorial authority and law" (Roshwald, 2006, p. 297). Johann Neem has provided a powerful critique of postnational forms of history writing and instead argued in favour of telling "collective narratives that shape present identity," for "nations deserve our loyalty" (Neem, 2011, p. 48 f). Such essentializing perspectives on national identities that claim to know about "human nature" find it hard to come to terms with the constructed nature of all national identities. They evade questions about who constructs national histories and national identities and for what purpose these are constructed. However, asking who, how and why is crucial for understanding both national histories and national identities.

Liberal nationalists have attempted to distinguish between bad nationalism and good patriotism. They have argued that good patriotism involves love for one's country not connected to negative feelings towards other nations. However, the voluminous scholarship on nationalism has established (beyond reasonable doubt) that any kind of collective national identity vitally depends on the conception of others who do not belong to the nation.[2] It is near-impossible not to construct a positive view of self without at the same time building a negative view of others. To what extent these constructions are xenophobic and intolerant has varied historically. We can perhaps best talk about a sliding scale between patriotism and national-ism, as historical examples of one merging and morphing into the other are certainly numerous. Patriotism and nationalism blend into one another precisely because they share construction features such as the search for enemies and "others." And this raises the question: how do we diffuse the high negative potential of national histories? How do we arrive at more self-reflexive, playful and less essentialist constructions of national history? To what extent do we need to attempt to construct different national histories or even denationalize our histories? And what consequences do answers to all these questions have for our teaching of history? If national history indeed is indispensable as an analytical framework for our understanding of the past, how do we tell national tales and avoid nationalist pitfalls? The current article provides some tentative suggestions on how we can begin to find answers to these conundrums.

NATIONAL HISTORY AND NATIONAL IDENTITY IN NINETEENTH- AND TWENTIETH-CENTURY EUROPE

Between 2003 and 2008 the European Science Foundation sponsored a five-year scientific programme that analyzed the interrelationship between national history writing and national identity formation in modern Europe. Involving over 250 historians from more than 20 European countries, the programme published fourteen books and special editions of journals and has set the benchmark for this topic for years to come.[3] Four different teams examined diverse facets of the overall topic. Thus, team 1 looked at processes of institutionalization and professionalization of history writ-ing, analyzing in great detail the intricate relationship between processes of professionalizing and nationalizing history writing. Team 2 examined the narratives of national history writing, looking in particular at the ways in which stories of the nation were interlinked with stories of ethnicity, race, religion, class and gender. The third team concentrated its analysis on the relationship between national history writing and diverse forms of sub- and transnational forms of history writing, such as regional history, European history, imperial history and world or global history. And the fourth team focused on the importance of contested borders, borderlands and territo-rial overlaps in national history writing. All teams aimed at providing com-parative perspectives on the topic. They asked comparative historians, or,

---

[2] For a good overview of the various theories of nationalism and the integral link between constructions of "us" and "them" in nationalist theory see Lawrence, 2005.

[3] For details see www.uni-leipzig.de/zhsesf [accessed 23 March 2011].

where possible, brought national historians together to write articles and develop comparative and transnational perspectives. The programme succeeded in dealing comprehensively with the whole of Europe. In particular it provided much-needed perspectives on Eastern Europe and contributed to the re-integration of Eastern and Western European historiographies, that had been divided by the Cold War and its legacy.

Many articles published under the programme emphasized the emancipatory potential of national history. National history was an important weapon in the armory of anti-feudal and anti-absolutist political forces in the nineteenth century. Both liberals and democrats across Europe used national narratives in order to further demands of greater participation of the people in politics and civil society. Within nineteenth-century European empires and outside of Europe, national histories fulfilled a vital function in contributing to the anti-colonial and anti-imperial struggles. For the Ukranian and Irish national movements, national histories were an important means to emancipate themselves from Russian and English domination respectively. History gave a voice to national minorities and it helped oppositional movements, from liberalism to socialism and communism, to formulate alternative visions of national history and national identity.

On the other hand national histories were also widely used to oppress people. Thus, xenophobia was furthered by the construction of internal and external enemies. National histories legitimated the repression and assimilation of national minorities. They legitimated wars and justified ethnic cleansing and genocide. In Franco's Spain, the Castilian construction of the Spanish nation made life difficult for Catalan, Basque, Galician and any other non-Castilian part of the multi-national state. The expansionist aims of Germany both in the First and Second World War clearly underlined the aggressive uses of national histories, and their catastrophic impact on some of the worst crimes committed against humanity in history. As Peter Fritzsche has argued in a memorable phrase: "the relationship between victimhood and violence is embedded in most national historiographies ... [The national idea] is first conjured up as being under threat. And it is this state of alarm that produces the energy to override competing identities, often violently. Violence is inscribed in the national narrative because the nation imagines itself first and foremost as a collective good that is incomplete and imperilled. In many ways, the national narrative must sustain itself by reproducing its own state of jeopardy. National histories tremble as a result" (Fritzsche, 2008). For better or worse, the power of national histories was visible in their success in subsuming all other potential master narratives (e.g. ethnicity, race, class and gender) under that of the nation (Berger & Lorenz, 2008).

THE CLOSE FIT BETWEEN NATIONAL HISTORY AND NATIONALIST POLITICS

Throughout the nineteenth and twentieth century we can observe the close fit between national history and nationalist politics in Europe. In the wars of liberty against Napoleon, Fichte mobilised the idea of national history. He sacralised the nation as the moral collective connecting the generations through the ages. Writing against the Napoleonic claims of French universalism, he followed Herder's emphasis on the ethnic and cultural particularity of nations, but additionally argued that those who maintained their particularities most purely were the best nations. Thus the problematic idea of a hierarchy of nations was born. Fichte specifically claimed a national history of the Germans to be the best defence against French universalism: "Amongst the means to strengthen the German spirit it would be a powerful one to have an enthusiastic history of the Germans, which would be a national as well as a people's book, just like the Bible or the Gesangbuch" (Fichte, 1808, p. 106; Hagemann, 1997).

In 1848 liberal revolutionaries sought to bring about a more unified and liberal German nation state, forming a constitutional assembly in Frankfurt/Main. They used notions of national history to underpin versions of national identity that undermined feudal practices and absolutist rule. They sought (to varying degrees) greater participation of people in public life and the establishment of constitutional forms of government. Hence the 1848 revolution can on a certain level be seen as a classic example of enlightened liberal nationalism. However, when it came to discussing the matter of Schleswig-Holstein, most enlightened liberal nationalists were capable of xenophobic and violent anti-Danish outbursts and unequivocal calls for a national people's war against Denmark to liberate the German breathren allegedly under the Danish yoke. This revolution, rather than being a straightforward instance of liberal nationalism, shows precisely the kind of sliding scale between patriotism and nationalism that I referred to above (Vick, 2002).

One of the most influential nineteenth-century German historians was Heinrich von Treitschke. He saw his task as a historian to "know how to arouse in the hearts of his readers [...] the joy of the Fatherland." His multivolume *History of Germany in the Nineteenth Century* became one of the most influential national histories in the late nineteenth and early twentieth centuries. His historical writings mirrored his political convictions: conservatism, anti-Semitism, colonialism and nationalism. The state, for him, was "the highest entity in historical life." He glorified power politics, authoritarian rule and war. "Only in war will a nation truly become a nation [...] if war was abolished, all movement, all development would cease." Treitschke graded the nations of the world according to racial characteristics. He was hostile towards virtually all foreign nations and particularly venomous in addressing the French and Slav nations. Treitschke was also an influential lecturer at the university. Admiral von Tirpitz, the motor behind the creation of a German battle fleet, and Heinrich Class, the ultra-nationalist leader of the Pan-German League, belonged to his most devoted pupils (Dorpalen, 1957).

The Ukraine also had a dominant national historian in the early twentieth century. Mikhailo Hrushevsky started his academic career with a professorship in history in Lviv in 1894. He was the author of the monumental 10-volume *History of the Ukranian Rus*, published between 1898 and 1936, *the* key national master narrative of the Ukraine. These tomes set out to refute the imperial claims of the Russian empire-nation over the Ukraine and asserted that three separate historical paths led to three separate ethno-national entities: Russian, Belorussian and Ukranian. It was a self-consciously "scientific" work, following the most advanced methodological and theoretical ground rules established by professional historians in the nineteenth century. Hrushevsky was also a major organiser of "Wissenschaft," overseeing the edition of dozens of volumes of historical sources as well as diverse journals and building an unofficial Ukranian Academy of Sciences in Austrian Galicia, the Shevchenko Scientific Society. It had permanent and corresponding members from all regions of the Ukraine, regardless of existing state borders and saw as its main task promoting scholarship in the Ukrainian language. In 1907 Hrushevsky also founded a Ukranian Scientific Society in Kiev, trying to link it to the Shevchenko Scientific Society. However, he was not content with mere *Wissenschaft*. As a towering public intellectual, he also wrote in newspapers and public journals, addressing audiences outside university. Actively involved in politics, he became one of the most important spokespersons for federalism in the pre-revolutionary Russian Empire and acted as first president of the Ukranian state in 1917–1918. Using a wide array of transnational contacts and putting into practice his internationalist outlook, Hrushevsky also became one of the most important lobbyist for the Ukranian cause abroad. It would be hard to describe Hrushevsky as a nationalist. Time and again he warned against national exclusiveness. He held strong federal and democratic principles, making him suspicious of those favouring majority domination of ethnic groups over minorities or claimed that their nation was superior to others. A staunch opponent of all forms of imperialism, especially of the Habsburg and Russian variants, he adhered to the idea of European culture to which all nations and ethnicities had something to contribute. His Herderian utopia was that of a world federation of nations, all regarding each other as equals. Hence he held a negative view of pan-Slavism and abhorred all forms of extreme nationalism. Also he had no difficulty in co-operating with Russian liberals and communists, even if the latter were making life very difficult for him after 1927 (Prymak, 1987).

Treitschke and Hrushevsky in many respects mark out the extremes on the spectrum of historiographical nationalism in nineteenth century Europe. Whilst Hrushevsky stood for a Herderian, cosmopolitan and liberal nationalism, Treitschke was the epitome of a Social Darwinist, ethnocentric, and xenophobic nationalist historian. The work, activities and reception of both historians demonstrate once again that their positions were united on a sliding scale. The two ideal-typical positions blended into each other, combined with each other and changed shape over time. Nevertheless, as we shall outline below, it was Treitschke's ideal-typical variant of a narrow nationalist historiography which was to play a more influential role in Europe during the second half of the nineteenth and the first half of the twentieth century.

The First World War undoubtedly marked the peak of nineteenth-century historiographical nationalism (Berger & Conrad, 2013, chap. 5). The historians' role as prophets of the nation state found ample expression during the conflict. In the belligerent countries, historians like many other scholars and intellectuals, signed petitions, made speeches and published pamphlets to justify their countries' involvement and denigrate the enemy's claims. Take for example Britain. The vast majority of British historians before the First World War had been pro-German (Siak, 1998). Many who had admired German historiography, now argued that two Germanies existed: one cultural and one militarist. In 1914, they insisted, militarism had won the upper hand against culture, and it was this militarism which needed to be defeated.[4] The Manchester-based historian Ramsay Muir wrote in the autumn of 1914 that the origins of the war lay in "a poison which has been working in the European system for more than two centuries, and the chief source of this poison is Prussia." (Muir, 1914, p. vii).

After the defeat of Germany and the ratification of the Versailles Treaty, the poison of historiographical nationalism began to reach new heights. The war guilt debate involved—on all sides—huge mobilisation of resources to demonstrate one thing only: that Germany either had or had not been the sole guilty party in the outbreak of the First World War. In the interwar period, all states published substantial document collections that had the explicit purpose of proving their actions right. Whilst they were keen on disseminating this official scholarship nationally and internationally to academic and popular audiences, they also tightly controlled the archives using censorship, in order to prevent other than the officially sanctioned views to emerge from the documents. Germany was first off the mark to produce a major government-funded source collection on the origins of the conflict. It set out to prove one thing only: that Germany was not, as ar-

---

[4] The historian and social reformer W. H. Dawson is a typical example of such an admirer of Germany who, in wartime, took refuge to the idea of "two Germanies" (Berger, 2001).

ticle 231 of the Versailles Treaty stated, the sole guilty party in the outbreak of war in August 1914. *Die grosse Politik der europäischen Kabinette, 1871–1914* was published in 40 volumes between 1922 and 1927—under the general editorship of Friedrich Thimme, who willingly sacrificed his own scholarly benchmarks when they clashed with political expediency (Epstein, 1973, p. 174). As Holger Herwig has argued: "By selectively editing documentary collections, suppressing honest scholarship, subsidizing pseudo-scholarship, underwriting mass propaganda and overseeing the export of this propaganda, especially to Britain, France and the United States, the patriotic self-censors in Berlin exerted a powerful influence on public and elite opinion in Germany and, to a lesser extent, outside Germany. Their efforts polluted historical understanding both at home and abroad well into the post-1945 period" (Herwig, 1996, p. 88 f).

And in the context of the Second World War, a number of historians directly collaborated with the National Socialist regime in the attempt to legitimate the territorial expansion of the German nation both west- and eastwards. So-called Westforschung, under historians such as Franz Petri, justified the inclusion of parts of France and the Low Countries into Germany, whilst Ostforschung, under historians such as Werner Conze, Theodor Schieder and Herman Aubin, worked out plans which foresaw the ethnic cleansing of wide parts of Eastern Europe of its Slav population and the resettlement of those territories with ethnic Germans. Historians thus belonged to those intellectuals who Susanne Heym and Götz Aly have called *Vordenker der Vernichtung*: "intellectuals preparing the road to annihilation" (Haar & Fahlbusch, 2005; Heim & Aly, 1991; Schönwälder, 1992).

When it was the turn of the Germans to be ethnically cleansed at the end of the Second World War, historians were again to the fore justifying such actions. With reference to the Beneš decrees, historians in Czechoslovakia argued that the expulsions were legal. Furthermore, many East-Central European historiographies justified the expulsion of Germans as necessary precondition for the socialist/ communist transformation which followed. In Poland historians provided justification for the political argument that Poles were just returning to "ancient Polish territories." Their sacrifices under German occupation and the heroism of Polish units fighting alongside French, English and Russian armies in the Second World War, were additional arguments why Poland was entitled to these territories after 1945. After 1958 the Commission for German Issues Studies established at the Historical Institute of the Czechoslovak Academy of Science published many tomes on the Sudeten Germans in particular, all aimed at demonstrating the collective guilt of the Germans in the crimes committed against the Czechoslovak nation in the Second World War. The legitimatory function of these works was obvious. By contrast, Polish historians did not deal in a major way with the expulsions apart from echoing the euphemisms which were politically decreed. "Repatriation" and "transfer" were the terms which described forms of ethnic cleansing. State censorship in this politically sensitive research area was considerable. Occasionally, dissidents and exile historians attempted to make the expulsions a topic for debate and questioned the official justification for the expulsions, but these voices only reached a very limited circle of people during the Cold War in those countries (Benthin, 2007; Kraft, 2005).

The final example I would like to give for the tight fit between national history and nationalist history comes from the bloody Yugoslav civil war of the 1990s. The war disrupted previous ties between historians belonging to different ethnicities. So, for example, Serb, Croat and Bosniak historians worked alongside each other at the history departments of Bosnia-Herzegovina before the Civil War, but thereafter practically all such cooperation stopped. Bosniak historians had been engaged on constructing a Bosniak Muslim identity long before the civil war, but in the context of war, they radicalised their nationalist positions, as did many Serb and Croat historians. Historians in the Republica Srbska constructed a Serb nationalist history which explicitly excluded Bosniaks. In Montenegro historians engaged in a major debate throughout the 1990s whether Montenegrin ethnic identity was different from Serb ethnic identity or not—with the proponents of a separate Montenegrin nationalism setting up their own Doclean Academy of Sciences and Arts in 1999.[5] Everywhere in the former Yugoslavia historians contributed to national histories which were ethnically exclusive and sometimes lent their support to forms of ethnic cleansing. Most Kosovo-Albanian historians had to leave higher education after Serbia ended Kosovan autonomy in 1989/90. Their positions were taken by Serbs. However, in 1999, the Serbs had to go, after Kosovo had come under UN administration. Kosovo-Albanian historiography has been strongly nationalist, seeking directly to support the political claims for full independence of Kosovo by giving it historical legitimacy. In Croatia, the nationalist president Franjo Tudjman (1991–1999) was himself a historian, who had founded the Institute for the History of the Labour Movement in Zagreb in 1961. Thirty years later, he sought to enlist history in the direct service of nationalism, using in particular the renamed Institute for Contemporary History (in 1996 it became the Croatian Institute for History) and the newly founded Croatian Studies Department at Zagreb University. He even created new departments of history in areas of Croatia perceived to be in danger of separatism, such as Istria or Slavonia. In fairness to the Croatian historians, it should be said that many of them did not support Tudjman's nationalism

---

[5] The name referred to the medieval state of Dukleja, which, to Montenegrin nationalists, was the first Montenegrin nation state.

and opposed attempts to instrumentalize history in this way (Brunnbauer, 2004).

ALTERNATIVES TO NATIONAL HISTORY

Given this track record of national history and its high potential for violence, exclusion and murder, one might be forgiven for wanting to search for alternatives to national history writing. For a start, rather than teach national history or indeed any history of collectives (because all collective histories have identitarian concerns and prejudices), one might consider teaching history as Radical Individualism. This kind of history would be geared towards highlighting what makes us special as individuals, thereby strengthening the individual ego and weakening the collective egos that come with master narratives of nation and other spatial or non-spatial collectives. This does not necessarily mean reducing history to a series of individual biographies, although biographical approaches may well be an appropriate way of highlighting individuation. But one can think of many topics where stories about individuals and their complex and contradictory identities can be foregrounded. One can also use history to celebrate cases of non-conformism to collective pressure, i.e. tell the stories of people who stood out against the crowd. Of course, this might also mean telling the story of some nationalists—in cases where nationalism was historically a form of non-conformism.

Furthermore, one can imagine the teaching of history that highlights cosmopolitan values and ideas in the past, i.e. instances where levels of tolerance and mutual acceptance of difference helped to reduce cultural antagonisms, class differences, racial hatreds, or religious zealotry (Appiah, 2006). Finally, one can also think of history teaching as demonstrating the limits of national approaches and national borders. Over the last twenty years historians have rightly pointed to the interconnectedness of allegedly unique and special national trajectories. They have highlighted instances of transfers, adaptations, connections, flows and migrations. These histories can help demystify "the national" and prevent essentializing it as authentic and natural (Werner & Zimmermann, 2006). Over the last fifty years Europe has not only been the description of a physical place; it has also become a political project to overcome and ameliorate the worst excesses of nationalism that had ravaged Europe during the first half of the twentieth century. Whilst Europeanization can be taught as one instance of the importance of transnational processes, one has to be careful not to re-erect exclusions, "others" and enemies at a supra-national level. The European Union, in its haphazard attempts to construct European identity, (Shore, 2000) might yet repeat the mistakes that nationalism and nationalists made in the nineteenth century, i.e. essentializing and naturalizing the spatial categories and constructing them vis-à-vis a host of enemies. Few people would doubt the effectiveness of such processes in the past, but all would do well to consider the considerable costs that came with such success. As I have tried to indicate here, there are various forms of teaching history in a post-national way. However, even if all our suggestions above would be taken up, there remains the argument with which we opened this essay. National history might be inadequate in so many ways, but it is also indispensable. Certain historical developments only make sense if we teach them within a national framework—this is true for much of modern political history, but also for many areas of social, economic and cultural history. It would be foolish to ignore the national frame completely. Hence the next question has to be:

CAN NATIONAL HISTORY BE TAUGHT DIFFERENTLY?

It seems to me to be essential that we try and break the strong link between national history and national identity formation. The real task is to accept the national framework for histories where that national framework is appropriate and sensible without allowing national histories to become the basis for national identity formation. For, if we want to avoid the pitfalls of nationalist histories, the task is surely, as Alan Megill has formulated it, to build solidarities below the level of identities (Megill, 2008). But how can we square this circle? For a start, national histories need to become more self-reflective, laying open their own perspectivity and relativity, allowing for a plurality of national perspectives. The task is no longer to produce historical national master narratives which underpin a sense of collective identity, but rather to give students of history a sense of the contestation over historical interpretation of specific phenomena, for which the national framework was important in the past. Konrad Jarausch and Michael Geyer have suggested that German national history after 1945 resembled a "broken mirror." The image can undoubtedly carry notions of nostalgia—the desire to make whole again what has been broken. Perhaps there is even a sense of melancholy—that the shattered glass cannot be put together again. But let me suggest here that we can also use the image of the "broken mirror" in a more positive constructive sense: anyone looking into a broken mirror sees not one reflection, but many reflections. National history as a broken mirror would allow the observer to recognize that national history can come in many guises, depending on the positionality and perspectivity of the speaker who is narrating that history. It would raise the awareness of the constructedness of national histories and the invention of national traditions for particular purposes. It would thus help to de-essentialize national history writing and throw a spanner in the works of those who are still intent on constructing national master narratives in order to underpin essentialized and exclusive versions of national identity. All of this will not be an easy task, but apart from the individualizing, cosmopolitan and transnationalizing strategies discussed above, the teaching of national history in such a self-reflexive way might be another opportunity to defuse the explosive potential of national histories.

CONCLUSION

In 2008 the Russian civil rights organization MEMORIAL issued a call for an International History Forum, on which to discuss the national master narratives still prevalent in European historical consciousness. Its explicit aim was to move beyond conflict and towards cooperation in Europe by building a loose confederation of associations, research centres, cultural and educational organisations who begin a transnational dialogue: "We have to work towards bringing the common tragic memories of the people of Europe together, so that they do not separate them. We can do this, if we are successful in coming to terms with the past not in an isolated country by country fashion, but in a common effort." [6]

There are today many efforts to construct a European memory culture which will bring the people of Europe together. As national history has traditionally divided Europeans and constructed neighbours as foes, this is a difficult task and will necessitate the transformation of a historical consciousness of warfare, ethnic cleansing and genocide into something that will commit Europeans to work towards a less conflictual future. True, there are elements of European history which are not primarily connected to violence. The classical heritage of Greece and Rome has been presented as the basis of a European humanism. For some Christianity and its ethics form a common bond for the building of a more united Europe. The Renaissance and the Enlightenment form periods in European history, which are presented as pinnacles of Europeanism with iconic figures such as Erasmus and Immanuel Kant putting forward ideas for a more peaceful, civilised and co-operative political entity called Europe. None of these underpinnings of Europeanism are without their dark side: Was the history of ancient Greece not continuously punctured by warfare between the different Greek city states and between alliances of them with Persia? Was Rome not an empire subjugating large parts of Europe? Did the ancient world not include large parts of Northern Africa and does this not present a geographical challenge for today's definitions of Europe? Have there not been wars, persecution of minorities, torture and unbelievable acts of cruelty committed in the name of Christianity? Witch hunts and the Inquisition as well as the Crusades and the religious wars of the seventeenth centuries, above all the Thirty Years' War are hardly foundations on which to build a more tolerant, peaceful and united Europe. The confessional divisions between

---

[6] The call can be found at http://www.memo.ru/2008/03/27/Memorial_obrazu_proschlo-go_De.htm (accessed 17 April 2011).

Catholics, Orthodox and Protestants continue to divide Christians today and have done so for many centuries. By no means all humanists had a cosmopolitan outlook on the world; the Renaissance already saw many expressions of proto-nationalism and xenophobia, whilst the indictment of the dialectics of the Enlightenment by Theodor Adorno and Max Horkheimer remains a powerful warning not to overlook the dark side of the European Enlightenment (Adorno & Horkheimer, 1972).

All of this does not mean that we should give up looking for ways in which we can Europeanize and transnationalize our historical consciousness. Decentering our still predominant national histories and weakening the strong links between national histories and national identities remains very much a task for today, if we want to build a less conflictual and less painful future and overcome the problematic legacies of historiographial nationalism.

REFERENCES

Adorno, T., & Horkheimer, M. (2002). *Dialectics of the enlightenment.* Stanford, CA: Stanford University Press.

Appiah, K. A. (2006). *Cosmopolitanism: Ethics in a world of strangers.* London: Allen Lane.

Benthin, M. (2007). *Die Vertreibung der Deutschen aus Ostmitteleuropa. Deutsche und Tschechische Erinnerungskulturen im Vergleich.* [*The expulsion of Germans from Eastern Middle Europe. A comparison between German and Czech recollection cultures.*] Hannover: Hahnsche Buchhandlung.

Berger, S. (2001). William Harbutt Dawson and Germany in the inter-war period, *English Historical Review, 116*(1), 76–112.

Berger, S. (2007). History and national identity: Why they should remain divorced, *History and Policy:* http://www.historyandpolicy.org/papers/policy-paper-66.html

Berger, S. (2011). Le "Tournant Linguistique" en Histoire: une perspective Anglo-Saxonne [The Linguistic Turn in History: an Anglo-Saxon perspective], *Diogenes, 229–230,* 6–29.

Berger, S., with Conrad, C. (2013). *The past as history: Historical consciousness and national identity in modern Europe.* Basingstoke: Palgrave MacMillan.

Berger, S., & Lorenz, C. (Eds.) (2008). *The contested nation: Ethnicity, class, religion and gender in national histories.* Basingstoke: Palgrave MacMillan.

Berger, S., Feldner, H,, & Passmore, K. (Eds.). (2010). *Writing history: Theory and practice.* London: Bloomsbury

Brunnbauer, U. (Ed.). (2004). *(Re)writing history: Historiography in southeast Europe after socialism.* Münster: Lit.

Chakrabarty, D. (2000). *Provincializing Europe: Postcolonial thought and historical difference.* Princeton, NJ: Princeton University Press.

Dorpalen, A. (1957). *Heinrich von Treitschke.* New Haven: Yale University Press.

Epstein, F. T. (1973). The accessibility of source materials illuminating the history of german foreign policy. The publication of documents of the German foreign ministry after both World Wars. In R. F. Byrnes (Ed.), *Germany and the east.* Bloomington/Indiana: Indiana University Press.

Fichte, J. G. (2008; first published 1808). *Reden an die deutsche Nation* [Speech to the German Nation]. Hamburg: Meiner.

Fritzsche, P. (2008). *National Narrative and Untimely Death.* Unpublished paper, given to the final conference of the NHIST Programme in Manchester, 23 October 2008.

Haar, I., & Fahlbusch, M. (Eds.) (2005). *German scholars and ethnic cleansing 1919–1945.* Oxford: Berghahn.

Hagemann, K. (1997). Of "manly valor" and "German honour": Nation, war and masculinity in the age of the Prussian uprising against Napoleon. *Central European History, 30,* 187–220.

Haupt, H. G., & Kocka, J. (Eds.) (2009). *Comparative and transnational history: Central European approaches and new perspectives.* Oxford: Berghahn.

Heim, S., & Aly, G. (1991). *Vordenker der Vernichtung: Auschwitz und die deutschen Pläne für eine neue europäische Ordnung* [*Intellectuals preparing the road to annihilation: Auschwitz and the German plans for a new European order*]. Hamburg: Fischer.

Herwig, H. (1996). Clio deceived: Patriotic self-censorship in Germany after the great war. In K. Wilson (Ed.), *Forging the collective memory. government and international historians through two world wars.* Oxford: Berghahn.

Iriye, A. (1996). The internationalization of history. *American Historical Review, 94*(1), 1–10.

Iriye, A., & Saunier, P. Y. (Eds.). (2009). *The Palgrave dictionary of transnational history.* Basingstoke: Palgrave MacMillan.

Kraft, C. (2005). Der Platz der Vertreibung der Deutschen im historischen Gedächtnis Polens und der Tschechoslowakei/Tschechiens [The place of the expulsion of the Germans in Polish and Czechoslovak/Czech historical remembrance]. In C. Cornelißen, R. Holec and J. Pešek (Eds.) *Diktatur—Krieg—Vertreibung. Erinnerungskulturen in Tschechien, der Slowakei und Deutschland seit 1945 [Dictatorship—War—Expulsion. Cultures of remembrance in Czech Republic, Slovakia and Germany since 1945]* (pp. 329–354). Essen: Klartext.

Lawrence, P. (2005). *Nationalism: History and theory.* London: Longman.

McNeill, W. (1986). *Poly-ethnicity and national unity in world history.* Toronto: Toronto University Press.

Megill, A. (2008). Historical representation, identity, allegiance. In S. Berger, L. Eriksonas, & A. Mycock (Eds.), *Narrating the nation: Representations in history, the media and the arts* (pp. 19–34). Oxford: Berghahn.

Muir, R. (1914). *Britain's case against Germany: An examination of the historical background of the German action in 1914.* Manchester: Manchester University Press.

Neem, J. N. (2011). American history in a global age. *History and Theory, 50*(1), 41–70.

Prymak, T. M. (1987). *Mykhailo Hrushevsky: The politics of national culture.* Toronto: Toronto University Press.

Roshwald, A. (2006). *The endurance of nationalism: Ancient roots and modern dilemmas.* Cambridge: Cambridge University Press.

Schönwälder, K. (1992). *Historiker und Politik. Geschichtswissenschaft im Nationalsozialismus* [Historians and politics. The historical profession during national socialism]. Frankfurt/Main: Campus.

Shore, C. (2000). *Building Europe: The cultural politics of European integration.* London: Routledge.

Siak, S. W. (1998). The blood that is in our veins comes from German ancestors: British historians and the coming of the first world war, *Albion, 30*(2), 221–252.

Tamir, Y. (1993). *Liberal nationalism.* Princeton, NY: Princeton University Press.

Vick, B. (2002). *Defining Germany: The 1848 Frankfurt parliamentarians and national identity.* Cambridge, MA: Harvard University Press.

Werner, M., & Zimmermann, B. (2006). Beyond comparison: "Histoire Croisee" and the challenge of reflexivity, *History and Theory, 45*(1), 30–50.

CHAPTER 4

RE-THINKING HISTORY TEXTBOOKS IN A GLOBALIZED WORLD

Stuart Foster[1]

INTRODUCTION AND OVERVIEW

Despite some important exceptions, this paper will outline how school history textbooks in many nations across the world typically are shaped by two characteristics. First, they are often overtly nationalistic. Second, they commonly adopt an official, single "best story" narrative style. As a result, these authoritative textbooks often serve as instruments of propaganda attempting both to reinforce ideologically constructed national identities and to appease social and political agendas in the present. It will be argued that these common textbook practices are problematic because they present students with a selective, narrow, and uncritical view of the world around them. To counter this deficiency it will be argued that in an increasingly globalized world it is vital that students are provided with a deeper under-

[1] s.foster@ioe.ac.uk

History Education and the Construction of National Identities, pages 49–62
Copyright © 2012 by Information Age Publishing
49

standing of the interpretive, contested, or disciplinary nature of history. In this context, drawing on the example of "new history" resources produced in England in recent decades, a different vision of history textbooks is proposed which encourage students to understand the disciplinary nature of history. An approach which holds the potential to help students make sense of different, and often conflicting, versions of the past and the present.

HISTORY TEXTBOOKS:
DIFFERENT SYSTEMS, DIFFERENT PRACTICES

For several centuries history textbooks have enjoyed a prominent place in the education landscape. Certainly, by the end of the nineteenth century history textbooks were a common feature in classrooms in many countries throughout the world (Marsden, 2001). Today, history textbooks continue to play a major role in educational systems and practices around the globe. However, despite these commonalities, the production, selection, and deployment of history textbooks differs considerably in international settings (Hein & Selden, 2000; Nicholls, 2006; Pingel, 1999; Vickers & Jones, 2005).[2] In Japan, China and many East Asian societies, for example, the textbook plays a central role in history classrooms. Routinely the teacher's duty is to teach the textbook. With education geared towards passing university entrance examinations that emphasise knowledge retention, students are required to memorise textbook information in preparation for the all-important tests. Likewise, in the United States, high school subjects commonly are dominated by survey courses in which "general knowledge" and breadth are emphasized. School subject textbooks in the United States are often large, some more than a thousand pages. With the need to cover an extensive range of content over relatively short periods of time, teaching and learning activities are often centred on the textbook. In contrast, the use of textbooks in Sweden, for example, varies widely across classrooms. This is due in part to the highly decentralised nature of the Swedish education system, where teachers are encouraged to design their own syllabi, often in consultation with students. Swedish schoolbooks typically are small, designed to "complement" teaching and learning (Foster & Nicholls, 2005; Nicholls & Foster, 2005; Sewall & Cannon, 1991).

The whole process of textbook selection and use is further complicated when consideration is given to the possibility that what is "in" the textbook may not be taught and, even if it is taught, it may not be understood by students in the way desired by national governments, textbook authors,

---

[2] These differences are graphically illustrated in Foster and Crawford's *What Shall We Tell the Children? International Perspectives in History Education* (2006a), which outlines how textbooks enjoy different authority and status in various nations in East Asia, Europe, the Middle East, Africa, the USA, and South Asia.

and teachers. Consequently, to easily accept that textbook content neatly equates to what teachers teach, or, more importantly, to what students learn would be unwise (Apple & Christian-Smith, 1991). The many ways in which students and teachers variously understand, negotiate, and transform their personal understandings of textual material is a complex process. Rarely is textbook content simply accepted, absorbed, and then regurgitated by students (see, for example, Apple, 1991; Barthes, 1976; Foster & Crawford, 2006a; Porat, 2004).

TWO IMPORTANT GENERALIZATIONS ABOUT TEXTBOOKS

Despite these cautions and considerations enough research exists to suggest that textbooks remain an important factor in determining how students learn history (Anyon, 1978, 1979; Apple & Christian-Smith, 1991; Foster, 1999; Marsden, 2001). Furthermore, although it is difficult to make sweeping generalisations about history textbooks, international research in textbook production and use suggests that textbooks in many nations share similar perspectives and characteristics.[3] Indeed, these commonalities appear more pronounced in countries where textbooks are approved centrally. In these settings two features prove salient. First, textbooks often adopt a nationalistic perspective on historical events.[4] Second, textbooks typically present students with an "official," single narrative.

Almost without exception education systems throughout the world play a vital role in shaping the collective memory of its citizens. As an increasingly rich body of scholarship reveals (Apple & Christian-Smith, 1991; Foster & Crawford, 2006a; Hein & Selden, 2000; Marsden, 2001; Nicholls, 2006; Pingel, 2000; Schissler & Soysal, 2005; Vickers & Jones, 2005) the history curriculum and history textbooks often serve as the principal means to influence, if not control, how children understand their nation's past. For example, Crawford and Foster's recent book, *War, Nation, Memory* (2007), which examines interpretations of the Second World War in school textbooks in China, France, Germany, Japan, USA, and the UK offers revealing insights into the ways in which selected interpretations of World War II serve

---

[3] It would be misleading, however, to argue that all nations share these characteristics. For example, in Germany conscious efforts have been made on the part of national and regional government to de-emphasise a nationalistic agenda. Rather, German textbooks are more likely to appeal to a sense of European identity. For an interesting discussion of this development see Soysal, Bertilotti, and Mannitz (2005). Similarly, Kaat Wils (2009) has argued that in Belgium the notion of a shared national canon has "evaporated" from the curriculum in recent decades.

[4] Not all scholars share this perspective. For example Schissler and Soyal (2005) argue that in Europe national identities are becoming less important. However, this view is contested by Joke van der Leeuw-Roord (2008) who argues that, "since 2000 the focus on national history in Europe is again increasing" (p. 79).

an important cultural function in the ongoing process of nation building. History textbooks in China, for example, deliberately focus on "the Nanjing Massacre" (1937), a genocidal war crime committed by the invading Japanese army. As an emotive issue, the "massacre" plays a deliberate role in presenting specific images of the Chinese "us" against the demonic Japanese "other" to construct a shared national history and consciousness. In a similar vein, in the United States, impassioned and celebratory textbook portrayals of Pearl Harbor, D-Day, Victory in Europe, and the Pacific War offer a context in which bravery, moral fortitude, determination, and endeavour are depicted as enduring characteristics of the American people. The same is evident in Russian textbooks where the conflict is described as the "Great Patriotic War" and where, in order to create a sense of national unity and pride, school books emphasize the courage, duty, and sacrifice of the Russian people. Similarly, in Britain, where the twin themes of heroism and victimization feature prominently, the "Battle of Britain," the retreat from Dunkirk, "the Blitz," and the defeat of Hitler's Germany appear as defining events that continue to shape and influence British identity.[5]

In fact, history textbook authors in almost every nation embroiled in war deliberately construct narratives to serve national and ideological agendas. This is perhaps not surprising for as Michel Apple and Linda Christian-Smith (1991) remind us, textbooks do not appear in a vacuum. Rather they are "conceived, designed, and authored by real people with real interests" and are "published with political and economic constraints of markets resources and power" (p. 9). Textbooks emerge from what Williams (1989) has called "the machinery of selective tradition" (p. 33) in which a highly selected version of knowledge typically is privileged while other knowledge is marginalised or excluded. In this context what is most evident is that the stories that nations choose to tell their young about World War II do not represent a universally accepted "truth" about events during the war. Rather, wartime narratives contained in school textbooks typically are selected to instil in the young a sense of national pride, a common identity, and a shared collective memory.

In nations throughout the world it is inescapable, therefore, that textbooks represent a powerful means to render a particular version of the nation's past in the history classroom. Largely influenced by official policies, textbook authors consciously attempt to shape and inform students' understanding of their national history and the relationship between their country and other nations. As Foster and Crawford (2006a) have written:

---

[5] Indeed, in 1999, Michael Naumann, the German Culture Minister, claimed, 'There is only one nation in the world that has decided to make the Second World War a sort of spiritual core of its national self, understanding and pride...' (*The Independent*, 15 February 1999).

In some nation states history teaching is used openly and unashamedly to promote specific ideologies and sets of political ideas. In other countries, under the guise of patriotism, the history of a nation served up for student consumption is what its leaders decide it is to be. In states which consider their existence to be under threat, or in states which are struggling to create an identity, or in those which are re-inventing themselves following a period of colonial rule, teaching a nationalistic and mono-cultural form of history can prove to be the cement which binds people together. In its worst form the manufacture and teaching of such an official past can create, sponsor, maintain and justify xenophobic hatred, racism and the obscenity of ethnic cleansing (pp. 6–7).

Embedded in history textbooks, therefore, are narratives that nation states choose to tell about themselves and their relationships with other nations. Often they represent a body of core cultural knowledge which the younger generation is expected both to assimilate and to support. As a result, textbooks often are used to convey a story of past as a means to unite people in the present and to emphasise national unity and pride. Similarly, textbooks typically focus on national achievements and triumphs and ignore or downplay the contributions of other nations. Revealingly, in some nations, textbook narratives use expressions such as "we," "our" and "us" to differentiate national citizens from the "them," "their," and "they" assigned to "other" peoples.

The second characteristic of textbooks used in many nations is the appearance of a single, authoritative, "official" narrative.[6] In these textbooks historical content typically is presented as uncontested and objective. Accounts are authoritative, detached, and technical and no source material or alternative evidence is presented. Furthermore, opinions often are stated as facts and in-text questions for students either do not exist or are based on factual recall of given information. These two common textbook characteristics (i.e., nationalist and single story narratives) typically produced in nations where education is centrally controlled are, of course, inexorably linked. Nations that use their education systems to promote feelings of pride unity and common heritage have no reason to encourage multiple narratives or competing evidence.

TEXTBOOKS AND THE DISCIPLINE OF HISTORY

Unfortunately, however, textbooks that present both a narrow nationalistic perspective and an uncontested singular narrative fail to provide students with any respect for the disciplinary nature of history. Often what students

---

[6] For example, an interesting discussion of the perpetuation of a single "master narrative" in the United States, is offered by Keith Barton and Linda Levstik (2004). See, specifically, chapter 9 "The Story of National Freedom and Progress."

are presented with is not history but propaganda and polemic. Rather than presenting young people with an understanding of how different interpretations of the past exist, students are too often confronted with narratives that adopt a particular (and often insular and limited) perspective. Typically these "history" textbooks offer no sense of dispute or interpretation, no appreciation of historical evidence or argument, and no understanding of the basis on which historical accounts are constructed. As Peter Lee (1991) has argued this is serious failing because,

> ...it is absurd...to say that schoolchildren know any history if they have no understanding of how historical knowledge is attained...the ability to recall accounts without any understanding of the problems involved in constructing them or the criteria involved in evaluating them has nothing historical about it (pp. 48–49).

From a disciplinary perspective, therefore, providing students with a single, unquestioned version of the past is hugely problematic. For true historical appreciation of any event requires a greater respect for evidence, an appreciation that other interpretations exist, and a critical and rational examination of competing claims to historical truth. Embracing and understanding a disciplinary perspective, students would learn to appreciate that history textbooks offer only *one* selected version of past events and that any historical account is, by its very nature, a social construction that requires critical analysis and careful evaluation. They would also appreciate that history represents a form of knowledge rather than just a body of knowledge. Ultimately, they would develop the capacity to appreciate that not *any* story of the past will do, but that some stories—provided they are firmly based on the available evidence—are more legitimate than others.

Producing textbooks that both eschew national narratives and help students appreciate the disciplinary nature of history is a huge undertaking and extremely difficult to achieve. Not surprisingly, therefore, few countries offer examples of textbooks, which strive for such ambitious goals. Nevertheless, during the past 40 years significant developments in England have seen a move away from traditional, single narrative textbooks to ones that adopt a more discipline-based approach to history. In most textbooks written prior to the 1970s authors' opinions were stated as objective fact and historical accounts typically were presented as uncontested "truths." Routinely they offered a nationalistic, single narrative, which focused on Britain's imperial past, the achievements of great men, and the activities of ruling monarchs. Attention to constitutional, military, and political events dominated and insular reference to "we" and "us" proved commonplace amidst ubiquitous patriotic narratives. Students never were exposed to alternative accounts or source material and visual representations proved exceptional. Textbook pages were crammed full with detailed information and densely written text dominated. Beginning in the late 1970s and early 1980s, however, dramatic and important changes occurred in history education and history textbook production. Indeed, by the end of the 1980s "traditional" textbooks based on conventions established for generations largely disappeared from the educational landscape.

Whilst changes in textbooks in England are not held up as an exemplary model for all nations, the dramatic shift in the character and content of history textbooks in England does offer some opportunities for reflection and consideration. Certainly the shift from the widespread use of "traditional textbooks" to "new history" textbooks that occurred during the past four decades offers intriguing insights into the possibilities and appropriateness of change.

DRAMATIC CHANGES: "NEW HISTORY" TEXTBOOKS

During the late 1970s and early 1980s, important developments took place in history education in England. In particular the 1980s proved a fascinating and dynamic time as the decade witnessed the clash between "traditional history" teaching and "new history." Essentially the "clash" resulted in a fierce and ideologically driven debate between, on the one hand, proponents of a traditional chronological and nationalistic approach to history teaching and those who, on the other, argued for a "new" history which placed greater emphasis on the structure of the discipline and the interpretive nature of history (Crawford, 2000; Dickinson, 2000; Foster, 1998; Haydn, 2004; Phillips, 1998; Sylvester, 1994).[7] The reasons why "new history" increasingly offered a serious challenge to established practices are numerous and complex. Fundamental to this important shift in practice and philosophy however was the increasing concern that history education needed to be revitalized with a more considered and contemporary approach. Undoubtedly the cognitive revolution in the psychology of learning proved influential in challenging existing theories of how children acquired knowledge and understandings. Constructivist approaches to learning also seriously challenged the widespread use of didactic teaching methods common in the period before the 1970s. Similarly, a number of influential researchers in England (e.g., Booth, Fines, Lee, Shemilt) challenged the domination of Piagetian thinking and suggested that students' abilities in history previously had been underestimated. Significantly, an

---

[7] Although educational and ideological battles over history surfaced most acutely in arguments over the introduction of the national curriculum for history in the late 1980s, the clash between competing traditions was apparent many years earlier. For example, the shift, in 1986, from the traditional and stratified "O" level and CSE examination courses to the more inclusive and arguably more innovative GCSE examination course already ensured that history teachers would have to embrace (or at least accept) many of the key influences and ideas of "new history."

increasing number of researchers and educators pursued the notion that students of all ages could and should acquire a greater appreciation of history as a discipline (not just as a body of knowledge to be learned).[8]

In addition to these important developments, it is no coincidence that "new history" emerged in a period in which socio-cultural shifts in society led to the ubiquitous questioning of tradition and "inherited thinking." An important aspect of the "new history" revolution therefore was also the increased attention given to more social, inclusive and critical history. Finally, the emergence of "new history" occurred at a time when history education was perceived to be seriously under threat. Unquestionably, a growing anxiety existed among history educators that the subject was in crisis and that traditional history appeared increasingly irrelevant to young people. As Shemilt (1980) wrote in the opening page to the classic Schools Council Project (SHP) "Evaluation Study,"

> The Schools Council Project *History 13–16* was established in 1972 as a result of teacher's dissatisfaction with "traditional history" and their concern at the apparent erosion of its position within the secondary curriculum (p. 1).

At its core "new history" challenged the notion of history as a "received" subject. Advocates of "new history" wanted students to understand how history was created and become more active in their study of the subject. They recognised that in order to know history students must understand the structure of the discipline and be concerned not only with knowing *that* but also with knowing *how*. The most effective embodiment of these changes was the Schools History Project (SHP) which, from the late 1970s onwards, offered teachers and students an innovative, thoughtful, and publicly examined curriculum driven by the philosophy of new history (Dickinson, 2000; Haydn, 2004; Phillips, 1998; Shemilt, 1980; Sylvester, 1994; Wineburg, 2001). It was widely applauded the history profession. According to John Slater (1989) the project remained,

> ...the most significant and beneficent influence on the learning of history and the raising of its standard to emerge this century. It gives young people not just knowledge, but the tools to reflect on, critically to evaluate, and to apply that knowledge. It proclaims the crucial distinction between knowing the past and thinking historically. It sums up what is often called "the new history" (pp. 2–3).

"New history" gradually grew in popularity among teachers and although some reactionary forces harked back to "traditional" history teaching, at

---

[8] In this respect "new history" followed Bruner's classic assertion that "any subject can be taught effectively in some intellectually honest form to any child at any stage of development" (Bruner, 1960).

the time of the implementation of National Curriculum history in 1988, few educators in England were willing to return to "old" ways (Dickinson, 2000; Haydn, 2004; Lee, 1999). Accordingly, most textbooks produced during the 1980s undoubtedly bore many of the hallmarks of "new history." Although narrative structures often were preserved, textbooks typically contained an array of source material that both supported and, at times, questioned accepted interpretations. Books invited enquiry and pupil engagement. Activities and questions typically asked students to assess and analyse evidence to reach historical conclusions. Textbooks also began to support the notion that historical narratives were not given and agreed, but were constructed and contested.

Above all, "new history" textbooks were more appreciative of history as a discipline. A typical example of a new history textbook was, *Peace and War*, authored by Shephard, Reid and Shephard. It was published in 1993 under the auspices of the SHP and it exemplified a number of features typical of the "new history" genre. In particular four elements stood out. First, the book chapters were organised around a question to be investigated. For example on two double-pages students were asked to consider: "Why did the USA drop the atomic bomb on Japan in August 1945?" In other sections of the book other similarly provocative questions invited student exploration (e.g., were the Victorians racist? Was there an Industrial Revolution?). Second, sources (which included photographs, newspaper extracts, maps, and political cartoons) dominated textbooks pages, while explicit narrative proved very limited. Moreover, the central narrative was less authoritative, and the language used appeared more tentative and conditional. For example, the book used phrases like "some historians argue..." or "several reasons have been suggested." Third, historical sources often provided different perspectives on an event or issue (for example, the section on Truman's decision to drop the bombs on Japan included sources from other Americans who argued against the fateful decision). Accordingly historical accounts were often left open to interpretation. Fourth, in-text questions rarely focused on comprehension or factual recall. Instead, textbook questions appeared more likely to focus on the utility and reliability of sources, the competing claims of evidence, or ask for evidence from sources that refuted or supported statements made.

As a result of important changes in textbook development begun in the 1980s, many students studying history today encounter history in a very different way to those who studied history in previous generations. Although the textbooks alone cannot guarantee a shift in students' understanding of the nature of history, young people today are more likely to appreciate that history is a discipline based on the interpretation and construction of historical evidence.[9] Furthermore "new history" textbooks are more likely to help students acquire important understandings. These include an appreciation that that history is not the past, but a reconstruction of the past. An awareness that although history provides us with stories and explanations, the past did not happen in stories and explanations any more than it does in the present. And, as a result of these understandings, students should begin to appreciate what sort of knowledge history is and understand the legitimacy of that knowledge.

NEW HISTORY TEXTBOOKS: LESSONS TO LEARN?

Although dramatic and often salutary changes in textbook production and development undoubtedly occurred in England during the past 40 years, it would be unwise and inappropriate to suggest that developments in England stand as a model to other nations. What is certain, however, is that significant change in textbook writing and provision requires a massive commitment on the part of any local, regional or national education system. At its core it involves a widespread re-assessment of the aims and purposes of history education. Changes might also include revisions to the history curriculum with less emphasis on coverage and more on promoting disciplinary understandings; the abandonment of examination systems solely based on factual recall and multiple choice testing; changes in teacher education in keeping with shifts in philosophy; and serious changes in the remit given to educational publishers.

Given the political, educational, and philosophical complexities of advancing such changes in any regional or national system of education it is, perhaps, worth considering what individual teachers might do to promote a more informed and enlightened appreciation of historical knowledge among their students. Of course the choices of individual teachers are context-dependent and are often directly related to the amount of pedagogical freedom a teacher perceives he or she possesses. Individual teachers always will make curriculum and pedagogical choices based on a number of considerations including the political context in which they work and the sys-

---

[9] Of course this is not to say that "new history" textbooks were (or are) without critics. It might be argued for example that the inclusion of a mosaic of competing sources at the expense of a clear and coherent narrative invites confusion among students. Also, it is widely recognised that if more attention is given to providing students with alternative historical evidence and interpretations then less time will be devoted to covering a range of "important" historical topics. Furthermore, the inclusion of sources alone cannot guarantee more sophisticated learning. The inclusion of sources ripped out of context, unattributed, and devoid of provenance are unlikely to help students develop their historical understandings. Finally, and perhaps most importantly, it is vital to recognise that textbook content never represents neutral knowledge. Indeed, the selection and inclusion of some source material and the exclusion of others arguably can lead students to certain conclusions and opinions about the past.

tem of examination to which they and their students are held accountable. Accordingly the following are offered as examples of possibilities rather than as a blueprint for action. Nevertheless teachers who often are restricted by the domination of a single, authoritative text might introduce other alternative accounts into the history classroom and further discuss how and why the accounts differ. Importantly teachers may consider with their students how different accounts can be reconciled and evaluated.

Other possibilities also exist. Teachers might, for example, introduce a range of historical evidence into the classroom and ask students to construct a narrative account based on this evidence. This activity could then be broadened to an informed discussion about what legitimately can, and cannot, be said based on this evidence. Another possibility is to ask students to read a given textbook topic. Then require students to research the topic to identity and evaluate information that may have been excluded from the text. An interesting discussion might then take place that requires students to consider why some information is included and why some is not.

Naturally teachers in different contexts will have to consider carefully their pedagogical approach. On the one hand some teachers will enjoy the freedom to be innovative and to challenge textbook conventions in the ways outlined above. On the other hand, many teachers will find themselves more constrained by political, curriculum, assessment, or parental pressures. How individual teachers operate in their given context will therefore be driven to a large extent by a practical assessment of what is possible and desirable. Nevertheless if, as educators, we want to seriously challenge the authority of one dimensional, nationalist textbook and encourage a broader appreciation of the interpretive nature of history, then new approaches must be explored. In particular, students living in a globalised world in which real or virtual interactions among peoples with different faiths, ideologies, cultures and histories are more frequent, need to acquire respectful and rational dispositions. Developed historical understanding is fundamental to this process as it encourages or obliges a respect for evidence, a reflexive approach to knowledge, a willingness to recognise value and strive for well-grounded judgements and the freedom to offer an account of the past that is sanctioned by available evidence. Ultimately, therefore, students should learn history not as a fixed story underpinned by vested social or political agendas, but because it provides them with the tools to evaluate the competing stories and evidence they encounter and it instantiates the values of an open democratic society.

CONCLUSIONS

This paper has briefly mapped out some of the characteristics commonly featured in textbooks across the world. In particular, it has critiqued those textbooks that offer nationalistic, single story narratives. As an alternative, a vision of a different form of textbooks, based on "new history" developments in England is advanced. Of note, however, it is important to realise that textbooks alone guarantee nothing. Textbooks can only be effective when they are employed by thoughtful teachers and considered by willing pupils. In the right hands, however, history textbooks have the potential to shape and deepen understandings. In this respect good history textbooks offer students the opportunity to appreciate the complexities of uncovering and understanding the past. They are not driven by nationalistic sentiments or propaganda, nor are they based on a single, authoritative story line. Rather, good history textbooks allow students to appreciate that history is a constructed discipline worthy of interrogation. Good textbooks also allow students to be comfortable with the idea that that different versions of the past always will exist. One of our primary goals as educators is, therefore, not to require students to learn a single official account of the past, but to give students the tools and mental apparatus to help them make sense of different versions of the past. If we can accomplish this we will have gone a long way to ensuring that students have a worthwhile and meaningful education in history and, by extension, a more informed understanding of the world around them.

REFERENCES

Anyon, J. (1978). Elementary social studies textbooks and legitimate knowledge. *Theory and Research in Social Education, 6,* 40–55.

Anyon, J. (1979). Ideology and United States history textbooks. *Harvard Educational Review, 49,* 361–386.

Apple, M. W. (1991). Culture and commerce of the textbook. In M. W. Apple & L. K. Christian-Smith (Eds.), *The politics of the textbook.* New York: Routledge.

Apple, M. W., & Christian-Smith, L. K. (1991). The politics of the textbook. In M. W. Apple & L. K. Christian-Smith (Eds.), *The politics of the textbook.* New York: Routledge.

Barthes, R. (1976). *The pleasure of text.* London: Cape.

Barton, K. C., & Levstik, L. S. (2004). *Teaching history for the common good.* Mahwah, NJ: Lawrence Earlbaum.

Bruner, J. (1960). *The process of education.* Cambridge, MA: Harvard University Press.

Crawford, K. A. (2000). Researching the ideological and political role of the history textbook: Issues and methods. *International Journal of Historical Learning Teaching and Research, 1,* 1–11.

Crawford, K. A., & Foster, S. J. (2007). *War nation memory: International perspectives on world war II in school history textbooks.* Greenwich, CT: Information Age Publishing.

Dickinson, A. (2000). What should history be? In A. Kent (Ed.), *School subject teaching: The history and future of the curriculum.* London: KoganPage.

Foster, S. J. (1998). Politics, parallels, and perennial curriculum questions: The battle over school history in England and the United States. *The Curriculum Journal, 9,* 153–164.

Foster, S. J. (1999). The struggle for American identity: Treatment of ethnic groups in United States history textbooks. *History of Education, 28*, 251–279.

Foster, S. J., & Crawford, K. A. (Eds.) (2006a). *What shall we tell the children? International perspectives on school history textbooks.* Greenwich, CT: Information Age Publishing.

Foster, S. J., & Crawford, K. A. (2006b). The critical importance of history textbook research. In S. J. Foster & K. A. Crawford (Eds.), *What shall we tell the children? International perspectives on school history textbooks.* Greenwich, CT: Information Age Publishing.

Foster, S. J., & Nicholls, J. (2005). America in world war II: An analysis of history textbooks from England, Japan, Sweden, and the United States. *The Journal of Curriculum and Supervision, 20*, 214–234.

Hein, L., & Selden, M. (Eds.) (2000). *Censoring history: History, citizenship and memory in Japan, Germany and the United States.* London: M. E. Sharpe.

Haydn, T. (2004). History. In J. White (Ed.), *Rethinking the school curriculum* (pp. 87–103). London: RoutledgeFalmer.

Lee, P. J. (1991). Historical knowledge and the national curriculum. In R. Aldrich (Ed.), *History in the national curriculum.* London: KoganPage.

Lee, P. J. (1999). Learning the right stories or learning history? Developments in history education in England. *Newsletter of the Organization of American Historians, 27*, 7–9.

Leeuw-Roord, J. (2008). Yearning for yesterday: Efforts of history professionals in Europe at designing meaningful and effective school history curricula. In L. Symcox & A. Wilschut (Eds.), *National history standards: The problem of the canon and the future of history teaching.* Charlotte, NC: Information Age Publishing.

Marsden, W. E. (2001). *The school textbook: Geography, history and social studies,* London: Routledge.

Nicholls, J., & Foster, S. J. (2005). Interpreting the past, serving the present: US and English textbook portrayals of the Soviet Union during world war II. In R. Ashby, P. Gordon, & P. Lee (Eds.), *International review of history education, Volume IV.* London: Woburn Press.

Nicholls, J. (2006). *School history textbooks across cultures: International debates and perspectives.* Oxford: Symposium Books.

Phillips, R. (1998). *History teaching, nationhood, and the state: A study in educational politics.* London: Cassell.

Pingel, F. (1999). *UNESCO guidebook on textbook research and textbook revision.* Hannover: Hahnsche Buchhandlung, Studien zur Internationalen Schulbuchforschung.

Pingel, F. (2000). *The European home: Representations of 20th century Europe in history textbooks.* Strasbourg: Council of Europe.

Porat, D. (2004). 'It's not written here, but this is what happened': Students' cultural comprehension of textbook narratives on the Israeli-Arab conflict. *American Educational Research Journal, 41*, 963–996.

Schissler, H., & Soysal, Y. (Eds.). (2005). *The nation Europe and the world: Textbooks and curricula in transition.* Oxford: Beghahn Press.

Sewall, G. T., & Cannon, P. (1991). New world of textbooks: Industry consolidation and its consequences. In P. G. Altbach, G. P. Kelly, H. G. Petrie., & L. Weis

(Eds.), *Textbooks in American society: Politics, policy, and pedagogy* (pp. 61–69). New York: State University of New York Press.

Shemilt, D. (1980). *History 13–16, Evaluation study: Schools council; history 13–16 project*. Edinburgh: Holmes McDougall.

Shepard, C., Reid, A., & Shepherd, K. (1993). *Peace and war: Discovering the past, year 9*. London: John Murray.

Slater, J. (1989). *The politics of history teaching: A humanity dehumanized?* London: Institute of Education.

Soysal, Y., Bertilotti, T., & Mannitz, S. (2005). Projections of identity in French and German history textbooks. In H. Schissler & Y. Soysal (Eds.), *The nation Europe and the world: Textbooks and curricula in transition*. Oxford: Beghahn Press.

Sylvester, D. (1994). Change and continuity in history teaching, 1900–93. In H. Bourdillon (Ed.), *Teaching history*. London: Routledge.

Vickers, E., & Jones, A. (Eds.) (2005). *History education and national identity in east Asia*. London: Routledge.

Williams, R. (1989). Hegemony and the selective tradition. In S. de Castell, A. Luke & C. Luke (Eds.), *Language, authority and criticism: Readings on the school textbook*. London: Falmer Press.

Wils, K. (2009). The evaporated canon and the overvalued source: History education in Belgium. In L. Symcox & A. Wilschut (Eds.), *National history standards: The problem of the canon and the future of history teaching*. Charlotte, NC: Information Age Publishing.

Wineburg, S. (2001). *Historical thinking and other unnatural acts*. Philadelphia: Temple University Press.

CHAPTER 5

COMMENTARY

What History to Teach? Whose History?

Alberto Rosa

HISTORY AND IDENTITY

History teaching in schools mainly consists of narratives about how we became what we are now. Narratives inevitably produce a fictionalization of
events of the past; they have a performative ability, create events, agents
and agencies. Historical narratives shape social representations about us
and others. They also have the ability to produce strong feelings, apprais-
ing events and characters in particular ways. They provide a *nar-rationality*
for events, making one identify with some and counter-identify with others. In sum, history is a way of producing values and inoculating them via
discourse.

History does not have the monopoly for distribution of discourses about
the past. Family and community life are full of souvenirs from the past.
Rituals and stories also contribute to establish feelings about what really
matters (family, community, symbols, etc). These settings very often include
networks of objects (pictures, souvenirs, monuments), narratives and ritu-

History Education and the Construction of National Identities, pages 63–72
Copyright © 2012 by Information Age Publishing
63

als, providing a ground on which individual and public memories get interweaved, and so personal, social and national identities get intermingled with lived experiences (Billig, 1995; Middleton & Edwards, 1990).

These elements shape together the collective memory of a community. They are among the goods present in a symbolic market (Bourdieu, 1991) capable of acting as tools for understanding, thinking and decision-making. History entered into the curriculum of public education as one of the key resources of the nation-states, to secure a loyal citizenry sharing a sense of belonging to the same imagined community (Anderson, 1983). The school history to be taught was then that of the community one belonged to and felt committed (or should be committed) to. But this was old wine in new wineskins; it came to play a role similar to that of Sacred History in old religious schools—to give sense and meaning to community life and moral. This could hardly be a surprise, since the very term nation had a religious meaning before taking a political one (Smith, 1991). This religious origin, well ingrained in the European past, makes Country to be placed above anything else (e.g., "no salvation outside the Church," "Todo por la Patria," "Deutschland über Alles"). It too often implied the drive to impose some kind of uniformity in the population (religious, ethnic, linguistic, and sometimes all of them together) so the true meaning and mission of the community gets preserved, even if this requires ideological or ethnic cleansing to keep and refine its pretended essence.

Memory, Identity and History are a trinity impossible to disentangle. The three chapters in this section share a concern for defusing the deleterious potential of nationalist history, as well as reflecting on possible alternatives. But they also point out the difficulties of so doing, precisely because of the connection between history teaching and the cement it provides for keeping a sense of shared identity and solidarity in the population. I will focus in this commentary on two of the main issues these papers touch upon: what history to teach and how to teach history.

HISTORY OF WHAT? WHOSE HISTORY?

Berger (2012) points out that "national history might be inadequate in many ways, but it is also indispensable," since "certain historical developments only make sense if we teach them within a national framework." I agree, but I also think that attention should be paid to how several kinds of identities interplay within nation-states. The structure of the population, the values cherished by individuals, and the very efficiency of nation-states may be changing. This makes one wonder how this could affect to the solidarity of the citizenry, and the role history teaching could play within the new unfolding landscape. Something must be happening when national leaders felt the urge to claim the necessity of enforcing the values of the Republic upon migrants (Nicholas Sarkozy, 2010), or to defend some kind of core national identity by declaring the failure of multiculturalism (Merkel, 2010).

History is about interpreting social affairs of the past to understand the present and to prepare for the future. For history teaching to be instrumental for the shaping of identity, it has to relate to one's own experience and feelings. It has to relate to *me*, to *us*. Whatever the case, this *we* has to include me, although I may not like to fare throughout time always with the same *you*'s (those I take as my fellows to shape the *we* I may identify with). Something similar happens with the others, different to *us*. Some of them may become a *you*, equal to me, one of *us*. And perhaps some of those who belonged to the *we* I may have had to identify with before, may end up being part of the *others*.

Diversity is now well established within the population of current nation-states. In spite of the myth of uniformity, *Polis* (the State), *Demos* (political community), *Ethnos* (cultural community) and *Cives* (spaces for the exercise of rights) do not coincide anymore, and even overlap in different ways inside and outside national borders.

Identity is something personal and social. I belong to a *we* to which some *you*'s (equal to me) also belong. Beyond is the world of otherness. But there are two kind of othernesses: external (outside Polis) and internal (inside Polis, but outside Ethnos). People living within national borders are from assorted origins. They have different languages, religion, culture and values. They want the State to do different and sometimes diverging things. *Demos* and *Ethnos* are not synonymous anymore, if they ever were.

Values can be highly emotional. Each individual (and collective) has final values (beliefs about 'what really matters' in life as goals) as well as means for reaching those ends, which are also valued. Final values are those which provide sense, which make experience (and what experience presents—objects, actions, agents, feelings, desires, even oneself) to have significance. Each culture, each *Ethnos*, provides final values about *what makes a life worthy of being lived*. That is why these values are so deeply ingrained in personal and cultural identity.

Ecological issues and globalization are putting the State sovereignty in jeopardy. Even the State monopoly of the legitimate use of violence within its territory is now being contested. Instrumental practices (economics, the media) are also following rules operating across national borders, so that they are beyond the control of any particular State. When this happens, States get deprived of some of their means to mediate between the natural and the social orders, so that its operational role for the governance of social systems of solidarity diminishes. When this happens there is no guarantee that a rational *Rule of Law* will be applied. As a consequence, individuals start to withdraw from participating in political and civil life. Ethnic belonging and cultural identities (old or new—religion, sects, gender, gangs, etc.)

come then to the forefront in public life, particularly among those who are left in the margins of society and have no way of defining themselves by their social role. New spaces for civil life develop aside and beyond the control of the State (Touraine, 1995). *Cives* and *Polis* get more and more separated from each other.

If culture appears as a tricky issue in political discussions, this is because in real life culture cannot be pronounced in singular. When referring to what is going on in concrete societies one should better speak of one culture as different from others. One adheres to a religion or a group, loves or hates particular symbols, some food or landscapes, but does not feel strongly committed to the Transit Control Administration or the National Revenue Service. If one wants *Polis*, *Cives* and *Demos* to hold together, both types of values (final and instrumental) have to reach some kind of *status quo*, so that they are able to coexist in the vital experience of individuals in such a way that the ends of one's own (cultural) identity are not at odds with the rationality of means (the State). Touraine (1995) suggests that this is possible by being very careful in not imposing some cultural values upon others, and so keeping political rationality restricted to the means and not the ends, as it is the case in the secular and democratic State. For individual citizens to feel committed to the State, the latter has to be felt as a resource rather than an obstacle for reaching their ends. This requires formulae for civic solidarity to be devised so that the social pact does not become ineffective for some, because a part of the population becomes instrumentally unequal. The key issue is to make compatible different kinds of cultural identity within one particular *Polis*.

THE NATION AS SPACE FOR THE EXERCISE OF LIBERTY AND RIGHTS

John Stuart Mill (*Essay on Liberty*) said that liberty cannot be taken as something primordial or natural at all. Liberty is not the capability of reaching the objects of desire whenever one wants—that would be being a slave to the received stimuli. Rather, it is the result of freeing oneself from the tyranny of immediacy and open new possible paths for action. So viewed, liberty is not something natural, but something historically reached by painfully conquering some spaces for autonomy. Rights are a historical product of socio-cultural efforts to open new possibilities for acting with lesser degrees of dependency from the existing powers (of nature or society). That is why Rights are so fragile—they are not natural properties but cultural creatures born from social pacts. For Rights to be kept alive, resources and institutions are required, as well as the willingness of citizens to honor their duties.

All kinds of Rights, whether they are Legal (property, justice), Civic (participation in communal life, vote), Social (health, education, housing, work) or Human Rights (preservation of life, freedom of thought, speech), result from efforts to open spaces for liberty. They are fully artificial; they are a consequence of the creation of norms ordering social life in such a manner that individuals acquire new properties as subjects—in the double sense of agents and citizens of the State. Rights belong to the ethical domain and provide humans with a very unnatural feature—dignity (Marina, 1995).

Rights are a product of Law, and these are created by States. The State, the Law opens paths for transiting between otherness and citizenship. It instantiates balances between Ethnos and Demos. This requires a new view of the social pact taking into account the porous nature of national borders, and how Demos and Ethnos overlap over and across national borders. Rights and Law are becoming transnational, but perhaps not necessarily cosmopolitan.

The continuous presence of Otherness is a challenge for the development of Civic values. The re-instantiation of the social pact requires the Other. This makes active defense of diversity to be a necessity. Caring for the Other is not only a principle different to that of justice (Gilligan, 1982), but is also a resource for increasing one's own freedom. Taking the Other into account is not only a resource for increasing one's consciousness, but also provides an indispensable open space for the possibility of liberating oneself from the values of one's own culture, even from one's own identity.

It is the continuous presence of the Other what keeps freedom of consciousness alive, together with the separation of the private and the public realms. The social pact has then to be re-worked within the new scenery of increasing cultural diversity. The new social pacts require new overlapping consensus to be reached (Rawls, 1999), something that cannot be done without caring for the internal and external other. This is what makes possible instrumental values to become themselves some kind of final values. Values that made possible to say "I disapprove of what you say, but I will defend to the death your right to say it" (Hall, 1906—frequently attributed to Voltaire).

So viewed, Ethnos is to be left for the private realm, although it cannot be ignored when devising any kind of social pact. Civil Rights are a product of the State. There cannot be Cives without Polis, but once Cives is well grown up it can flourish above State borders, although never can be operational without the law of each individual Polis granting particular rights. But this is not enough, Civil Rights can only be kept alive if citizens feel driven to act according to them, to practice civic duties in their actions; i.e., if they get embodied as traits of character of the citizens—virtues of citizenship: reasonableness, solidarity, justice, tolerance, commitment, but also patriotism. I believe history teaching can play some role for this purpose.

PATRIOTISM AND COSMOPOLITANISM

If one wants history teaching to contribute to the shaping of an active citizenship, there is little doubt that Ethnos is not to be taken as its main subject, but it also may be worthy to consider what weight school history should give to Polis and Cives when devising its curriculum.

Hansen (2012) points out that no democracy can exist without borders. Quoting Benhabib, he reminds us that accountability and representation come together, and that requires institutions, laws and policies to operate within borders, even if these are of a porous nature. Ours is a world of nation-states, and thanks to that we can enjoy Rights and exercise our civic and political agency.

It seems then that, as Berger (2012) and Foster (2012) point out, we cannot dispense with national history. We all belong to one particular nation-state, and our direct experiences are linked to events happening within its boundaries that can be historically explained. However, there is widespread agreement that a nationalist history requires another against whom to exercise national identity. That is why sometimes a distinction is made between (bad) nationalism and (good) patriotism, as Berger puts it.

Patriotism is not well regarded nowadays. In spite of the efforts of some (e.g., Habermas, 1989; Sternberger, 1947) it keeps being understood by many as synonymous to nationalism, or even worst, to jingoism. However I believe it is worthy going into examining some of the possible meanings it can gather within its complexity.

Patriotism derives from the Latin word *Patria*, meaning fatherland—native country. This primitive meaning is what makes patriotism have such bad press. However, there is a long past of different uses of this word. Cicero in *De Legibus* differentiated between *patria naturae* and *patria civitatis* (civic, political). Jerónimo Feijoo (a Spanish writer of the 18th century) called to differentiate between love for the *patria*, linked to the rule of law, and national passion—to take the region in which one was born as better and above anywhere else. The latter for him is no other thing but a kind of idolatry.

Mario Onandía (2002, quoted by Blanco, 2005) offers a constitutional and republican conception of *Patria*, elaborating on previous ideas of Milton, Shaftsbury, Bolinbroke, d'Holbach, and Montesquieu. For him Patria is the ensemble of institutions and laws that guarantees liberty. Human Rights and dignity may be of universal value, but it gets its concrete realization in a concrete constitutional State. Patriotism is grounded on identifying with some others for carrying out a particular common enterprise (Taylor, 1989, quoted by Blanco, 2005). It is a commitment to concrete solidarity. It is upon these principles that Sternberger and Habermas coined and spread the concept of *constitutional patriotism*. As Pettit (1999, quoted by Blanco,

2005; p. 411) puts it, "my country for the values it realizes, my country for the freedom that gives us."

These views embody one's rights and liberty in the concrete institutions and laws of one's country, which also provides the ground, but also sets boundaries, for the exercise of solidarity. Patriotism is a commitment with the *you*'s who, together with *me*, shape the *we*—*us*, the nationals of *our* nation-state. Patriotism is not Cosmopolitism. Or, should it be?

Patriotism, as here presented, seems to constrain the limits of Cives within the borders of Polis, making them somehow synonymous. But the argument previously developed rejects both terms to be co-extensive. Transnational institutions, law and rights, even if fragile, witness that they are not identical, but not independent either. It seems to me that now that we are well aware of the complexities of the relations between *Ethnos* and *Demos,* and are busily trying to deal with them, even if not too well, we should also pay some attention to the subtleties of the overlaps, gaps and frictions between Polis and Cives.

I believe that Hansen's essay in this section sheds some light upon this point. Far from a naïve optimistic view of cosmopolitism, he goes into a careful discussion of the complexities it involves. He refrains from the easy dualism of communitarianism and cosmopolitism and calls attention to the difficulties of the clashing of values and customs between different communities, as well as on the dangers of taking for granted that one's ideas about Cives are of universal nature. Following Appiah and Addams, he states his confidence in cultural change and everyday efforts for reaching common understanding by doing common work, in the neighborhood as well as in international cooperation.

I believe some of Addams' ideas quoted by Hansen, are particularly at issue here. The Cives to be built is to be reached by working in the heart of the cosmopolitan city, where people from different origins live and work together and create bonds by the power of association, rather than by the old powers of State discipline and coercion. Rather than refusing patriotism, or searching for the creation of some kind of international patriotism, a certain sense of duty soaking up old national patriotism is needed. Patriotism and international fair play are not only compatible, but indistinguishable.

The argument takes one to believe that Cives is a product of Polis, but it cannot span beyond the borders of the State but through the effort of Demos. In turn, Demos transforms itself by negotiating pacts among different Ethnos. This requires the citizenry to work towards this end, as well as exercising Civic virtues. As Domingo Blanco (2005) points out, "Demos' civic virtue is indispensable for the democratic State. It cannot be guaranteed by the State, and even less to be imposed—that would be contradictory. For constitutional principles to become a drive for action, they have to engage with the motivation and mentality of citizens; i.e., they have to be supported by habits of respect for the law, for preference of the public upon the private, for a sufficient level of enlightenment" (p. 420). There is little doubt that school history is not foreign to the purpose of creating an informed citizenry.

WHAT HISTORY TO TEACH?

It seems then that if the history taught at school is that of the nation-state, it might be impossible to avoid the dual danger of nationalism and presentism. A possible alternative is centering on a history of Cives, rather than Polis. But, before going further into this idea, I believe some consideration of what kind of History to teach is worthwhile.

Rosa (1994) pointed out that, in spite of sharing the same verbal label, School history and disciplined history are not the same subject. The first, as Foster (2012) reports when reviewing school history textbooks around the world, tends to be overtly nationalistic, as well as presenting a single official narrative. This contrasts with disciplined history, well aware of the interpretative, contested nature of the historical accounts it provides. As Foster says, historical accounts are social constructions requiring careful analysis and evaluation. It may end up providing a story, but some are more legitimate than others. So viewed, History is more a form of knowledge than a body of knowledge. That is why he calls for a kind of history teaching that goes more into training students on understanding how histories were and are created, so students can get to support the notion that historical narratives were not given and agreed, but constructed and contested. As Holt (1990) said, "rather than teaching [students] to be consumers of stories, 'someone else's facts', we might better develop their critical faculties by letting them create stories of their own" (p. 10). This obviously requires refraining from providing ready-made stories, and promoting the discussion of alternatives narratives, as well as the use of texts and data to build their own accounts about the past.

If such a conception is adopted, the issue of whether to teach national history or not disappears. Disciplined history is to be taught, and this requires selecting issues of current interest and going into their critical examination. This may include the examination of how nation-states developed, but may also be prepared "to dissipate illusions and recall what has been forgotten by the uses of history by the powers of each moment" (Carreras & Forcadell, 2003, p. 42), to recover the voice of the defeated of the past (Leone, 2000), that the victorious hurried to bury (Benjamin, 1974). A critical history has the duty of showing how some of the *we* one may too easily identify with, have sometimes in the past been executioners, and some other times victims. But each time, they were different *we*, and for different reasons. That is why I believe that the teaching of history should focus more on the changes of Cives, than on the building of Polis, although the latter is unavoidable. It should not be forgotten that many of the values of Cives one cherishes were forged in a Polis different to that of the nation-state one belongs to.

Álvarez Junco (2003) suggests that school history should not keep the same historical subject all time. It should consider in turn the actors and agencies operating in particular relevant events. In addition, he recommends taking an ironic approach in history teaching. This will favor a more detached view of one's belongings, and history, and so helping to avoid a too quick identification with the agents involved in the events under scrutiny. Such a history will resemble more a post-modern movie, than a classical novel. Perhaps this will help historical events to appear more human, more close to our understanding. This may make history less glorious, but also less dangerous.

A critical history of the shaping of Cives cannot be a history of whatever *we* the powers may choose (*one's* Ethnos or Polis) for the student to identify with. It has to be a history of what concerns us now: the kind of *we* wanted for the future, or better the kind of *we* are now ready to work for, in cooperation with the others.

REFERENCES

Álvarez Junco, J. (2003). Historia e identidades colectivas [History and collective identities]. In J. J. Carreras & L. Forcadell (Eds.), *Usos Públicos de la Historia* [Public uses of history] (pp. 47–68). Madrid: Marcial Pons Historia.

Anderson, B. (1983). *Imagined communities.* London: Verso

Benjamin, W. (1974). *La Dialéctica en suspenso. Fragmentos sobre la Historia* [Dialectics in suspense. Fragments about History]. Santiago de Chile: Lom, 1996.

Berger, S. (2012). De-nationalizing history teaching and nationalizing it differently! Some reflections on how to defuse the negative potential of national(ist) history teaching. In M. Carretero, M. Asensio, & M. Rodríguez-Moneo (Eds.), *History education and the construction of national identities* (pp. 33–47). Charlotte, NC: Information Age Publishing.

Billig, M. (1995). *Banal nationalism.* London: Sage.

Blanco, D. (2005). Patriotismo [Patriotism]. In P. Cerezo Galán (Ed.), *Democracia y virtudes cívicas* [Democracy and civic virtues] (pp. 383–422). Madrid: Biblioteca Nueva.

Bourdieu, P. (1991). *Language and Symbolic Power.* Cambridge, Mass.: Harvard University Press.

Carreras, J. J., & Forcadell, L. (2003). Historia y Política: Los Usos [History and politics: The applications]. In J. J. Carreras & L. Forcadell (Eds.), *Usos Públicos de la Historia* [Public uses of history] (pp. 11–46). Madrid: Marcial Pons Historia.

Foster, S. (2012). Re-thinking history textbooks in a globalised world. In M. Carretero, M. Asensio, & M. Rodríguez-Moneo (Eds.), *History education and the construction of national identities* (pp. 49–62). Charlotte, NC: Information Age Publishing.

Gilligan, C. (1982). *In a different voice.* Cambridge: Harvard University Press. 1982.

Habermas, J. (1989). *Identidades nacionales y postnacionales* [National and postnational identities]. Madrid: Tecnos.

Hansen, J. (2012). De-nationalize history and what have we done? Ontology, essentialism, and the search for a cosmopolitan alternative. In M. Carretero, M. Asensio, & M. Rodríguez-Moneo (Eds.), *History Education and the Construction of National Identities* (pp. 17–31). Charlotte, NC: Information Age Publishing.

Holt, T. (1990). *Thinking historically. Narrative, imagination and understanding.* New York: College Entrance Examination Board.

Leone, G. (2000). ¿Qué hay de social en la memoria? [What is social in memory?] In A. Rosa, G. Bellelli & D. Bakhurst (Eds.), *Memoria colectiva e identidad nacional* [Collective memory and national identity]. Madrid: Biblioteca Nueva.

Marina, J. A. (1995). *Ética para náufragos* [Ethics for the shipwrecked]. Madrid: Anagrama.

Middleton, D., & Edwards, D. (Eds.). (1990). *Collective remembering.* London Sage.

Onandía, M. (2002). *La construcción de la nación española. Republicanismo y nacionalismo en la ilustración* [The construction of the Spanish nation. Republicanism and nationalism in the Enlightenment]. Barcelona.: Ediciones B.

Pettit, P. (1999). *Republicanismo.* Barcelona: Paidós.

Rawls, J. (1999). *A theory of justice.* Cambridge, Massachusetts: Belknap Press of Harvard University Press.

Rosa, A. (1994). What do people consume history for? (If they do). Learning history as a process of knowledge consumption and construction of meaning. In M. Carretero & J. Voss (Eds.), *Learning processes in history and social sciences.* Hillsdale, N.J.: Lawrence Erlbaum.

Smith, A. (1991). *National identity.* London: Penguin.

Sternberger, D. (2001). *Patriotismo constitucional* [Constitutional patriotism]. Bogotá: Universidad Externado de Colombia.

Taylor, C. (1989). Cross-purposes: The liberal-communitarian debate. In M. Rosemblum (Ed.), *Liberalism and the moral life* (pp. 159–182). Cambridge, Mass: Harvard University Press.

Touraine, A. (1995). ¿Qué es una sociedad multicultural? [What is a multicultural society?] *Claves de Razón Práctica, 56,* 14–25.

SECTION 2

PURPOSES OF HISTORY EDUCATION

CHAPTER 6

DILEMMAS OF COMMON AND PLURAL HISTORY

Reflections on History Education and Heritage in a Globalizing World

Maria Grever

In 2007 six high school students (16–17 years) in Rotterdam were asked to express their views on school history. A student of Turkish descent stated:

> There are many people here from different cultures and backgrounds and I don't hear anything about that. I miss that. It is mainly European history here.[1]

---

[1] Group interview with six students of Havo-Vwo (upper high school level), Nova College Montfort. Rotterdam (The Netherlands), February 2, 2007. In 2006 and 2007 we conducted four focus group interviews with 16 students in Rotterdam from different ethnic backgrounds; the semi-structured interviews were taped and transcribed with anonymous names. First quote see Grever and Ribbens (2007, p. 117).

History Education and the Construction of National Identities, pages 75–91

The answer of this student is at odds with the current tendency in Western society to stress the teaching of a *common history* within the framework of the nation. A frequent complaint is that young people are ignorant of the history of their country of residence. Politicians assume that furthering historical knowledge and awareness about the nation will avoid fragmentation, support social cohesion and strengthen national identity (e.g., Grever & Stuurman, 2007; Phillips, 2000; Symcox & Wilschut, 2009). Several Western governments interfere with historical culture by revitalizing national institutions, rituals or symbols and by establishing an increasing grip on the subject matter of history education. However, in the globalizing world both popular culture and the pursuit of history have become increasingly pluralistic (Berger & Lorenz, 2008). Hence the emphasis on a common -national- history and the heterogeneous reality of society evoke tensions which have a profound impact on the aims and tasks of education in general, and on history education in particular (Seixas, 2004, p. 5).

Educationalists have researched multiperspectivity and cultural pluralism in (history) education (Klein, 2010; Meijer, 1993; Stradling, 2003; Von Borries, 2001b), but little attention is paid to the construction of common history in the classroom. Common history in the sense of *shared* historical knowledge is not the same as harnessing history in a top-down canon to promote national unity (Osler, 2009, p. 85). This kind of policy not only ignores crucial teaching insights, it also undermines history as a critical discipline and its potential function for democracy (Grever, 2007; Seixas, 2007). Moreover, in professional historiography (Berger et al., 2008) and in school history (Barton & Levstik, 2004) the nation was never an uncontested principle. Over the years historians were sometimes deeply engaged in building up the Fatherland, whereas others treated the nation critically. What exactly is the meaning of common history? Is this a (perceived) "common past" of the nation or another community? Or does common history refer to a specific historical approach? And how does a common history relate to plural history?[2] Focusing on these questions, I will examine in this article the meaning of common history from the perspective of critical hermeneutics.

After a brief explanation of the conceptual differences between plurality and diversity, I shall argue why common history does not necessarily contradict plural history. Subsequently, I will point to some dilemmas of these approaches in history education. I shall illustrate my argument with results of comparative research on students' views on history and identity and a recent education project on sensitive heritage.

---

[2] These questions are the central issues of a research program, granted by the Netherlands Organization for Scientific Research (NWO), that I am currently directing at Erasmus University Rotterdam with Carla van Boxtel. We investigate how heritage education might contribute to shared historical knowledge in a globalizing society, while acknowledging a plurality of narratives. See www.eshcc.eur.nl/english/chc/home/.

PLURAL HISTORY AND DIVERSITY

To clarify my approach it is necessary to make an analytical distinction between plurality and diversity, although I realize that these two concepts are related. *Plurality*—here in the sense of plural history—refers to distinct, sometimes opposing points of view or perspectives on a historical subject matter, derived from and influenced by a selection of *sources* (e.g. eyewitnesses, chronicles, images), *geographical levels* (e.g. Europe, Asia; local, global), *historical agents* (e.g. poor, rich; men, women); *plotlines* (e.g. progress, decline; linear, multi-linear) and *historiographies* (e.g. political history, colonial history, gender history) (Stradling, 2003, pp. 9–10, 18). To select their sources, agents, plotlines and historiographies, historians and history teachers use criteria which are based on outcomes of historical research, scientific paradigms and ideological views. Hence, historical narratives are always created from specific perspectives. Within the context of history didactics, the concept "plurality" is part of historical reasoning to stimulate students to critically reflect on the diverse perspectives of historical narratives and accounts (e.g., Lee, 2007; Seixas, 2006; Van Boxtel, 2009; Van Drie & Van Boxtel, 2008). I will come back to this issue later.

I use *diversity* for the "given" situation that students bring different histories and narrative templates into the classroom they have received from various cultures and mental worlds they grow up in. This situation refers to social characteristics or identity dimensions of human beings such as nationality, age, gender, religion and educational level. However, we have to realize that this identity is never a static phenomenon. Paul Ricoeur's approach (1988, pp. 246–247) to overcome the dilemma between a subject identical with itself through the diversity of its different states—the formal category of identity (being the same)—and sheer change, is to pose the dynamic category of narrative identity (oneself as self-same). That identity consists of a constant narrative refiguration in view of new happenings, knowledge and experiences. Today teachers increasingly deal with heterogeneous groups of students from migrant descent who have layered past relationships, influenced by different religions, countries of origin, and family stories. Like everyone else, these students attempt to understand themselves and the world surrounding them by adapting and incorporating discourses from their family, teachers, peer groups, the Internet and other sources, and integrating these into a coherent narrative.

The research I have conducted with Kees Ribbens on high school students' views of history and identity (Grever & Ribbens, 2007), unmistakably revealed the immense diversity of the student population in large Western European cities. We focused on twelve multicultural high schools with altogether 678 young adults in three urban areas who attended history classes: Rotterdam (the Netherlands), Greater London (United Kingdom) and Nord-Pas-de-Calais (an urban conglomeration in Northern France). Students of five high schools in Rotterdam came from 42 different countries, reaching from China, Zimbabwe and Poland to Peru and France. Moreover, many of them had parents born in different countries: a Chinese mother married to a Dutch father, or a French mother to a Surinam father. To create an atmosphere in these classrooms in which students are willing to learn and to master a body of historical knowledge, partly related to their country of residence with which they are often unfamiliar, is rather difficult. To get them to truly understand the narratives of textbooks, expositions and DVDs, is time-consuming. It seems even harder for a teacher to do justice to various perspectives on the provided subject matter and to leave room for dialogue. Genuine interaction in these classes about different interpretations requires of teachers both broad historical knowledge and considerable teaching skills (Klein, 2010, pp. 615, 628).

For our study we investigated the meaning of history for students' identity construction. We then concentrated on the major ethnic groups in the three urban areas. Furthermore we only selected respondents whose parents were both born in the same country. This resulted in ten different "parental-country of birth groups" of 448 respondents in the three urban areas: three native (Dutch, English, French) groups and seven groups of non-western migrant descent, mainly second generation. Our research entailed a questionnaire survey, consisting of fourteen questions. Two questions, each consisting of 15 items, particularly focused on the meaning of history for students' *personal lives* and how, in their view, history may be relevant for *society*. Using factor-analysis, five factors or "profiles of historical interest" have been constructed, related to social characteristics of the students, such as gender and cultural ethnicity.[3]

The analyses were conducted for each country separately. Relevant for this article is profile 3: I have a common history with others. This profile shows only for one French category of migrants significant differences (Grever et al., 2011).

Profile 3 Common History with Others

- I have a common history with other inhabitants of my city or village
- I have a common history with other inhabitants of the Netherlands/ UK/France
- I have a common history with other inhabitants of Europe
- I have a common history with other people in the world

---

[3] For the Dutch and English data the same five profiles could be identified, whereas the French data reveal only three of the five profiles. The items were measured on a five-point scale ranging from 1 (totally disagree) to 5 (totally agree). See Grever et al. (2011).

Apparently, these students consider history, among other things, as something that is shared with other people. They seem to articulate that they share a framework of historical reference with others, whether living nearby or far away: a common history on various geographical levels—local, national, European and global. Consequently, this profile also implies having a common history on different *ideological* levels, since geography or spatiality is never a neutral concept (Lorenz, 2004, pp. 36–39). In the next section I explore the concept of common history from a hermeneutic approach.

CONSTRUCTING COMMON HISTORY AND SHARED UNDERSTANDING

People do not live in different worlds, they live in the same world. Although individuals draw borderlines to situate and differentiate themselves in relation to others, they do that within the locality and temporality of that world (Rüsen, 2005, p. 2; Van den Akker, 2009). People live in the same world, performing themselves through language, politics, religion, media, leisure, and other interactions in the public and private sphere. These articulations provide people with an idea of having a common past and a common future. Without that there would not be a livable world, nor would it be possible to understand the world we live in. This does not necessarily mean that people have the same convictions, values and norms. The Rotterdam students we interviewed had different interests and priorities, and different views on school history. Nevertheless, they were able to describe the behavior of people from the past and to understand more or less their actions in the light of past circumstances, what philosopher R. G. Collingwood (1994, pp. 282–302) has called the *re-enactment of past thoughts.*

In the 1980s, Collingwood's ideas on re-enactment have affected the construction of second-order concepts in the Dutch field of history didactics, in particular the concept "Empathy, perspective bound" (Dalhuisen, 1993, p. 29). The re-enactment of past thought is a cognitive procedure. It implies the *rational* re-thinking of specific decisions of historical actors in order to explain their actions and behavior. Although it is not possible to actually re-think past thoughts, Collingwood (1994, p. 427) emphasizes the possibility of re-enacting the logical "structure" of past thought: "(...) the historian is enabled, indeed not to "know" the past as it actually happened (...) but to solve with accuracy and certainty the particular historical problems which present themselves to his mind, in terms of the evidence at his disposal." So we can basically understand past beliefs and utterances, even when those beliefs differ strongly from those of the interpreters. It is therefore important that students are aware of the distinction between being capable of understanding sentences and actions, taking the historical circumstances into account, and to raise the question how they judge these beliefs and views as articulated in sentences and actions. This kind of reflection can only be realized in the awareness of living in a *common* world, in what we call a society.

Whereas Collingwood considers re-enactment as a procedure for historical understanding, Hans-Georg Gadamer elaborates a hermeneutic-onto-logical conception of understanding, as a way of *being*. His hermeneutics has inspired American and Canadian research on historical consciousness and historical understanding concerning history teaching (Gadamer, 1987; Seixas, 2004, pp. 8–9; Wineburg, 2001, p. 10). Gadamer presents the possibility of shared understanding by pointing out that sharing the same world makes it possible to value and exchange interpretations. In the case of our Rotterdam students: despite national, religious or ethnic differences, they all attend the same class at the same high school, have the same teacher, acquire the same school subject and skills, and they all may come under the spell of a story and get excited by an argument. However, they probably attribute different meanings to that same situation. Gadamer (2006, pp. 470–471) acknowledges the existence of different cultures and view points, but he holds on to the presupposition of a common world and to the possibility to reach agreement. In his view language constitutes "commonality" or sharedness, because language discloses the world we share with others, allowing to understand each other. From early childhood we learn to speak and to write, hence we learn to participate in a *linguistic community*. Because languages are translatable into one another, we can also understand foreign people, cultures and worlds (Gadamer, 2006, pp. 386–389). Language supersedes the ego, it always implies a dialogue.

Gadamer (2006, p. 285) also claims that "our historical consciousness is always filled with a variety of voices in which the echo of the past is heard. Only in the multifariousness of such voices does it exist: this constitutes the nature of the tradition in which we want to share and have a part." On an individual level it involves the mastering and appropriation of knowledge, norms and stories which circulate in families, schools, communities, and society. This means that human beings are both part of pre-existing traditions passively and that they reinterpret them actively according to future desires (Meijer, 2006, p. 329). A total awareness of this tradition can never be completely achieved, just as it is impossible to be complete free from tradition. According to Gadamer (2006, p. 301): "To be historically means that knowledge of oneself can never be complete."

What is the significance of these philosophies to history teaching in multicultural classrooms? To what extent is it possible to achieve the situation that students are willing to listen to each other, to take the perspective of a specific historical agent, and to reach shared understanding?

When we interviewed the Rotterdam students, they told us about the emotional debates they often had about religion, particularly after history classes. Another small-scale study on Dutch multicultural classes (Blanken et al., 2003) shows even more antagonism between students. The study reports that children with an Islamic background are often less familiar with the history of the Second World War and the Holocaust. They know more about the history of the Maghreb and the Gulf war. Whereas Dutch native students are more involved in collective memories that have been transmitted by their parents and grandparents, those students do not share collective memories of the Second World War. According to the teachers, differences manifest themselves both on the level of knowledge and in the way they experience this (transmitted) history. Students with an Islamic background hardly understand the sensitive aspects of the Holocaust. During history classes on the Holocaust, particularly Moroccan Dutch students identify with the current situation of the Palestinian people and regularly express anti-Jewish views under the guise of freedom of expression (Blanken et al., 2003, pp. 20–27).[4]

The researchers concluded that students from migrant descent in the pre-vocational schools lack the necessary skills of debate and dialogue. Some teachers were shocked about the radical ideas of students and stopped discussions.[5] They explained that it was really difficult to unravel the different layers of the debate, particularly the anachronistic and presentist mixture of the history of the Holocaust with the current violent situation in the Middle East.

THE LIMITS OF UNDERSTANDING

According to Gadamer (2006, p. 180), people meet each other through language: in a dialogue they come to understand each other with respect to a subject-matter. Hence, it is essential that history teachers are well trained in listening, asking questions, and summarizing different standpoints. It requires the mastery of the skills to apply historical reasoning in history teaching practices, such as the identification of causes and consequences, facts and opinions, continuity and change, intended and unintended effects of people's actions.

But suppose the students of the above-mentioned research are capable of applying historical reasoning in a classroom conversation, will they reach shared understanding or agreement? I doubt that, because the emphasis on verbalization and rational analysis ignores two phenomena. First, the assumption that every experience can be translated into a narrative is too optimistic. Second, following Vasterling's critique of Gadamer, his herme-

---

[4] It also became evident that Islamic students are not a homogeneous group either. There are differences concerning gender and country of origin.

[5] In 2008 I delivered a lecture at a high school teacher training at the Leiden University. Some history teachers expressed the same kind of experiences they had when they teach about the Holocaust.

neutic approach does not acknowledge the distinction between understanding and agreement. This distinction is, however, essential in view of plural perspectives.

I will start with the first point. Although cognitive skills are necessary conditions for history learning, emotions often play an incredibly important role in the process of historical understanding. Focusing just on evidence and rational explanations would ignore the impact of excitement, euphoria, eagerness, fear, pain or trauma. Sometimes a topic might suddenly evoke intense negative emotions amongst students due to frightening experiences related to that subject. In that case it makes little sense to apply Collingwood's logic of question and answer to solve this kind of historical "problem." Nevertheless, in *The principles of history* Collingwood (1999, p. 45) acknowledges that emotions and irrational thoughts are both involved in the actions of historical agents, and that it is not impossible for historians to understand these. So we can re-think the reasons why Hitler was vindictive against the French, and why this emotion incited his decision to occupy France. However, although we are able to re-think the logical "structure" of past thought, we never can re-think why Hitler expressed this specific past thought and not another. We cannot reveal why he selected some arguments and not other ones, since every selection of arguments also depends on a person's emotional involvement. It is not possible to investigate the *specific* underlying emotions of a decision. But these emotions are still there and might influence a person's actions. Collingwood does not address that issue.

Ricoeur (1988) reflects on the issue. Through narrative, he argues, we construct an identity: telling a story articulates experiences through emplotment, thereby integrating heterogeneous elements into a synthetic whole. But the idea of a narrative identity disregards the possibility of not being able to verbalize experiences. There are situations in which people are not in charge of their memories and are unable to integrate them into a whole, refiguring story-fragments into a narrative that constitutes a personal identity. Sometimes the past is so horrific, evoking such painful emotions in a person, that narrative understanding is not possible. According to Ricoeur (1988, p. 187) events such as Auschwitz generate feelings of considerable ethical intensity. In that case the ethical neutralization that may be fitting in the case of history of a past—keeping the past at a distance in order to better understand and to explain—is not possible nor desirable. He points at the risk of ending up in a ruinous dichotomy between a history that would dissolve the event in explanation and a purely emotional retort that would dispense us from thinking the unthinkable. Ricoeur (1988, p. 186) sees a solution in the role of fiction, but it is not clear what this exactly means. In the last chapter of his magnum opus *Time and narrative*, he concludes optimistically that the bits and pieces of stories that are unbearable can be transformed into a coherent and acceptable story, "in which the analysand can recognize his or her self-constancy" (Ricoeur, 1988, pp. 246–247). In a recent article Ricoeur (2008) acknowledges the difficulties of integrating traumatic memories. He differentiates between memories that are transformed into healing narratives and traumatic memories, resulting in a compulsive perpetuation of violence as a form of acting out. This distinction is important in the context of history teaching.

Telling stories about a past event in a classroom with interactive reflection afterwards, will offer children and students the possibility to identify with other persons, cultures and times. Many histories deal with fear, adventure, pain, victory, evoking all kinds of emotions and commitment. Young students are often fond of "adventure stories." However, when history teachers tell about the large-scale violent conflicts of the twentieth century—such as colonial wars, the Holocaust, Cambodia or Srebrenica—we must realize that these past atrocities might come too close to the experience of some students, or that stories like these might be too terrible to re-enact in their minds and too complex to put into language. If teachers have students with relatives who have traumatic experiences and deal with a repressed past,[6] or students who have recently escaped dangerous regions involved in a war, it seems even more difficult.

The second point refers to what Gadamer calls full or true understanding which entails, according to him, agreement. Although Gadamer is right to emphasize that understanding is sharing the world, Vasterling (2003, p. 166) argues he is wrong in assuming that understanding, or sharing the world, entails agreement. The distinction between understanding and agreement is essential in order to do justice to the different perspectives people, including the students in our classrooms, have on the world they inhabit. Understanding means being able to take into account the diversity of perspectives on the same (historical) subject matter or situation. It does not mean agreeing to all and every perspective.

Both the small-scale study of Blanken et al. (2003) and our own research indicate that native students and students from migrant descent differ in their evaluative standards. Because Dutch native students are part of the hegemonic culture in the Netherlands, it is sometimes hard—if not impossible—to achieve full understanding of students from other cultures. Habermas (1990) has rightly criticized Gadamer's hermeneutic model of understanding for neglecting power-relations. A necessary condition of any dialogue is a commitment of the interlocutors as equals in a spirit of mutual respect and concern (Lefstein, 2006). Hence, it would not be realistic nor desirable to expect from the students that they agree with each other's

---

[6] See the example about a Chinese student Carmen in Canada whose stories of her family involve the war with Japan and the Cultural Revolution in Seixas (1993, pp. 311–313).

evaluative standards. They have to learn to respect these differences and to reflect on that situation by making them aware of the fact that it is possible to understand each other's perspective without necessarily consenting to it. This important exercise is particularly difficult to perform with an issue like the Holocaust, because of its resonance in the fraught situation in the Middle East and the current anti-Islam rhetoric of public debates in many Western countries such as the Netherlands. Last but not least, let us not forget the reality of high school life—the energy of students, the tensions with their peers, the role of teachers—which makes the organization of classroom conversations demanding.

Being part of different cultures correlates with specific historical interests, as the outcome of our research concerning students' interests in different *kinds of history* will show. This is the issue of the next paragraph.

A VARIETY OF HISTORICAL INTERESTS

The Rotterdam students complained that in their history lessons topics, such as the Ottoman Empire, the Atlantic Slave Trade and Migration, were hardly addressed. They also emphasized the importance of historical knowledge about the Netherlands. Perhaps this last statement was a socially desirable answer, because the data derived from our survey research show something else. We investigated the interest of the Dutch, English and French students in a given set of ten particular kinds of history (Grever & Ribbens, 2007, pp. 111–125; Grever et al., 2011). They had to select and rank five—out of the ten—kinds of history into a top-5, from most important (place 1) to less important (place 5).

Native students in the three urban areas clearly appreciate the *national history* of the country of residence; this kind of history belongs for them to the five most important kinds of history. Yet, nobody put this kind of history on the first place. The Dutch data significantly shows that students from migrant descent are less interested in Dutch history. About 44% of them place Dutch history in the top 5 of most interesting kinds of history against 87% of the native Dutch. The differences are greatest for the *history of religion*. In the three urban areas this kind of history scores high among all (first and second generation) migrant groups. In contrast, native youth demonstrates much less identification with the history of religion; this kind of history did not belong to the five most often mentioned kinds of history that native students were interested in. Remarkably, all students declare an interest in *world history*; there are no significant differences between native students and students of migrant descent in this respect in all three urban areas. Dutch and British students showed significantly more interest in world history than their French peers. In *European history* students are hardly interested; only native students show some interest, significantly more in the Netherlands and France. These outcomes, particularly with respect to national history and the history of Europe, confirm other studies (Angvik & Von Borries, 1997; Von Borries, 2001a).

With respect to national history, the outcomes of our research demonstrate that native respondents consider the history of the country of residence relevant (although not very much) and that respondents from non-western migrant descent are less interested. Furthermore, there is a statistically significant relation between the different cultures of students (related to country of residence and country of origin) and their interest in various kinds of history (Grever et al., 2011).

Several educationalists stress the importance for young people to acquire historical knowledge about the country they live in. For instance Keith Barton and Linda Levstik (2004, pp. 59–60) argue that the legitimacy of the state's demands and benefits in a democratic nation, rests on a *shared* sense of identity—anchored in history—among its citizens, which is a precondition for participatory citizenship. Indeed, although transnational communities have become increasingly influential, nation-states are still important sovereign entities. Yet the authors do not state that students should learn exclusively about the history of the nation.

In any case, global history—the history of civilizations, global networks, large-scale conflicts, migrations, and other global interactions—has become increasingly indispensable if young people are to grow up with an understanding of the issues and problems that will shape their lives. Moreover, our research has revealed that many of these 14–18 years old students are interested in world history. If teachers use a broad framework of historical knowledge with a coherent chronology from a global perspective, then the national history of the country of residence could be linked to world history topics and developments (Grever, 2007, p. 43; VanSledright, 2008).

Now the purpose of history teaching in secondary high schools is also to help young people to discover and to evaluate various vantage points and perspectives. In what way then are common history and plural history related, and how is it possible to find a balance between the two approaches in a classroom with students who are part of different traditions and show interest in various kinds of history?

I have explained that plural history refers to distinct perspectives on a historical subject matter, achieved by the choice of sources, historical agents, plotlines and historiographies. So there are traces of a past reality and there is a plurality of meaning of that past reality which generates plural history. Hence, plural history deals with different viewpoints of people in the past, different viewpoints between historical actors and readers in the present, and different historiographical viewpoints. The assumption is that historians, readers and students who try to understand past beliefs and actions, share the world with the historical agents having those beliefs and performing those actions (Van den Akker, 2009, p. 216). Whereas diversity refers to a "given" identity in a specific situation, plurality is the result of "action." Becoming aware of different perspectives concerning the same historical subject matter constitutes the possibility of common history. There is no plurality waiting to be discovered. Whereas historians create plurality in the context of academic historiography, history teachers evoke plurality in a classroom. Without it they lose the idea of living in a common world. Why is that?

Using *plural perspectives* with respect to past events or processes opens up reasoned discussion about the interpretation of contingent facts and the assessment of different views in practicing history. It helps to overcome historical determinism (Huizinga, 1912, pp. 432–433; Ricoeur, 2008, p. 15). In order to reach historical understanding it is crucial to make students aware of the significance of unfulfilled possibilities. Indeed the past is factual. But in any given historical situation there have been multiple options. The development of historical processes turns possibilities into "reality." Hence, deploying a singular (canonized) perspective transforms history into a series of relics (Grever, 2007). If historical facts will be discussed from several—competing or opposing—perspectives, it will generate more visibility and a deeper sense of historical reality. This is the epistemological argument.

Identifying and comparing various perspectives stimulate students to examine the sources carefully and critically, to present plausible arguments and to exchange different views. The very act of discussing and comparing perspectives in a classroom engenders reflexivity, that is "the human possibility of reflecting on one's own assumptions as well as on those of others" (Meijer, 2006, p. 325). If the circumstances in a classroom allow such a dialogue, then the use of diverse perspectives might create an awareness of living in a pluralist yet common world. This is the social and political argument.

Summing up: *exploring the same world (or the same history) from various perspectives, transforms the world (history) into a common world (common history).*[7] There are, however, at least three dilemmas in finding a balance between common and plural history.

First, students coming from other cultures can articulate their stories and points of view without being ostracized, marginalized or ridiculed by their peers or teachers. There are many telling examples in the past of excluding cultural minorities from expressing their narrative; this exclusion is no less today. Second, teachers have to make well-informed choices which perspectives on a specific topic they select. It is simply not possible to apply an infinite range of perspectives in view of effective learning processes. Related to that issue, teachers should consider how to deal with Arendt's state-

---

[7] I owe much to the inspiring discussions with Veronica Vasterling about this line of thinking.

ment (1993, p. 51) about looking *upon the same world from one another's standpoint.* To what extent is this approach applicable to histories of large-scale conflicts and genocide? It is rather problematic to require that high school students take the perspective of perpetrators such as concentration camp guards or war criminals (Hondius, 2010, pp. 42–43). We cannot avoid nor escape these morally and politically charged issues. The preliminary answer to this dilemma is that historians, teachers and educationalists should jointly reflect more on this problem. Third, to achieve genuine dialogue, the interlocutors are willing to listen to each other and to recognize perspectives and interpretations other than their own. This requires that students are psychologically capable to articulate their view on the subject-matter. With respect to violent histories, it is therefore important to acknowledge that historical reasoning is not always or not yet possible. In that case a teacher could better take another approach.

An interesting approach with respect to sensitive heritage in the Netherlands is the elaboration of the education program "Telling stories" for Remembrance Centre Camp Westerbork (Tijenk, 2010). One heritage education project, *Fragments in the night—fugitives of all times,*[8] involves twelve-year old students from primary schools who listen to a story of a camp survivor, collect and investigate factual information about daily life in the camp, and make their own little artefacts. Next, they put their self made artefacts in a story-chest that can be used later to transmit the stories of Jewish fugitives and survivors to class-mates, parents or visitors. In this way the young students have "translated" the incomprehensible atrocities—i.e. the exportation of 107.000 Dutch Jews from Westerbork to the concentration camps of whom 102.000 have been killed—into more comprehensible dimensions. The active construction of meaning refers to the network of relations between people, places and material culture that is subject to variation (Jones, 2010), generating a dynamic approach of heritage. Moreover, the combination of listening/telling stories and making/preserving artefacts provides room for young students to cope with this horrific past, appropriated to their own feelings in that situation without a direct pressure of verbalizing.

CONCLUSION

In this article I have explored the meaning of common and plural history, and the dilemmas of finding a balance between the two. The problem is urgent because schools in large urban areas are increasingly confronted with heterogeneous student populations. In these classrooms some topics such as the Holocaust have become more sensitive than before. High school teachers have the responsibility to teach in such a way that students

---

[8] The Dutch title of the project is *Scherven in de nacht—vluchtelingen aller tijden.* The project is based on the children's book with the same title of the author Martine Letterie.

acquire both historical knowledge about the world and their country of residence, and the skills of historical reasoning in order to understand the contingency and complexity of the past.

Hence, history education should focus on different spatial levels: from local to national to global. It is important that all students learn about global history. Concerning national history, teachers better include the variety of people in the country of residence, the impact of immigration on its development, and the nation's historical position in the world. Then there is a possibility that students experience a sense of belonging to their country of residence. Not in the sense of a nationalistic point of view, but from the perspective that they are emergent cosmopolitan citizens living in an age of globalization and universal human rights as well.

Furthermore, historical reasoning has the potential to create common history for students in a classroom. Particularly the actual use of plural perspectives provides for a common ground. The pursuit of history always implies a dialogue on interpretations. If students explore the same historical text or the same heritage and exchange various perspectives, they are transforming that revealed past into a common history. To reach that goal it is important that students feel safe to express their views, and that teachers have the skills and the time to supervise them in carrying out their interpretations.

Finally, although people live in the same world, they are part of different cultures. Today, history lessons about a horrific or repressed past in multicultural classrooms might cause quite different responses. For some students a war is linked to national heroism, for others that war evokes such painful memories that it is hard for them to articulate a comprehensive narrative. Using various assignments related both to texts and to heritage traces that appeal to the senses, might provide more room for them to cope with their emotions. In that sense the emerging dynamic approach of heritage education in countries such as the Netherlands and England is promising. The use of museum pieces, relics or monuments as primary source of instruction seems to offer other opportunities to imagine the past than history textbooks do. At the same time it remains important to apply historical reasoning in heritage education settings. The condition, however, is that we have to be aware that sensitive heritage might evoke conflicts amongst students or negative emotions they cannot verbalize. If we do not take that into account, we achieve dissension instead of shared understanding.

REFERENCES

Angvik, M., & Von Borries, B. (Eds.). (1997). *Youth and history. A comparative European survey on historical consciousness and political attitudes among adolescents. Vol. A: Description; vol. B: Documentation.* Hamburg: Körber Stiftung.

Arendt, H. (1993). *Between past and future. Eight exercises in political thought* (1st ed., 1961). New York: Penguin Group.

Barton, K., & Levstik, L. (2004). *Teaching history for the common good.* Mahwah, New York/London: Lawrence Erlbaum.

Berger, S., Eriksonas, L,. & Mycock (Eds.) (2008). *Narrating the nation. Representations in history, media and the arts.* New York/Oxford: Berghahn Books.

Berger, S., & Lorenz, C. (2008). Introduction; national history writing in Europe in a global age. In S. Berger & C. Lorenz (Eds.), *The contested nation. Ethnicity, class, religion and gender in national histories* (pp. 1–23). Basingstoke: Palgrave Macmillan.

Blanken, C., Tuinier, J.D., & Visser, G. (2003). *Antisemitisme op school? Verslag van een onderzoek naar leerlingen met een islamitische achtergrond in confrontatie met de geschiedenis van de jodenvervolging* [*Anti-Semitism at school? Report of an investigation of students with an Islamic background in confrontation with the history of the persecution of the Jews*]. Utrecht: St. Vredeseducatie.

Collingwood, R. G. (1994). *The idea of history* (rev. edition with *Lectures* 1926–1928). Oxford/New York: Oxford University Press.

Collingwood, R. G. (1999). *The principles of history and other writings in philosophy of history* (W. H. Dray & W. J. Van der Dussen, Eds.). Oxford: Oxford University Press.

Dalhuisen, L. (1993). Structuurbegrippen voor het schoolvak geschiedenis. Inleving, standplaatsgebondenheid [Structural concepts voor school history. Empathy, restriction by point of view]. *Geschiedenis in de klas, 14,* 29–40.

Gadamer, H.-G. (1987). The problem of historical consciousness. In P. Rabinow & W. M. Sullivan (Eds.), *Interpretive social science: a second look.* Berkeley: University of California Press, 103–160.

Gadamer, H.-G. (2006). *Truth and method* (1st ed., 1975). New York: Continuum.

Grever, M. (2007). Plurality, narrative and the historical canon. In M. Grever & S. Stuurman (Eds.), *Beyond the canon. History for the twenty-first century* (pp. 31–47). Basingstoke: Palgrave Macmillan.

Grever, M. (2009). Fear of plurality. Historical culture and historiographical canonization in Western Europe. In A. Epple & A. Schaser (Eds.), *Gendering historiography: beyond national canons* (pp. 45–62). Frankfurt am M./New York: Campus Verlag.

Grever, M., Pelzer, B., & Haydn, T. (2011). High school students' views on history. *Journal of Curriculum Studies, 43* (in press).

Grever, M., & Ribbens, K. (2007). *Nationale identiteit en meervoudig verleden* [National identity and plural past]. Amsterdam: Amsterdam University Press.

Grever, M., & Stuurman, S. (Eds.). (2007). *Beyond the canon. History for the twenty-first century.* Basingstoke: Palgrave Macmillan.

Habermas, J. (1990). The hermeneutic claim to universality. In G. L. Ormiston & A.D. Schrift (Eds.), *The hermeneutic tradition: from Ast to Ricoeur* (pp. 245–272). Albany NY: State University of New York Press.

Hondius, D. (2010). *Oorlogslessen. Onderwijs over de oorlog sinds 1945* [*Lessons of war. Education about the war since 1945*]. Amsterdam: Bert Bakker.

Huizinga, J. (1912). Uit de voorgeschiedenis van ons nationaal besef [*From the ancenstry of our national sense*]. *De Gids, 76,* 432–487.

Jones, I. (2010). Negotiating authentic objects and authentic selves. *Journal of Material Culture, 15,* 181–203.

Klein, S. (2010). Teaching history in the Netherlands: teachers' experiences of a plurality of perspectives. *Curriculum Inquiry, 40,* 614–634.

Lee, P. (2007) From national canon to historical literacy. In M. Grever & S. Stuurman (Eds.), *Beyond the canon. History for the twenty-first century* (pp. 48–62). Basingstoke: Palgrave Macmillan.

Lefstein, A. (2006). Dialogue in schools: towards a pragmatic approach (paper 33). In *Working papers in urban language and literacies.* London: King's College.

Lorenz, C. (2004). Towards a theoretical framework for comparing historiographies: some preliminary considerations. In P. Seixas (Ed.), *Theorizing historical consciousness* (pp. 25–48). Toronto: University of Toronto Press.

Megill, A. (2007). *Historical knowledge, historical error. A contemporary guide to practice.* Chicago: The University of Chicago Press.

Meijer, W. (1993). Plurality and commonality in basic education. *Paedagogica Historica, 29,* 767–775.

Meijer, W. (2006). Plural selves, and living traditions: A hermeneutical view on identity and diversity, tradition and historicity. In M. de Souza, G. Durka, K. Engebretson, R. Jackson, & A. McGrady (Eds.), *International handbook of the religious, moral and spiritual dimensions in education* (pp. 321–332). Dordrecht: Springer Academic Publishers.

Osler, A. (2009). Patriotism, multiculturalism and belonging: Political discourse and the teaching of history. *Educational Review, 61,* 85–100.

Phillips, R. (2000). Government policies, the State and the teaching of history. In J. Arthur & R. Phillips (Eds.), *Issues in history teaching* (pp. 10–23) London: Routledge.

Ricoeur, P. (1988), *Time and narrative* III. Chicago/London: The University of Chicago Press.

Ricoeur, P. (2008). Memory, forgetting, history. In J. Rüsen (Ed.), *Meaning and representation in history* (pp. 9–19) New York & Oxford: Berghahn Books.

Rüsen, J. (Ed.). (2005). Introduction. Historical thinking and intercultural discourse. In J. Rüsen (Ed.), *Western historical thinking. An intercultural debate* (pp. 1–11). New York & Oxford: Berghahn Books.

Seixas, P. (1993). Historical understanding among adolescents in a multicultural setting. *Curriculum Inquiry, 23,* 301–327.

Seixas, P. (Ed.) (2004). *Theorizing historical consciousness.* Toronto: University of Toronto Press.

Seixas, P. (2004). Introduction. In P. Seixas (Ed.), *Theorizing historical consciousness* (pp. 3–20). Toronto: University of Toronto Press.

Seixas, P. (2006). *Benchmarks of historical thinking: a framework for assessment in Canada.* Vancouver: Centre for the Study of Historical Consciousness.

Seixas, P. (2007). Who needs a canon? In M. Grever & S. Stuurman (Eds.), *Beyond the canon. History for the twenty-first century* (pp. 19–30). Basingstoke: Palgrave Macmillan.

Stradling, R. (2003). *Multiperspectivity in history teaching: A guide for teachers.* Strasbourg: Council of Europe.

Symcox, L., & Wilschut, A. (Eds.). (2009). *National history standards: the problem of the canon and the future of teaching history*. Charlotte, NC: Information Age Publishing.

Tijenk, C. (2010). Verhaal centraal in het Herinneringscentrum Kamp Westerbork [Central story in Memorial Centre Camp Westerbork]. In C. van der Kooij & I. Mulder (Eds.), *Van canon tot klaslokaal. Slotsymposium project Verhaal Centraal* [*From canon to classroom. Final conference project Central Story*] (pp. 9–14). Borger: Projectbureau Verhaal Centraal.

Van Boxtel, C. (2009). *Geschiedenis, erfgoed en didactiek* [*History, heritage and didactics*]. Amsterdam: Erfgoed Nederland.

Van den Akker, C. (2009). *Beweren en tonen. Waarheid, taal en verleden* [*To claim and to demonstrate. Truth, language and past*]. Nijmegen: University Library.

Van der Dussen, W. J. (1997). Collingwood's "Lost" manuscript of *The Principles of history*. *History and Theory, 36,* 32–62.

Van der Kooij, C., & Mulder, I. (Eds.). (2010). *Van canon tot klaslokaal. Slotsymposium project Verhaal Centraal* [*From canon to classroom. Final conference project Central Story*]. Borger: Projectbureau Verhaal Centraal.

Van Drie, J. & Van Boxtel, C. (2008). Historical reasoning: towards a framework for analyzing students' reasoning about the past. *Educational Psychology Review, 20,* 87–110.

VanSledright, B. (2008). Narratives of nation-state, historical knowledge, and school history education. *Review of Research in Education, 32,* 109–146.

Vasterling, V. (2003). Postmodern hermeneutics? Towards a critical hermeneutics. In L. Code (Ed.), *Feminist interpretations of Hans-George Gadamer* (pp. 149–180). University Park: University Pennsylvania Press.

Von Borries, B. (2001a). Europe's past present and future—perceived by European adolescents. A cross-cultural study. In J. van der Leeuw-Roord (Ed.), *History for today and tomorrow: what does Europe mean for school history?* (pp. 179–204). Hamburg: Körber Stiftung.

Von Borries, B. (2001b). "Multiperspectivity"—Utopian pretensions of feasible fundament of historical learning in Europe?. In J. van der Leeuw-Roord (Ed.), *History for today and tomorrow: what does Europe mean for school history?* (pp. 269–295). Hamburg: Körber Stiftung.

Wineburg, S. (2001). *Historical thinking and other unnatural acts. Charting the future of teaching the past*. Philadelphia: Temple University Press.

CHAPTER 7

SCHOOL HISTORY AS A RESOURCE FOR CONSTRUCTING IDENTITIES

Implications of Research from the United States, Northern Ireland, and New Zealand

Keith C. Barton

History education and issues of national identity have long been connected. The rise of nationalism in the nineteenth century was linked to the creation of historical narratives that explained and justified emerging nation states (Anderson, 1983; Hobsbawm & Ranger, 1983), and from a modern perspective, it is hard to imagine a nation without a history, because history justifies the very existence of a nation. The creation of these national narratives coincided with the rise of universal public schooling and the development of museums, both of which arose during the nineteenth century, and both of which took on responsibility for transmitting historical identities—conceived in national terms—to both young people and adults. Still today, the use of history to create a sense of national identity is a source of ongoing controversy in countries around the world, as textbooks and cur-

History Education and the Construction of National Identities, pages 93–107
Copyright © 2012 by Information Age Publishing

ricula are constantly revised to reflect changing ideas about how a given nation should think of itself.

The relationship between students' identities and their understanding of history has been an active field of research in recent years, and studies have established that students' national, ethnic, political, and religious backgrounds all play a role in their interpretation of the meaning and significance of the history they encounter in school (e.g., Barton & McCully, 2005; Epstein, 2008; Goldberg, Porat, & Schwarz, 2006; Peck, 2010; Seixas, 1993). In order to move forward, however, a clearer conceptualization of identity is needed. Most studies in this area have not used an explicit theoretical framework for understanding identity or its influence on students' understanding, nor have they provided a clear definition of what identity entails. It is commonplace to claim that identity is fluid and dynamic, that it is socially constructed, and that students can hold multiple identities simultaneously, but just what these identities consist of has not been explicitly addressed. Such conceptual clarification is necessary, however, not only to improve the precision of research on the topic but to address the educational implications of such research. Although this chapter cannot provide a comprehensive definition of identity, by examining research from three countries in which the relationship between school history and nationhood is very different, it may be able to offer insight into some relevant aspects of identity with which educators must contend.

Three different perspectives on identity and school history have characterized most scholarship in the field, as well as having informed most policy debates related to the history curriculum. The first assumes that one task of school history is to "provide" students an identity, almost always conceived of in national terms. By learning about the history of the nation, students will learn what it means to be an American or Russian or Netherlander, and presumably they will then give their allegiance to the nation. This perspective often is associated with nationalist politicians, but even scholars who consider such an approach wrong-headed may assume that school history currently functions in this way; that is, they often characterize school curricula as straightforward attempts to impose such identities on students. On the other hand, a second approach (based sometimes on ideological commitments, sometimes on empirical findings) notes that attempts to impose identity are likely doomed to failure, because students have pre-existing identities that are grounded in ethnicity, religion, or nationalities other than those represented in the curriculum. In the strong version of this perspective, students resist the historical identities offered in school; in a weaker version, students' alternative identities simply influence how they make sense of what they learn there. Finally, some educators regard the relationship of identity to history to be nonexistent or, perhaps, a mistake. From this perspective, the study of history at school can—and perhaps should—safely ignore questions of identity altogether, both by declining to impose a national identity on students, and by failing to take into consideration the identities that students already bring with them; mixing history and identity, it is suggested, corrupts the subject's disciplinary integrity. The research discussed in this chapter, however, suggest that a fourth way of thinking about history and identity may better characterize students' own perspectives. School history may provide important resources (among many others) that students draw upon in constructing the historical dimensions of their identities.

THE UNITED STATES

The history curriculum in the United States conforms in many ways to the stereotype of a pervasive attempt to inculcate an exclusive identity conceived of in national terms. From the first years of primary school, students celebrate holidays and other events that are meant to give them a sense of their national identity. Later they encounter a systematic, chronological treatment of U.S. history at least three more times, and the emphasis again is on the origin and development of the current social, political, and demographic status of the country. World history, meanwhile—and particularly modern world history—receives little attention. The very fact that this pattern is so prevalent in the United States, despite the lack of an official national curriculum, indicates just how widely U.S. educators share an assumption that the purpose of studying history is to learn about the origin and development of the nation.

This approach influences students' thinking in two important ways, each of which highlights a crucial component of what historically-grounded identity entails. The first is that U.S. students consistently refer to the people and events in the national past by using first-person, plural pronouns: *we, us,* and *our.* They talk about how the American Revolution was the beginning of *our* country, how the Bill of Rights represents *our* freedoms, how *we* almost came apart during the Civil War, how immigration shows where *we* came from. This pattern, notably, holds true for students from different ethnic groups, as well as for recent immigrants. Students whose families have only immigrated to the United States in the last year will nonetheless refer to the actions of people in the Revolutionary Era as though they were their own direct ancestors—which, in a historical sense, they consider them to be (Barton, 2001b; Barton & Levstik, 1998). Creating this sense of national community is a major element of history education in the United States, and it is largely successful.

Students also learn what kind of experiences "we" have had as Americans. For students in the United States, the basic narrative template is one of people seeking freedom from oppression, progressively solving a variety of social and technological problems, and always doing what is right. People came to the United States for freedom; we cast off British oppression during the Revolution; we solved the problems of racial and gender discrimination; we invented technologies to make life easier; we fought wars to help others. Even when things have not gone well—the Great Depression or the Vietnam War, for instance—we have learned lessons from our mistakes, and thus the overall narrative of freedom and progress is preserved. It is very difficult for students to break away from this narrative and to make sense of discrepant events—such as ongoing racism or sexism—even when they recognize its limitations (Barton, 2001a; Barton & Levstik, 1998). This too is a crucial element of historical identity: establishing not only who "we" are, but what *kind* of people we are—in the case of the United States, morally upright, freedom-seeking, problem-solving people.

Yet there are visible cracks in both these elements of identity. Sometimes, for example, the unity of imagined community begins to fall apart, and it becomes less clear to whom "we" refers, particularly when talking about controversial historical issues. When discussing slavery or civil rights, for example, White and African American students sometimes begin to talk about not only "we" but "they." For White students, "we" still refers to the national community, but "they" is more specifically a single ethnic group that does not include themselves. For African Americans, on the other hand, both "we" and "they" refer to racially defined groups—African Americans and Whites respectively. Recent immigrants, meanwhile, may think of themselves as part of the national community, but others may not. Such immigrants may become "they" rather than being included in the shared national identifications of others. And students with conflicting loyalties may struggle to integrate the different communities with which they identify. Muslim teenagers, for example, use the word "we" to identify with the U.S. national community when talking about actions directed at the United States in other countries (such as people in the Middle East burning a U.S. flag), but they switch to using "we" to refer to an international community of Muslims when considering issues such as the U.S. torture of prisoners at Abu Ghraib prison in Iraq.[1] In each of these circumstances, students' identification with a unified national community begins to break down into more particularistic identifications. Their identifications might be better characterized not as flexible, but as situational.

Some students may also experience difficulty accepting the stories that are meant to define U.S. identity. African American students, for example, although they accept the narrative of freedom and progress, define the role of African Americans within that story differently than White students do. For them, social progress was not something bestowed by the nation (as

---

[1] These findings are based on unpublished masters research with Muslim American adolescents conducted by Kaukeb Malik at the University of Cincinnati.

White students see it) but something wrested from the nation by African Americans, not without great struggle and hardship (Epstein, 2008). For other students, the requirements of accepting the narrative template of the U.S. experience may be even more difficult, if they consistently fail to see reflections of the historical experiences of other, more specific groups with whom they identify—such as people whose behaviors do not match gender expectations, or who have been the victims of continuing economic oppression, or who have continued to experience racism or sexism. Students with such competing identities may draw from the dominant narrative less thoroughly and enthusiastically than other students.

NORTHERN IRELAND

Northern Ireland presents a distinct contrast to the United States. All schools follow the same curriculum, but for political reasons, no single story can be told about the national past. Nationalists and Unionists have their own historical interpretations, and although they focus on many of the same events, they use very different narrative frameworks to make sense of those events. For Nationalists, history is the story of British conquest and exploitation, indifference to Irish suffering, and opposition to the national aspirations of the Irish people. For Unionists, history is the story of the development of British institutions, particularly political and religious freedoms; it's the story of Irish treachery, and of their own steadfast defense of liberty. Thus it is impossible to talk about "we" the way that U.S. students and teachers do, because there are two communities—the Catholic/Nationalist one, and the Protestant/Unionist one.

At the primary level, schools avoid issues that might have direct relevance to national identity. There is no attempt at that level to teach about the history of Northern Ireland as a political unit; instead, students learn about the social life of people in different times and places—Mesolithic people, Vikings, Victorians, and so on. At the secondary level, on the other hand, students do study events important in understanding the political and demographic origins of the region, at least up through partition in 1921. In doing so, they confront many of the most controversial topics in the region's past. But there is still no attempt to create a shared identity. Students study Unionist and Nationalist viewpoints in careful balance, and neither perspective is presented as the version with which students themselves should identify. Moreover, there is no separate, consensus view of the past that is presented as an alternative to Unionist or Nationalist views of history. Although many of the topics at this level are directly relevant to students' identities, there is no explicit attempt to create a particular identity, because doing so would be politically unacceptable.

At both primary and secondary levels in Northern Ireland, however, there is a tacit recognition that students' identities are important, and schools aim to provide students with ways of thinking about the past other than in terms of partisan narratives. In its emphasis on inquiry, evidence, and the comparison of perspectives, the curriculum aims to give students access to a more balanced and academic way of understanding history, so that they will—presumably—be less influenced by the histories they may encounter in their families and communities. This attempt remains almost entirely implicit, however; although educators may hope to lessen the appeal of historically-grounded sectarian identities, they do not usually broach issues of identity directly in the classroom, nor do they often challenge students' community-based ideas about history. Indeed, some observers consider history teaching in Northern Ireland to be so neutral and balanced that it is altogether bland (Kitson, 2007). And, notably, the required component of the curriculum ends in 1921; schools thus avoid dealing with the more immediately relevant period of Troubles since the early 1970s.[2]

What effect does this neutral and balanced curriculum have? At the primary level, students talk about history very differently than their counterparts in the United States, and they almost never use words that indicate historically-grounded identities such as *we* and *our*. In fact, they often do just the opposite: they talk about history's purpose in terms of the need to understand *others*, to understand people who were different than themselves. Unlike those in the United States, primary students in Northern Ireland do not see history as a way of explaining the development of the country of which they consider themselves a part, nor do they invoke history as a way of establishing their own community identifications (Barton, 2001b).

At the secondary level, students' responses are more complicated. When asked about the purpose of studying history, secondary students are adamant that history should help them understand the present state of affairs in Northern Ireland, particularly by providing insight into the origins of community conflict. They also are consciously aware that the curriculum provides a neutral and balanced approach to history, and they appreciate the fact that they are exposed to perspectives other than those they are likely to encounter in their own communities. They do not, however, necessarily see this exposure to alternative ways of understanding history to be a direct challenge to their own identities. They maintain that they will remain committed Unionists or Nationalist, but by studying history, they will become more informed and less prejudiced members of those communities (Barton & McCully, 2010).

---

[2] The national curriculum in Northern Ireland has recently been revised to place stronger emphasis on the utility of the subject in addressing societal division. The revised curriculum gives teachers greater freedom to choose subject knowledge appropriate to the needs of their students and asks teachers to engage their classes in exploring links between history and national identity, including events of the recent past. The impact of these curriculum changes on classroom practice remains to be seen.

But that is not the whole story. Secondary students are resolute about the benefits of considering multiple perspectives, but the more they study the subject, the more they become interested in the history of their own political and religious communities, and the more they identify with those communities. Near the beginning of secondary school, students identify with a wide variety of historical topics—some sectarian, but more often related to the Troubles in general or to noncontroversial aspects of local history. By the end of their required study of history three years later, their identifications have narrowed considerably—they are much more likely to identify with historical events related to their own communities, and all other identifications (except the Troubles generally) decrease dramatically. In addition, their community-based identifications become more specific; rather than identifying with general symbols such as the British flag, as first-year students might do, students who have studied history for three years point to the role of specific individuals in defending the community they identify with. Rather than developing an alternative to sectarian identities, these students draw selectively from the school curriculum to bolster those identities (Barton & McCully, 2005).

Although schools do not promote identity, then, the pull of identities that students develop outside school is so strong that it affects their encounter with the content of the curriculum. Just as important, schools do not provide alternative identities, and thus students are largely limited to those to which they have access outside school. By not directly addressing issues of identity, the curriculum allows students to fit comfortably into Northern Ireland's polarized divisions. In some ways, the country presents a mirror image of the United States: In the United States, school history aims to develop a shared national identity but has difficulty acknowledging the diversity of the country's experiences and perspectives; in Northern Ireland, schools are so concerned not to challenge diverse identifications that they fail to provide—or even to enable—the kind of shared identity that might contribute to overcoming the region's conflict.

NEW ZEALAND

The majority of New Zealand's population descends from immigrants from the current or former United Kingdom (including Ireland), and many people feel very strong ties to Britain. Yet approximately 15% of the population is made up of members of the country's indigenous Māori population, while another 10% is of Asian descent, and yet another 7% come from several Pacific Islands; in addition, intermarriage and cultural hybridity lead to identifications that do not always correspond to neat categories (Byrnes, 2007; Statistics New Zealand, 2008). Despite initiatives that recognize the diverse nature of New Zealand society, residents whose ancestry is not exclusively Anglo-European often confront problems of prejudice, discrimination, and marginalization, and conflicts over both material and symbolic resources often are expressed in ethnic terms. Little of this, however, would be apparent from the content of the history curriculum, which largely ignores not only New Zealand's diversity but even the history of New Zealand itself. The messages about identity found in the history curriculum there are entirely implicit but nonetheless powerful.

The formal study of history in New Zealand exists only at the secondary level, and it is purely an elective subject, chosen by only about 15% of students. During each year, teachers address only two or three topics in depth, which they can choose from a list of numerous possibilities. In practice, however, there is a great deal of uniformity in the topics chosen.[3] These focus almost entirely on European history, with occasional forays into the United States or New Zealand. Many of the most popular topics are those in which the United Kingdom figured prominently, such as the world wars and the Tudor-Stuart period. Largely missing is consideration of the history of Africa, Asia and the Pacific, or indigenous peoples throughout the world. This sends a strong message about what counts as important: If only a handful of topics can be covered in three years of historical study, then choosing to include those that deal almost entirely with Europe and selected English-speaking countries makes it clear that other regions have little to offer. In addition, these choices signal that history is primarily the study of Britain's involvement in world affairs. The association of the subject with New Zealand's former governing power is largely taken for granted.

The effect of this is to distance the history curriculum from students who do not identify primarily with British ancestry. For these students to choose history as an option, they must make a conscious decision to spend most (or all) of their time studying people whose ethnic origins and national, political, and religious experiences are dissimilar to their own. As a result, non-White students are underrepresented among those who elect to study history, and in my conversations with those who do select the subject, they sometimes express a desire for greater attention to non-Western topics.[4]

But just as significant is the relative absence of New Zealand itself from the curriculum. Even those secondary topics that emphasize New Zealand do so primarily within the context of international affairs (such as the Cold War). One topic in New Zealand history, however, is not only taught consis-

---

[3] As in Northern Ireland, the official New Zealand history curriculum has recently undergone a significant revision that provides even greater flexibility for teachers; in addition, the revised curriculum emphasizes the relevance of historical topics for New Zealanders. Just as in the United States, a great deal of local variation exists within larger national patterns. The characterization of the enacted New Zealand Curriculum in this chapter is based on Derbyshire (2004), Manning (2008), and New Zealand History Teachers Association (2005).

[4] The research presented in this section is based on unpublished data collected by the author in 2009-2010 and is currently under analysis.

tently but also taught before the senior secondary level—the Treaty of Waitangi (the 1840 agreement between representatives of the British Crown and some Māori chiefs). Today, this treaty is considered the founding document of the nation, and through later interpretations of the "principles of the Treaty," it has served as a cornerstone for attempts to bring about a more just and equitable society (Orange, 2004). In schools, many teachers devote attention to the Treaty on Waitangi Day, each February 6. Students agree that it is important to understand the Treaty, but they suggest that their study of it has been over simplified. These simplifications are evident in their explanations of the Treaty's signing.

When asked why the Treaty was signed, most students give one of two explanations. They explain either that it was signed to bring peace between Whites and Māori, or that it was an attempt by Whites to rob Māori of their land. Both interpretations oversimplify the time period by portraying the Treaty as an agreement between two monolithic ethnic groups who had single-minded motivations. In fact, both Whites and Māori entered into the Treaty for a variety of reasons (neither "bringing peace" nor "cheating Māori out of their land" were prominent), and many Māori chiefs had no involvement in the process at all. Moreover, the common "land-robbing" explanation fails to provide either White or Māori students with a source of identification. White students are unlikely to identify with ancestors who seem so single-mindedly exploitative, and Māori students may not want to think of their ancestors as lacking in power or agency. Asian, Pasifika, and other groups, meanwhile, are not part of this story at all, and so there is even less reason for them to identify with school history. Students who feel connected to their British origins find much to like in the curriculum, but many others simply ignore it.

HISTORY AND IDENTITY

Research from the United States, Northern Ireland, and New Zealand suggests that the relationship between identity and the history curriculum cannot be ignored, because students' identifications not only are shaped by the curriculum but also influence how they interpret history both in school and out. Differences in the relationship between history and identity in these countries allow us to think about what is involved in historical identification, and how schools might respond. First, what exactly *is* historical identification? The U.S. and Northern Ireland examples in particular suggest that historical identification involves asserting one's membership in a group that has existed over time; talking about the American Revolution by saying that "*we* broke away from England" is an example of such identification, and Northern Ireland students who say that events involving Protestants or Catholics in the past are related to who they themselves *are* engage in a similar act of identification. Such groups can be based on nationality, religion, ethnicity, or other characteristics—or some combination of these.

But historical identification involves more than simple membership; it also involves selecting certain experiences as representative of the perspectives or experiences of that group. In the United States, to be an "American" is not simply a matter of having residence or citizenship in a particular location; it means being part of a narrative that involves moral rectitude, the quest for freedom, and continual social and material progress; Americans are the kind of people who have those experiences. Similarly, in Northern Ireland to be Catholic is to be part of a community that has stood up for itself against Protestant and/or British oppression; to be Protestant is to have supported and sacrificed for Britain and to have resisted the loss of British liberties.

And perhaps most important, historical identification involves paying more attention to some groups than others. In each of these three countries, students pay more attention to the groups they identify with than those they do not. In the United States, the national experience is more important than the history of other countries; world history is only a small part of the curriculum, and because it does not relate to the object of most students' historical identification, it may have little salience for them. African Americans, meanwhile, are more likely to regard the achievements of African Americans in history as significant than are Whites. In Northern Ireland, the curriculum itself is carefully balanced between Unionists and Nationalists, but students attend more closely to the history of their own community; as a result, their understanding of that community's history outpaces their knowledge of the other. And in New Zealand, students who do not identify with the topics of the curriculum often simply choose not to study the subject at all.

These relationships lead to a number of questions that history educators must grapple with. Should schools encourage students to identify with groups that have existed over time, and if so, which ones, and in what combinations? The U.S. experience suggests that schools can effectively encourage identification with the national community, but it is less clear whether young people can balance that identity with others to which they feel committed. Can they be both American and African American, or American and Muslim? In Northern Ireland, can a shared identity be promoted without asking students to reject Nationalist and Unionist identities? In addition, whether aiming to promote identity or not, schools must carefully consider the choices they make in selecting some experiences and perspectives as representative of any particular group, because students draw from these portrayals in thinking about what it means to be a member of groups they identify with. Does being a Protestant mean that one must forever be opposed to the perspectives of Catholics? Does being an American mean that one always believes in the rightness of the country's foreign policy? Does being a New Zealander mean that one is either a land-hungry Englishman or a powerless Māori? And how can educators convince students to pay attention to a variety of groups within history, when their divergent identities might lead them in the opposite direction?

In order to begin answering these questions, we need a clearer conceptualization of the relationship between school history and students' identities. Contrary to common perspectives on this relationship detailed earlier, schools neither provide students with identities, nor remain irrelevant to identities they develop elsewhere. Rather, school history provides *resources* for students as they develop historically-grounded identities, whether it is the intent of the curriculum to do so or not. By studying history in school, students learn about groups of people (national, ethnic, religious, etc.) who have existed over time, and these suggest some of the range of groups of which they may consider themselves part. Even more importantly, students learn about the historical experiences of these groups, and in doing so they learn what it means to be a member of that group—what patterns of experience have endured over time for each. But because both the definition of each group and the representation of its experiences are simply resources for students in their construction of identity, they select from the content of the curriculum in different ways. Within any nation, students choose to identify with different groups, to identify more or less strongly with those groups, and to select different experiences as representative. And because schools are only one resource for developing historical identities, students invariably combine the content of the curriculum with ideas and perspectives they have encountered elsewhere.

Given this relationship, educators should seek to expand rather than constrict the range of identity resources available to students. Narrowing the range only ensures that school history will play a less important role for students than the alternatives, and that it will fail to address the kinds of issues students consider important (Barton, 2009). As Grever, Haydn, & Ribbens (2008) put it, "The attempt to singularize or simplify young people's ideas about identity may well be a doomed or even counterproductive enterprise" (p. 89). Expanding and complicating students' ideas, rather than simplifying them, would involve, first of all, diversifying the portrayals of each of the groups with which students might identify. In the United States, nearly all students identify to some extent as "American," but rather than portraying Americans as a monolithic category—diverse in background but similar in experience—schools might encourage students to learn about people in the nation's past whose motivations and experiences have differed from the canonical narrative of freedom and progress. Students might learn about Loyalists who wanted to remain part of Britain, Native Americans who were forced off their land (as well as those who assimilated), African Americans who continued to be lynched long after slavery was over, Japanese Americans who were forced out of their homes during World War II, workers whose conditions deteriorated with technological changes, men and women whose appearance and behavior have not accorded with established gender norms, and so on.

In Northern Ireland, meanwhile, schools might move beyond the tendency to portray the region's past as a dichotomous and never-ending struggle between two monolithic and unchanging groups. Students might learn about Catholics who fought on the side of King William and Protestants who fought for King James, about Protestants who supported Home Rule for Ireland and Catholics who fought for Britain in the First World War, and about both Catholics and Protestants who have sought peace and reconciliation rather than violence or division. In New Zealand, students might learn about the variety of ways that Whites, Māori, and other groups have interacted over the years—Whites who sought to protect native land rights, Māori who fought on the side of the British against other Māori, Chinese who migrated to New Zealand at the beginning of the early twentieth century, Samoans who have been deported or denied New Zealand citizenship, and so on. Not only would such diverse portrayals be more historically accurate and comprehensive, but they would expand the variety of possible identifications open to students. Some students might be better able to find themselves in the curriculum if it were diversified in this way, while others might draw from the curriculum to develop different ideas about the range of what it could mean to be American, Unionist or Nationalist, New Zealander, and so on.

But schools also need to be careful not to provide only resources for particularistic identifications; one of the dangers of diversifying the curriculum is that although students may be better able to find themselves in the curriculum, they may also become less interested in paying attention to anyone else. This means that schools must also give students the chance to identify with superordinate groups (Banks et al., 2001), so that they do not see identity as exclusive, or as operative at only one level (Smith, 2003). That is, students should be able to identify with the varied experiences of all Americans at the same time that they are identifying with the experiences of African Americans, Latinos, or others. Students in Northern Ireland should be able to identify with the experiences of all of the region's population, while at the same time identifying with more specific groups, as well as with nationalities such as Ireland or the United Kingdom. And in all cases, students should also have the chance to identify with groupings that extend beyond national boundaries; this is particularly critical in the United States, where the nation has traditionally been the largest unit of identification, and the effect has been that many Americans show little regard for the rest of the world.

This is asking a lot of schools, this attempt to encourage both diverse and superordinate identifications, and there are no easy formulas for success—particularly given that no nations have made the attempt in any significant way. Helping students develop multiple and overlapping identities—affirming their membership in more than one group, and paying attention to the experiences of each of those—may require one fundamental change in the way that history is taught: Schools may have to include historical identification as an explicit topic of study. For many years now, historians, sociologists, anthropologists, and educational researchers have been investigating the way in which people link history to their sense of identity. If this is an appropriate topic for those of us in academia, then why not for students as well?

Students could, for example, examine how identities are socially constructed, and how history is—and has been—part of this process. They could examine how the rise of nationalism was linked to the invention of historical narratives. What stories that are now taken for granted were created in the nineteenth century, and how were these stories promulgated? They could explore how people in the past thought of their own identities (if they thought of them at all), and the sources of these identifications—including the ways in which they were manipulated by others. U.S. students learning about the Revolutionary War, for example, could examine the diverse and changing identities of people before, during, and after the war. Students in Northern Ireland could study how commemoration of historical events has become increasingly sectarian and exclusive in recent decades. Those in New Zealand could examine when and how participation in the British military became a defining characteristic of the country's history. And perhaps most importantly, students could seek to understand the consequences of these historical processes. What have been the effects of defining identity in particular ways? Who has been excluded from these definitions, and with what costs to themselves or others? By asking students to consider such questions, schools might not only expand the range of identity resources available to students but might better ensure that they can draw from those resources thoughtfully, with a fuller recognition of their consequences and limitations.

CONCLUSION

Ultimately, we cannot force students to develop any particular historical identification. We cannot impose identifications on them (as some people would like), because there are too many other social forces at play—families, communities, media, popular culture, and so on. Yet at the same time, research makes it clear that schools are not irrelevant in the formation of students' historical identities, because students do indeed make use of that content. In order to play a more productive role in this process, then, educators need to be conscious of how the curriculum serves as a resource in students' active construction of identity. They need to make sure that the curriculum provides the kind of resources that will enable students to make reasonable and informed choices about identification, with greater knowledge of the range of experiences people have had in the past, of the social forces that influence people's identities, and perhaps most importantly, of the consequences for defining one's historical identification in particular ways. If schools can provide these kinds of resources for thinking about historical identity, then they will surely have made an important contribution to contemporary society.

Acknowledgements: The author would like to thank Claire Sinnema, Michael Harcourt, Mark Sheehan, and Alan McCully for their valuable insights into the role of history in New Zealand and Northern Ireland.

REFERENCES

Anderson, B. R. O. (1983). *Imagined communities: Reflections on the origin and spread of nationalism.* London: Verso.

Banks, J. A., Cookson, P., Gay, G., Hawley, W. D., Irvine, J. J., Nieto, S., Schofield, J. W., & Stephan, W. G. (2001). Diversity within unity: Essential principles for teaching and learning in a multicultural society. *Phi Delta Kappan, 83,* 196–198, 200–203.

Barton, K. C. (2009). The denial of desire: How to make history education meaningless. In L. Symcox & A. Wilschut (Eds.), *National history standards: The problem of the canon and the future of teaching history* (pp. 265–282). Greenwich, CT: Information Age Publishing.

Barton, K. C. (2001a). A sociocultural perspective on children's understanding of historical change: Comparative findings from Northern Ireland & the United States. *American Educational Research Journal, 38,* 881–913.

Barton, K. C. (2001b). "You'd be wanting to know about the past": Social contexts of children's historical understanding in Northern Ireland and the United States. *Comparative Education, 37,* 89–106.

Barton, K. C., & Levstik, L. S. (1998). "It wasn't a good part of history": Ambiguity and identity in middle grade students' judgments of historical significance. *Teachers College Record, 99,* 478–513.

Barton, K. C., & Levstik, L. S. (2004). *Teaching history for the common good.* New York: Routledge.

Barton, K. C., & McCully, A. W. (2005). History, identity, and the school curriculum in Northern Ireland: An empirical study of secondary students' ideas and perspectives. *Journal of Curriculum Studies, 37,* 85–116.

Barton, K. C., & McCully, A. W. (2010). "You can form your own point of view": Internally persuasive discourse in Northern Ireland students' encounters with history. *Teachers College Record, 112,* 142–181.

Byrnes, G. (2007, September). *Rethinking national identity in New Zealand's history.* Address to the Concepts of the Nation Symposium, Wellington, New Zealand.

Retrieved March 12, 2008, from http://www.mch.govt.nz/dominion/byrnes. html#_ednref15.

Derbyshire, A. (2004). *Anyone's but our own: The teaching of New Zealand history in New Zealand secondary schools, 1925–2000.* Unpublished masters thesis, University of Auckland, New Zealand.

Epstein, T. (2008). *Interpreting national history: Race, identity, and pedagogy in classrooms and communities.* New York: Routledge.

Goldberg, T., Porat, D., & Schwarz, B. (2006). "Here started the rift we see today": Student and textbook narratives between official and counter memory. *Narrative Inquiry, 16,* 319–347.

Grever, M., Haydn, T., & Ribbens, K. (2008). Identity and school history: The perspective of young people from the Netherlands and England. *British Journal of Educational Studies, 56,* 76–94.

Hobsbawm, E. J., & Ranger, T. O. (1983). *The invention of tradition.* New York: Cambridge University Press.

Kitson, A. (2007). History education and reconciliation in Northern Ireland. In E. A. Cole (Ed.), *Teaching the violent past: History education and reconciliation* (pp. 123–154). Lanham, MD: Rowman & Littlefield.

Manning, R. F. (2008). *Place, power and pedagogy: A critical analysis of the status of Te Atiawa histories of place in Port Nicholson Block secondary schools and the possible application of place-based education models.* Unpublished doctoral dissertation, Victoria University, Wellington, New Zealand.

New Zealand History Teachers' Association. (2005). *NZHTA survey results, May 2005.* Retrieved 1 June, 2005, from http://www.nzhta.org.nz.

Orange, C. (2004). *An illustrated history of the Treaty of Waitangi.* Wellington, New Zealand: Bridget Williams Books.

Peck, C. (2010). "It's not like [I'm] Chinese and Canadian. I am in between": Ethnicity and students' conceptions of historical significance. *Theory and Research in Social Education, 38,* 574–617.

Seixas, P. (1993). Historical understanding among adolescents in a multicultural setting. *Curriculum Inquiry, 23,* 301–327.

Smith, R. M. (2003). *Stories of peoplehood: The politics and morals of political membership.* Cambridge: Cambridge University Press.

Statistics New Zealand. (2008). *Quickstats about culture and identity.* Retrieved March 11, 2008, from http://www.stats.govt.nz/census/2006-census-data/ quickstats-about-culture-identity/quickstats-about-culture-and-identity. htm?page=para002Master

CHAPTER 8

A TRADITIONAL FRAME FOR GLOBAL HISTORY

The Narrative of Modernity in French Secondary School

Nicole Tutiaux-Guillon

Whereas in France primary school history tended—and still tends today—to pass on a narrative of nation, the general history framework in secondary school is rather different, more versatile and more potent. Since the seventies, more than eight new history curricula have been implemented, mainly in secondary education (Garcia & Leduc, 2003). However, the school history aims are quite steady. History in secondary school is not nationalistic. It supports and is supported by values granted to be the ideal for humanity, particularly human rights, democracy, scientific and economical progress, equality, and openness to otherness. The institutional aims insist on the priority of these values over any national identity. The curricula are shaped through interpretations from a universalist perspective. The grand narrative shapes how politics, society and economy have developed from archaism and barbarism to modernity and political and social rights, even through acute crises. This provides an opportunity to teach both the history

History Education and the Construction of National Identities, pages 109–123
Copyright © 2012 by Information Age Publishing

109

of France and that of Europe or the World, interpreted through the same values. Also it provides an opportunity to change the contents of the curricula, and thus to implement global perspectives, without changing the core structure of the narrative. Nevertheless the chosen topics, and the chronological context in which they are set, results in and from ethnocentrism. This might be problematic in a society more and more sensitive to ethnical diversity.

This general argumentation will be supported by the current analysis of 20th century curricula in France, especially of the most recent ones: 2008 (lower secondary school) and 2009 (upper secondary school). The first part will focus on the universalistic values underlying the curricula, the second on the "*mise en intrigue*" organized by the tale of modernity. The third part will specify the tensions between openness to others and ethnocentrism in French history curricula. The last part attempts to question the relations to the student's identities.

TEACHING HISTORY FOR UNIVERSALIST VALUES

As in many Western countries, French school history has been subject to ideological and pedagogical criticism since the 1970s. Especially the nationalist historical narrative has been condemned as historically obsolete, politically irrelevant and ethically harmful. This critical discourse is far more relevant for primary school than for secondary school history.[1] The French history curriculum in secondary education has several official goals: promoting political and cultural collective identity, encouraging social cohesion, fostering citizenship and developing intellectual abilities. The latter particularly concerns critical thinking, and more recently a burgeoning personality. A core aim is fostering adherence to universal values such as human rights, democracy, justice, solidarity, tolerance etcetera, besides the French republican values of *Liberté, Egalité*, and *Laïcité*. These values are part of the legitimate culture, particularly of the political one, and also are reputed to provide sound basis for social and political judgements. Of course universalism has been a part of French intellectual and political tradition since the Enlightenment. But also in the curricula, since 1890, the priority has been explicitly the greater good of humanity, over the greater good of France. Even in the ministerial prescriptions of the late 19th and early 20th century for secondary school, universalism prevailed over French identity.

---

[1] During the 6 first decades of the 20th century, the difference between primary and secondary school has not been a matter of age but of social background. Presently, the primary school is for pupils from 2 to 11, and is followed by secondary school: *collège* (4 years, from 11 to 15, respectively 6th, 5th, 4th, 3rd grades) and *lycée* (3 years from 15 to 18, 2nd, 1st, terminal grades). The *lycée* offers 3 streams: general, technical and vocational. This paper will deal only with the general stream.

The stress on human rights has increased over the last three decades. Let's consider some examples. Since probably 50 years the nationalistic narrative regarding colonization has disappeared. For thirty years, teachings on French or European colonization are accompanied by documents and information presenting its negative effects. Since the seventies, the textbooks mention that the French army used torture in dealing with Algerian patriots/rebels. The same goes for some dark pages of French history as the "*affaire Dreyfus*" or as the Collaboration in 1940–44 and the Shoah. The lessons on these topics focus on the French social minority that defended human rights: the *dreyfusards*, the intellectual demonstrating against torture during the 1950s, the Righteous among nations etcetera. In such a narrative, the positive reference is no longer France as a nation state, but the imaginary native country of Human Rights (Lantheaume, 2009). The tendency to select history contents that support universal values explains how the issues of past crimes (even committed by the French) and of victims can be integrated in school history. Specific histories of minorities can be integrated in the school narrative when they are told from this universal perspective. Teaching about the suffering of a particular community in the past is not fostering *communautarisme*[2] but working for human rights. All victims, outcasts, dominated or oppressed people (medieval peasant, poor *Tiers Etat*, industrial worker, slaves...), in French classrooms are considered as the People. However, this approach is not suggested in the official texts. The prescriptions focus more on citizenship.

The French Republican citizenship is based on the transcendence of any specific interest in favour of the common interest, and of private matters in favour of the public ones. The French citizen is somehow an "abstract" being, free from any distinctive identity, such as religion, gender, ethnicity or class, basing his or her political judgements and actions on reason and on universal values. Thus, even if citizenship and nationality are legally bound together, citizenship is not explicitly rooted in a national heritage. Of course, the focus on French political history conveyed a perspective that fostered nationalism and ethnocentrism. At the same time, however, it aimed at extending the universal values of progress, human rights and democracy. And presently these components are far more relevant and legitimate for teachers and for students than any nationalism. When asked about the purpose of school history, 80% of high-school teachers affirmed the civic function of history (Lautier, 1997, Tutiaux-Guillon, 2004). They believed that understanding history would "naturally" evolve into the development of positive attitudes to politics, culture, "otherness," and human rights. Their main attempt is to foster citizenship and critical thinking

---

[2] A "community-ism," that in France is a threat to political unity and a promotion of politically irrelevant private interests.

(Bonafous et al., 2007; Lantheaume, 2009; Lautier, 1997; Tutiaux-Guillon et al, 2004). Identity comes far behind citizenship in the teachers' preoccupation (Lautier, 2001). Usually, most teachers give a priority to topics that aim at tolerance and social harmony. For example, when studying the medieval Mediterranean area, they emphasize more Al Andalus and the Sicily ruled by Roger II than the crusades.[3] Thereby they hope to provide examples of people from different religions living peacefully and even fruitfully together. Personally and collectively, they discuss, criticize or possibly reject some explicit or presumed political demands for school history, if they judge these aims opposed to human rights and to historical truth.[4] For example in 2005–2006, there was a huge and strong protest against a legal obligation to teach "the positive effects of colonization,"[5] in which not only historians,[6] trade unions and the Human Rights League, but also history teachers and their inspectors took an active part. The teachers might even decide to teach about some issues that are not prescribed. Before 1962 some taught about France in the period of 1940–1944, while school chronology ended before that. Some have taught colonization and slavery in French colonies before the recent prescriptions. During the 1990s some engaged in pedagogical works on the students' familial memories, etcetera (De Cock & Picard, 2009). Generally there is no discussion about the consensual historical narrative, the tale of the progress and achievements of humanity (at least of western humanity).

A NARRATIVE OF PROGRESS AND MODERNITY

"The utility of teaching history is to inform the young men of the evolution of humanity since the cave ages to the century of aviation" (quotation translated from official prescriptions, 1925). Researchers analyzing the former history curricula have stressed that in secondary school they were centred on political, economical, social or cultural human progress (Bruter, 2005; Garcia & Leduc, 2003; Mousseau et al., 1994). It is no more explicit but still underlying the present curricula for the *collège*.

> Each of the 4 years, at least 3 topics point at some type of progress (political, scientific/cultural, economical or social). This means roughly 40% of the

---

[3] The resulting historical perspective might be rather mythical. See for example the analysis developed by Rodriguez (2009).

[4] See the website of the Professional Association Historiens et Géographes, <www.aphg.fr> and specifically the column <http://www.aphg.fr/Actualites.htm> or the website for teachers <http://www.cafepedagogique.org/disci/histoire.php> ; see also for example the rubrics on <http://www.snes.edu/-Enseignant-.html> (a trade union website).

[5] On this specific content, the paragraph 4 of the law voted on 02/23/2005 has been abrogated by the French president (02/15/2006)

[6] See <www.lph-asso.fr> and <cvuh.free.fr>

contents. Whatever the period, the contents insist on the apogee of the civilizations (European, Indian, Asian, Muslim-Arabic, African).

The scientific/cultural progress is studied each year: Greek scientists and philosophers, cultural and scientific revolution (16th–17th centuries), scientists and philosophers of Enlightenment, scientific and technical evolutions of present time.

The political progress is not as continuous. Two main streams coexist: the conquest of democracy (Antique Athens, French Revolution, 19th and 20th century—with the counter-example of dictatorial regimes and totalitarianism), and the building of a State (medieval and modern France, 19th century). The building of European union, studied in the last year of *collège* might be added to this list.

The economical progress seems limited to industrialization and capitalism that figure the economical modernity. But what is not explicit in the prescriptions might be detailed in the textbooks : the social progress, for example, appears through the documents and is connected with either scientific progress (health, school) or the political ones (social claims and conquests, equality).

The same general narrative gives its consistence to the new curriculum for the first grade of the *lycée*, which has no chronological continuity: 7 of 11 topics echo the ones referring to progress in the history curricula of *collège*. Also the textbooks now and then used the issue of progress as the sense and significance of history. The recent textbooks, even for the older students, still picture colonization through school, health care and modern agriculture, as before the sixties—even if some documents of the same chapters refer to colonial exactions (Lantheaume 2006, Tutiaux-Guillon, 2006). In the years 2000 textbooks characterized monotheism as a social and intellectual progress compared with polytheism (Baquès & Tutiaux-Guillon, 2006). The newest textbooks for the 5th grade presented the role of the Church during the Medieval age as socially progressive.[7] At the same time the progress might be at least "qualified" because past difficulties and violence are not omitted, even for the periods that are set as birth of modernity, as 19th and overall 20th centuries.

This narrative of progress has probably two main origins. Since 1830, the development of a secular teaching of history has substituted the holy history with the national history: the narrative is of course different, but the structure is still teleologic. The end is no more a godly eschatology, but the fulfilment of socioeconomical progress and of democracy (Bruter,

---

[7] For example in the textbook edited by Ivernel one of the subchapters is titled "l'Eglise au service de la société" (Church serving society; elaborated in the chapter as protecting against violence, caring of ill and poor people, schooling and encouraging intellectual development, *Histoire-Géographie, 5e,* Hatier, 2010)

2005). Historical time and progress just keep the same pace. Also, one of the persistent aims of school history was providing the students with means to understand the present times. This meant selecting from the past what prefigured or explained the society and the world in which they live. Now, the place allotted in school to the victims' narratives is taken as a way of healing the social wounds of the past, of developing tolerance and social cohesion. Opening the school history to others, particularly to wounded self-proclaimed heirs of slaves or of colonized peoples, is supposed to foster democratic progress.

BETWEEN "OUR" HISTORY AND "THEIR" HISTORY: OPENESS AND ETHNOCENTRICISM

The contents of the *socle commun des connaissance et des compétences* (common base of knowledge and competencies), compulsory for schools since 2006, seem to prioritize the World and Europe above France. The prescribed attitudes are set in the field of universality, as mind-opening to any culture. The abilities do not focus on any cultural, historical or geographical area. In the detailed knowledge a frequent wording is "France, Europe and World" and the cultural references are both European and Global. If the history of France has to be known, the same goes for the history of the European union. It cannot be said that such aims, prescribed for primary and lower secondary school, are focused on national identity. These developments do not mean that school history in secondary education does not take the national history into account at all: the curricula are a compromise between different actors and tendencies, often contradictory (De Cock & Picard, 2009). In the recent detailed prescription for *collège* (50 pages), the "*histoire nationale*" is mentioned less than 10 times and mostly to characterise what the students have learnt in primary school. The contents in secondary school are explicitly presented as enlarging the scope. They deal mostly with European/Western history (24 topics), and present less national history (10 topics), but still less non Western history (5 topics). The time prescribed for history lessons might roughly be divided between 20% allotted to the history of France (mostly political history), 26% allotted to topics that deal both with France and Europe, 26% allotted to the history of Europe or Western countries without mentioning France, and 17% to non Western history. But this rather open view contrasts with a more unobtrusive one: taking into account the titles, subtitles and prescribed examples, "France" appears 19 times. If we add every moment devoted to the study of topics explicitly mentioning France, the total is close to half of the school history hours! Furthermore, the 57 dates that a student must know for the final exam[8] contains 30 "French" dates and 11 that are part of

---

[8] The *Brevet*, at the end of *collège*.

French history. This is close to 72%! The tale of progress is not mainly a national one. But in every secondary curriculum, political progress is treated largely referring to France, and cultural, scientific and economical progress is referring to Europe.

In fact, the issue of "opening up to others" is not simple nor unequivocal. Defining who we will consider as "others" in the curricula and courses would be a first step—and suggests the first difficulties. Would it mean other than French? Then any topic about European history or Western history has to be taken in account. This option is not really convincing. In the first place, since the nineties, the ministries of education in the European union have stressed the importance of teaching a European history as a self-history for new European generations. Secondly, France has taken an active part in what might be called the European political, cultural and economical history, and for some period in Western history as well. Teaching about Europe—or about Western history—is also teaching about France. Thirdly, Europe is not a reality, but a social construct, as was nation: its history recycles former canons.

If we consider "others" as non-Western, then they were introduced in the secondary history education during the sixties[9], and had been sporadically present in different curricula ever since. The Chinese and African civilisations, for example, had been prescribed contents for 2nd grade from 1976 to 1985 and are now prescribed for 6th and 5th grades. In the present curricula for *collège,* the part of non-Western history represents 17% of the time and 15% of the topics. But when colonization is at issue, must we take it as Western or non Western? An example of the new contents for 2nd grade demonstrates the ambiguity: the topic "enlarging the [European] world, 15th–16th centuries," articulates a European navigator, a European port, Constantinople-Istanbul, a pre-Columbian city facing colonization, and Peking. Now, is the case of Istanbul and of the American city focused on "others" or not? They might be—as they might make a larger place to European merchants or soldiers: only a close study of the textbooks or of the effective teaching would allow to decide if the focus is on "them" or on "us." Furthermore some topics correspond to a projection in the past of present issues in French society. The main example is the Islamic civilization. Since 1977, Islam is a topic of the curriculum for 5th grade, firstly focused on the political aspects of the Muslim and Arab Medieval age, then on the civilization. The parallel with the importance of a so-called Muslim immigration in France is clear: between 1962 and 1982 the migrant population com-

---

[9] It is often said that this was the innovation implemented by the so-called "programme Braudel" for terminal grade, because of the historian's involvement in 1962. But some information on history and civilization of non-Western people was developed in the geography textbooks since the early 20th century.

ing from North Africa grew from 407,000 to 1,930,000[10]. Currently Islam is the second religion in France. From 1995 till 2009, the French pupils had to study the medieval Islam in primary school, in 5th grade and in 2nd grade[11]. In 1995, the Koran became a "heritage document" that all students had to know as historical source and as meaningful for humanity. Its study is still prescribed in the 2008 curricula. The date of the Hegira is ranked as compulsory knowledge. But most textbooks during the years 1990 and 2000 selected the documents on Jihad[12], sometimes on Sharia and on women's status. These aspects of Islamic civilization are debated in French society and emphasise otherness. On the other hand teachers seemed to avoid what could stir cultural conflicts in the classroom, and chose a consensual content—omitting the sensitive issues. As for other courses on non-Western civilisation, the effect might be a stress on the supposedly "alien" character of some people living in France (Bonafous et al., 2007). Textbooks and teachers focused on the knowledge and techniques that the Western Christian civilization had drawn from exchanges with Muslims. Furthermore this presentation of Islamic civilization emphasized techniques, medicine and sciences, the achievements which are known to converge with the common meaning of progress in "our" society, and just briefly mentioned poetry, law and philosophy, that are of core importance in the islamic culture. The point of view in the textbooks is clearly Eurocentric (Baquès & Tutiaux-Guillon, 2008). This means that there is often a lapse from past civilizations to present society.

Another key concern for school history is to foster social cohesion, and it has been increasing since the nineties (Tutiaux-Guillon, 2007). Young people have to be educated as members of a same society and a same political community: sharing cultural references, values and interpretations of the past, useful for living together, important for understanding each other, and necessary for understanding present times and imagining a future. Ten history teachers who were interviewed in 2003, unanimously declared that their objective was to integrate everyone, especially the children of migrants, in one common culture. Some identified this common culture as French, others opted for European, or even Mediterranean. All of them wanted to provide the pupils with intellectual resources to understand present French society. Yet, even though they favoured national identity over sub-cultural

---

[10]This is partly due to the demand of workers in industry and partly to the option of accepting not only the workers but their family. In the same period, the Portuguese immigration grew too and comparatively faster.

[11]The new contents for 2nd grade (2009) do not include it any more.

[12]Nearly always defined only as struggle to convert or submit the non-Muslim; the inner struggle against the believer's tendency to act against God's will and the effort for becoming a better Muslim is mentioned only in a textbook published by Nathan (Histoire-Géographie, 4ème, s.d. M. Bernier, Paris, Nathan, 2002)

community identities, they rated individual identity higher than national identity (Tutiaux-Guillon et al., 2004). A recent but strong view is that the youth must learn how to make sense of its own history (Delacroix & Garcia, 1999). Fostering social cohesion also means, for policy makers and often for teachers, providing the youth with non-European ancestry some glimpses at its supposed cultural roots. This raises questions about both the young people's identities and on the educators' representation of these identities.

THE DIFFICULT ISSUE OF THE
YOUTHS' COLLECTIVE IDENTITIES

We do not have much information on the relations between the youth's collective identities and their conception of the past. Some teachers testified that they feared to teach about Shoah and about Israel (even about Antique Jews), about women's history or about Islam, even if vigorous or violent oppositions to study such issues are scarce (Falaize, 2009). They react to the incidents often spontaneously, sometimes without caution and subtleness.[13] They rely on a widespread discourse stigmatizing young suburban males as Arabs, thus as Muslim, and therefore as sexist, violent, anti-Semitic, anti-West. The international context from 2000 onwards has stirred up both this discourse and this fear. However, these are not reliable data on the students' attitudes.

Researchers point out that the main publications about the controversial issues of sensitive memories in school, deal with prescriptions or with teaching, but not usually with *learning* (Bonafous et al,, 2007, Tutiaux-Guillon, 2008). The inquiries among students are still to be developed (Tutiaux-Guillon, 2008). Suburban youth cannot be defined plainly as "Muslims," "Arabs," "*Maghrébins*" (North-Africans), "African" etc. Most are born in France, where also most of their parents have grown up. The supposed link with the so-called "native culture" is very weak.[14] As a rule, in France, the students who have migrant ancestry do not ask for ethnically tailored history lessons. Their familial history has little to do with medieval Islam or with the black kingdoms of the past, however prestigious. When such young people are asked about their identity, they declare themselves "French," because they are born there and live there, as do other young people whatever their ancestry (Frydmann, 2004). Furthermore, the familial memories are not always passed on and not always focused on sensitive historical issues as colonialism and French domination (De Cock-Pierrepont, 2007; Lepoutre, 2005). When these youths claim an ethnic identity, it is mostly to contest the demands

---

[13]Representative of these rough and abusively generalized statements, is the book edited by Emmanuel Brenner (2002).

[14]It is also well-known in sociology that this "native culture" is re-constructed in the context of migrations, both by adaptation to the dominant culture and by mythification.

of the authorities, or to protest against injustice and discrimination. Their living culture is a mixed, creative and fast-changing one, in which in ethnicity is weak (Lorcerie, 2003). Moreover, their claims refer rather to the conception of French citizenship as universal, abstract and as setting apart the private interests and identities. But from a 2006 research (Grever & Ribbens, 2007; Grever & Tutiaux-Guillon, 2008), some disturbing figures arose. Of the youth from French descent 12.9% grant God historical influence; the majority conforms to the secular politics in France and the ideal of *laïcité*. Of the youth from migrant descent 32.3% adheres to the proposal that "History shows what are God's intentions for the people and the world." Quite contradictory to French civic (and historical) tradition. This might point at a divide between school history and some young believers.

The French inquiries on learning history focus more on intellectual abilities than on collective identities: this issue is somehow intellectually suspect. The core distinction, proposed by Lautier (1997) and corroborated by the *Youth and History* inquiry (Tutiaux-Guillon & Mousseau, 1998), has been that some students make sense of history for themselves and their lives (Lautier named them "internal" to history), some do not ("external" to history, roughly one third of the students). The first display more commitment to values, while the last are from lower social classes and more often fail in school. In France the question about the relations between ethnic identities, views of the past and school history has become a legitimate one for researchers only recently.[15] In the comparative inquiry developed by Grever and Ribbens (2007), the students from migrant ancestry in northern France were more committed to the history of the Nation State than the ones living in England or the Netherlands. Could we directly attribute this result to the French curricula? The same inquiry showed that both the French students from "French" descent and the students from migrant descent considered that "the migrants' history is part of French history" (respectively 57.6% and 81%; often more than the youth in England and The Netherlands, respectively 62.5% and 52.6%, and 41.6% and 52.8%). Notably, at the time, migrant history was not a part of school history.[16] And whatever the curriculum, in several quantitative and comparative inquiries, the French youth ranked among other European youth as the least committed to their national identity and the most committed to the importance of history (Grever & Tutiaux-Guillon, 2008; Tutiaux-Guillon, 2000; Tutiaux-Guillon & Mousseau, 1998).

What is complicated is that we cannot assume that the curricula have a direct effect on the youth's historical culture. Public opinion and politicians seem to assume naively that the school is the main medium for (legitimate)

---

[15]The same could be said for gender identities.
[16]And not taught except by a few innovative teachers. The topic has recently been introduced in the 2008 and 2009 curricula for *collège* and *lycée*.

historical culture, and do not always separate historical knowledge and so-cial memory. The underlying equation (social memory equals learning his-tory in school equals teaching history that equals prescribed contents) is not validated through research in history didactics (Lautier, 1997; Tutiaux-Guillon, 1998, 2000; Tutiaux-Guillon & Mousseau, 1998). Most information passed on in school is also passed on elsewhere in society, by social interac-tions and by media (music, television, cinema, video-games, comics, novels, role-play etc.). In France at least political argumentation and communica-tion, advertisement, tourism, entertainment and the press use and some-times abuse historical images, or representations and interpretations of the past. This contributes, a lot or even more than school, to the shared histori-cal culture. And this information, however biased regarding the historians' works, is weighted as reliable and true to the past, as much as what is learnt in school. The research focused on social representations of the past has stated how any type of knowledge might combine, and combine with values and affective views of it (Cariou, 2003; Lautier, 1997; Tutiaux-Guillon, 1998; Tutiaux-Guillon & Mousseau, 1998). We do not have enough reliable infor-mation on the specific effects of French school history on young attitudes and understanding of themselves, of the society and of the past, or on their identities, at least since the late nineties.

Thus the teachers might act more from their own social representation of the students than from exact information regarding the links between familial origins, identities and attitudes towards school history. And the students/young people might react against the stigmatizing stereotypes by expressing strongly their distrust and their exasperation. This could induce them, in history lessons, to criticize vehemently the contradiction between the French ambition (or pretense?) to support universal values and the past acts of the French people or State against the same values. Is this adherence to collective French identity or anti-nationalism? The most sensitive issues of young people's collective identity do not mainly revolve around national-ity and around common French or European history. The attitudes of some students regarding particular contents of school history seem to be support-ed by political opposition against the USA and Israel. This means that the world perspective, however biased, is prevalent. However, in most cases the anti-established school history attitudes are generally anti-establishment, more likely a matter of erratic disorientation, of poverty, unstructured so-cial context and gang affiliation, than a matter of historical consciousness (Ernst, 2008). In such a context, it seems right that State and teachers aim at a shared heritage and at a common identity. The school also has to in-troduce the new generation into the society, especially when other supports for social integration and social self-structuring are lacking. Perhaps the interest for history, including both common history and critical history of the dark pages that the French students displayed, whatever their origin, allows us to be a little optimistic (Grever & Ribbens, 2007). Also, we have to keep in mind the complexity of the process involved in self-identification, especially during adolescence.

CONCLUSION

The French curriculum for secondary education is partly contradictory. It fits with a tradition more keen on universalism and on human progress than on national identity. This focus provides opportunities to include topics about Europe and about "Others" without disturbing traditional narratives. Since the sixties, the curricular contents have included, although sporadically, glimpses at other civilizations. This has been renewed in the recent curricula (2008, 2009) for secondary school. But the underlying trend is still towards France This is not what the teachers attempt to do, at least if the results of several inquiries might be generalized. We have to keep in mind that school history is more a matter of effective teaching than of prescriptions. Probably present history teachers in France do not aim at any collective identity, except perhaps when they teach to students displaying a large cultural diversity.[17] The aim of fostering social cohesion and passing on a "common" culture (this does not mean a nationalistic one) is shared between institution and teachers, and seems a legitimate way to deal with the young students socially at a loss.

Research on historical consciousness of the youth, or on the links between what is learnt in school and identities, is scarce. It is perhaps partly out-of-date (the context has changed since the nineties), and, when it deals with ethnic/cultural identities, suspected of stirring social conflicts and *communautarisme*. The strength of the French model of citizenship—presently threatened but still a basis for school and politics—might explain this blank. It might also be, as stated by Ernst (2008) that the teachers' preoccupation is practice and not content. That is on discipline in the classroom, especially when they work in a social context where a lot of students drop out of school and where there is a large distance between familial cultures and school culture. If the teacher has to "open the lessons up to a range of interpretations, controversial discussions about ethnic or religious identities, or "burning questions" related to present-day society, the familiar routines of teaching will no longer work, and teaching will become a harder job" (Tutiaux-Guillon, 2007). And presently, who would like that?

---

[17] It is not usual in France to speak of "ethnic diversity." Statistically and legally, ethnicity has no visibility. In the language of the state, migrant children who receive French nationality, are just "French" like all the others. Ethnic labeling could be taken as a discreet form of racism, a reason to "sort out" the (bad) students, a sense of guilt, or, worse, a claim for communitarism. "Ethnicity" is also a trap because there is no ethnicity as "suburban youth"! In the context, ethnicity is more an argument than a fact, more a social construct than a legacy and more a fictive identity, useful for supporting claims, than a cultural heritage (Lorcerie, 2003).

REFERENCES

Baquès, M.-C., & Tutiaux-Guillon, N. (2008). Los Arabes, el islam y los turcos en la enseñanza de la historia en el sistema educativo francès contemporaneo: entre la tradicion educativa y el contexto sensible [The Arabs, the Islam and the Turks in contemporary French school system history teaching: between educational tradition and delicate context]. In L. Cajiani (Ed.), *Conociendo al otro. El Islam y Europa en sus manuales de historia* [*Knowing the other. Islam and Europe and its history manuals.*] Fundacion Atman y Santillana, España.

Bonafous, C., De Cock-Pierrepont, L., & Falaize, B. (2007). *Mémoires et histoire à l'Ecole de la Republique, quels enjeux?* [*Memories and history at the School of the Republic, what is at stake?*] Paris: Armand Colin.

Brenner, E. (Ed.) (2002). *Les territoires perdus de la République: Milieu scolaire, antisémitisme, sexisme* [*The lost territories of the Republic: School environment, anti-Semitism, sexism*]. Paris: Fayard-Mille et Une Nuits (republished 2004).

Bruter, A. (2005). Les créations successives de l'enseignement de l'histoire au cours du premier XIXe siècle [The successive creations of history teaching during the beginning of the 19th century]. In P. Caspard, J.-N.l. Luc, & P. Savoie (Eds.), *Lycées, lycéens, lycéennes. Deux siècles d'histoire* (pp. 177–197). Lyon: INRP.

Cariou, D. (2003). *Le raisonnement par analogie: un outil au service de la construction du savoir en histoire par les élèves* [*Reasoning by analogy: A tool for knowledge construction in history by students*]. Thèse, Amiens, Université de Picardie.

Chervel, A. (1998). *La culture scolaire—une approche historique* [*School culture—a historical approach*]. Paris: Belin.

De Cock-Pierrepont, L. (2007). Enseigner la controverse au miroir des questionnements épistémologiques, socioculturels et didactiques, l'exemple du fait colonial [Teaching controversy in the reflection of epistemological, sociocultural and didactic questioning, the example of the colonial fact], *Le cartable de Clio*, 7, 196–206.

De Cock, L., & Picard, E. (2009). *La fabrique scolaire de l'histoire* [*The educational factory of history*]. Marseille: Agone.

Delacroix, C., & Garcia, P. (1998). L'inflexion patrimoniale: l'enseignement de l'histoire au risque de l'identité [The patrimonial inclination: History teaching at the risk of identity]. *EspacesTemps*, *65/66*, 111–136. <http://www.espacestemps.net/index.html>

Durpaire, F. (2002). *Enseignement de l'histoire et diversité culturelle, « nos ancêtres ne sont pas les Gaulois »* [*History teaching and cultural diversity, « our ancesters aren't Gaulish »*]. Paris: CNDP, Hachette éducation.

Ernst, S. (2003). L'école et les mémoires de l'immigration, au milieu du gué [School and memories of immigration, halfway through]. In F. Lorcerie, *L'école et le défi ethnique, éducation et intégration* [*School and the ethnic challenge, education and integration*] (pp.245–260). Paris: INRP, ESF.

Ernst S. (Ed.). (2008). *Quand les mémoires déstabilisent l'école. Mémoire de la Shoah et enseignement* [*When memories destabilise school. The memory of the Shoah and teaching*]. Lyon: INRP.

Falaize, B. (2009). Esquisse d'une histoire des génocides à l'école [*A sketch of the history of genocide at school*]. In L. De Cock, & E. Picard, *La fabrique scolaire de l'histoire* (pp.127–146). Marseille: Agone.

Frydmann, D. (2004). *L'enseignement du patrimoine en Seine Saint Denis et construction identitaire des élèves* [*Heritage teching in Seine Saint Denis and the identity construction of the students*] (unpublished research study).

Garcia, P., & Leduc, J. (2003). *L'enseignement de l'histoire en France de l'Ancien Régime à nos jours* [*The teaching of history in France from the Ancient Regime until our present time*]. Paris: A. Colin.

Grever, M., & Ribbens, K. (2007). *Nationale identiteit en meervoudig verleden* [*National identity and plural past*]. WRR Verkenning, 17. Amsterdam: Amsterdam University Press.

Grever, M., & Tutiaux-Guillon, N. (2008). Insegnamento della storia, pluralità culturale e coscienza storica: approci teorici e ricerca empirica [*History teaching, cultural plurality and historical consciousness: Theoretical approaches and empirical investigations*]. *Mundus, rivista di didactica della storia, 2*, 59–73. Palerme: Palumbo & C. editore.

Jacquet-Francillon, F. (2008). Le discours de la mémoire [The discourse of memory]. *Revue Française de Pédagogie, 165*, 5–15.

Lantheaume, F. (2006). Les difficultés de la transmission scolaire: le lien Algérie-France dans les programmes d'histoire, les manuels et l'enseignement en France [The difficulties of educational transmission: The relation Algeria-France in history curricula, manuals and teaching in France]. *Colloque Pour une histoire critique et citoyenne*, INRP-ENS. <http://colloque-algerie.ens-lyon.fr/communication.php3?id_article=208>

Lantheaume, F. (2009). Enseignement du fait colonial et politique de la reconnaissance [Teaching the colonial fact and the politics of recognition]. In L. De Cock & E. Picard, *La fabrique scolaire de l'histoire* (pp. 111–126). Marseille: Agone.

Lautier, N. (1997). *Á la rencontre de l'histoire* [In encounter with history]. Villeneuve d'Ascq: Septentrion.

Lautier, N (2001). *Psychosociologie de l'éducation, regards sur les situations d'enseignement* [*Psychosociology of education, views on teaching situations*]. Paris: Armand Colin.

Lepoutre, D. (2005). *Souvenirs de familles d'immigrés* [*Recollections of immigrant families*]. Paris: Odile Jacob.

Lorecerie, F. (2003). *L'école et le défi ethnique, éducation et intégration* [*School and the ethnic challenge, education and integration*]. Paris: INRP, ESF.

Mousseau, M.-J., Jakob, P., & Cremieux, C. (1994). Regard didactique sur les productions scolaires en histoire-géographie [A didactical approach to school productions in history-geography]. *Revue Française de Pédagogie, 106*, 47–54.

Rodriguez, M.C. (2009). Al-Andalus, "l'Orient de l'Occident"? Autour d'une approche nuancée d'al-Andalus au-delà de ses représentations mythiques [Al-Andalus, "Orient of the Occident"? On a nuanced approach of Al Andalus beyond its mythical representations]. *Le cartable de Clio, 9*, 57–68.

Tutiaux-Guillon, N. (2000). *L'enseignement et la compréhension de l'histoire sociale au collège et au lycée, l'exemple de la société d'Ancien régime et de la société du XIXe siècle*

[*Teaching and comprehesion of school history at college and high school*]. *Lille: thèses à la carte.* (Thèse, Université de Paris 7—Denis Diderot, 1998).

Tutiaux-Guillon, N. (Ed.) (2000). *l'Europe entre projet politique et objet scolaire* [*Europe between political project and educational object*]. Paris: INRP.

Tutiaux-Guillon, N. (2004). *L'enseignement de l'histoire-géographie dans le secondaire, analyses didactiques d'une inertie scolaire* [*Teaching historical geography in secondary school, didactical analysis of educational inertia*]. Mémoire pour l'Habilitation à Diriger des Recherches, Université Lyon 2-Lumière.

Tutiaux-Guillon, N. (2006). Altérité et enseignement de l'histoire: quelques pistes de réflexions et de recherche à partir de la situation française [Otherness and history teaching: some hints of reflection and research proceeding from the French situation]. In M. Hassani Idrissi, *Rencontre de l'histoire et rencontre de l'autre, l'enseignement de l'histoire comme dialogue interculturel* [*Meeting history and meeting the other, teaching history as an intercultural dialogue*] (pp.257–274). Rabat, presses de l'université Mohamed V.

Tutiaux-Guillon, N. (2007). French school history confronts multiculturalism. In M. Grever & S. Stuurman. *Beyond the canon, history for the 21st century* (pp. 173–187). London: Palgrave- Macmilan,.

Tutiaux-Guillon, N. (2008). Mémoires et histoire scolaire en France: quelques inter-rogations didactiques [Memories and school history in France: some didactical interrogations]. *Revue Française de Pédagogie, 165,* 31–42.

Tutiaux-Guillon, N., & Mousseau, M.-J. (1998). *Les jeunes et l'histoire, identités, mémoires, conscience historique* [*The young and history, identities, memories and historical conscience*]. Paris: INRP.

Tutiaux-Guillon, N., Boyer, G., Ogier, A., & Vercueil-Simion, C. (2004). *Enseignement et apprentissage de l'histoire et de la géographie en CM1/CM2 et en 6e/5e: la prise en compte des finalités civiques et culturelles* [*Teaching and learning history and geography in CM1/CM2 and 6th/5th grades: taking into account civic and cultural goals*]. The research conclusions were published online on <www.lyon.iufm.f/ recherche.htmlr>, but are no more available.

CHAPTER 9

INDIGENOUS HISTORICAL CONSCIOUSNESS

An Oxymoron or a Dialogue?[1]

Peter Seixas

In some ways, Canada has been a multinational state since the British North America Act of 1867. Different historical experiences, languages, and religions, thrust relations between Quebec and the Anglophone provinces onto center stage in the negotiations that led to the modern Canada. Tension, rebalancing and renegotiation comprise a large theme in the subsequent history of the country.[2]

---

[1] I am indebted to Keith Carlson and Kristina Fagan for an invitation to a symposium, *Theorizing and Grounding Indigenous Historical Consciousness and Voice.* University of Saskatchewan, 23–24 Sept. 2010, which stimulated my thinking about the issues confronted in this paper. Keith Carlson, Penney Clark, Margaret Conrad, Kadriye Ercikan, Susan Inman, Michael Marker and Carla Peck offered helpful comments.

[2] The leading proponent of the notion that Quebec is a "nation that failed to become a state" is Gerard Bouchard (2000); For contrasting views of the history and future of Quebec, see Jocelyn Létourneau, (2000).

History Education and the Construction of National Identities, pages 125–138

The Anglophone/Francophone divide has, not surprisingly, been expressed in the historiographic narration of Canada. But that division took place within a common European Enlightenment framework of historical epistemology and method. Though interpretive disagreements raged, epistemological and methodological issues did not fracture across the linguistic line (Smith, 2007).[3]

Immigration, a second key theme in Canadian history, has not challenged or threatened the idea of two European founding peoples. While many immigrants have maintained ties and loyalties to their countries of origin, and have, particularly in recent years, sought *cultural* accommodation, none has claimed *national* status within the state of Canada (Kymlicka, 1998).

Moreover, the expansion of Canadian historiography to include more attention to immigrant communities within Canada was relatively unproblematic. Some, most notably Jack Granatstein (1998) and Michael Bliss (1991) complained of historiographic fragmentation. But immigrants were included in the narratives of the modern Canadian state as successfully as they had been integrated into the fabric of Canadian society: that is to say relatively easily, from the standpoint of 2012 and a purview of the world at large, notwithstanding some painful and shameful episodes.

None of this worked in the same way for the Aboriginal peoples of Canada, or, as they are known in northern North America, First Nations. First, as the term suggests, they *do* claim status as many geographically dispersed nations. Secondly, they claim rights and title to the land on the basis of tenure *prior to* European colonization. Most importantly, there is claim to a distinct "way of knowing," an indigenous epistemology, a non-European, non-Enlightenment sense of the relation between past, present and future that puts the understanding of history on an entirely different ground from that developed by English, French, Dutch and German historical thinkers.

Formal, state-sponsored history education represents a crucial engagement with historical consciousness. While extracurricular narratives have strong impacts on young people's understanding of the past, there is no other institution which enjoys compulsory attendance over the entire course of childhood and adolescence, and which can potentially exercise (however fitfully and partially, in fact) planned, systematic, goal-oriented shaping of historical consciousness.[4]

Canadian ministries of education have recently framed strongly stated goals, aiming to incorporate First Nations more fully and more legitimately into their programs and curricula.[5] Achieving this goal will entail a change

---

[3] This lack of confrontation might otherwise be explained simply as a consequence of "two solitudes," with little dialogue.

[4] On unofficial and extracurricular impacts, see Wineburg (2001) and Wertsch (2000).

[5] See, e.g., British Columbia Ministry of Education (2006); Ontario Ministry of Education (n.d.).

in the emplotment of Canadian history, a process that has begun at least in a piecemeal way. But more profoundly revolutionary will be the consequences of taking seriously the claims to alternative epistemologies. What, exactly, is at stake?

WHAT IS HISTORICAL CONSCIOUSNESS?

In Gadamer's seminal formulation, historical consciousness is the awareness of—as well as the need to understand—profound change in human affairs over time. Time is conceptualized as a series of eras, periods, or epochs, each of which has not only different technologies and material circumstances, but also different intellectual, moral and emotional orientations. The term *Weltanschauung*, or, as Carl Becker rendered it in more prosaic English, "climate of opinion," only makes sense in the context of historical consciousness. There is a break between the present and the past: the past is a "foreign country." Most importantly, no matter how hard we strive for universal truths, the knowledge that we possess today is, as is all earlier knowledge, rooted in a moment in time (Becker, 1932; Gadamer, 1987; Koselleck, 1985; Lowenthal, 1985).

In brief, we are immersed in change, and it is a difficult challenge (ever only partially overcome) to transcend our own changeable historical situation, to interpret texts from a different era, and to see things from outside the flux of which we are nevertheless aware. This profoundly relativized state is the situation of modernity. Gadamer located its development in the late 18th–early 19th centuries:

> The appearance of historical self-consciousness is very likely the most important revolution among those we have undergone since the beginning of the modern epoch…The historical consciousness which characterizes contemporary man is a privilege, perhaps even a burden, the like of which has never been imposed on any previous generation (Gadamer, 1987, p. 89).

Yosef Yerushalmi concurred as to the burden of historical consciousness:

> The very ability to conceive a time when men and women think differently than we, be it in the future or in the past, is the fruit of that historical consciousness which is ours in the present. We cannot avoid it without an inner violence and betrayal, even if we know that what we do may be only provisional. But that is all right. In the terrifying time in which we live and create, eternity is not our immediate concern (Yerushalmi, 1989, p. 103).

Beyond a particular relationship between past, present and future, these conceptual orientations place human agency at the center of history. Knowledge of the past is important—for science, politics and every other sphere of human endeavor—because it allows those in the present to take informed collective action. Just as they recognize a different past, they envision the possibility of a different future. Though such knowledge does not ensure development, it makes development possible. Historical consciousness is likewise necessary for a populace undertaking the democratic governance of a state.

Jörn Rüsen provides a more inclusive definition by mapping four different types of historical consciousness, arrayed in a developmental hierarchy, from the most basic "traditional," which supports "the continuity of fixed and unchanging moral obligations, without acknowledging any significant change over time" to the most advanced, "genetic," which acknowledges "the ongoing legacy of the past, at the same time that it comprehends radically changed present circumstances and mores."[6] Again, human actors are at the center of a morally inflected historical universe.

While Rüsen's hierarchy opens up the boundaries of "historical consciousness," it poses as much of a problem as Gadamer and Yerushalmi for anyone who is interested in the cross-cultural study of collective memory: is all historical consciousness to be measured against a standard set by modern Europe?[7] Yet *some* attainment target is indispensable for those who work in history education, which bears an obligation to define the desired ends of the pedagogical project.

INDIGENOUS COMMUNITY MEMORY IN CANADA

Michael Marker (2011) has identified four characteristics of indigenous ways of understanding the past, all of which pose difficulties for Western historiographies.[8]

1. The circular nature of time and the ways oral tradition is integrated into recurring events; notions of "progress" are problematic in this way of understanding history;
2. The often central theme of relationships with landscape and non-humans;
3. An emphasis on the local landscape as containing the meaning of both time and place rather than an analysis of global social and political change; and
4. Indigenous narratives and perspectives on the histories of colonization that attempted to displace and replace Indigenous knowledge.

---

[6] See the discussion of Rüsen in Seixas (2004).

[7] This problem is addressed in Rüsen (2002) and Chakrabarty (2000).

[8] What Marker has done in this chapter is both important and dangerous: it articulates key differences in organization of thinking about the past, while potentially fraught with over-generalization. As Alfonso Ortiz put it, "There is simply no *the* Indian viewpoint in the writing of history." Quoted in Nabokov (2002, p. vii).

In Marker's account, "indigenous worldviews tend to emphasize the moral and spiritual structure of events. These are immersed in recurring stories that circulate to bind reality together." As Julie Cruikshank found (as cited by Marker), Yukon Aboriginal elders' stories wove events and individuals from the 1940s with much older oral traditions. "A sense of linear time was folded and curved to account for the merging of events and characters creating a circular and recurring moral universe within an Indigenous epistemology" (Marker, 2011, pp. 126–7). The indigenous notion of time articulated by Marker, Cruikshank and others thus differs significantly from the time articulated by theorists of historical consciousness.[9]

There is a similar disjunction about the role of human agency in history. According to Marker, "Indigenous systems of knowledge and understandings of the past are different from . . . [non-Aboriginal] approaches in that they place the relationship of animals as unsegmented from human beings" (p. 128). The intentional actions of human beings do not occupy a special place in Aboriginal consciousness. Marker suggests that Indigenous categories "merge human and animal histories" (p. 131).

Marker's third characteristic again contrasts dramatically with Western historiography. "The Indigenous vision of the past is sublimely local," he claims (p. 132).[10] In non-Aboriginal historiography even the intensely local microhistories of Laurel Thatcher Ulrich, Natalie Zemon Davis, and Carlo Ginzburg elevate their formerly unknown protagonists to a level of historical significance by embedding their stories in larger historical developments, such as evolving medical practice, gender relations and religious belief (Davis, 1983; Ginzburg, 1992; Ulrich, 1990).

Marker does not explicitly identify the final node of contention. That is the idea that historical knowledge, or stories about the past, can be the exclusive possession of certain individuals. There are two aspects of this: ownership—that some stories, for spiritual reasons, can only be told at certain times by certain people; and authority—that the credibility of an account rests upon the identity of the teller. While in practice, historians in Western academia may claim some authority on the basis of their scholarly seniority, disciplinary standards require that they remain open to challenge. Indeed the whole historiographic enterprise depends on new scholars criticizing the interpretations of their forerunners. Moreover, while politicians and public figures may try to protect their own historical secrets, historians, by

---

[9] This generalization has not gone unchallenged. Shepard Krech III (2006) complicates the picture considerably, noting the multiple ways that aboriginal peoples marked linear time, as well as the "unfortunate conflation of circular with cyclical" (p. 573). Krech attributes the conventional wisdom of a simple, widely held dichotomy to the influence of Benjamin Whorf, Mircea Eliade, and Claude Levi-Strauss.

[10] Like Shepard Krech, Keith Carlson (2010) challenges this simple dichotomy, based on work with the Coast Salish of British Columbia.

the nature of the discipline, place themselves at the forefront of efforts to make knowledge public.

WHAT HAPPENS AT THE BORDER?

Recent attempts to deal with these disjunctions are sometimes awkward, sometimes creative. In Canadian historiography, Margaret Conrad and James Hiller's *Atlantic Canada: A History* offers the following in Chapter 1, "Beginnings." After a brief summary of the Biblical creation story...

> Aboriginal creation stories also attributed the earth's origins to powerful gods. According to Mi'kmaq beliefs, Kji-kinap made the world and breathed life into a large, flat stone that he named Kluskap...
>
> The implications of the scientific view of creation that now dominates most textbooks also take a leap of faith to grasp...
>
> Scientists now think that the earth is at least 4.5 billion years old, and explain the creation of continents and oceans in the framework of plate tectonics... (Conrad & Hiller, 2010, p. 3)

The remainder of this orienting section leaves both the Bible and the Mi'kmaq beliefs behind and carries on, leap of faith or not, with a straight-forward account of the geological history of the region. The inclusion of various belief systems (and even the Bible) in a chapter about Maritimes geology clearly exists as a nod to Aboriginal ways of knowing. The Bible would not otherwise have been in there.

More ambitious is John Ralston Saul's (2009) *A Fair Country: Telling Truths About Canada.* Saul is one of Canada's most visible public intellectuals: author of thirteen books, husband of former Governor-General Adrienne Clarkson, Massey Lecturer, among other honors. Saul argues for a wholesale reinterpretation of the history of Canada as a "Métis nation," meaning that Aboriginal ideas are at least as foundational as Enlightenment Europe in Canadian government, society and culture. Not a work of serious scholarship, but rather a polemic whose rhetorical power is based on a series of anecdotes, Saul seeks to find roots for what he thinks the country *should be*—one based on fairness and inclusion—in what it *has been*, even if most people—historians, politicians, and most everyone else—don't recognize the latter.

In her survey *Canada's First Nations: A History of Founding Peoples from Earliest Times*, Métis historian Olive Dickason (2002, p. 21) has a clear and efficient solution to conflicts over Aboriginal origin stories: "Many Indians believe this is the land of their origins; ... their different perceptions of time and nature place these tales at another level of reality than that of this work."

CANADIAN HISTORY EDUCATION TODAY

Constitutionally, education in Canada lies within the jurisdiction of 10 provinces and 3 territories. There has been relatively little problem including more of the aboriginal experience in school textbooks and academic histories. Indeed, more thorough accounts of the fur trade, the treaties in 19th century Western Canada, the elimination of the bison, the residential school system, and the various attempts to protest against, mitigate and compensate for the most disastrous aspects of the colonial relationships are increasingly making their way into new textbooks across the provinces and, even more so in the northern territories. The problem lies elsewhere.

These changes come at just the moment when Canadian history curricula are moving towards a more explicit emphasis on historical thinking.[11] This movement, at least at the outset, involves neither more nor less focus on "the nation" than earlier curricula. Both reflecting this movement and stimulating it, the federal Department of Canadian Heritage has supported the Benchmarks of Historical Thinking, a project based at the University of British Columbia, of which the author is director (Peck & Seixas, 2008; Seixas, 2010).[12] A Project report summarized its objective,

> The project was designed to foster a new approach to history education—with the potential to shift how teachers teach and how students learn, in line with recent international research on history learning . . . It revolves around the proposition—like scientific thinking in science instruction and mathematical thinking in math instruction—that *historical thinking* is central to history instruction and that students should become more competent as historical thinkers as they progress through their schooling. (Seixas, 2008, p. 5)

For the purposes of the project, historical thinking has been framed around six "structural" historical thinking concepts, drawing on earlier British work, but not unlike similar frameworks internationally (Lee, 2004). Since 2008, these concepts have informed new provincial curriculum documents and history textbook production from all of the major Canadian publishers.

They capture major facets of disciplinary practices even at their most sophisticated, but they are articulated in such a way as to be meaningful to teachers and students across the years of schooling. The six concepts, defined very briefly as student competencies, are: to establish *historical significance* (why we care, today, about certain events, trends and issues in his-

---

[11]Personal communication, Tom Morton, who recently (2009–10) completed a comprehensive, unpublished survey of provincial social studies and history curricula across Canada, one part of a larger study *Historical Thinking in Canadian Schools.*

[12]In the Spring of 2011, the name of the project was changed from "Benchmarks of Historical Thinking" to "The Historical Thinking Project."

tory); to use primary source *evidence* (how to find, select, contextualize, and interpret sources for a historical argument); to identify *continuity and change* (what has changed and what has remained the same over time); to analyze *cause and consequence* (how and why certain conditions and actions led to others); to take *historical perspectives* (understanding the "past as a foreign country," with its different social, cultural, intellectual, and even emotional contexts that shaped people's lives and actions); and to understand the *ethical dimension* of historical interpretations (how we, in the present, judge actors in different circumstances in the past; how different interpretations of the past reflect different moral stances today; when and how injustices of the past bear consequences today) (The Historical Thinking Project, n.d.).

Every one of these could be used to support the inclusion of more Aboriginal topics, more sensitively treated, in the school curriculum. Yet every one potentially runs up against contradictions and problems when faced with Aboriginal ways of knowing the past. What follows below are a series of questions and puzzles, which can best be addressed in ongoing dialogue with Aboriginal scholars.

A. Historical Significance

At one point, establishing historical significance in Western historiography primarily involved identifying events whose outcomes, and people whose actions had deep consequences for many people over a long period of time. Their significance was established through narrative accounts of those outcomes. The historiographic revolution of the past forty years has challenged that criterion as the sole standard of significance. Its attention to the powerless, oppressed, and subaltern peoples has brought women, immigrants, workers, the poor, and the colonized onto center stage. But establishing their significance still involved linking their lives to larger historical movements of which they were a part and showing how their actions helped shape historical developments, often in relation to those who were closer to the reins of power. Even a historian like Alain Corbin (2001), whose *The Life of an Unknown* is the product of a search for a vanished, 19th century illiterate, is described by his publisher as offering an "exploration into the life of the common man in nineteenth-century France." This is not to say that his *life* was historically significant, but the account is made so by being located in a larger narrative of French and European histories. Is there overlap, or conflict, between methods for establishing historical significance in an aboriginal story? If we take Marker seriously, then "emphasis on the local landscape as containing the meaning of both time and place" suggests no need to contextualize the specific and local in a larger narrative.

B. Primary Source Evidence

The foundations for modern historical research are the procedures used in handling primary source evidence, traces of the past that have survived into the present. As with the problem of historical significance, the new questions posed in the course of the historiographic revolution of the past forty years have dramatically opened the kinds of traces that are utilized, including oral tradition and testimony. Moreover, historians are more openly conscious about the uses and limitations of the archives themselves (Steedman, 2002). Some ideas have not changed, however. Sources, in order to contribute to historical understanding, need to be contextualized, that is, read through the historical circumstances, different from ours today, in which they were produced.[13] The position of the authors (or artists or photographers, etc.) is always of interest, but their authority always demands a critical stance. The historian never takes their words at face value. How different is the Aboriginal approach to the interpretation of traditional stories of elders?[14]

C. Continuity and Change

In the Benchmarks Framework, the concepts of continuity and change provide a large category into which fall the ideas of progress and decline, periodization and chronological time. The modern idea of progress, a normative stance towards change over time, linked both to the nation and scientific knowledge, has ebbed and flowed since its articulation by the French *philosophes*, reaching an apogee in the early 20th century with J. B. Bury's (1932) *Idea of Progress*, and arguably, again, with modernization theory of the 1960s (e.g., Rostow, 1960). Today's assessments of world historical trajectories, as we stare down environmental catastrophe, are not as rosy. Moreover, historians making explicit or implicit claims of progress *or* decline are more likely to parse the judgment more finely, noting progress for whom. Finally, any historian who embedded a teleological notion of progress into a historical account would be roundly criticized as a Whig historian. Nevertheless, the concept of progress provides a seminal yardstick for gauging change. Can it be reconciled with a belief in the "circular nature of time"?

---

[13]Actually, along the fringes, there are critics of this fundamental practice. See Harlan (1997) and Jenkins (1991).

[14]The legal analog of this educational question was played out in the *Delgamuukw* decision of the Supreme Court of Canada in 1997. As J. R. Miller (2000, p. 387) summarizes, "The court upheld the significance of oral history evidence, a clear sign that the judiciary was now willing to accord *Aboriginal standards of reality and Aboriginal forms of history* (italics added) the same respect Euro-Canadian ones received." I am indebted to Penney Clark for alerting me to this reference.

D. Cause and Consequence

The concepts of cause and consequence introduce more trouble. In the Historical Thinking Framework, the goal is to introduce students to increasingly complex notions of cause. There are multiple layers, which might have designations of "underlying" and "immediate;" there are enabling conditions, necessary and sufficient causes; causation can be explored with counterfactuals; and the causes that are highlighted in one account of an event might be downplayed or omitted in another, as a result of the focus of the questions that the historian is asking. Informing all of this complexity is the notion that human beings, acting intentionally, individually and in groups, have roles to play in historical development. Their actions are constrained by the conditions in which they find themselves, and more often than not have unintended consequences. But humans remain at the center of the story. Serious historians cannot today invoke the "will of God" or "national destiny" as causal explanations for events. So where does this leave Western historiography in relation to indigenous notions of causation, where, according to Marker (p. 130), "histories include moral teachings from encounters with animals such as Owl, Raven, Wolf, and Bear"? Animals and landscapes can be central to Western historiography; environmental history is alive and well in North America (see Network in Canadian History and Environment, 2005–11). But in this literature, animals are not invested with the historical agency that can only be a consequence of intentional action: they cannot occupy the moral ground that is the province of human beings. Is there common ground between these modes of narration and explanation?

E. Historical Perspective-Taking

Taking historical perspectives is the quintessential act of historical consciousness. The first step is to recognize the possibility that change affects all levels of human activity, from the material circumstances of life to the ways we think about the world, moral values, ourselves. The second is to try to interpret and reconstruct life from different eras. Historiography in the wake of Michel Foucault has relentlessly historicized more and more domains of existence, from crime to gender relations, to sexuality, to historical knowledge itself. An epistemology grounded on tradition that valorizes continuity over change, which seeks primarily to preserve old accounts rather than to critique them publicly and write new ones, seems, at least, *prima facie*, to be profoundly at odds with this notion of historical consciousness. Is there more complexity beneath the surface?

F. The Ethical Dimension

The ethical dimension in Western historiography is plagued by the dilemma posed by the distance between past and present. Judgments of people and events in distant times must account for differences in vocabulary ("sexism," for example, is a relatively recent neologism), beliefs and mores, and yet those judgments are inescapable. The moral tales of First Nations' ways of knowing escape this dilemma. There is an aspect of the ethical dimension, however, where the two epistemologies may be more in harmony, which comes into play in considering the present legacies of past injustices and sacrifices. Western and First Nations historiography have a chance to come together around debts of memory, and obligations for reparations and restitution. Canada's residential schools are one of the most stunning examples where oral memory and Western modes of scholarship have reinforced each other to uncover and make public histories that might otherwise have remained unknown (Truth and Reconciliation Commission of Canada, n.d.).

Are there ways in which other aspects of historical thinking might be brought into similar productive dialogue with each other in order to map a trajectory for a cosmopolitan history education in Canada?

MAKÚK

John Lutz explains the Chinook word, *makúk*, in all its polysemous possibility (Lutz, 2008). The word was part of trading jargon, an argot stripped to the simplest terms in order to make negotiations across language barriers possible. Within the jargon, it meant "to exchange," either to buy or to sell. As Lutz (pp. x–xi) explains, "It was a language of approximate meaning." Can we *makúk* in the realm of history education? With each of the historical thinking concepts in the section above, I have attempted to outline the contradictions and difficulties in as stark a way as possible, in order that we can begin to know what is at stake in the exchange. Built into *makúk* is the possibility of adjustment, accommodation, and negotiation. Moving beyond totalizing dichotomies of circular vs. linear and local vs. global, as Shepard Krech III and Keith Thor Carlson suggest, is one step in the process.

Stories are part of history education, but stories are not the whole story. Adding more topics to the curriculum in an increasingly diverse society is not the solution. Nor is simply telling different stories. We need to teach students how to assess the significance of stories, how to analyze the evidence behind stories, how to relate micro-stories to larger pictures of historical development, and how to unearth stories' underlying structures and implicit ethical messages. Only with a populace able to read and share stories across borders, across difference, can we shape a future together. The multicultural, multinational Canada of today demands a cosmopolitan approach to the teaching of history to its young people in schools. There is little room for exclusive claims to insular knowledge. At the same time, cosmopolitanism demands respect for others with different belief systems.

Herein lies the conundrum for modern, secular Canada. Opening the door of Canadian education to Aboriginal stories poses no problem. Publisher Prentice-Hall could comfortably include "Why the Salmon Came to Squamish Waters" as a special-colored insert in their Grade 10 offering (Cranny, 1998, pp. 182–5). In standard textbook form, its short caption explains what a "myth" is, and then claims, "In this story, the origins of the salmon are revealed." If the publisher decided to take out the special colors and captions, and genuinely integrate this story as part of the historical geography of British Columbia, the ride would not be so easy. Once indigenous ways of knowing are actually part of the textbook's way of knowing, then who will be able to object to histories based on Islamic cosmology, Biblical fundamentalism and Haitian voodoo? What does it mean, then, to teach students to think historically, in a way that is appropriate for a multicultural society, pedagogically sound, and true to the most current practices in the discipline?

REFERENCES

Becker, C. (1932). *The heavenly city of the eighteenth-century philosophers.* New Haven: Yale University Press.

Bliss, M. (1991). Privatizing the mind. *Journal of Canadian Studies, 26*(4), 5–17.

Bouchard, G. (2000). *Génèse des nations et cultures du nouveau monde: Essai d'histoire comparée* [*Genesis of nations and cultures of the new world: An attempt to comparative history*]. Montréal: Boréal.

British Columbia Ministry of Education (2006). *BC First Nations Studies 12.* www.bced.gov.bc.ca/irp/ (accessed 9 Oct 2010).

Bury, J. B. (1932). *The idea of progress.* New York: Dover.

Carlson, K. T. (2010). *The power of place, the problem of time: Aboriginal identity and historical consciousness in the cauldron of colonialism.* Vancouver: UBC Press.

Chakrabarty, D. (2000). *Provincializing Europe: Postcolonial thought and historical difference.* Princeton NJ: Princeton University Press.

Conrad, M. R., & Hiller, J. K. (2010). *Atlantic Canada: A history.* Toronto: Oxford University Press.

Corbin, A. (2001). *The life of an unknown: The rediscovered world of a clog maker in 19th century France* (A. Goldhammer, Trans.). New York: Columbia University Press.

Cranny, M. (1998). *Crossroads: A meeting of nations.* Scarborough, ON: Prentice Hall Ginn Canada.

Davis, N. Z. (1983). *The return of Martin Guerre.* Cambridge: Harvard University Press.

Dickason, O. P. (2002). *Canada's first nations: A history of founding peoples from earliest times* (3rd ed.). Don Mills ON: Oxford University Press.

Gadamer, H.-G. (1987). The problem of historical consciousness. In P. Rabinow & W. M. Sullivan (Eds.), *Interpretive social science: A second look* (pp. 82–140). Berkeley, CA: University of California Press.

Ginzburg, C. (1992). *The cheese and the worms: The cosmos of a sixteenth-century miller* (J. A. A. C. Tedeschi, Trans.). Baltimore: John Hopkins Univeristy Press.

Granatstein, J. (1998). *Who killed Canadian history?* Toronto: Harper-Collins.

Harlan, D. (1997). *The degradation of American history.* Chicago & London, UK: University of Chicago Press.

Jenkins, K. (1991). *Rethinking history.* London, UK: Routledge.

Koselleck, R. (1985). *Futures past* (K. Tribe, Trans.). Cambridge MA: MIT Press.

Krech III, S. (2006). Bringing linear time back in. *Ethnohistory, 53,* 567–593.

Kymlicka, W. (1998). *Finding our way: Rethinking ethnocultural relations in Canada.* Toronto: Oxford University Press.

Lee, P. (2004). Understanding history. In P. Seixas (Ed.), *Theorizing historical consciousness* (pp. 129–164). Toronto: University of Toronto Press.

Létourneau, J. (2000). *Passer à l'avenir. Histoire, mémoire, identité dans le Québec d'aujourd'hui* [Passing to the future. History, memory, identity in the Québec of today]. Montréal: Boréal.

Lowenthal, D. (1985). *The past is a foreign country.* New York: Cambridge.

Lutz, J. S. (2008). *Makúk: A new history of Aboriginal-white relations.* Vancouver: University of British Columbia Press.

Marker, M. (2011). Teaching history from an indigenous perspective: Four winding paths up the mountain. In P. Clark (Ed.), *New perspectives on the past: Teaching and learning history in Canada.* Vancouver: University of British Columbia Press.

Miller, J.R. (2000). *Skyscrapers hide the heavens: A history of Indian-white relations in Canada* (3rd ed.). Toronto: University of Toronto Press.

Nabokov, P. (2002). *A forest of time: American Indian ways of history.* Cambridge UK: Cambridge University Press.

Network in Canadian History and Environment (2005–2011). http://niche-canada. org/ (accessed 4 September 2011).

Ontario Ministry of Education (n.d.) Aboriginal perspectives: A guide to the teacher's toolkit, http://www.edu.gov.on.ca/eng/aboriginal/toolkit.html (accessed 9 Oct 2010).

Peck, C., & Seixas, P. (2008). Benchmarks of historical thinking: First steps. *Canadian Journal of Education, 31*(4).

Rostow, W. W. (1960). *The stages of economic growth: A non-communist manifesto.* Cambridge: Cambridge University Press.

Rüsen, J. (Ed.). (2002). *Western historical thinking: An intercultural debate.* New York: Bergahn Books.

Saul, J. R. (2009). *A fair country: Telling truths about Canada.* Toronto: Viking Canada.

Seixas, P. (2004). Introduction. In P. Seixas (Ed.), *Theorizing historical consciousness* (pp. 3–20). Toronto: University of Toronto Press.

Seixas, P. (2008). *'Scaling up' the benchmarks of historical thinking: A report on the Vancouver meetings, Feb. 14–15, 2008.* Vancouver: University of British Columbia.

Seixas, P. (2010). A modest proposal for change in Canadian History Education. *International Review of History Education, 6,* 11–26.

Smith, A. (2007). Seven narratives in North American history: Thinking the nation in Canada, Quebec and the United States. In S. Berger (Ed.), *Writing the nation* (pp. 63–83). New York: Palgrave Macmillan.

Steedman, C. (2002). *Dust: The archive and cultural history.* New Brunswick NJ: Rutgers University Press.

The Historical Thinking Project (n.d.). www.historicalthinking.ca (accessed 3 September 2011).

Truth and Reconciliation Commission of Canada (n.d.). http://www.trc.ca/ (accessed 4 September 2011).

Ulrich, L. T. (1990). *A midwife's tale: The life of Martha Ballard, based on her diary.* New York: Knopf.

Wertsch, J. V. (2000). Is it possible to teach beliefs, as well as knowledge about history? In P. Stearns, P. Seixas, & S. S. Wineburg (Eds.), *Knowing, teaching and learning history: National and international perspectives.* New York: New York University Press.

Wineburg, S. S. (2001). *Historical thinking and other unnatural acts: Charting the future of teaching the past.* Philadelphia: Temple University Press.

Yerushalmi, Y. H. (1989). *Zakhor: Jewish history and Jewish tz.* New York: Schocken Books.

CHAPTER 10

COMMENTARY

Identity Construction and the Goals of History Education

Cesar López and Mario Carretero

A pioneering writer on the topics covered in this book, the French historian M. Ferro (1981) affirmed in his work *How the Past is Taught to Children* that:

> Our images of other people, or of ourselves for that matter, reflect the history we are taught as children. This history marks us for life. Its representation (…) of the past of societies, embraced all of our passing or permanent opinions, so that the traces of our first questioning, our first emotions, remain indelible. (p. vii)

We have discussed Ferro's assertion a number of times in recent years, and we must confess that we have occasionally thought it, if not wrong, at least exaggerated. However, thirty years after the publication of the original work, which is seminal in the field, his statement seems more accurate than ever. The history taught in most countries (Carretero, 2011; Foster & Crawford, 2006; Symcox & Wilschut, 2009) is composed of versions of the past that in addition to giving historiographic meaning to the study of causal temporal relationships, also amplify the nation-state's official voice—often

History Education and the Construction of National Identities, pages 139–150
139

its only voice. Similar to how our minds are influenced by fairy tales—as Bettelheim described some time ago in another seminal book (2005) the historical accounts learned in school have a decisive influence on our view of the past, present, and future.

Some readers may find this parallel somewhat exaggerated; however, we could cite the daily press accounts of the growing influence of the conservative Tea Party movement in the United States. In that case, a historical metaphor from the American revolution of 200 years ago is used in its most literal version, out of its historical context, to inspire an ultraconservative critique of the present and construct a political direction for the future. We believe that the present-day example of the Tea Party is a clear demonstration of the role that history-based metaphors can play in our understanding and behavior as human beings.

One of the most important sources of such metaphors is the school curriculum, particularly the teaching of history, which commonly generates and disseminates national narratives called master narratives. Strangely enough, we believe in these stories as though they were indisputable, erecting them in the center of the past. However, contemporary historiographic investigations show that in reality, such narratives are based more on the interests of certain social groups than on the objective investigation of past events.

Textbooks and other teaching devices used inside and outside of schools express a certain vision of the past, and in the end, the students and future citizens imbibe these productions because the school transmits them through historical narratives. This practice results in deep internalization; students across social groups believe these narratives to be true. Moreover, students believe that they are self-evident, empirical truths and that it is impossible to doubt any of narrative's key elements. It is not only the school that contributes to this state of affairs through its formal and informal mechanisms, of which patriotic rituals are undoubtedly the most prominent example, but society as a whole also contributes through family socialization, the media, and other cultural instruments, such as museums and films.

In many countries, one finds an almost perfect internalization of these narratives; however, in some cases, obvious dissenting voices emerge among students and professors, giving rise to tension between acceptance and resistance. We believe the work in this book clearly and convincingly demonstrates that this tension is possible but often unlikely to arise because the nation-state tends to be effective in using its instruments. Therefore, educational mechanisms, even if they do not meet the objective of providing a good education, do appear to meet the objective of instilling ideology—and in the case of the teaching of history, even indoctrination.

The accounts usually found within various patriotic rituals shape national identities by having students aged six to eight affirm with certainty that "I am Argentine," "English," or "Spanish." As this concept is instilled in at that young age, students come to feel like heirs to the heroes who used their swords to build the political institutions of the places to which they claim to belong. This feeling, which is observable by any educator who has a relationship with their students, actually encompasses inherent contradictions that students do not detect but that education should help make them aware of.

Such help would primarily be not attributing an essentialist status to nationality. Students tend to think that nations, particularly their own nation, have always existed and that things could not be otherwise (see Carretero, Lopez, Gonzáles, & Rodríguez-Moneo, 2012). Students have difficulty understanding that although nations are well-defined political entities, they are also the result of social and political tensions and structures that have come together in a particular way but not the only possible way. There are clear, well-known examples of these effects, such as how the boundaries of European countries changed after each world war. In Latin America, there were substantial changes in most countries throughout the nineteenth and twentieth centuries. For example, Argentina, a country in which we have conducted extensive research, only became independent in 1816, and even then it was very different from the current situation. However, most of the Argentinean students we interviewed, including adolescents and youth, thought that the country had always existed as a nation and that its destiny was predetermined in a teleological sense. Conceptualizations such as these indicate that education in history has been strongly influenced by identity issues. This influence has been greater than an adequate understanding of history as a discipline.

The four papers in this section present theoretical issues in both general discussions and in detailed analyses of specific countries, including the Netherlands (Grever, 2012), the United States, Ireland, New Zealand (Barton, 2012), France (Tutiaux-Guillon, 2012), and Canada (Seixas, 2012). One of the strengths of this section is the range of educational contexts that are analyzed, which allows for more broad-based comparisons. We believe that these four papers share the recognition of the failure of traditional national narratives as a basis for teaching history. Notably, there has been a growing awareness of this failure in recent years. It has been recognized in previous works (Grever & Stuurman, 2010) and is clearly expressed in Tutiaux-Guillon's paper in this section, which states the following:

> [T]he history of France has to be known... [I]t cannot be said that such aims, prescribed for primary and lower secondary school, are focused on national identity. These developments do not mean that school history in secondary education does not take the national history into account at all: the curricula

are compromises between different actors and tendencies, often contradictory. (p. 114)

Current research appears to have strongly established that we must rethink
the relationship between the goals of teaching history and identity construction. This relationship has been discussed frequently in recent years
(Barton & Levstik, 2008; Carretero, 2011; Grever & Stuurman, 2008). It
is a complex phenomenon that manifests itself in a variety of ways due to
the complexity of each element in the relationship. In both the specialized
literature on the purposes of teaching history and the literature on identity
aspects, it is difficult to find similar approaches or common conclusions.

The goals of teaching history continue to be the subject of frequent
debate. These debates have occurred both within the discipline of history
(Foster & Crawford, 2006; Nakou & Barca, 2010) and outside of it as part
of political, social, and cultural discussions (Evans, 2004; Nash, Crabtree,
& Dunn, 2000). One of the key elements that undoubtedly contribute to
the complexity of debates on the goals of history teaching is its association
with the transmission of values and identity construction (Barton & Levstik,
2004; Hobsbawm, 1997; Wertsch, 2002).

It is well known that the centralization of teaching history in schools
began at the end of the eighteenth and beginning of the nineteenth centuries, coinciding with the emergence of nation-states. Since that time, a clear
purpose has been established for teaching history, namely the construction
of national identity. The classic statement by Massimo d'Azeglio in the first
session of parliament of the united Italy is very revealing in this regard: "We
have made Italy; now we have to make Italians" (Hobsbawm, 1997, p. 44).
In the chapter by Tutiaux-Guillon, the origins of the teaching of history are
clearly described:

> This narrative of progress (about the nation) has probably two main origins.
> Since 1830, the development of a secular teaching of history has substituted
> the holy history with the national history: the narrative is of course different,
> but the structure is still teleological. The end is no more a godly eschatology,
> but the fulfillment of socioeconomical progress and of democracy (Bruter,
> 2005)... (p. 113)

However, after World War II and especially in the 1960s and 1970s, educators began to advocate history as an important subject in its own right
and the importance of historical knowledge. Without a doubt, the changes within the discipline of history after World War II played an important
role, when a stronger relationship was established between historiographic
research and the social sciences. At that time, history curricula began to
incorporate scholarly objectives related to "thinking historically," such as
evaluating evidence and understanding historical causation. Current schol-

arship continues to develop the skills used by historians, making the transmission of such skills the primary objective of teaching history (Carretero & López, 2010; Reisman & Wineburg, 2012; Seixas, 2012).

Yet, the traditional role of teaching history as a means of constructing national identity has never been completely forgotten. Several studies have shown that the teaching of history continues to substantially focus on national histories (Berger & Lorenz, 2008; Van der Leeuw-Roord, 2009; Van Sledright, 2008). Tutiaux-Guillon (2012) notes that the construction of national identity is still the main objective of primary-school history teaching in France.

According to Grever (2012), this construction occurs within an international context of mass migration and growing multiculturalism. As VanSledright (2008; also see Barton, 2012) demonstrates, in the United States, the fundamental goal of current education in history is teaching the "American creed," while history as it is understood in the discipline itself is rarely taught. Because of this phenomenon, significant sectors of the population not matching the official identity do not feel that they are reflected in the national historical narratives. This situation is true of African Americans in the USA (Epstein & Schiller, 2009) and indigenous groups in Latin America (Carretero & Kriger, 2011), Canada (Peck, 2011; Seixas, 2012), and New Zealand (Barton, 2012).

HOW SHOULD THE TEACHING OF HISTORY ADDRESS IDENTITY ISSUES?

There are different approaches to defining the role of teaching history in identity construction. We can group these approaches into three types, summarized here in general terms.

The first approach advocates a total separation between the two. The teaching of history should focus only on developing an understanding of the past through the lens of the social sciences and be completely disconnected from processes of identity construction (see, for example, Álvarez Junco, 2011). The construction of an identity of any kind is outside of the purview of the historical discipline.

A second approach advocates the use of history to help build one type of collective identity or another. As we previously observed, the most common type of identity linked to the teaching of history has traditionally been national identity.

A third approach takes into account the issues addressed by the other two approaches but that is more nuanced. This approach recognizes both the importance of historical thinking for its own sake and students' identities as a key element in learning. In this respect, the third approach is more focused on understanding the issues of identity and their influence on learning history than constructing a particular identity.

If we consider that a combination of these approaches commonly occurs in the classroom, we can begin to understand the complexity of this phenomenon for both historians and those who conduct research on these issues.

HOW DO IDENTITY ISSUES INFLUENCE TEACHING AND LEARNING HISTORY?

Aspects of identity are a factor in the teaching and understanding of history on at least two levels. On the one hand, students bring their various collective identities into the classroom, which are expressed in different ways (Barton, 2012; Epstein & Schiller, 2005). History pedagogy must therefore be able to account for this diversity of identities (Grever, 2012). On the other hand, as we have observed previously, the teaching of history itself occasionally attempts to construct such collective identities *a posteriori*. We believe that it is necessary to address both of these influences.

It seems clear that students' existing identities influence their construction of historical knowledge. Studies have shown that students as young as three participate in activities such as patriotic historical celebrations that involve a form of initiation into the national identity (Carretero, 2011). In a similar vein, Michael Billig (1995) described how our daily activities in society reinforce—often implicitly—our national identity. National anthems, national flags, street names, holidays, movies, and our passports constantly remind us that we are part of a society organized into nations. It is well-known that this organization is arbitrary and attributable to a variety of political, cultural, and economic factors of a historical nature. However, various social actors commonly present this organization of the world as if it were due to natural causes rather than convention. When people later encounter historical facts, they tend to resort to group identities, which usually results in positive biases towards those they consider as of their own group and negative biases towards those they consider outsiders. It is in this way that historical facts are reinterpreted as confrontations between "us" and "them."

Consequently, the existing identities that students bring to a class can occasionally form an obstacle to an adequate understanding of history, as they prevent the students from achieving the emotional distance required to critically interpret historical events. However, identity has also been viewed as a beneficial element in learning history (Hammack, 2010). One of the main difficulties educators encounter is that students tend to think that history is not a personally useful or meaningful subject. Furthermore, as indicated above, students frequently are confronted with historical issues laden with identity implications outside of the classroom. Acknowledging students' preexisting identities in history class can, in addition to motivating them, help them better understand the relationships they address outside of the classroom, which in turn gives more meaning to what they learn in class.

In other cases, identity is relevant in history classrooms not only in terms of the identities the students bring with them but also in the schools' versions of history, which are intended to build identities. In authoritarian regimes, this identity construction can be more similar to indoctrination (Ahonen, 2001; Carretero, 2011; Janmaat, 2006, 2008). Traditionally, national identities have been formed around ethnicity, i.e., they are based on race, culture, and tradition, presented as if they are permanent and natural. Today, we also find history-teaching methods intended to promote aspects that are more closely linked to a civic national identity (Barton & Levstik, 2008; Janowitz, 1983; Von Heyking, 2006). This civic national identity is based on ideas such as the future citizen's active participation in society and the challenges posed in that society within a changing social context. The goal of such teaching methods is to transmit skills that will enable the student to participate in society as a good citizen and foster values such as universality and plurality (Grever, 2012; Tutiaux-Guillon, 2012). There is no doubt that the construction of an ethnic national identity differs greatly from the construction of a civic national identity. However, in both cases, teaching history is more important as a means to the end of building identity than solely as a social science.

As we have discussed, the relationships between identity issues and the goals of teaching history are complex and far from resolved. Identity can be seen as an obstacle or benefit to understanding history. It is certain that identity can be both in practice, depending primarily on how identity is treated within the discipline of history.

HOW DOES HISTORIOGRAPHY
ADDRESS ISSUES OF IDENTITY?

Historical research often addresses subjects closely linked to identity issues. The role of women in history, civil-rights movements and struggles for national independence are only a few of the examples that reflect the connection between history and identity. Examining the way historiography itself treats identity issues can help us understand the relationship between the two.

In the nineteenth and part of the twentieth century, history was primarily responsible for propagating romantic ideas about national identity; national identities were thus cloaked in an aura of naturalness and timelessness. History was tasked with demonstrating how national identities—and ethnic and even religious identities—have been an essential part of human nature from time immemorial. History strove to justify the emerging division of societies into nation-states on an almost biological basis. National identities were therefore considered in historiography to be innate and permanent properties that constituted an essential aspect of human nature (Calhoun, 1997; Smith, 1991).

Within this perspective, national and other identities were understood to have a clear function in group cohesion. Each national group was observed to have some common essential characteristics, usually based on cultural, historical, ethnic, and other traditional elements, that had been handed down since time immemorial within a well-defined territory that coincided with the emerging nation-state (Smith, 1991). However, while national identity has a cohesive function for a given group in this understanding, it is also disruptive for other groups (Triandafyllidou, 1998). In practice, these essential characteristics of national identity are not only considered to be permanent, objective characteristics of the national group, but also exclusive to that group. In other words, each national group must have an identity that is not only its own but also clearly distinct from other identities, which distinguishes who belongs to our nation and who does not (Cruz Prados, 2005; Smith, 1991).

However, in the mid-twentieth century, a modernist or instrumentalist approach to the phenomenon of nationality emerged within the field of history. National identities began to be understood as artificial realities motivated by political interests rather than as natural realities. National identity was no longer understood as an innate and spontaneous property of human beings but as something acquired and inculcated inside and outside of school (Álvarez Junco, 2011). The supposed naturalness and timelessness of national identities was discredited. National-ancestral traditions were revealed to be invented traditions (Hobsbawn & Ranger, 1983). Identities came to be viewed as changing social constructions.

Current historiography views identities as complex, multifaceted phenomena that are constantly changing and never permanent nor exclusive. However, people continue to be passionate about their identities, and identity is often a major factor in intergroup conflict (Ashmore, Jussim, & Wilder, 2001); in many cases, people even kill in its name (Maalouf, 1998).

Studies have shown that students' ideas about their identity are closer to the natural, timeless, and static conception held in the nineteenth century than the manner in which current historiography understands identity (Lopez, Carretero, & Rodríguez-Moneo, 2012; Carretero, Lopez, & Rodríguez-Moneo, 2012). This conceptualization is reflected, for example, in students' reinterpretation of historical conflicts that occurred long before the emergence of nations as struggles between national groups. This understanding of national identities as timeless and permanent produces a simplistic and narrow interpretation of historical events and is often associated with a tendency to make positive judgments about one's own group but not those perceived as "foreign" (Carretero & Bermudez, 2012). Perhaps, as Barton suggests (2012), teaching students how current historiography views these aspects of identity and highlighting its complex, social, and dynamic character should be an explicit objective of history pedagogy.

As we have discussed, understanding the relationships between identity issues and the goals of history education is one of the most difficult challenges in teaching and learning history. The complexity and diversity of students' identities on the one hand and different objectives associated with the teaching of history on the other make for a particularly problematic area of study. However, a deep understanding of each aspect enables us to shed some light on these interrelationships that are established in history classrooms.

We believe that there are two important questions to examine in this regard. First, it is important to understand the explicit role the state assigns to education in constructing a national identity. For example, countries such as Ireland and New Zealand (see Barton, 2012) do not assign any role for the schools in constructing a national identity; this is also the case in a number of other European countries, such as Spain. In such nations, these phenomena are therefore more implicit. In contrast, in Latin America and the United States, national-identity formation is explicitly considered a function of schools and is conducted intensely (Carretero, 2011). Second, we believe that these differences are also related to the particular variety of nationalism involved and its role in the given society. In some nations, such as France (Tutiaux-Guillon, 2012) and the USA (Barton, 2012), nationalism may be (or may not be) intense, but it is never challenged by alternative nationalisms within the state itself. In contrast, in other nations such as Ireland (Barton, 2012), Irish nationalism is opposed to British nationalism, and in Spain (Carretero, 2011), there is both Catalan and Basque nationalism.

REFERENCES

Ahonen, S. (2001). Politics of identity through history curriculum: Narratives of the past for social exclusion—or inclusion? *Journal of Curriculum Studies, 33*(2), 179—194.

Álvarez Junco, J. (2011). *Spanish identity in the age of nations*. Manchester: Manchester University Press.

Ashmore, R. D., Jussim, L. J., & Wilder, D. (Eds.). (2001). *Social identity, intergroup conflict, and conflict reduction*. New York: Oxford University Press.

Barton (2012). School history as a resource for constructing identities: Implications of research from the United States, Northern Ireland, and New Zealand. In M. Carretero, M. Asensio, & M. Rodríguez-Moneo (Eds.), *History education and the construction of national identities* (pp. 93–107). Charlotte, NC: Information Age Publishing.

Barton, K. C., & Levstik, L. (Eds.). (2004). *Teaching history for the common good*. Mahwah, NJ: Lawrence Erlbaum Associates.

Barton, K. C., & Levstik, L. S. (2008). History. In J. Arthur, C. Hahn, & I. Davies (Eds.), *Handbook of education for citizenship and democracy* (pp. 355–366). London: Sage.

Berger, S., & Lorenz, C. (Eds.). (2008). *The contested nation: Ethnicity, class, religion and gender in national histories.* Basingstoke: Palgrave Macmillan.

Bettelheim, B. (2005). *Psicoanálisis de los cuentos de hadas.* Barcelona: Crítica.

Billig, M. (1995). *Banal nationalism.* London: Sage.

Bruter, M. (2005) *Citizens of Europe? The emergence of a mass European identity.* Palgrave Macmillan.

Calhoun, C. J. (1997). *Nationalism.* Minneapolis: University of Minnesota Press.

Carretero, M. (2011) *Constructing patriotism. Teaching of history and historical memory in globalized world.* Charlotte CT: Information Age Publisher.

Carretero, M., & Bermúdez, A. (2012). Constructing histories. In: J. Valsiner (Ed.), *Oxford handbook of culture and psychology* (pp. 625–646). Oxford: Oxford University Press.

Carretero, M., & Kriger, M. (2011). Historical representations and conflicts about indigenous people as national identities. *Culture and Psychology, 17*(2), 177–195.

Carretero, M., & Lopez, C. (2010). Studies in learning and teaching history: Implications for the development of historical literacy. In C. Lundholm, G. Peterson, & I. Wisted (Eds.), *Begreppsbildning i ett intentionellt perspektiv. [Conceptual change and intentional perspective]* (pp. 167–187). Stockholm: Stockholm University Press.

Carretero, M., Lopez, C., Gonzáles, M. F., & Rodríguez-Moneo, M. (2012). Students historical narratives and concepts about the nation. In M. Carretero, M. Asensio, & M. Rodríguez-Moneo (Eds.), *History education and the construction of national identities* (pp. 153–170). Charlotte, NC: Information Age Publishing.

Cruz Prados, A. (2005). *El nacionalismo, una ideología.* Madrid: Tecnos.

Epstein, T., & Schiller, J. (2005). Perspective matters: social identity and the teaching and learning of national history. *Social Education, 69*(4), 201–204.

Epstein, T., & Shiller, J. (2009). Race, gender, and the teaching and learning of national history. In W. C. Parker (Ed.), *Social Studies Today: Research and Practice* (pp. 95–101). New York: Routledge.

Evans, R. W. (2004). *The social studies wars: What should we teach the children?* New York: Teachers College Press.

Ferro, M. (1984). *The use and abuse of history, or, how the past is taught after the great fire.* London: Routledge.

Foster, S. J., & Crawford, K. A. (Eds.). (2006). *What shall we tell the children? International perspectives on school history textbooks.* Greenwich, CT: Information Age Publishing.

Grever, M. (2012). Dilemmas of common and plural history: Reflections on history education and heritage in a globalizing world. In M. Carretero, M. Asensio, & M. Rodríguez-Moneo (Eds.), *History education and the construction of national identities* (pp. 75–91). Charlotte, NC: Information Age Publishing.

Grever, M., & Stuurman, S. (2007). *Beyond the canon: History for the 21st century.* Basingstoke & New Cork: Macmillan.

Hammack, P. L. (2010). Identity as burden or benefit? Youth, historical narrative, and the legacy of political conflict. *Human Development, 53*, 173–201.

Heyking, A. J. V. (2006). *Creating citizens: History and identity in Alberta's schools, 1905–1980.* Calgary: University of Calgary Press.

Hobsbawm, E. (1997). *Nations and nationalism since 1780: Programme, myth, reality.* Cambridge: Cambridge University Press.

Hobsbawm, E., & Ranger, T. (Eds.). (1983). *The invention of tradition.* Cambridge: Cambridge University Press.

Janmaat, J. G. (2006). Popular conceptions of nationhood in old and new European member states: Partial support for the ethnic—civic framework. *Ethnic and Racial Studies, 29*(1), 50–78.

Janmaat, J. G. (2008). The civic attitudes of ethnic minority youth and the impact of citizenship education. *Journal of Ethnic and Migration Studies, 34*(1), 27–54.

Janowitz, M. (1983). *The reconstruction of patriotism: education for civic consciousness:* University of Chicago Press.

Lopez, C., Carretero, M., & Rodríguez-Moneo, M. (2012). *Is the nation a historical concept on students' minds?* In preparation.

Maalouf, A. (1998). *Identidades asesinas.* Madrid: Alianza.

Nakou, I., & Barca, I. (Eds.). (2010). *Contemporary public debates over history education.* International Review of History Education Series. Charlotte, NC: Information Age Publishing.

Nash, G. B., Crabtree, C. A., & Dunn, R. E. (2000). *History on trial: Culture wars and the teaching of the past.* Pensilvania: Vintage Books.

Peck, C. L. (2011). Ethnicity and students' historical understandings In P. Clark (Ed.), *New possibilities for the past: Shaping history education in Canada* (pp. 305–324). Vancouver: UBC Press.

Reisman, A., & Wineburg, S. (2012). Ways of knowing and the history classroom. In M. Carretero, M. Asensio, & M. Rodríguez-Moneo (Eds.), *History education and the construction of national identities* (pp. 171–188). Charlotte, NC: Information Age Publishing.

Seixas, P. (2012). Indigenous historical consciousness: An oxymoron or a dialogue? In M. Carretero, M. Asensio, & M. Rodríguez-Moneo (Eds.), *History education and the construction of national identities* (pp. 125–138). Charlotte, NC: Information Age Publishing.

Smith, A. D. (1991). *National identity.* London: Penguin.

Symcox, L., & Wilschut, A. (Eds.). (2009). *National history standards: The problem of the canon and the future of teaching history.* Charlotte, NC: Information Age Publishing.

Triandafyllidou, A. (1998). National identity and the 'other.' *Ethnic and Racial Studies. 21*(4), 593–612.

Tutiaux-Guillon, N. (2012). A traditional frame for global history: The narrative of modernity in French secondary school. In M. Carretero, M. Asensio, & M. Rodríguez-Moneo (Eds.). *History education and the construction of national identities* (pp. 109–123). Charlotte, NC: Information Age Publishing.

Van der Leeuw-Roord, J. (2009). Yearning for yesterday. Efforts of history professionals in Europe at designing meaningful and effective school Histoy curricula. In Symcox, L. & Wilschut, A. (Eds.). *International review of History educa-*

tion National History Standars. The problem of the canon and the future of teaching History. (Vol. 5. pp. 73–94). Charlotte, NC: Information Age Publishing.

VanSledright, B. (2008). Narratives of nation-state, historical knowledge, and school history education. *Review of Research in Education, 32*(1), 109–146.

Wertsch, J. (2002). *Voices of collective remembering.* Cambridge: Cambridge University Press.

SECTION 3

STUDENTS IDEAS AND IDENTITIES

CHAPTER 11

STUDENTS HISTORICAL NARRATIVES AND CONCEPTS ABOUT THE NATION

Mario Carretero, Cesar Lopez,
María Fernanda González, and Maria Rodríguez-Moneo

History is mainly taught through narratives. Particularly national narratives are central in the educational field (Barton & McCully, 2005; Carretero & Lopez, 2010a). As Ballantyne (2005) notes, nation-states remain the organizing axis of school narratives and historical analyses. In the nineteenth century nation-centered narratives became the basis of national history within the European colonies and in much of Asia (Duara, 1995). The tight relationship between history and the nation continues to be active in the curricula of several countries (see Alridge, 2006; Van Sledright, 2008 for the United States. Grever, 2006; Grever & Stuurman, 2007; Van der Leeuw-Roord, 2009 for Europe). Despite the emergence of the disciplinary and civic approaches to history education, the national foundations of curricula and textbooks in Europe have changed little since 1989 (Foster & Crawford, 2006; Van der Leeuw-Roord, 2009). Furthermore, the number of

History Education and the Construction of National Identities, pages 153–170

nation-based approaches, which use a traditional methodology of teaching history, has increased (Mak, 2005). National narratives attempt to bring continuity to the past, present and future, making the nation a perpetual protagonist. In such narratives, the stories that are told—and how they are told—are as important as those that must be forgotten. As noted by Renan (2004), forgetting and even historical error-making are essential factors in the creation of a nation.

The influence of the narrative in the field of history is molded by two different processes: the production of historical accounts by historians and the consumption and appropriation of these narratives by students (Carretero & Kriger, 2011; Wertsch, 2002). The narratives produced by historians serve as schematic narrative templates. These are generated in a social context, constituting a fixed model for the specific narratives that people create in the process of consuming them. Therefore, the preexisting national narratives provide the individual with a fixed model for inserting the narratives that he or she constructs. These narratives also explain or discuss historical events. As we have noted thus far, the main characteristic of these national narratives is that they are organized around a continuous and a temporal protagonist, the nation, which is at once the origin and final destination of the narrative (Carretero & Lopez, 2010a).

In several countries, the main objective of national narratives is the creation of a sense of national identity. Epstein and Shiller (2005) underscore how the viewpoints of students, in addition to those of professors and historians, regarding social problems are molded by their identities as members of a family, community, region or nation. These identities influence how students establish relationships with historical content. It is important to take into account that the students' social identities influence not only what they know about their nation's history but also their values and what they are willing to accept about their nation (Hammack, 2011).

Linking identity and emotional aspects with historical events does not necessarily present an obstacle to an adequate historical understanding, as suggested by Bellino and Selman (2012). Nonetheless, the type of national identity pursued by these traditional national narratives seeks to create a positive emotional evaluation—frequently uncritical of the nation's history. From the viewpoint of history education, it seems that these identity-based objectives usually imply successful learning.

Research on history education and school textbooks (Carretero, 2011) shows that history has been recurrently positioned in the school curriculum to instill in the future citizens the symbolic representations that guarantee:

a. A positive assessment of their own social group's past, present and future; both local and national.
b. A positive assessment of the country's political evolution.

c.   Identification with past's events and characters and national heroes.

These goals of history education could be considered *romantic* because the emerging of the nation-states cannot be fully understood without the influence of the romantic ideas and their intellectual context. The whole idea of the nation as a specific ethnic group which is under a process of awakening and finally constituting itself in a community of destiny, cannot be conceived of without the romantic ideal.

On the other hand, there have been *the enlightened or disciplinary goals* of fostering critical citizens capable of informed and effective participation in the progress of the nation, including a possible criticism to the own local or national community. In general they consist of:

a.   Understanding the past in a complex manner, according to age and educational level,

b.   Distinguishing different historic periods, through the appropriate comprehension of historical time,

c.   Understanding the complex historical multiple causality,

d.   Approaching the methodology used by historians (Wineburg, 2001),

e.   Relating the past with the present and the future.

These romantic and enlightened goals of history education coexisted from the very beginning and developed over time, being the first the most important goals in many countries until approximately 1960. After that, the disciplinary goals started having an increasing importance in many nations. But we think, the romantic goals are still having an important influence on students historical representations. As it will be shown later in this paper, these romantic goals tend to produce an essentialist understanding of the nation.

Understanding and discussing the past from the national present, in an uncritical and essentialist manner, assumes a nationalization of the events of the past and its protagonists. The essentialist idea of the very concept of a nation is at the core of the national narratives, whereby the nation is seen as an invariable and timeless element of history on which people base their explanations about historical topics. Similarly, the main characters of history are nationalized, becoming members of the national group, even if they couldn't have been at a time that the nation did not exist (Carretero, 2011; Carretero & Gonzalez, 2012).

If we consider the informal sphere of the transmission of historical themes, we find a similar situation. As Michael Billig (1995; also see Hansen, 2012, and Rosa, 2012) indicates, a world order built on nations is part of current common sense, as if it were the only possible order and no others could have ever existed. Effectively, the nationalist idea that solely recognizes a political organization of the world based on the nation-state has become the norm. However, where does this powerful idea about nation originate? How did it become a global norm?

According to authors such as Renan (2004) or Gellner (1978), nations are focused on identity-based aspects related to will, unity and self-determination. The nation is understood as something mutable and negotiable, which depends on the will of its members to continue existing. For nations to be perceived as stable and natural, a group of beliefs, assumptions, rituals, representations and practices contributes to modeling this collective will and developing this idea of the nation as a natural reality. Billig (1995) refers to this process as banal nationalism.

The informal sphere of history education contains several examples of the mechanisms that reinforce an essentialist idea of history and the concept of the nation. Numerous countries have celebrations and patriotic rituals that commemorate historical events, such as Independence Day. These rituals play an important role in the formation of citizens' national identity. In several countries, students begin participating in these rituals from a very early age in school, which fosters an emotional link between citizens and the nation (Carretero, 2011).

As analyzed above, we find different educational mechanisms within both the formal and informal spheres of history through which historical content concerning the concept of nation is transmitted. These mechanisms contribute—according to Benedict Anderson (1983)—to *imagining* the community that we call a nation. The representations of the historical problems and questions are made through both narrative explanation and historical concepts with a greater or lesser degree of abstraction. Without these concepts, it would be impossible to generate sophisticated historical explanations (Koselleck, 1975).

CONCEPTIONS OF NATION IN THE CONTEXT OF HISTORICAL NARRATIVES

Most of cognitive analysis of historical thinking and expertise agrees that historical concepts are used by both experts and novices in their historical narratives (VanSledright & Limon, 2006; Voss & Wiley, 2006; Wertsch, 2002). There is no doubt that most of causal explanations of the students about historical problems are of narrative nature. Whether they use abstract concepts (Halldén, 2000; Riviere, Nuñez, Barquero, & Fontela, 1998) or concrete ones (Carretero, Lopez Manjon, & Jacott, 1997).

Elsewhere (Carretero, 2011; Carretero & Bermudez, 2012; Carretero, Castorina & Levinas, in press) we have presented a theoretical analysis of the interactive processes of production-consumption of school historical narratives, specifying the role played by concepts in those narratives. Based on previous work about students´ historical master narratives and its cultural and educational significance (Wertsch & Rozin, 2000) and also in our comparative analysis of history textbooks of different nations, most of them from Latin America (Carretero & Gonzalez, 2012; Carretero, Jacott, & Lopez Manjon, 2002). In the present chapter, we try to present an analysis of the historical master narratives features and the way they are related to the features of nation as a concept, showing some of our empirical studies and results. Our proposal distinguishes six common features of historical master narratives:

1. *Exclusion-inclusion as a logical operation contributing to establish the historical subject.* This logical operation is performed in such a way that any positive aspect will be almost always assigned to the national "we", and any critical or negative aspect will be assigned to "the others". This logical operation is very critical because it determines both the main voice and the logical actions for that national subject.

2. *Identification processes as both cognitive and affective anchor.* It is very probable that this emotional feature will facilitate at a very early age the formation of the nation as a concept, through a strong identification process, instead of a cognitive rational understanding.

3. *Frequent presence of mythical and heroic characters and motives.* Myths, mythical figures and narratives are usually beyond time restrictions (Barton & Levstik, 1996; Carretero, Asensio & Pozo, 1991; Egan, 1997). When time and its constraints are introduced history, as a discipline, is making its appearance.

4. *Search of freedom or territory as a main and common narrative theme.* The narrative is based almost uniquely on the intention of a group of persons to be free from some domination and trying to obtain a specific territory. Usually, the territory is presented as having no differences with the present one.

5. *Historical school narratives contain basic moral orientations.* Of particular importance is the right to the mentioned specific territory, that logically includes the various violent acts performed and political decisions made to achieve it.

6. *Romantic and essentialist concept of both the nation and the nationals.* This implies the view of the nation and the nationals as pre-existing political entities, having a kind of eternal and essentialist nature. As it will be shown below, we have studied how the understanding of the nation, as a concept, is very much related to the way previous narratives features are being represented by citizens of different ages.

LEARNED HISTORY: CONCEPTIONS OF STUDENTS ABOUT THEIR OWN NATION

The main objectives of our empirical research in the last years have been to analyze the concept of nation of 12 to 18 year old students and adults (Carretero, 2011; Carretero & Kriger, 2011). More specifically we were interested in analyzing whether their conceptions change as a result of both cognitive development and school history learning. Theoretically our objectives were also related to examining whether both Romantic and Enlightened goals of history teaching were having an influence on students' and adults' conceptions. As stated above, we expected that traditional teaching of national history would hinder conceptual change in historical contents instead of favoring it (Carretero, 2011).

Most of the tasks used in our investigations have to do with national foundational or national historical themes and concepts, particularly in relation to the past of both Spain and Argentina. Yet these themes have clear similarities to those in other parts of the world. We will present some of our main findings as to how participants were employing the concept of nation in their narrative. Some of these uses will be related to the six narratives features previously mentioned. We will not be presenting a detailed analysis of every feature, as it can be found elsewhere (Carretero & Gonzalez, 2012; Carretero & Kriger, 2011; Lopez, Carretero, & Rodriguez-Moneo, 2012). We will be focusing in the last feature, about the specific and explicit use of the concept of nation in the context of national narratives.

As has been mentioned, the concept of a nation seems to be one of the central concepts of history education, especially throughout national narratives, both inside and outside of the school. As a matter of fact, about the half of the school historical contents of any nation are about the own nation.

Medieval Times in Spain. Conquest or Reconquest as a Foundational Event?

In a study conducted with Spanish university students, we attempted to analyze their ideas about the concept of the nation through the narratives that they generated about one of the foundational events of Spanish history. The main objective of the study was to examine whether their conceptions had romantic characteristics or whether, after completing the obligatory schooling, their conceptions were closer to a disciplinary approach (see Lopez, Carretero, & Rodriguez-Moneo, 2012, for details).

Semi-structured individual interviews were conductedabout the Reconquest, a period of nearly 800 years during which different Christian kingdoms made a series of conquests in the Iberian peninsula. The peninsula had been dominated by Muslims since their arrival in 711 and their victory over the ruling Visigoth Kingdom. The Reconquest, which occurred before the existence of the Spanish nation, began in 718 and finally ended in 1492 with the expulsion of the Muslims from the peninsula. This process was reinterpreted by historiography throughout the centuries and converted into an enterprise of national character, through which the monarchy was legitimized and on which Spanish national identity was built (Álvarez Junco, 2011; Ríos Saloma, 2005).

During the interviews, students were asked to indicate the political situation relative to four different moments of the Reconquest on four different mute maps. They were then asked about such topics as

a.   The inhabitants of the Iberian Peninsula at that time,
b.   The causes and motivations of the conquests,
c.   The legitimacy of the conquests, and
d.   The possession of territory.

Towards the end of the interview, both participants who had used the term "Reconquista" spontaneously and those who had not were asked about the use of this term.

The results showed that 51.6% of the interviewees constructed a narrative based on a nationalist notion of the concept of the Spanish nation, while 22.6% created a narrative closer to the disciplinary concept of the nation. The remaining 25.8% displayed an intermediate conception.

The large majority of the participants (80.6%) showed a general interpretation of the process based on the loss and subsequent recovery of the national territory. Similar percentages were found while analyzing conceptions of the existence of the Spanish nation and the Spanish people in this historical period. Most (70%) of the participants explicitly used the terms "Spain" and/or "Spanish" to describe the territory under dispute and the inhabitants of such a territory. We find these data particularly relevant because, although the creation of nations did not occur before the end of the XVIII century, most participants considered the Spanish nation and the Spanish people to be the protagonists of the Reconquest.

In addition, nearly half of the participants (45.2%) showed a spontaneous and explicit identification with the national group. These identity connections were reflected in the use of the first person plural to reference the national group.

In this manner, expressions such as "In 711, we were colonized by the Muslims" or "1492 was when we kicked them out of Granada" showed this romantic identity connection with the national group, which was never used to make reference to the Muslims. Again, although the disciplinary sphere considers national identity to be a modern concept that emerged with the concept of nationalism in the XIX century, these participants identified with the main characters of the historical process based on an alleged common nationality already established from times as early as the VIII century.

Another important result of this study is related to the different ways in which the participants legitimized the conquests made during this period. More than half of the participants (63.3%) considered the conquests accomplished by their own national group to be more legitimate, while the remaining 26.7% considered the conquests made by Muslims and Christians to be equally legitimate. The majority of the participants used justifications such as the recovery of national territory or argued that the Spanish had more rights than the Muslims to occupy such territory "because they had lived there since the beginning."

The identity connection with an essentialist character—in the sense that it applies a national characteristic to moments long before the very origin of the nation—contributes to the creation of an "us" in opposition to the "them" of the foreign group. This issue clearly constitutes an important element of analysis, along with the different methods of legitimizing the conquests of different groups. Related to the findings regarding the different approaches to history analyzed in this chapter, we can observe how these types of historical arguments adapt to the objectives of the romantic approach. The disciplinary approach would suppose a multi-causal analysis of the so-called "Reconquista," an analysis of the viewpoints of the different groups participating in the process. However, the majority of participants showed an essentialist narrative scheme based on the recovery of an alleged national territory as the main explanatory argument.

An Essentialist Understanding of Nation and Independence of Argentina

Another study was carried out in Argentina (see Carretero & Gonzalez, 2012, for details). The topic the participants were asked about was the Independence, which took place in 1816 but was preceded by an important political event in 1810, usually called "May Revolution". It consisted of both a meeting and a demonstration against the political domination of the Spanish Crown. In general terms, it could be compared to the Tea Party events in the United States.

Semi structured interviews were carried out with 80 Argentinean subjects, they were girls and boys in equal proportions. Twenty were 12 year olds in the 7th grade, 20 were 14 year olds in the 9th grade, 20 were 16 year olds in tenth grade and 20 were adults (average age: 35) that did not have any specific education in history. The students came from two public secondary schools from the urban area of La Plata, Argentina and came from middle class families.

The interview had two parts. In the first part we asked the subjects to provide a narrative about the independence. The following questions were asked: When did this event take place? Who participated? How did it occur? Why did it occur?

In the second part of the interview, we asked specifically about the people who were present at the "May Revolution"

a.   If they thought these people were Argentinean,
b.   If these people felt that they were Argentinean at that specific moment, and
c.   If they were just as Argentinean as actual (current) Argentineans.

With these three questions, we sought to investigate the ideas the subjects had about the process of "becoming Argentinean". In a strict sense, they were not yet Argentineans as the country of Argentina did not exist yet. The first constitution of the Argentinean state was not sanctioned until 1853. Between 1816 and 1853 several civil wars took place motivated by different forms of organization proposed by different groups of power. It is also important to mention that the Independence was declared by 1816 under the name of the "United Provinces of the South", which was a territory quite different compared to the present Argentina.

The first question was asked to probe the ideas about the origin and process of creating nationality and national identity. The second question looked to investigate the affective aspects of nationality: to feel Argentine. With this question, the subjects were asked to explain their beliefs about the existence of a feeling of being Argentine among the people of 1810 and 1816. With the third question they were asked to compare their own 'Argentineness' with that of the inhabitants of the Spanish colony in 1810 and 1816.

Answers to the first question were categorized into two groups:

1.   *Affirmative.* These subjects considered that the people depicted in the images were Argentines. Therefore they believe that a nationality—in this case the Argentine—existed before the constitution of a Nation State, in this case in 1810 and 1816.
2.   *Negative.* These subjects considered that the people depicted in the images were not Argentine.

The following results were obtained. At age 12, students gave 65% affirmative answers and 35% negative answers. At age 14, the answer distribution was 70% and 30%; at age 16, 65% and 35; and finally 50% of the adults answered affirmatively and 50% negatively.

The results indicate that the majority of subjects in our study (62%), independent of their age affirm that the people that inhabited the territory in 1810 and 1816 were Argentine. The adult group was the only group that was different, indicating the same proportion of positive and negative answers. Nevertheless, the difference in the adult group was not statistically significant.

The narrative elements that appear when the subjects have to justify the "Argentineness" of the people are strongly essentialist. Among them, we can consider the following:

a.   The metaphor of "blood and spirit". Nationality seems to be characterized as something natural and intrinsic, something a priori and without regard to the history of the subjects. As 16 year old Santiago explains:

"*No, they were not officially Argentine, but, they really were in their spirit because what they wanted was their territory being independent and what they did was to fight for what belonged to them, and anyone who would fight for their territory and for their country deserves to be Argentine...*" Interviewer: Some people argued that they were not Argentine because they were from the Spanish territory and Argentina did not exist yet... What do you think? Santiago: "*Even though Argentina did not exist in that moment, I think that they were Argentine because from the beginning, they rebelled against the established power... and they confronted it to become independent and to be Argentine; and they wanted to become Argentine... and if they wanted to be argentine more than to be Spanish... they were Argentine in their blood.*

b.   The territory as a repository of "Argentineness": the territory is understood as always having been Argentine and transforming people into Argentines, as can be seen in the narrative of 12 year old Nehuén:

"*If they were born here, it was because they were Argentine, they were born in Argentine territory, not in Spain... it was here, it was owned by the Spanish, but it was an Argentine place*".

Or 14 year old Luciana: "*No, I think they were Argentine because even though they were born when the Spanish came to take over, if they were born here, in this place, they were Argentine*".

c.   Nationality is previous to the formation of a nation; nation and nationality are confused and they mean the same thing.

This is the case for 12 year old Jessica who said about the people: "*In order to become free from spain, they had to be Argentine because if not...*" Interviewer: Why not? Jessica: "*Well, how are they going to gain freedom from their own country*"

It is also demonstrated by an adult, Lali. Interviewer: Were they Argentine? Lali: *"Yes, from the moment they began to fight for their freedom, yes…"*

Another interesting argumentation given by the interviewees is based on the patriotic feelings that the people in the images had. The question of feelings of national identity also appeared in subjects narratives as justifying the right of the colonists to become independent. In this sense, our subjects repeat the essentialist a historical line of argumentation that is also present in the teaching of national history (Chiaramonte, 1991).

Fourteen year old Constanza responds to our counterarguments in the following way:

> Interviewer: And, some people say hat they were not argentine because the territory was Spanish and Argentina did not exist yet. What do you think? Constanza: *"Even though it was a Spanish territory, it does not have anything to do with the feelings that someone has. Even though I am living in Spain, it does not have anything to do with whether I feel Argentine and I want to fight for my country".*

Lastly, we have selected the parts of the interviews where the subjects believe that the people depicted are not Argentine and others that show the conflictive character of this essentialist view of nationality.

Among the negative responses, which we consider as disciplinary, is that of 16-year-old Matías, who explains:

> *"They were not Argentine. Some, a large majority, had Spanish parents… they were not yet Argentine… they were… territory of… the territory was called the United Provinces of la Rio de la Plata, they were from there, born in the United Provinces of la Rio de la Plata."* Interviewer: That was Spanish territory before… Matías: *"Exactly."* Interviewer: So, we cannot really say that they were Argentine… Matías: *"Argentine, no. In order to be Argentine they have to go through an entire process".*

We also found answers that allow us to see the conflict that implies to explain in historical terms the origins of the own nation. Although there are very few of these cases, they are very interesting. Take 12-year-old Juan:

> Interviewer: Can it be said that the people in this image are Argentine? Juan: *"No, most of them are Spanish (doubt) the majority were Argentine because the majority were people that…* (He doubts again and repeats with security) *At this moment they were not Argentine. In this moment they were not Argentine because obviously, it was not Argentina, how is it possible to be American if the United Stated did not exist yet. What was said was quite contradictory."* Interviewer: So, what do you think? Were they or were they not Argentine? Juan: *"They were not Argentine if Argentina did not exist. It was just a project at that moment."*

Juan is conscious of his own contradiction and he resolves it by taking focus away the formation of his own national identity. He uses the example of the formation of the United States and the formation of national identity in order to understand that one cannot come before the other and in this way, he introduces the idea of historical process.

In the next case, the construction of identity is understood as a process in which the juxtaposition of different identifiable projects causes a kind of identity crisis in modern Argentine society:

> "*They were not Argentine because... because the Republic was not yet formed but, but they were not Spanish either. They were in a process of formation.*" Interviewer: So, you mean to say that they were not Spanish but they were not Argentine either... "*And they were looking for their identity and we are still looking for it (...)*" (Manuel, adult)·

Natives and Nationals. Difficulties Understanding Historical Changes of the Own Nation.

Another particular event we studied in Argentina is the so called "Desert Campaign". This was a national crusade that began 1878 with the primary objective of extending the territory of the nation and finally exterminating the indigenous people who were already living in those areas for centuries.

By the late nineteenth century, the Argentine territory was significantly smaller than the current territory. Among other places it did not include much of what is now Patagonia. The land was inhabited and dominated by indigenous populations. In those days there used to be frequent conflicts over disputed border territory. The Argentine government applied different policies trying to gain territory, and finally conducted a fierce campaign to achieve their goals of conquest.

The investigation considered whether the conception of students of the nation and national character was of essentialist nature or disciplinary, according to our previous distinctions.

Twenty students attending the Common Basic Cycle of the University of Buenos Aires were interviewed. They were between 18 and 20 years old with a mean age of 18 years and 8 months. We asked them what they knew about the Desert Campaign. More specifically, what the main goal of the campaign was, what individual and collective subjects were involved, who had the right over the territory and why. Also it was asked whether the conquered territory was or was not part of Argentina and whether or not they were native Argentines and finally they were asked for their overall assessment of the historical event.

We found that 65% of interviewees display an essentialist conception, that is, one that conceives the territory as essentially Argentinean, independently from its historical construction.

Thirty five per cent of participants maintained a disciplinary conception about the territorial construction of the nation itself. This means that they claimed throughout the interview that the territory of the nation was a historical construction, over time, and that Argentinean national territory changed considerably from the Desert Campaign onwards.

Daniela (19 years old), for example, asserts that the territory was Argentina long before the Desert Campaign, and therefore this territory's indigenous inhabitants were Argentinean too. She shows a clearly essentialist conception of the national territory, affirming a clear a *historicity* with regard to the construction of the nation (Carretero & Kriger, 2011).

> I: Did the Argentinean State have a right over the territory it conquered?
> D: Yes, as a State, that is, as an institution, the State itself should have a right over the territory where we live.
> I: The territory that was conquered in the Desert Campaign, was it Argentinean before the Campaign?
> D: [She thinks] Yes. Yes, yes. It was Argentinean territory.
> I: So the territory was already Argentinean. And the Indians, who were born in that territory, were they Argentinean?
> D: Yes, obviously.

It is interesting to highlight the time gap in Daniela's account, with reference to identity. When she refers to the conquered territory, she unites two times: the past, suggesting that the State "should have a right"; and the present ("we live") referring to where she lives today. In this statement, Daniela clearly includes herself as a subject, and this is why she needs to refer to the present when she speaks of the past event. We may infer that the romantic objective is speaking through Daniela's words, and this is how past and present are united in an identitary key.

An example of the disciplinary conception is demonstrated by Lautaro (19 years old):

> I: What do you remember about the Desert Campaign?
> La: What I know is the basics, the government of President Roca ... the three governments and the liberal policies of the guys and the mentality of progress and civilization, all imported from Europe and the vision of the native people ... or whatever, and that they mobilized to try to eliminate all ... all types of Indian life or whatever, to get new land, right? Expanding that, basically. (...)
> I: Was the territory conquered in the Desert Campaign part of Argentina?
> La: I guess part of what is now Argentina and what was just forming with [the campaign], right? To end the shaping of the country, they ended up removing everything that was not supposed to be part of the country.

I: The indigenous groups living in that territory, were they Argentineans?

La: No, they were not Argentineans. They were not recognized as Argentineans by themselves or by others .... Only now they can be seen as Argentineans but then ... after it transcended that time, the Desert Campaign. And now that they also understand themselves belonging to what was organized from then onwards.

I: What do you think? At that time, they were or not Argentineans? La.: No, at that time they were not. Definitely not.

I: Why?

La: Because neither they considered themselves as such, nor others considered them as such. That is, the mentality of the moment would not have been considered as such because it was something completely alien to what was to be Argentinean.

I: The territory inhabited by them was or was not Argentina?

La: I do not know where you want to reach, but this ... No, it was not Argentina because Argentina had not been shaped yet. To my knowledge Argentina is a modern convention.

Lautaro has a clear historiographical perspective regarding the Desert Campaign. His narrative shows an understanding of the nation and the national territory as a historical construction developed over time. We can infer from his claims that to be "Argentinean" is a quality that the natives do not have. In other words, Lautaro thinks the natives lack the necessary qualities to be considered in Argentineans.

DISCUSSION

In the very same days we are writing this chapter, a number of dramatic social, economical and political problems are taking place in the world. The most important economic crisis after 1929 is producing devastating effects on numerous European countries in the short-term, but also forms a much more serious problem for the long term. Would it be possible to understand the EU crisis without considering the very concept of the EU? Is the EU a new concept of nation? Is the EU a nation of nations? What would that mean? What is the role of each particular nation in relation to the whole set of EU?

In the context of this chapter, we would like to emphasize two main issues related to these questions. First, it is important to take into account that fully understanding those, and similar problems, from a social, economic and political points of view, implies a historical point of view. For this reason historical knowledge is necessary in our schools and societies. There is no way to understand the present without understanding the past. And there is no way to make sense of the possible future without establishing a meaningful relation with the present and the past (Carretero & Solcoff, 2012). In other words, historical understanding implies social and political comprehension, adding also a unique temporal dimension.

However, according to our studies it looks like the concept of nation is not understood in a proper historical manner. Students have a rather essentialist idea of the nation, closer to a romantic than to a disciplinary conception. The romantic conception has essentialist features, such as an eternal territory, legitimized in a tautological way. Present nations appear in the mind of citizens as immutable political objects whose historical origin is misunderstood, as if they existed "since always", as some of the research participants would say. The stability of these conceptions appear very clearly: no differences were found across different age groups of 12, 14, 16, 18 year olds and adults.

In the three studies, participants understood the territory as a natural entity belonging to the nation which is, in turn, a predetermined entity. This essentialist conception of the territory also promotes an essentialist conception of the whole nation as the unit of unchanging and eternal destiny. The conception of the nation our participants showed is linked to the concept of territory, and that is why the essentialist character that is given to the territory might expand to the concept of nation in general.

We can consider the narratives as expressing the tension between the two types of objectives for teaching history we have outlined above. This is to say, between the enlightened and romantic. As it was mentioned the first pretends the consolidation of a critical and academic conception of history, and the second relates to the construction of national identities.

There are two probable causes of this, even though much more research is needed. On one hand, it is important to consider what Billig (1995) has considered "banal nationalism", frequent in and out the school. In reaction to an intense process of globalization, in many societies nationalist ideas are even more supported than before. Certainly, any nationalist idea promotes and is even based on the romantic conception of the nation (Carretero, 2011). On the other hand the teaching of history in many schools around the world still is something that should be seriously improved. Specifically, the excessive emphasis of national narratives and the romantic manner in which the nation is portrayed in those narratives. A number of significant contributors to history education have been trying to develop new proposals. Most of them are in the line of developing disciplinary historical thinking in the schools. Peter Lee (2004) has pointed out how, on numerous occasions, learning to think historically (Levesque, 2008) entails navigating counterintuitive ideas. Historical thinking is even described as an "unnatural process" (Wineburg, 2001). This historical thinking is based on acquiring a set of skills that are characteristic of historical experts (Carretero & Lopez, 2010b; Wineburg, 1991a; 1991b). Through these proposals, the complex and dynamic nature of concepts such as nation and national identities are acknowledged. Thus, students are given the opportunity to address these issues in a deep, critical way.

REFERENCES

Alridge, D. P. (2006). The limits of master narratives in history textbooks: An analysis of representations of Martin Luther King, Jr. *Teachers College Record, 108.*

Álvarez Junco, J. (2011). *Spanish identity in the age of nations.* Manchester University Press.

Anderson, B. (1983). *Imagined communities: Reflections on the origin and spread of nationalism.* London: Verso.

Ballantyne, T. (2005). Putting the nation in its place? World history and C. A. Bayly's The birth of the modern world. In A. Curthoys & M. Lake (Eds.), *Connected worlds: History in transnational perspective* (pp. 23–44). Canberra: ANUE press.

Barton, K. C., & Levstik, L. S. (1996). Back when god was around and everything: Elementary children's understanding of historical time. *American Educational Research Journal, 33*(2), 419–454

Barton, K. C., & McCully, A. W. (2005). History, identity, and the school curriculum in Northern Ireland: An empirical study of secondary students' ideas and perspectives. *Journal of Curriculum Studies, 37*, 85–116.

Bellino, M. J., & Selman, R. L. (2012). The intersection of historical understanding and ethical reflection during early adolescence. A place where time is squared. In M. Carretero, M. Asensio, & M. Rodriguez-Moneo (Eds.), *History education and the construction of national identities.* Charlotte, NC: Information Age Publishing.

Billig, M. (1995). *Banal nationalism.* London: Sage.

Carretero, M. (2011) *Constructing patriotism. Teaching of history and memories in global worlds.* Charlotte, NC: Information Age Publishing.

Carretero, M., Asensio, M., & Pozo, J. I. (1991). Cognitive development, historical time representation and causal explanations in adolescence. In M. Carretero, M. Pope, R. J. Simons, & J. I. Pozo. (Eds.) *Learning and instruction. Vol.III. European research in an international context* (pp. 27–48). Oxford: Pergamon Press.

Carretero, M. & Bermudez, A. (2012). Constructing histories. In. J. Valsiner (Ed.), *Oxford handbook of culture and psychology.* Oxford : Oxford University Press.

Carretero, M., Castorina, J .A., & Levinas, L. (in press). Conceptual change of the historical knowledge about the nation. In S. Vosniadou (Ed.) *International Handbook of Research on Conceptual Change.* New York: Routledge.

Carretero, M., & Gonzalez, M. F. (submitted). Historical narratives and conceptual change about the nation. *Cognition & Instruction.*

Carretero, M., Jacott, L., & López Manjón, A. (2002). Learning history through textbooks: Are Mexican and Spanish Children taught the same story? *Learning and Instruction, 12,* 651–665.

Carretero, M., & Kriger, M. (2011). Historical representations and conflicts about indigenous people as national identities. *Culture and Psychology, 17* (2), 177–195.

Carretero, M., & Lopez, C. (2010a). The Narrative mediation on historical remembering. In S. Salvatore, J. Valsiner, J. Travers, & A. Gennaro (Eds.), *Yearbook of idiographic science* (Vol. 2, pp. 285–294). Roma: Firera & Liuzzo.

Carretero, M., & Lopez, C. (2010b). Studies in learning and teaching history: implications for the development of historical literacy. In C. Lundholm, G. Peterson, & I. Wisted (Eds.), *Begreppsbildning i ett intentionellt perspektiv. [Conceptual change and intentional perspective]* (pp. 167–187). Stockholm: Stockholm University Press.

Carretero, M., Lopez Manjón, A., & Jacott, A. (1997). Explaining historical events. *International Journal of Educational Research, 27*(3), 245–253.

Carretero, M., & Solcoff, K. (2012). Comments on "After the archive: remapping memory." *Culture and Psychology, 18.*

Chiaramonte, J. (1991) El mito de los orígenes en la historiografía latinoamericana. [The myth of the origins in Latin American historiography] *Cuadernos del Instituto Ravignani, 2,* 5–39.

Duara, P. (Ed.). (1995). *Rescuing history from the nation: Questioning narratives of modern China.* Chicago: University of Chicago Press Chicago.

Egan, K. (1997). *The educated mind: How cognitive tools shape our understanding.* Chicago: University of Chicago Press.

Epstein, T. & Schiller, J. (2005). Perspective matters: social identity and the teaching and learning of national history. *Social Education, 69*(4), 201–204.

Foster, S. J., & Crawford, K. A. (Eds.). (2006). *What shall we tell the children? International perspectives on school history textbooks.* Greenwich, CT: Information Age Publishing.

Gellner, E. (1978). *Thought and change.* Chicago: University of Chicago Press.

Grever, M. (2006). Nationale identiteit en historisch besef. De risico's van een canon in de postmoderne samenleving [National identity and historical awareness. Risks of a canon in a postmodern society]. *Tijdschift voor Geschiedenis, 119,* 160–177.

Grever, M., & Stuurman, S. (Eds.) (2008). *Beyond the canon. History for the twenty-first century.* New York: Palgrave Macmillan.

Halldén, O. (2000). On reasoning in history. In J. F. Voss & M. Carretero (Eds.), *Learning and reasoning in history* (pp. 272–278). London: Routledge.

Hammack, P. (2011). *Narrative and the politics of identity: The cultural psychology of Israeli and Palestinian youth.* NY: Oxford University Press.

Hansen, J. M. (2012). De-nationalize history and what have we done? Ontology, essentialism, and the search for a cosmopolitan alternative. In M. Carretero, M. Asensio, & M. Rodriguez-Moneo (Eds.), *History education and the construction of national identities* (pp. 17–31). Charlotte, NC: Information Age Publishing.

Koselleck, R. (1975). Geschichte, Historie (Caps. I, V–VII). In *Geschichtliche Grundbegriffe,* Vol. 2 (pp. 593–595, 647–718), Stuttgart. [Spanish Translation, Antonio Gómez Ramos: *historia/Historia.* Madrid, 2004]

Lee, P. (2004). Understanding history. In Seixas, P. (Ed.), *Theorizing historical consciousness* (pp. 129–164). Toronto: University of Toronto Press.

Lévesque, S. (2008). *Thinking historically: Educating students for the twenty-first century.* Toronto: University of Toronto Press.

Lopez, C., Carretero, M., & Rodríguez-Moneo, M. (2012). *Is the nation a historical concept on in students' mind?* Manuscript in preparation.

Mak, G. (2005). *Gedoemd tot kwetsbaarheid.* Amsterdam: Atlas.

Renan, E. (2004). What is a nation? In H. K. Bhabha (Ed.). *Nation and narration* (pp. 8–22). Routledge: London.

Ríos Saloma, M. F. (2005). From the restoration to the reconquest: The construction of a national myth (An historiographical review. 16th–19th centuries). *España medieval, 28,* 379–414.

Rivière, A., Nuñez, M., Barquero, B., & Fontela, F. (1998). Influence of intentional and personal factors in recalling historical texts: A developmental perspective. In J. F. Voss, & M. Carretero (Eds.) *Learning and reasoning in history. International review of history education* (Vol. 2, pp. 214–226). London: Woburn.

Van Der Leeuw-Roord, J. (2009). Yearning for yesterday. Efforts of history professionals in Europe at designing meaningful and effective school history curricula. In L. Symcox & A. Wilschut (Eds.), *International review of history education National history standards. The problem of the canon and the future of teaching History* (Vol. 5, pp. 73–94). Charlotte, NC.: Information Age Publishing.

VanSledright, B. (2008). Narratives of nation-state, historical knowledge, and school history education. *Review of Research in Education, 32*(1), 109–146.

VanSledright, B., & Limón, M. (2006). Learning and teaching in social studies: Cognitive research on history and geography. In P. Alexander & P. Winne (Ed.), *The handbook of educational psychology* (2nd ed., pp. 545–570). Mahweh, NJ: Lawrence Erlbaum Associates.

Voss, J. F., & Wiley, J. (2006). Expertise in history. In N. C. K. A. Ericsson, P. Feltovich & R. R. Hoffman (Ed.), *The Cambridge handbook of expertise and expert performance,* (pp. 569–584). Cambridge: Cambridge University Press.

Wertsch, J. V. (2002). *Voices of collective remembering.* Cambridge: Cambridge University Press.

Wertsch, J. V., & Rozin, M. (2000). The Russian revolution: Official and unofficial accounts. In J. F. Voss, & M. Carretero (Eds.), *Learning and reasoning in history: International review of history education* (vol. 2, pp. 39–59). London: Routledge.

Wineburg, S. (1991a). Historical problem solving: A study of the cognitive processes used in the evaluation of documentary and pictoral evidence. *Journal of Educational Psychology, 83*(1), 73–87.

Wineburg, S. (1991b). The reading of historical texts: Notes on the breach between school and academy. *American Educational Research Journal, 28,* 495–519.

Wineburg, S. (2001) *Historical thinking and other unnatural acts: Charting the future of teaching the past.* Philadelphia: Temple University Press.

CHAPTER 12

WAYS OF KNOWING AND THE HISTORY CLASSROOM

Supporting Disciplinary Discussion and Reasoning About Texts

Avishag Reisman and Sam Wineburg

> The historian who is most conscious of his own situation is also more capable
> of transcending it, and more capable of appreciating the essential nature of
> the differences between his own society and outlook and those of other peri-
> ods and other countries....Man's capacity to rise above his social and histori-
> cal situation seems to be conditioned by the sensitivity with which he recog-
> nizes the extent of his involvement in it. (Carr, 1967, p. 54)

History education has always been justified on the grounds that it prepares
students for democratic citizenship, yet proponents disagree over what, exactly, constitutes effective citizenship (Hertzberg, 1981; Thornton, 1994).
To some, citizenship requires student mastery of a shared narrative that
provides a cohesive national identity. To others, citizenship demands an
awareness and stake in contemporary social problems; the past, in this view,
provides us with lessons that should inform our decisions. In this chap-

History Education and the Construction of National Identities, pages 171–188
Copyright © 2012 by Information Age Publishing
All rights of reproduction in any form reserved.

ter, we present the findings from a curriculum intervention that suggests a third argument for the importance of history instruction. We propose that the skills of disciplinary historical reading—the ability to read and interpret written text; the ability to evaluate and reconcile competing truth claims; and the ability to temper one's rush to judgment in the face of competing worldviews—constitute the heart of participatory democracy. In a history classroom where students regularly practice such disciplinary reading skills and wrestle with the antiquated worldviews of their predecessors, whole-class discussion emerges as the site for reasoned deliberation (Dewey, 1985; Habermas, 1990). It is during classroom discussion that we would hope to see students develop consciousness of their own historical subjectivity, and transcend it in an effort to understand others.

The empirical research on discussion in history class is sparse. Much of the best-known work on classroom discussion has involved elementary math, science, or reading comprehension, rather than high school humanities classrooms (Wells & Arauz, 2006). Research on text-based discussion in secondary classrooms is especially limited, and has primarily occurred in English, rather than in history or social studies classrooms (e.g., Haroutunian-Gordon, 1991; Lee, 1995). Hess and Posselt (2002) examined student reactions to a controversial public issues (CPI) curriculum; however, the topics concerned contemporary policy issues, not the past. Wortham (1994, 2001) examined a classroom discussion about Plutarch's description of the Spartan practice of infanticide, but his analysis began when students departed from the text and used contemporary analogies and "participant examples," rather than close textual interpretation, to understand the past. The only research that has investigated how students in middle or high school marshaled textual evidence to support claims about the past has examined students in autonomous small groups, rather than in teacher-led, whole-class discussions (Dickinson & Lee, 1984; Martens, 2009; Pontecorvo & Girardet, 1993).

The present study examined whole-class text-based discussions in classrooms that participated in the Reading like a Historian (RLH) project, a six-month curriculum intervention in 11th grade history classrooms (Reisman, 2012a). The curriculum consisted of 83 stand-alone lessons that followed a particular sequence of activities. These "Document Based Lessons" (Reisman, 2012b) consisted of four distinct lesson segments: 1) Reviewing background knowledge; 2) Posing the central historical question; 3) Reading and interpreting historical documents; 4) Whole-class discussion. Students first reviewed relevant historical background information that prepared them to engage with the lesson's documents. Second, students were presented with a historical question that required documentary investigation. Students read between 2–5 primary documents that shed light on the central historical question from different perspectives. Guiding questions and graphic organizers were designed to help students apply the strategies of disciplinary historical reading, namely sourcing, close reading, contextualization, and corroboration (cf., Martin & Wineburg, 2008; Wineburg, 1991a, 1991b). Finally, students engaged in whole-class discussion about the central historical question, using evidence from the documents to substantiate their claims. The multiple documents were intentionally selected to increase the chance that students would arrive at conflicting interpretations that would have to be reconciled through discussion. Rather than requiring students to memorize state-sanctioned narratives, they were taught to form and justify their own interpretations. Figure 1 lays out the sequence for a typical Document-Based Lesson in our curriculum.

The quasi-experimental intervention compared students whose teachers used the documents-based RLH curriculum to students in traditional history classrooms. Students in treatment classes outperformed their counterparts on historical thinking, factual recall, and a measure of reading comprehension. However, the broad quantitative measures used in the larger

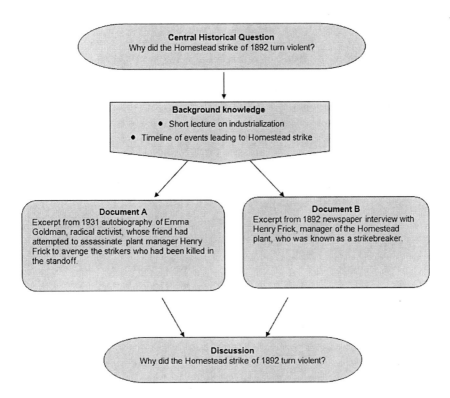

Central Historical Question
Why did the Homestead strike of 1892 turn violent?

Background knowledge
- Short lecture on industrialization
- Timeline of events leading to Homestead strike

Document A
Excerpt from 1931 autobiography of Emma Goldman, radical activist, whose friend had attempted to assassinate plant manager Henry Frick to avenge the strikers who had been killed in the standoff.

Document B
Excerpt from 1892 newspaper interview with Henry Frick, manager of the Homestead plant, who was known as a strikebreaker.

Discussion
Why did the Homestead strike of 1892 turn violent?

FIGURE 1. Outline of a sample "Document-Based Lesson"

study failed to capture the nuances of historical understanding evident in student speech. This paper focuses on teacher and student participation in the document-based whole-class discussions that should have occurred at the end of each RLH lesson. We identify emergent and sophisticated instances of historical understanding and explore the relationship between particular teacher moves and higher levels of student argumentation.

CONCEPTUAL FRAMEWORK

We examine classroom discussion in history class through the lens of pedagogical content knowledge (Shulman, 1986; Shulman & Quinlan, 1996). Rather than the simple mastery of discreet and easily transferable behaviors, pedagogical content knowledge holds that effective teaching requires the ability to represent subject matter knowledge to students in developmentally appropriate ways. Teachers must not only master the discipline's content knowledge—both its substantive concepts and the methods by which its practitioners verify truth claims (Schwab, 1978)—but also anticipate novices' common misconceptions and preconceptions, and have appropriate strategies to address them (Shulman, 1986).

For our purposes, pedagogical content knowledge provides a useful lens for understanding the distinction between *generic* and *disciplinary* discussion (in math, cf. Ball, 1993; Kazemi, & Stipek 2001; Lampert, 1990). Whereas the goals of generic discussion may include student interaction, participation, and even argumentation, the goal of disciplinary discussion must be the construction of historical knowledge. As philosophers of history contend, historical knowledge is characterized by paradox: by close attention to the particulars of historical context alongside the recognition that the past remains irretrievable and fundamentally unknowable (cf., Carr, 1967; Collingwood, 1946; Wineburg, 2001). We must rely on our cognitive tools to understand the past, but these tools will always preclude complete understanding.

To bring students into the *historical problem space*, teachers must move them beyond the binary that characterizes classroom historical knowledge. On one side of this binary lies a notion of history as a strange but retrievable past, lying dormant in dusty facts. By opening the floor to discussion, however, teachers often present a history that lies on the other side of the binary: a past familiar and recognizable, but subject to distortion in the face of contemporary interpretation. When students see the past as familiar, they leap to judgment, condoning or condemning the deeds of historical actions according to present values and contemporary standards. These favorable or critical judgments constitute a second binary that one commonly finds in history classrooms. To overcome these binaries and move towards historical understanding, students must see the paradox of the past/present divide: they must grasp that their existence in the present colors and therefore limits their perception of the past. In the words of Hans-Georg Gadamer, "Having an historical sense is to conquer in a consistent manner the natural naiveté which makes us judge the past by the so-called obvious scales of our current life, in the perspective our institutions, and from our acquired values and truths" (1979, p. 90).

We propose a quasi-developmental trajectory to describe the continuum between students' incoming notions about the past and their engagement with texts in the historical problem space. In doing so, we draw from research on the development of historical thinking, which has identified two intertwined trajectories for growth, one that describes students' relationship to historical texts, and one that describes students' perceptions of the continuity between past and present. Students initially regard historical texts as straightforward records of past events; in a subsequent developmental stage, they view accounts as pieces of testimony that should be accepted as truth or should be discarded. However, disciplinary thinking requires that students view historical documents as pieces of evidence that must be interrogated as one builds an account of what occurred in the past (Lee, 2005; Lee & Ashby, 2000; Shemilt, 1983; Wineburg, 1991a, 2001). Students move along a different trajectory when asked to explain unusual historical customs or behaviors towards a stage that scholars have called "contextual historical empathy" (Ashby & Lee, 1987; Shemilt, 1984). Assuming continuity between past and present, students initially occupy an evaluative stance towards historical actors, either judging them as stupid or morally deficient or imputing motivations without regard for contextual circumstances. At higher levels, students acknowledge an increasingly complex historical context that shaped the behaviors and worldviews of historical actors (Dickinson & Lee, 1984; Lee, Dickinson, & Ashby, 1997).

This study combined and modified these two developmental trajectories of historical thinking to account for student claims in text-based discussion about the past. Figure 2 lays out a model that includes four levels to account for student claims in whole-class discussion: in level 1, students evaluate historical actors without regard for the documentary evidence; in level 2, students regard the documentary evidence as given, without considering the author's perspective, purpose, or context; in level 3, students acknowledge the author's perspective and context, but these factors are perceived as static and descriptive, so as to render the author wholly untrustworthy or the historical context uniformly backwards. The model also includes a fourth level, which does not appear in prior developmental models, in which students demonstrate an awareness of their own subjectivity as historical actors and as *readers* of historical documents (cf. Gadamer, 1979). This historical consciousness tempers their rush to judgment and brings them to the heart of the historical problem space. Students who recognize that their personal experiences shape and limit their understanding of the past are best positioned to see the complexity of the past.

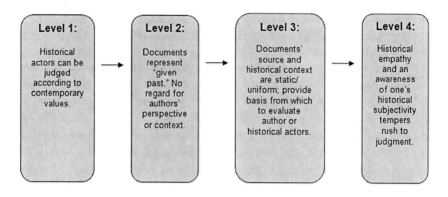

Level 1:

Historical actors can be judged according to contemporary values.

Level 2:

Documents represent "given past." No regard for authors' perspective or context.

Level 3:

Documents' source and historical context are static/uniform; provide basis from which to evaluate author or historical actors.

Level 4:

Historical empathy and an awareness of one's historical subjectivity tempers rush to judgment.

FIGURE 2. Developmental Trajectory for Student Argumentation in Text-Based Historical Discussion

METHOD

We examined teacher and student verbal participation in whole-class discussion. Over the course of the six-month RLH intervention, five treatment classrooms were observed twice per week and videotaped once per week, for a total of 20 videotaped lessons per teacher, 100 videotaped lessons total. Field notes were taken during observations and are occasionally referenced to paint a fuller picture of the teachers' instruction over the six-month intervention.

Participants

The Reading like a Historian Project (Reisman, 2012a; 2012b; cf., Wineburg, Martin, & Monte-Sano, 2011) included five treatment classrooms from five different San Francisco high schools. The schools represented

TABLE 1. School Demographics

	Total School Enrollment	Percent Free/ Reduced Lunch	Percent 11th graders at or above proficient on ELA	Treatment Teacher	Years Teaching	Undergraduate Degree
School 1	939	53.2	29.9	Mr. Peters	9	U.S. History
School 2	2500	47.5	42.1	Ms. Clay	17	Business
School 3	666	62	11.5	Ms. Addams	5	American Studies
School 4	637	57.4	35.2	Ms. Hudson	24	Art History
School 5	2400	44.8	43.9	Ms. Smith	7	U.S. History

a cross-section of the city's public high schools. One 11th grade classroom from each of the schools in Table 1 participated in the curriculum intervention. The teachers ranged in age, years of experience, and background in history.

Criteria for Discussion

Videotaped classroom lessons were analyzed and instances of whole-class discussion were identified using four criteria: 1) the teacher needed to pose the Central Historical Question explicitly at the start of the discussion; 2) students must have read at least two documents *prior to the discussion*; 3) the discussion had to include at least three distinct student turns, each of which qualified as an argument (see below for argument criteria); 4) the discussion needed to have lasted at least four minutes. These criteria were far more stringent than those used in prior research on discussion (cf., Nystrand et al., 1997).[1] However, they maximized the probability that the discussions would contain instances of substantive text-based discussion about the past.

RESULTS

Analysis of 100 videotaped lessons sought to determine whether teachers moved students beyond the binaries that characterize historical knowledge in classrooms and into the *historical problem space*. At the highest level of argumentation, students demonstrated an awareness of their own subjectivity as historical actors and as *readers* of historical documents. Only nine discussions satisfied all four criteria and they occurred in three of the five participating classrooms: Ms. Clay in School 2, Ms. Addams in School 3, and Ms. Smith in School 5 (see Table 1). These nine discussions were transcribed verbatim.[2] Of these nine discussions, only three included student

---

[1] Nystrand et al. (1997), for example, define discussion as "the free exchange of information among students and/or between at least three students and the teacher that lasted at least *half a minute*" (Italics added, p. 36).

[2] Numbers to the left of turns indicate the place of the utterance in the whole-class discussion, which begins when the teacher initially poses the Central Historical Question. "T" indicates teacher, students are identified with "S" followed by a number, according to the order of their contribution in the particular excerpt. Ss indicates multiple student voices simultaneously. I indicate when I have deleted turns and these turns only contain irrelevant material (e.g., student side talk or teacher disciplinary talk) or redundant material (e.g., arguments that are included in another segment of the excerpt, or students clarifying question before responding). I use italics to indicate when the speaker uses special emphasis. An equal sign at the start of a turn means "latching," that there was no elapsed time between the end of the preceding turn and the start of the new turn. A dash marks the sudden cut-off of speech. Material enclosed in parentheses is my best guess as to the content of inaudible utterances. Double parenthesis include transcriber's comments. Ellipses outside brackets indicate a pause within the speaker's utterance. Ellipses inside square brackets indicate deleted material inside a turn.

comments that reflected the highest level of student argumentation: an awareness of one's subjectivity as an historical actor. All three of these successful discussions occurred in Ms. Clay's classroom. Below we present a discussion from Ms. Clay's classroom where she moved students into the historical problem space.

Ms. Clay's WWI Discussion

The World War One lesson plan included four documents: (a) a 1914 speech by Woodrow Wilson, when he explained why the United States should remain neutral; (b) a famous 1917 speech by Woodrow Wilson when he explained that the United States had to enter the war to "make the world safe for democracy"; (c) a textbook excerpt that discussed the Zimmerman Telegram as well as the British blockade that preceded Germany's policy of unrestricted submarine warfare; and (d) an excerpt from Howard Zinn's *A People's History of the United States* (1980) that casts doubt on Wilson's claims and argues that the United States entered the war at the urging of bankers and industrialists, who fretted that a defeated Britain would default on its loans.

Clay divided the WWI discussion into three distinct discussions over the course of the lesson, all revolving around the Central Historical Question of whether Wilson had good reasons for entering the war. In the first discussion (approximately 5 minutes), students discussed Wilson's reasons for entering the war and whether they were good. In the second discussion (approximately 7 minutes), students discussed whether they found Zinn's argument convincing; in the third discussion, (approximately 12 minutes), students discussed which of the three documents—Wilson's second speech, the textbook, or Zinn—they found most trustworthy and why. To prepare for both the second and third discussion, Clay first had student discuss the questions in small groups. In the second discussion, students had unanimously said that they found Zinn's argument convincing. The segment below is from the third discussion. Ms. Clay's repeatedly asked students to consider the source note for the Zinn excerpt, which read: "Howard Zinn is a historian and activist who is best known today as the author of *A People's History of the United States*, a book that tells American history from the perspective of minorities, women, and poor people, and that is very critical of the United States government."

103   S1: I agree with Zinn because it seems like he just lists facts in his argument, and Wilson, like in his speech and stuff, he's just like telling people what they want to hear, you know like democracy and like they're taking our rights away, America, you know—

104   T: Okay.

105 S1: He wants—he's telling people what they want to hear so that they want to go to war and like if his economic reasons for going to war were legitimate, he would have told people, he wouldn't have hidden them from the people in his speech.

106 T: Um, a lot of you seem to agree with Zinn, thinking about what Jackson sourced for us on Zinn, how might Zinn also be talking about what people want to hear? Jackson, what did you tell us, who was his audience, his intended audience?

[Skip one turn.]

108 S2: Um ((inaudible)) the perspective of minorities, women and poor people. So I guess it's . . . I don't know.

109 T: So how might Zinn also be talk—So, if Michael's argument, which was a valid one, that Wilson was saying that people want to hear about democracy and things, how might Zinn also be speaking to his audience as well? Sure, Catherine.

110 S3: Because Zinn's talking to the poor people, the minorities, and the women, people who are not going to prosper from the war, so he's trying to get them to be against the war, so that no one prospers.

111 T: Okay, so, uh, against the war so that no one prospers, can you explain that to me?

112 S3: Like, if we didn't go the war, the rich wouldn't get any money, and the poor still wouldn't get any money anyways, so Zinn's trying to tell them all the bad things about how the rich is going to get all the money, and we're not going to get any money, either way they wouldn't get money, even if they went to the war or not.

113 T: Okay, and when is he writing this again?

114 S4: This is in 1980, so it's after the fact, so it doesn't matter if they disagreed or agreed because it already happened.

115 T: So let me ask you, Juan, he might not be speaking to poor people during World War 1, but who is Zinn speaking to in the 1980s?

116 S4: =Poor people

117 S5: To the general public

118 S6: =To everyone

119 T: Okay, so he's speaking to everyone, but why might he give that perspective that Catherine just pointed out, right? He's giving the perspective that's basically speaking to the poor people and that the rich people had, you know, they would have made money, and that was his thinking of why they went to war. Why does that matter in the 1980s and today and the fact that people, that it's selling out to go to Central High School next week to hear this guy?

120 S7: Because we're in a war.

121 T: Okay, keep going James.

122 S7: So, it's sort of the same thing before and now.

123 T: What do you mean?

124 S7: Like nothing really changed—there's still, like, rich people still get money. Like, with oil, like, rich people still get money from that—

[Skip three turns.]

128 T: So let's talk about, again, who the audience that he's writing to and why that might affect [. . .] Thinking about when we talk about what might be missing from that person's argument, right? So Zinn gives one perspective, Michael pointed out that Wilson gives one perspective, what else do you think about who Zinn was writing to? Why are all of you so convinced by his argument?

129 S3: Because we are the minority people.

130 T: So why would that convince you?

131 S3: Because he's telling us what we want to hear.

Ms. Clay is quite deliberate here about pushing students to consider their own subjectivity relative to the historical texts they have read. As it happened, Howard Zinn was scheduled to speak at a local school the following week. When students were informed of this at the start of class, they were palpably excited: few of the documents they had read over the course of the year were written by a contemporary author. And yet, the students did not consider that Zinn's perspective might have particular resonance for them as high school students in San Francisco in 2009. Clay posed the question four distinct times (in turns 106, 109, 119, 128) and each time students struggled to grasp her point: they labored to see Zinn's argument as a human construction and themselves as subjective readers with political preferences, just like President Wilson's audience in 1917.

This newfound awareness of their subjectivity unsettled the students. Ms. Clay continued her questioning by asking students whether Zinn's contemporary perspective makes his claims untrustworthy:

138 T: Okay. So does that mean you trust it and there's no fault in his argument either, because he's saying what you want to hear?

139 S5: There could be fault but I believe what he's saying 'cause why would he have to lie? He's speaking to the people, uh the poor people. Anyway, nobody's paying him to write this or whatever, or giving money to write this perspective, I mean, he's writing it from his own ordeals, or what he researched.

[Skip two turns.]

142 S8: We don't really know—

143 T: Okay, what do you mean, Amanda, you don't really know?

144 S8: You keep on trying to trick us! Like—

((Class laughs.))

145 T: *I* do?!?

146 S8: Anything we say you're like, you contradict what we're saying so now we're thinking we're being like—

[Skip two turns.]

149 T: I'm not contradicting, I'm pointing out the textbook said it was the bombing, you know, it was blowing up these ships, and in the beginning we said it was revenge—

150 S8: We don't know—we don't know for sure, like, why they went to war because both of them could lie for their benefit, telling like, different stories, you know, so we don't really know what the truth is.

At Clay's pressing, S5 and S8 quickly retreated into the two epistemological corners of historical knowledge: the first view, grounded in the past, sees history as the "objective compilation of facts," and the second view, grounded in the present, sees history as "the subjective product of the mind of the historian" (Carr, 1967, p. 34). S5 grasped for steady ground in turn 139: Zinn must be telling the truth because "why would he have to lie?" His only motivation to lie would be financial gain, which S5 dismissed. One either tells the truth or tells lies. Missing from S5's understanding is that historical argumentation relies on the interpretation of evidence and the historian's imaginative reconstruction of the past. Rather, for S5, Zinn's facts come from "his ordeals, or what he researched," so they must be true. Meanwhile, S8 descended into a spiral of relativism, realizing that Zinn, like Wilson and the textbook, could "lie for their benefit," and therefore, we can never "know what the truth is." Yet, Ms. Clay did not allow the conversation to end. She rejected S8's assertion that we can never know the truth, and reminded students that certain events happened:

163 T: Okay, [. . .] you have all these different sources, one thing that we know is that what *did* happen?

164 S: The ship blew up.

165 S: We went to war.

166 T: The U.S. goes to war, right? The same kind of thing that we ((inaudible)) so regardless of all these different perspectives, we know that the U.S. went to war. Any other comments about this before we move on? Anything that anyone has not had a chance to say? Yes?

167 S9: Like in the textbook it says that the British captured the telegram, but couldn't the British lie to the U.S. about it because they wanted ((inaudible))?

[Skip seven turns.]

175 T: Okay, so maybe [the Americans] could help the British win the war, I think that's a really valid point, that *none* of the things that we looked at addressed, right. The validity of the Zimmerman note, right. Was it really "sent secretly" or did they capture it or did the British, I mean—you know, I think there's definitely some potential questions there . . . Is there anything else anybody else would want to know more about? Anything else you'd want to look at? Sure, Sam.

176 S10: How Zinn got all these numbers and like –

177 T: So where Zinn got his facts. Absolutely. Right. I mean he's writing this in 1980, it's a long time later, where did he get this information that was never put out. Totally. Maybe if you go next Thursday you could raise your hand and ask him that. ((Laughter.)) So Sam would like to know where Zinn got his information, anything else anybody else would like to know about the causes of WWI that's not provided here? Yes, James.

178 S7: How did they know that the Germans attacked the ships?

179 T: How did they know the Germans attacked the ships? So what kind of evidence would you want to see?

[Five turns of students suggesting genres of evidence].

Clay, tied up the discussion by asserting that certain historical facts were irrefutable and then she opened the floor to further comment. What followed was a singular moment in the entire six-month study across five classrooms when students launched into a spontaneous series of inquiries into the textbook's claims. As the questions teetered into the realm of conspiracy theories, Clay brought students back to consider the evidence they would need to support a counter-claim. The final segment of the conversation, in effect, reversed the tone of S8's relativism and S5's simplistic distinction between truth and lies. Buoyed by their newfound awareness of their subjectivity, students began to question the basis of the historical claims made by both the textbook and Zinn. In doing so, they positioned themselves as legitimate arbiters of others' truth claims.

DISCUSSION

In our excitement over students' growth in reading comprehension and the strategies of historical thinking, we might be forgiven for overlooking the fact that only three discussions—from over 100 videotaped lessons—included moments where students grappled with their subjectivity and entered the historical problem space. To explain the rarity of this phenomenon, we must begin with ourselves. We *all* struggle to see ourselves historically, to recognize that our beliefs, our institutions, our values—our very reality—do not belong to some eternal, universal truth, but rather, to a particular socio-historical moment. Our struggle to get a fix on our own historicity shapes how we understand the past. We ignore the foreign and incomprehensible in an effort to render the past familiar and recognizable. We do this so that we may see ourselves. As we have noted in another context, the "familiar past entices us with the promise that we can locate our own place in the stream of time and solidify our identity in the present" (Wineburg, 2001, pp. 5–6). We need look no further than the rhetoric of the Tea Party to appreciate the powerful human desire to see the past through contemporary eyes, especially a past populated with heroes and villains, all agents in their destiny (Lepore, 2010). Historian Gordon Wood argues that this tendency masks a particular American fear: "We do not want to learn about the blindness of people in the past or about the inescapable boundaries of our actions. Such a history . . . is apt to remind us of our own powerlessness, of our own inability to control events and predict the future" (2008, p. 14). Whether national proclivity or human need, the urge to draw a continuous line from past to present has proven hard to resist. Presentism is our mental state at rest.

The culture of social studies classrooms often works against the development of historical consciousness. Distancing themselves from the didactic monotony of traditional study, social studies reformers frequently trumpet relevance, problem-solving, and student engagement. Throughout the 20th century, the call for relevance has taken different shapes, from approaches that emphasized social justice and student empowerment, to those that purport to address "multiple intelligences" and hands-on learning. The Reading like a Historian curriculum, with its emphasis on student inquiry and knowledge construction, appeared to follow in these traditions, and was especially embraced by teachers who were accustomed opening their classrooms to discussion, to encouraging student participation and engagement.

Yet, engagement and participation sometimes came at the expense of historical accuracy and intellectual rigor. Indeed, all nine discussions that fulfilled the criteria pivoted around Central Historical Questions that asked students to judge historical actors. These questions had purchase with students; the invitation to pass judgment lowered the initial threshold for participation. The problems arose when teachers were challenged to move students beyond the binary and to emphasize the disjuncture between past and present. Such goals stood in contrast to typical social studies goals that emphasized relevance and engagement, for they required teachers to correct students' misconceptions and redirect discussions that were tinted with presentism. These competing goals precluded student entry into the tough intellectual terrain of the historical problem space. Indeed, this study showed that it was easier to achieve statistically significant results on reading comprehension, than to create classroom conditions where students acknowledged their historical subjectivity.

Subject Matter Knowledge in Disciplinary Historical Discussion

Clay's relationship to subject matter knowledge distinguished her from the other teachers. Of the three teachers, only she consistently lectured and assessed students on factual recall. She connected Reading Like a Historian lessons with narrative arcs that allowed students to locate each topic chronologically and spatially in the unfolding story of American history. Clay did not permit discussions to stray from the facts and she corrected anachronistic thinking. Ironically, Clay's undergraduate degree in business made her the only treatment teacher who was not trained in the humanities, and she had taken the fewest history classes of the five teachers. Indeed, her emphasis on factual knowledge and chronology may have stemmed from an effort to compensate for lack of training in the subject. The effect, however, was that her students were constantly reminded of the difference between past and present.

Clay was also the only teacher to interrupt discussion to review students' content knowledge, or "stabilize" the historical context. This move corrected students' tendencies towards presentist thinking. Clay posed closed, "display" questions that barely required answers, in the midst of what would be considered "exploratory" discussion (Cazden, 2001). The following brief exchange occurred during the first week of school, when students discussed whether Thomas Jefferson opposed the slave trade:

S1: We wrote that Thomas Jefferson didn't want to end the slave trade because if he did he would have like fought against [the removal of the anti-slavery grievance in the Declaration of Independence], like he would have fought against the fact that it was taken out.

T: Okay so that's true, maybe he should've done something but is Jefferson the only one who writes the Declaration?

Ss: No.

T: No, so I'm trying to think about what happens here. There's all these men sitting around and they want to get this passed, because what is the purpose of getting the Declaration?

S: Complain.

T: Complain to who?

Ss: The king.

T: The king. Right. And so if they want to get this out and they have all these people agreeing, can Jefferson simply say I'm not going to sign this until we get that in there?

Ss: No.

T: Maybe he could have done that, but is it that easy?

Ss: No.

This interaction did not qualify as a discussion. Indeed, it could be argued that Clay squelched student participation by launching a recitation sequence just as students began to formulate their views on Jefferson. However, the exchange reveals Clay's insistence on historical accuracy. By marking certain aspects of the past irrefutable and "stabilizing the context," Clay effectively constrained the ground from which students could evaluate historical actors. In doing so, she lent the discussions a degree of substance and historical legitimacy.

In addition to stabilizing the context, Clay directed students' attention to the documents in discursive moves that highlighted the authors' historical context. These questions demanded that students do more than simply lift quotes from the page without regard to source or context. In doing so, Clay helped students note their own subjectivity as readers of historical texts. Students, in turn, allowed themselves to withhold judgment in the face of difference.

IMPLICATIONS

In many history classrooms, student engagement has become a proxy for substantive learning. Students see discussion or debate, in this context, as a welcome departure from the lecture and memorization. The discussion segment of the Document-Based Lesson was designed to overcome the binary between the substantive "stuff" of historical facts, and the subjective banter of presentist historical debate. Effective disciplinary discussion has the potential to produce substantive historical learning, as students appreciate the distance between past and present, and face the limitations and insufficiency of their own cognitive architecture. This study has shown that such moments are extremely rare but nonetheless attainable. Given the range of problems facing public schools, it may seem absurd to encourage teachers to reach for this disciplinary golden ring. That this same intervention found effects on historical thinking strategies, factual knowledge, and reading comprehension, demonstrates that much can be gained short of an awareness of subjectivity. Yet, it is the cultivation of humility, caution, and reason to which we should aspire.

Participatory democracy requires that citizens be capable of articulating their views without resorting to demagoguery or ideological warfare. Reasoned deliberation requires that we try to see the world through the eyes of our loudest detractors. It is the responsibility of schools to train students in these practices. Classroom discussion about the past affords students a unique opportunity to stretch themselves beyond the familiarity of their contemporary belief system. They need not become apologists for the misguided actions of historical actors. Yet, in permitting themselves to understand the choices and actions of those who lived in the past, they may become aware of their own historical subjectivity, and perhaps, their human fallibility.

REFERENCES

Ashby, R., & Lee, P. J. (1987). Children's concepts of empathy and understanding in history. In C. Portal (Ed.), *The history curriculum for teachers* (pp. 62–88). Basingstoke: Falmer Press.

Ball, D. L. (1993). With an eye on the mathematical horizon: Dilemmas of teaching elementary school mathematics. *Elementary School Journal, 93*(4), 373–397.

Carr, E. D. (1967). *What is history?* New York: Vintage Books.

Cazden, C. B. (2001). *Classroom discourse: The language of teaching and learning.* Postsmouth, NJ: Heinemann.

Collingwood, R.G. (1946). *The idea of history.* Oxford: Oxford University Press.

Dewey, J. (1985). Democracy and education. In J. A. Boydston (Ed.), *John Dewey: The middle works, 1899–1924* (Vol. 9). Carbondale: Southern Illinois University Press.

Dickinson, A. K., & Lee, P. J. (1984). Making sense of history. In A. K. Dickinson, P. Lee, & P. J. Rogers (Eds.), *Learning history* (pp. 117–153). London: Heinemann Educational.

Gadamer, H. G. (1979). The problem of historical consciousness. In R. Rabinow & W. M. Sullivan (Eds.), *Interpretive Social Science* (pp. 82–140). Berkeley: University of California Press.

Habermas, J. (1990). *Moral consciousness and communicative action.* Cambridge: MIT Press.

Haroutunian-Gordon, S. (1991). *Turning the soul: Teaching through conversation in the high school.* Chicago: The University of Chicago Press.

Hertzberg, H.W. (1981). *Social studies reform, 1880–1980.* Boulder, Colorado: Social Science Education Consortium Publications.

Hess, D., & Posselt, J. (2002). How high school students experience and learn from the discussion of controversial public issues. *Journal of Curriculum and Supervision, 17*(4), 283–314.

Kazemi, E., & Stipek, D. (2001). Promoting conceptual thinking in four upper-elementary mathematics classrooms. *Elementary School Journal, 102*(1), 59–80.

Lampert, M. (1990). When the problem is not the question and the solution is not the answer: Mathematical knowing and teaching. *American Educational Research Journal, 27*(1), 29–63.

Lee, C. D. (1995). A culturally based cognitive apprenticeship: Teaching African American high school students skills in literary interpretation. *Reading Research Quarterly, 30*(4), 608–631.

Lee, P. J. (2005). Putting principles into practice: Understanding history. In J. D. Bransford & M.S. Donovan (Eds.), *How students learn: History, math and science in the classroom* (pp. 29–78). Washington, D.C.: National Academy Press.

Lee, P. J., & Ashby, R. (2000). Progression in historical understanding among students ages 7–14. In P. Seixas, P. Stearns, & S. Wineburg (Eds.) *Teaching, learning and knowing history,* (pp. 199–222). New York: New York University Press.

Lee, P. J., Dickinson, A. K., & Ashby, R. (1997). "Just another emperor": Understanding action in the past. *International Journal of Educational Research, 27*(3), 233–244.

Lepore, J. (2010, May 3). Tea and sympathy: Who owns the American Revolution? *New Yorker,* 26–32.

Martens, M. (2009). Reconstructing historical understanding: How students deal with historical accounts. In M. Martens, U. Hartmann, M. Sauer, & M. Hasselhorn (Eds.), *Interpersonal understanding in historical context* (pp. 115–136). Rotterdam: Sense Publishers.

Martin, D., & Wineburg, S. (2008). Seeing thinking on the web [Electronic version]. *The History Teacher, 41*(3), 305–320.

Nystrand, M. (1997). *Opening dialogue: Understanding the dynamics of language and learning in the English classroom.* New York: Teachers College Press.

Pontecorvo, C., & Girardet, H. (1993). Arguing and reasoning in understanding historical topics. *Cognition and Instruction, 11*(3/4), 365–395.

Reisman, A. (2012a). Reading like a historian: A document-based history intervention in an urban high school. *Cognition and Instruction, 30*(1), 86–112.

Reisman, A. (2012b). The "document-based lesson:" Bringing disciplinary inquiry into high school history classrooms with adolescent struggling readers. *The Journal of Curriculum Studies 44*(2), 233–264.

Schwab, J. J. (1978). Education and the structure of the disciplines. In I. Westbury & N. J. Wilkof (Eds.), *Science, curriculum, and liberal education* (pp. 229–272). Chicago: University of Chicago Press.

Shemilt, D. (1983). The Devil's Locomotive. *History and Theory, 22*(4), 1–18.

Shemilt, D. (1984). Beauty and the philosopher: Empathy in history and classroom. In A. K. Dickinson, P. J. Lee, & P. J. Rogers (Eds.), *Learning history* (pp. 39–84). London: Heinemann Educational Books.

Shulman, L. S. (1986). Those who understand: Knowledge growth in teaching. *Educational Researcher, 15*(2), 4–14.

Shulman, L. S., & Quinlan, K. M. (1996). The comparative psychology of school subjects. In R. C. Calfee & D. C. Berliner (Eds.), *Handbook of educational psychology* (pp. 399–422). New York: Macmillan.

Thornton, S. J. (1994). The social studies near century's end: Reconsidering patterns of curriculum and instruction. In L. Darling-Hammond (Ed.), *Review of Research in Education, 20,* 223–254. Itasca, IL: Peacock Publishers.

Wells, G., & Arauz, R.M. (2006). Dialogue in the classroom. *The Journal of the Learning Sciences, 15*(3), 379–428.

Wilson, W. (1914). *Speech before Congress, August 19, 1914, 63rd Congress, 2nd Session,* Senate Document No. 566, Washington D.C.

Wilson, W. (1917). *Speech before Congress, April 2, 1917, 65th Congress, 1st Session,* Senate Document No. 5, Serial No. 7264, Washington, D.C.

Wineburg, S. S. (1991a). Historical problem solving: A study of the cognitive processes used in the evaluation of documentary and pictorial evidence. *Journal of Educational Psychology, 83*(1), 73–87.

Wineburg, S. (1991b). On the reading of historical texts: notes on the breach between school and academy. *American Educational Research Journal, 28*(3), 495–519.

Wineburg, S. (2001). *Historical thinking and other unnatural acts: Charting the future of teaching the past.* Philadelphia: Temple University Press.

Wineburg, S., Martin, D., & Monte-Sano, C. (2011). *Reading like a historian: Teaching literacy in middle and high school history classrooms.* New York: Teachers College Press.

Wood, G. S. (2008). *The purpose of the past: Reflections on the uses of history.* New York: Penguin Books.

Wortham, S. (1994). *Acting out participant examples in the classroom.* Philadelphia: John Benjamins.

Wortham, S. (2001). *Narratives in Action.* New York: Teachers College Press.

Zinn, H. (1980). *A people's history of the United States, 1492–present.* New York: Harper-Collins.

CHAPTER 13

THE INTERSECTION OF HISTORICAL UNDERSTANDING AND ETHICAL REFLECTION DURING EARLY ADOLESCENCE

A Place Where Time is Squared

Michelle J. Bellino and Robert L. Selman

INTELLECTUAL AND ETHICAL DISCIPLINARITY

To think historically is considered both inevitable (Holt, 1995) and un-natural (Wineburg, 2001), an amateur approach, but one that requires cognitive maturity (Lowenthal, 2000). In recent times, psychologists have applied theory and methods to historical thinking, linking children's and adolescents' emerging cognitive development to their capacity for histori-cal understanding, both as it develops "naturally," and as it is taught in mid-dle and high school. Accordingly, this growing body of research illustrates how historical understanding develops through a sequence of progressive differentiations and integrations, rather than simply as an aggregation of

History Education and the Construction of National Identities, pages 189–202
Copyright © 2012 by Information Age Publishing
189

information (Ashby, Gordon, & Lee, 2005; Duhlberg, 2002; Hartmann & Hasselhorn, 2008; Hartmann, Sauer, & Hasselhorn, 2009; Jensen, 2008; Lee & Ashby, 2000; Lee, Dickinson, & Ashby, 2001; Lee & Shemilt, 2003; Reisman & Wineburg, 2012; Seixas, 1996).

However, the interdisciplinary study of how human history is learned also hinges on the socio-emotional dimensions of empathic processes. Historical empathy entails recognition of the shared humanity among past and present actors, as well as an awareness of the often irreconcilable differences between actors' worldviews, and consequently, the way they interpret and exercise their agency (Lee & Shemilt, 2011; Seixas, 1996). Paradoxically then, the "rickety bridges of empathy" (Dunn, 2000, p. 133) are meant to be both imaginatively crossed and willfully acknowledged as boundaries that separate distinct subjectivities. As conscious as we may be of our presentist and personal beliefs, to varying degrees we are inevitably bound by them (Barton & Levstik, 2004; Lowenthal, 2000; Wineburg, 2001).

Learning about the choices of people in the past inevitably raises the question of how much to include or exclude ethical judgment from learning the tools of historical analysis (Selman & Barr, 2009). In pursuit of disciplinary understanding, many scholars and practitioners of history education believe that emotions (as in "easily swayed") and moral judgments (as in "opinionated") should be kept as separate and distinct as possible from rational, critical thought, and that the teaching of history is not primarily an emotional or ethical endeavor (e.g., Boix-Mansilla, 2000; Carretero, 2011; Lee & Shemilt, 2007; Lowenthal, 2000). Because history fused with moral or civic goals potentially "undermines deep historical understanding ... no matter how difficult and morally problematic the past may be" (Boix-Mansilla, 2000, p. 391), judging the past risks the presumption that historical agents subscribed to or deviated from the same social and moral norms we practice today. Emotionally driven opinions in the history classroom, therefore, often indicate uncritical thinking, over-identification with historical figures, or susceptibility to propaganda; similarly, moral responses are symptoms of presentistic bias.

In contrast, advocates of the "new" civic education are determined that any historical presentation of past injustice needs to be taught with a strong sense of emotional engagement and ethical reflection (Levine & Higgins-D'Alessandro, 2010; Rittner, 2004; Sleeter, 2008; Stern Strom, 1994). The motivation driving this perspective is both pedagogical and social, reinforcing students' engagement inside the classroom as active participants in discussion and debate, and outside the classroom as active society building citizens who thoughtfully draw lessons about themselves and society through informed social reflection.

Historians themselves debate whether the particularities of context defy our capacity to morally judge the actions of historical agents from any temporal position other than a concurrent historical moment (e.g., Rüsen, 2004). While some argue for strict historical relativism in order to accurately understand any decision made in the past, just or unjust (Lowenthal, 2000), others reach for universal criteria from which they can actively denounce wrongdoings, past and present (Totten, 2004). If this is confusing for historians, think what it must be like for typical early adolescents, who on one day can be abstractly and altruistically idealistic and on the next, contrite and concretely egocentric. Can these competing approaches, which represent distinct purposes for history education (Barton & Levstik, 2004; Carretero, 2011), be reconciled in the classroom, where students often respond emotionally before analytically? Given the developmental evidence that we will review, this is a particularly important consideration in middle and high school history pedagogy.

THEORY TO PRACTICE: EMPIRICAL REVIEWS AND EDUCATIONAL POSSIBILITIES

Empirical research from psychologists and history educators suggests that historical thinking can be learned by young students, though the range of learning outcomes varies along both a shared developmental continuum and across the more particular ecological or cultural contexts that individuals may not share. Using interview methods, Lee and Ashby (2000) have provided evidence that even in the lower elementary grades children can approach an awareness of historical agents as both actors and subjects with ideas and beliefs different from the students' own, especially if the different ideas are relatively straightforward and tangible (e.g., Corriveau, Kim, Schwalen, & Harris, 2009). Similarly, through ethnographic methods, Duhlberg (2002) has demonstrated how early adolescent (fifth grade) students' capacity for historical understanding is not only associated with chronological age, but also depends on their individual culture and experience. More recently, experimental (Ashby, Gordon, & Lee, 2005; Reisman & Wineburg, 2012) and action research (Jensen, 2008) have illustrated how shifts in classroom pedagogy can facilitate deeper historical thinking for both students and teachers.

In a recent program of quantitative studies, Hartmann and her colleagues (Hartmann & Hasselhorn, 2008; Hartmann, Sauer, & Hasselhorn, 2009) have paid attention to the need for psychometrically valid and standardized measures that take advantage of the emerging theory of historical thinking as a set of developmental progressions. These studies demonstrate that tenth grade students are less likely to apply presentistic notions and more likely to historically contextualize their interpretations of agency than seventh grade students from similar backgrounds. However, the differences in the use of presentist-based inferences among these age groups are surprisingly modest. In other words, presentism is still largely present in tenth graders' historical thinking, even in students on a high achieving academic track.

As Wineburg (2001) has suggested, the capacity for sophisticated historically contextualized thinking seems to rely on moments of heightened awareness of one's inherently partial ability to consider the past from a present perspective. However, scholars of history education have also fervently argued that historical thinking at its best actually should invite us to consider our present contexts—not as a hindrance to inquiry but as a condition of the constructed process of historical understanding. For instance, Barton and Levstik (2004) posit a typology of historical perspective recognition that includes a sense of otherness, shared normalcy, historical contextualization, differentiation of perspectives, and contextualization of the present (pp. 209–210). Within this typology, they identify contextualization of the present as both the most difficult type of historical empathy to grasp analytically and the most imperative aspect of this process to understand for civic participation. Somewhat differently, Lee and Shemilt (2011) illustrate historical empathy through a progression model, describing the extent to which students can access the meaning making processes of historical agents. This trajectory moves from "deficit and assimilation explanations" (p. 42), to recognizing in what ways and why the worldviews of historical actors were fundamentally distinct from those we have today, despite our seeming commonalities. Along this continuum, the most sophisticated "meta-empathetic explanation[s]" (p. 47) demonstrate attentiveness to the reflexive relationship between historical agents' structure (or context) and subjectivity.

While these typologies and models of progression do not adhere to an explicitly age-driven developmental lens, the movement to the more sophisticated practice of analytic skills denotes a developmental range of what students may be capable of expressing, with critical periods of transition. More specifically, during the middle school period, roughly between nine and fifteen years of age, students begin to develop the capacity for abstract thinking in social and moral domains, highly relevant to the continued development of historical empathy. Moving from an earlier phase of psychosocial egocentrism, early adolescents are on a fast-paced trajectory toward the increasing capacity to coordinate social perspectives, most importantly the facility of a "third person" perspective on human social behavior (Selman, 2003). This level of awareness sets the stage for the challenging movement to a fuller appreciation of historical perspective taking in its significantly maturing form: one that appreciates the role of cultures, climates, and contexts in making both interpretations of human behavior and judging them morally under the conditions of their particular time. There is historical understanding of a kind earlier in life, but at this point under the right conditions, adolescents' potential to think historically takes on greater analytic power and proficiency.

Yet despite their emergent moral idealism and recognition of differing, simultaneous perspectives, these same early adolescents remain highly self-centered, often overwhelmed by strong internal and external forces that drive their own need for security and satisfaction (Freud, 1965; Sullivan, 1953). As such, we consider the delicate work required to disentangle ethical and historical understanding to begin with the recognition of—and respect for—the value that a personal, evaluative, or judgmental point of view might have, in particular during the transitions that characterize early adolescence. We contemplate doing this even at the risk of their continued reliance on (some) judgmental thinking that may be associated with the disciplinary "sin of 'presentism'" (Lee & Shemilt, 2007, p. 16).

This does not by any means suggest that we abandon the promotion of multi-causal, evidentiary thinking for middle and early high school students of history, but it does suggest that student engagement in learning historical information may favor a pedagogy that allows for (even encourages) the expression of both personal opinion (*What would you have done if you were a historical agent in this particular context?*) and moral judgment (*What do you think about the actions of this historical agent in this particular context—are they fair and just?*), as well as the development of good logical arguments and analytic methods (*How did agency and context intersect and lead to this historical agent's choice to take this particular action within this particular context—and to what consequence?*).

Drawing on Werner's (1948) orthogenetic principle and classical developmental theory in psychology (Langer, 1978; Valsiner, 2004), we envision both the differentiation from and integration with the ethical as a complement to the historical rigor that teachers are trying to inculcate into middle and early high school history lessons (See Bermúdez, 2012). Werner (1948) persuasively argued that a key feature of any developmental phenomenon is the "organismic" emergence of domain specific progressions from a normative state, or phase, of conflation of mental parts and wholes, to a period where there is a differentiation of conceptual parts, and movement toward hierarchical integration of these parts into a restructured and more adequately integrated whole (exhibiting both stability and flexibility of mental functioning). The orthogenetic principle also posits the importance of recognizing transitional periods of construction, confusion, critique, and clarification in the developing mind as part of the natural processes and pathways of mental development, from differentiation to hierarchical integration.

Applying this principle to the corresponding developmental progressions of students' capacity for historical analysis and moral reflection, the dual trajectory emerges from their predisposed conflation in young chil-

dren's minds. Development can lead to students' differentiation of historical inquiry and ethical reflection as independent skillsets and orientations
toward the past, and ultimately, their purposeful integration. Once students
reach the point of conceptual integration, they have the capacity to recognize their own sense of morality as a dimension of their presentistic subjectivity (Reisman & Wineburg, 2012); from there, they can interpret the past
with both lenses.

The associated empirical question we pose is whether early adolescence
might be an ideal phase of time along students' developmental trajectory
to promote this differentiation and integration, and if so, how it might be
done in ways that are sensitive to both student learning and development.
In other words, what educational opportunities do we lose if we insist that
adolescents learn to think on strictly differentiated disciplinary terms before they are naturally disposed to do so?

SOME EMERGING EVIDENCE OF OUR OWN

Recently, we have begun to explore the relationship between historical
thinking and ethical reflection in a representative sample of ninth and
tenth graders across the United States (Bellino & Selman, 2011).[1] In that
study, we found that adolescents struggled to coordinate their evaluative
(moral and ethical) and explanatory (historical) responses to a complex
case of personal betrayal in an historical context of instability and intolerance.

In our study, we relied on a pilot measure originally designed to assess
the quality of students' historical understanding (along the dimensions of
historical evidence, causality, and agency) through their responses to questions asked in a case study about ethnic conflict in the former Yugoslavia
toward the end of the twentieth century (Stoskopf et al., 2007). Students
were first introduced to a series of primary and secondary source historical documents that provided background information on the country's
geography, economy, ethnic and religious makeup, and a brief historical
account of the conflict dating back to World War I. The seven documents
include: excerpts from Yugoslavia's 1976 Constitution guaranteeing the
freedom of ethnic and religious expression, a chart illustrating the economic turmoil that accompanied the escalation of conflict (a precipitous
fall in gross national product at the end of the decade, 1980–90), and direct

---

[1] The research we have conducted is a secondary analysis of data drawn from an experimental
evaluation of the Facing History and Ourselves program. Facing History and Ourselves
is an international organization that provides professional development to educators
and an educational approach for adolescents, positioned at the intersection of historical
understanding, civic engagement, and ethical reflection. (See Barr & Facing History and
Ourselves, 2010 for information about the evaluation design, instruments, and outcomes.)

testimony from Serbians and Bosnians, both Christians and Muslims, during the height of the conflict.[2]

The final questions are based on "Jasmina and Tanja's Story," a narrative centering on the lifelong friendship between Jasmina, a Bosnian Muslim, and her close friend Tanja, a Bosnian Serb. The document was excerpted and retold from a first-person memoir (Dervisevic-Cesic, 1994) into a third-person account. In the narrative, as the country becomes more divisive and intolerant, Tanja begins working as an informant for the Chetniks, an extremist paramilitary group that committed atrocities against non-ethnic Serbs. She betrays Jasmina and her family, who had protected Tanja from her abusive father prior to the war. Following their reading of this document, students were given this open ended prompt: "By the end of the story, Tanja was working for the Chetniks, helping them round up her Muslim neighbors. How would you explain what she did?" (Stoskopf et al., 2007).

Through qualitative analysis of 621 responses to this question from ninth and tenth graders in seven metropolitan locations across the United States, we were able to reliably code for students' degree of comprehension of the written text, and identify eleven distinct explanatory themes as to why Tanja chose to join the Chetniks (several themes are listed below; see Bellino & Selman, 2011, for full coding scheme). We were also able to distinguish three distinct kinds of moral responses students spontaneously offered to this ethically charged decision made in historical context, even though no moral judgment was asked for on the measure. Student moral responses were categorized as: valenced (explicitly either positive or negative judgments of Tanja's actions), neutral (descriptive reiteration of historical facts, and/or refusal to respond on the basis that "only Tanja knows why she did what she did"), and unresolved (implicit expressions of judgment or explicit acknowledgement of both positive and negative aspects of Tanja's decision).

Though we were not surprised that students responded morally to the historical case—as it implicitly provoked ethical questions about group loyalty during ethnic violence and personal connections through the lens of a friend's betrayal—we did not expect to see such visible gravitation toward evaluative judgment on a question that called for a "simple" historical interpretation or explanation for Tanja's actions. In order to investigate whether the often emotionally-driven, potentially ahistorical judgment response to the past and the more cognitively demanding disciplinary approach were oppositional or coexistent in student responses, we collapsed the number of explanations students offered for Tanja's actions into a dichotomous outcome variable, measuring the presence or absence of a sound histori-

---

[2] Students had approximately thirty minutes to complete the fourteen document-based questions, ranging from true/false, to item rating, and one open-ended question in response to the final document, "Jasmina and Tanja's Story."

cal explanation in relation to the type of judgment a student's response expressed. Our goal was to explore how adolescents interpreted Tanja's historical agency if they simultaneously responded by applying a moral judgment to her actions.

Our findings indicated that, on average, student responses were nearly two times more likely to offer an explanation based on historical understanding for Tanja's actions (e.g., ethnic group loyalty, fear and self-preservation, conformity, obedience to authority, dehumanization) when they exhibited "unresolved" moral judgment (expressions of confusion, ambivalence, uncertainty), than when they articulated a clearly valenced moral position. This relationship persisted across nearly all covariates (gender, age, parent education, etc.), including degree of comprehension of the narrative text. Though the historical explanations students offered ranged in their sophistication, what we find compelling is that students were not only significantly inclined to respond morally, but that their ethical reflection of historical actions did not necessarily preclude historical thinking.

In actuality, nearly all students positioned themselves as arbiters of Tanja's past actions, unable to neutrally explain an ethical decision made in historical context. Student responses, however, ranged in their capacity to reflect on Tanja's decision in ethical and/or moral terms, as well as their tendency to contextualize her actions within a particularly challenging socio-historical moment. Similarly, student responses that expressed unresolved moral judgment explained Tanja's actions from a variety of interpretive perspectives, with no predominant theme emerging. In some cases, responses consciously engaged with Tanja's positionality within her historical context ("*the pressure and fear created by this invasion was too much for her*"; "*when there is a strong political influence and you are on the 'safe' side*"); other times, they overlooked context in pursuit of more abstract universal moral invocations ("*she did not think one person could make a difference*"; "*she should have stood up for what was right*"). From the conflation of external forces and internal motivations for Tanja's actions, to the selective differentiation between the two, to their more complex integration, the students who exhibited unresolved moral judgment were most capable of reflecting on Tanja's decision, as indicative of their capacity to compare both moral and historical agency.

In one sense, we cannot be sure whether these "unresolved" responses demonstrate a space where students were consistently engaging in complex ethical reflection beyond their initial, possibly biased, moral reactions. But because students whose responses were considered "unresolved" moral claims were more likely to explain and not simply judge (e.g., *"Tanja is a traitor"; "what she did was not right"*), we believe this illuminates a space where disciplinary thinking, ethical reflection, and civic awareness can effectively meet, working toward historically contextualized ethical reflection, a more nuanced moral reasoning than a hasty, ahistorical judgment. Because of the nature of student responses, we are not able to make this claim definitively without further research. However, our findings suggest that adolescent students are either not always at risk for presentism when they express their moral beliefs about injustice in historical context—especially when they articulate moral complexity or uncertainty—or that a little bit of presentism might not be such a dangerous thing.

One challenge in reconciling the disciplinary approach with the ethics evoked in historical cases of injustice is that we do not have a clear grasp on adequate historical thinking about ethical issues (e.g., Rüsen, 2004), let alone a consensus on pedagogical objectives when moral and historical agency become inextricably tangled (Barton & Levstik, 2004). Like the bob of a pendulum, moral responses to historical events risk swinging toward ahistorical bounds: either falling victim to presentism (e.g., easy slippage into the stance of "essentialist apologetics" judging the past from a present "culture of contrition" (Lowenthal, 2000, p. 70)) or "relativist nihilism" (p. 71), where postmodernist skepticism gives way to cynicism and withdrawal. Similarly, these poles exemplify extremes in reflecting morally on the actions of others—either imposing one's conventional moral norms as universal and essential—or dismissing the task of critique altogether on the basis that moral views are too bound up with one's psychology and particular context.

How, then, can historical habits of mind assist in moral reflection; and how can we scrutinize moral reflection for anachronistic or historical thinking? It seems to us that both moral reflection and historical analysis implicitly intersect in the concentric circles of individual, social, and historical context. Moral claims exhibit historical understanding when they attend to historical specificity, potentially adjusting in response to the constraints of context. In this sense, responses in our study that displayed unresolved moral judgment suggest that the students were grappling with their own moral responses, sometimes in conflict with the particular limitations of Tanja's historical context (i.e., *I don't agree with her decision to betray her friend and support the Chetniks, no matter how fraught her context was*) and, most complexly, at the intersection between historical context and present-day subjectivity (i.e., *I may not agree with what she did, but I can never know what it felt like to be her, to be there, in that time, because I am me, here, now*).

For students at risk of conflating their own conventional morality with Tanja's moral outlook—as history education research and developmental theory suggests most early adolescents do (Duhlberg, 2002; Lowenthal, 2000; Selman, 2003)—the question is perhaps seldom heard as *why Tanja did what she did?*, but instead becomes *what would I do if I were in her situation?* To over-empathize is to simplify the range of human experience; to over-distance is to pretend that context does not influence how we are in the world, and navigating the uneven terrain requires recognition of one's subjectivity and its entrenched presentism. But under these "extreme" civil and social conditions, historical questions are no longer simply historical, but ethical, even existential encounters.

TOWARD HISTORICALLY CONTEXTUALIZED ETHICAL REFLECTION

It is a widespread concern that both adolescents and adults tend to use ahistorical morality in the guise of conventional values to subvert understanding of how past actors thought and acted (Lowenthal, 2000). The muddling of moral relevance and moral righteousness can exemplify the bad habit of privileging "kneejerk" emotional reactions at the expense of engaging in the labor of critical and contextual historical thinking. For the early adolescent, however, it may reveal a natural phase in a developmental process along the road from conflation of two emergent progressions in ontogenesis, the moral and the historical, to the differentiation of the two, to a clarification of their relation to one another through hierarchical integration. In sum, historical rigor and ethical reflection are not necessarily oppositional courses, though during a swath of time in early adolescence their development appears to travel separate, but intersecting, pathways. Adolescents may get lost, or lose their interest along the way without a pedagogy that allows them to work out for (and among) themselves where they are going in both their analysis and their judgment, where they sit and where they stand.

One question in need of study is when or whether growth in historical understanding benefits from moments of disorientation—not regression but temporary disequilibrium where students are afforded the space to struggle with decisions made in the past and the choices they themselves face as civic agents and narrators of the past. Perhaps the best we can do is slow that process down, help students feel safely puzzled about why people made the choices they did. We cannot be certain whether all historical thinking might reflect this synergetic interpenetration of historical agency and ethical reflection, but we feel that the demands for pure disciplinary rigor may be an emotional mismatch for a developmental phase when early adolescents are struggling to find a moral voice, whether in the symbolic order of the past or the present. For this reason, we need to consider not only how social and historical decentration develops, but also how, during the arc of adolescence, contextualization becomes an appropriate lens through which human action, agency, and autonomy come more clearly into focus (Selman & Kwok, 2010).

An analogous case can be found in the field of literacy, where youth face a crucial and difficult transition, shifting from *learning to read* to *reading to learn* (Chall, 1983). Students begin by learning the formal qualities of text: decoding letters, words, and sentences, while developing simple comprehension skills. Somewhere around age 9–10 there comes an inflection point where students need to develop deep comprehension to understand what they are reading, by integrating information, making inferences, and building up background knowledge (Snow, Lawrence, & White, 2009). Learners move beyond reading as an essential act of "simple" comprehension, regarding it as an invitation to consider author perspective and intent, persuasive voice, reader response—a space to inquire and explore.

During the era of early adolescence there may be a similarly challenging crossover between learning "simple" (conventional) morality and the capacity for historically contextualized thinking to expand students' moral as well as historical vision. As young learners begin to develop their sense of human relationships, social ethics, and moral reasoning, the language of human behavior becomes the structure on which to build their historical understanding. In other words, until adolescents are able to coordinate multiple perspectives and take a third person perspective in everyday social interactions, they are ill-equipped for the temporal leaps required of historical perspective taking. Similarly, until they can put human events into historical perspective, they are not able to morally distance themselves from decisions made elsewhere (e.g., in the past) that do not fit their conventional sense of right and wrong.

History, possibly more than any other school subject, makes apparent the reflexivity between human agency and social context (Bermúdez & Jaramillo, 2001; Seixas, 2000). The mastery of this requires an experiential recognition of one's own agency and the antecedent causes and future consequences of the choices we make in the present. At some point there is an acute awareness that an historical analysis of human actions and interactions in context, especially under conditions students can recognize as similar to their own, has personal meaning for the self, e.g., for the self's identity, perspective, and ethical choices. It is at this time that historical analysis becomes a tool students see as useful for understanding the world and their role in it, and not simply one more thing that adults think youth need to store up on. But, for history to matter, adolescents must sort out to some degree on their own, their historical identity (what is and was) and their moral identity (what ought to or should have been—and what can be). There is no such thing, really, as history for history's sake.

REFERENCES

Ashby, R., Gordon, P. & Lee, P. (Eds.). (2005). *Understanding history: Recent research in history education. Volume 4, International review of history education.* Oxford, UK: Routledge.

Barr, D. J., & Facing History and Ourselves. (2010). *The Facing History and Ourselves national professional development and evaluation project: Continuing a tradition of research on the foundations of democratic education.* Brookline MA: Facing History and Ourselves National Foundation, Inc.

Barton, K. C., & Levstik, L. S. (2004). *Teaching history for the common good.* Mahwah, NJ: Lawrence Erlbaum Associates, Publishers.

Bellino, M. J., & Selman, R. L. (2011). High school students' understanding of personal betrayal in a socio-historical context of ethnic conflict: Implications for teaching history. *International Journal of History Teaching, Learning and Research* 10(1), 29–43.

Bermúdez, A. (2012). The discursive negotiation of narrative and identities in learning history. In M. Carretero, M. Asensio, & M. Rodriguez (Eds.), *History education and the construction of national identities.* Charlotte, NC: Information Age Publishing.

Bermúdez, A., & Jaramillo, R. (2001). Development of historical explanation in children, adolescents and adults. In A. Dickinson, P. Gordon, & P. Lee (Eds.), *Raising standards in history education* (pp. 146–167). London; Portland, OR: Woburn Press.

Boix-Mansilla, V. (2000). Historical understanding: Beyond the past and into the present. In P. N. Stearns, P. Seixas, & S. Wineburg (Eds.), *Knowing, teaching, and learning history: National and international perspectives,* (pp. 390–418). New York and London: New York University Press.

Carretero, M. (2011). *Constructing patriotism: Teaching history and memories in global worlds.* Charlotte, NC: Information Age Publishing.

Chall, J. S. (1983). *Stages of reading development.* New York: McGraw Hill.

Corriveau, K. H., Kim, A. L., Schwalen, C. E., & Harris, P. L. (2009). Abraham Lincoln and Harry Potter: Children's differentiation between historical and fantasy characters. *Cognition, 113*: 213–225.

Dervisevic-Cesic, J. (1994). *The river runs salt, runs sweet: A memoir of Visegrad, Bosnia.* Eugene, OR: Panisphere.

Dulberg, N. (2002, April). *Engaging in history: Empathy and perspective-taking in children's historical thinking.* Paper presented at the annual meeting of the American Educational Research Association, New Orleans, LA.

Dunn, R. (2000). Constructing world history in the classroom. In P. Stearns, P. Seixas, & S. Wineburg (Eds.), *Knowing, teaching, and learning history: National and international perspectives,* (pp. 121–140). New York and London: New York University Press.

Freud, A. (1965). *The writings of Anna Freud: Normality and pathology in childhood: Assessments of development* (Vol. 6). New York: Indiana University of Pennsylvania.

Hartmann, U., & Hasselhorn, M. (2008). Historical perspective taking: A standardized measure for an aspect of students' historical thinking. *Learning and Individual Differences, 18*(2), 264–270.

Hartmann, U., Sauer, M., & Hasselhorn, M. (2009). Perspektive nübernahme als Kompetenz für den Geschichtsunterricht [Perspective taking as a competence for history education: Theoretical and empirical relations between subject-specific and socio-cognitive characteristics in students]. *Zeitschrift für Erziehungswissenschaft 12,* 321–342.

Holt, T. (1995). *Thinking historically: Narrative, imagination, and understanding.* New York: The College Board.

Jensen, J. (2008). Developing historical empathy through debate: An action research study. *Social Studies Research and Practice, 3*(1), 55–67.

Langer, J. (1978). Werner's comparative organismic theory. In P. Mussen (Ed.), *Charmichael's manual of child psychology* (3rd ed., pp. 773–771). New York: John Wiley & Sons.

Lee, P. & Ashby, R. (2000). Progression in historical understanding among students ages 7–14. In P. Stearns, P. Seixas, & S. Wineburg (Eds.), *Knowing, teaching, and learning history: National and international perspectives*, (pp. 199–222). New York and London: New York University Press.

Lee, P., Dickinson, A., & Ashby, R. (2001). Children's ideas about historical explanation. In A. Dickinson, P. Gordon & P. Lee (Eds.), *Raising standards in history education* (pp. 97–115). London: Woburn Press.

Lee, P. & Shemilt, D. (2003). A scaffold, not a cage: Progression and progression models in history. *Teaching History, 113*, 13–22.

Lee, P. & Shemilt, D. (2007). New alchemy or fatal attraction?: History and citizenship. *Teaching History, 129*, 14–19.

Lee, P., & Shemilt, D. (2011). The concept that dares not speak its name: Should empathy come out of the closet? *Teaching History, 143*, 39–48.

Levine, P., & Higgins-D'Alessandro, A. (2010). Youth civic engagement: Normative issues. In L. R. Sherrod, J. Torney-Purta, & C. A. Flanagan (Eds.), *Handbook of research on civic engagement in youth*, (pp. 115–138), Hoboken, N.J.: Wiley.

Lowenthal, D. (2000). Dilemmas and delights of learning history. In P. Stearns, P. Seixas & S. Wineburg (Eds.), *Knowing, teaching, and learning history: National and international perspectives*, (pp. 63–82). New York and London: New York University Press.

Reisman, A., & Wineburg, S. (2012). Ways of knowing and the history classroom: Supporting disciplinary discussion and reasoning about texts. In M. Carretero, M. Asensio, & M. Rodriguez (Eds.), *History education and the construction of national identities*. Charlotte, NC: Information Age Publishing.

Rittner, C. (2004). Educating about genocide, yes: But what kind of education? In S. Totten (Ed.) *Teaching about genocide: Issues, approaches, and resources*, (pp. 1–5). Greenwich, CT: Information Age Publishing.

Rüsen, J. (2004). Responsibility and irresponsibility in historical studies: A critical consideration of the ethical dimension of the historian's work. In D. Carr, T. R. Flynn, & R. A. Makkreel (Eds.), *The ethics of history*, (pp. 195–213). Evanston, IL: Northwestern University Press.

Seixas, P. (1996). Conceptualizing the growth of historical understanding. In D. R. Olson, & N. Torrance (Eds.), *Handbook of education and human development: New models of learning, teaching, and schooling*, (pp. 765–784). Malden, MA: Blackwell.

Seixas, P. (2000). Schweigen! die Kinder! or, Does postmodern history have a place in the schools? In P. Stearns, P. Seixas & S. Wineburg (Eds.), *Knowing, teaching, and learning history: National and international perspectives*, (pp. 19–37). New York and London: New York University Press.

Selman, R. L. (2003). *The promotion of social awareness: Powerful lessons from the partnership of developmental theory and classroom practice*. New York: Russell Sage Foundation.

Selman, R. L., & Barr, D. (2009). Can adolescents learn to create ethical relationships for themselves in the future by reflecting on ethical violations faced by others in the past? In M. Martens, U. Hartmann, M.Sauer, & M.Hasselhorn (Eds.) *Interpersonal understanding in historical context*, (pp. 19–41). Rotterdam, The Netherlands: Sense Publishers.

Selman, R. L., & Kwok, J. (2010). Informed social reflection: Its development and importance for adolescents' civic engagement. In L. R. Sherrod, J. Torney-Purta, & C. A. Flanagan (Eds.), *Handbook of research on civic engagement in youth*, (pp. 212–246), Hoboken, N.J.: Wiley.

Sleeter, C. E. (2008). Involving students in selecting reading materials. In M. Pollock (Ed.), *Everyday antiracism: Getting real about race in school* (pp. 150–153). New York and London: The New Press.

Snow, C. E., Lawrence, L. F., & White, C. (2009). Generating knowledge of academic language among urban middle school students. *Journal of Research on Educational Effectiveness* 2(4), 325–344.

Stern Strom, M. (Ed.). (1994). *Facing history and ourselves: Holocaust and human behavior resource book*. Boston: Facing History and Ourselves National Foundation, Inc.

Stoskopf, A., Bermudez, A. Hartmann, U., Selman, R. L., Barr, D. J., & Facing History and Ourselves. (2007). *An Assessment Measure for Students' Historical Understanding*. Brookline, MA: Facing History and Ourselves National Foundation, Inc.

Sullivan, H. S. (1953). *The interpersonal theory of psychiatry*. New York: Norton.

Totten, S. (Ed.) (2004). *Teaching about genocide: Issues, approaches, and resources*, (pp. 1–5). Greenwich, CT: Information Age Publishing.

Valsiner, J. (Ed.) (2004). *Heinz Werner and developmental science*. New York: Kluwer Academic/ Plenum Press.

Werner, H. (1948). *Comparative psychology of mental development*. New York: Science Editions.

Wineburg, S. (2001). *Historical thinking and other unnatural acts: Charting the future of teaching the past*. Philadelphia: Temple University Press.

CHAPTER 14

THE DISCURSIVE NEGOTIATION OF NARRATIVES AND IDENTITIES IN LEARNING HISTORY

Angela Bermúdez[1]

INTRODUCTION

What role do values and emotions play in the development of historical understanding by youth? Do they hinder good understanding? Do they foster meaningful learning? These are fundamental questions for the advancement of both research and practice. However, with few exceptions (Barton & Levstik, 2004; Hahn, 1994; Von Borries, 1994) they have received remarkably little attention in the field of research on history education. For the most part, this issue has slipped into a gap between two prominent lines of inquiry; one that focuses on the individual process of developing rational

[1] Data for this study were kindly provided by Facing History and Ourselves (www.facing.org). Data analysis, interpretation, and conclusions are the sole responsibility of the author of this paper.

abilities for historical thinking, and one that focuses on the social production and consumption of historical narratives.

CONSTRUCTIVIST RESEARCH

The first line of inquiry, influenced by a constructivist paradigm, has focused on the individual process of developing historical thinking capacities, that is, how students learn increasingly sophisticated cognitive or logical operations that underlie the development of historical understanding. Abundant work has documented how students improve in the analysis of evidence, the reconstruction of causal relationships, the analysis of change and continuity, or the coordination of different perspectives (Dickinson, Gordon, & Lee, 2001; Dickinson, Lee, & Rogers, 1984; Leinhardt, Beck, & Stainton, 1994; Stearns, Seixas, & Wineburg, 2000; Voss & Carretero, 1998; Wineburg, 2001). This research has left us with rich models of how children and adolescents develop the competencies needed to engage in 'rigorous historical inquiry' that are useful to plan and guide teaching (Barton & Levstik, 2001; Portal, 1987; Shemilt, 1980).

However, while this line of inquiry prioritizes the analysis of rational abilities that allow students to understand the complexities of historical events, it tends to marginalize the analysis of students' management of personal values and emotions. A common rationale is that values and emotions may cloud rational understanding and hinder any attempt to think about the past in a disciplined way. Critics argue that an unqualified integration of moral questions and emotions in the analysis of the past may distort both the authenticity of historical experience, and the rigor of historical thinking (Lee, 1984). As a result, this tradition tends to regard values and emotions as obstacles to rationality, and thus to give them little attention in its research agenda.

SOCIO-CULTURAL RESEARCH

A second line of inquiry, often influenced by socio-cultural perspectives, has investigated the processes of production and consumption of historical narratives (Alridge, 2006; Barton & McCully, 2010; Carretero, 2011; Ferro, 1984; Luczynski, 1997). This tradition tends to reposition sentiments and values at the core of historical consciousness formation, and is therefore more attentive to the role they play in how individuals make meaning of the social narratives they consume.

Studies in this tradition emphasize the narrative structure of historical knowledge and the connection between knowing the past and constructing identities in the present (Barton & Levstik, 1998, 2004; Barton & McCully, 2010; Hammack, 2010; Wertsch, 1997). Indeed, the social construction of historical narratives has been a typical vehicle used to build cohesive identities, whether they are based on nationality, ethnicity, gender, or political beliefs. This connection between historical narrative and identity has important implications as it recognizes that a) narratives usually have an ideological and political sub-text, b) because they are meant to build identity, they have deep personal meaning for individuals, and c) historical accounts are cultural artifacts that communicate diverse and often controversial views of the past. Altogether, this explains why the role of values and emotions is highly visible in this body of work. More importantly, these studies point to important ways in which values and emotions are mobilized in the process of teaching and learning history. We have learned, for example, that historical understanding involves a fluid interplay between a student's sense of past and present, society and self, or that students engage with a variety of historical narratives in active processes of negotiation that involve actions of endorsement, editing or challenge that may support their developing identities (Barton & McCully, 2010).

A shortfall of this line of inquiry, however, is that because it has directed the focus of attention to the social processes of production and consumption of narratives, less attention has been paid to students' development of the skills of historical inquiry, precisely what the first line of inquiry focuses on. Yet, in order to fully understand the role that emotions and values play in historical understanding, we need to examine how they interplay with historical thinking capacities, and how they shape or modulate their use. This paper intends to contribute to these questions.

Summing up the knowledge afforded by each line of inquiry, we know that learning history involves three interactive dimensions: a) disciplined thinking about the past, b) ethical reflection, and c) emotional engagement (Stoskopf & Bermudez, 2012). They are not one and the same thing, but they interact in the learning process. In this interaction, values and emotions may indeed set obstacles to a mature understanding of the past. However, it is also reasonable to think that they may open avenues for a reflective and transformative understanding of the past and the present. In any case, for good or for bad, the interplay between values, emotions and historical thinking needs to be better understood than we currently do. For example, if values and emotions generate obstacles for a disciplined thinking about the past, how does that happen? How do these obstacles operate? What other roles may values and emotions play? How can they be harnessed to support the development of deep and relevant understanding?

In this paper I explore the interplay between these three dimensions in a case in which values and emotions hold back the development of sophisticated historical understanding. In order to do so, I analyze excerpts of an online discussion among high school students about a historical controversy, which illustrates how the management of values and emotions shapes students' historical thinking, and more in particular, their use of core historical concepts such as change and continuity, perspective coordination or causality.

CONTEXT OF DATA

The data analyzed in this paper come from the archives of the Twilight L.A. Forum, an online discussion among a group of 120 high school students from different socio-cultural backgrounds.[2] They met in 2002 to discuss about issues of justice, discrimination, and violence around the 10th anniversary of Los Angeles "riots" (1992), which followed the non-guilty verdict of the police officers accused of beating Rodney King.[3]

One of the discussion threads involved 20 students arguing about the roots of current racism in the experience of slavery, and the role of historic legacies and memory. A particularly contentious issue developed regarding how to locate the incidents of 1991–1992 in relation to the past. Students invoked different narratives about the role and significance of the past in the present, and more in particular, about when and how it is appropriate to bring up the past in order to explain current affairs.

The excerpts presented here are a good example of a discussion gone bad, one in which participants evoke popular stereotypes without questioning or complicating them. In this sense, they illustrate a case in which personal values and emotions set "obstacles" for sophisticated historical understanding. These data were selected precisely because they provide a unique opportunity to examine these "obstacles," and *how* they operate in students' process of thinking and arguing[4].

DISCURSIVE-RHETORICAL FRAMEWORK

At first sight, all that students seem to do in this discussion thread is talk past each other. However, if we look carefully, we find a rich and intricate process of negotiation of meaning and identity at play, which seems to modulate how students *use* the historical thinking capacities at their disposal. This process of negotiation sets in motion a social dynamic of conversation and learning in which students cannot be seen as individual thinkers, but rather as thinkers-in-relation-to-others. Situated in context, learning history

---

[2] Facing History and Ourselves. www.facing.org

[3] Rodney King is an African-American citizen who was brutally beaten by L.A. Police Officers in 1991, when he was arrested for speeding and was detected as having consumed drugs. Four police officers were tried in a state court a year later and found not guilty (1992). The announcement of their acquittal sparked the 1992 uprisings in Los Angeles. A later federal trial for civil rights violations (1993) convicted two of the officers, and awarded King 3.8 million in damages.

[4] Due to restrictions of space and the particular purpose of this paper, I do not discuss the various pedagogical interventions that teachers initiated in response to the discussion between students.

amounts to *thinking-and-talking-about-the past-with-others-in-the-present.* In doing so, students engage in discursive activities of negotiation, affirmation, recognition and contestation around competing social narratives, value conflicts, and power differences. As we will see, these discursive activities intertwine with the processes of historical thinking.

Theories of discursive and rhetorical analysis offer a particularly useful lens to examine this social dynamic, allowing one to dissect the various discursive activities that compose it, as well as to reconstruct the meaning of the interactions between participants. I will draw upon the following specific propositions of discursive-rhetorical theory which suggest different ways in which culture, social context and relationships, and with them, values and emotions, shape students' historical thinking.

Rhetorical stances—A foundational idea in this approach is that thinking consists primarily a process of arguing with others (or with yourself). Billig (1987) claims that the ideas expressed by an individual are modeled on outward dialogue, rather than on internal structures of the mind. In the process of arguing individuals adopt different 'rhetorical stances' depending on whether their arguments *expose* certain ideas that others take for granted, *justify* personal beliefs that are disregarded by others, *challenge* what others believe or claim, or *resist* meanings and labels imposed on them. These concepts are helpful to unveil the discursive content of arguments.

Narrative—Narratives reflect the cultural systems of representation and construction of meaning that are particular to historical times and cultural contexts (Hall, 1997). Individuals draw upon these cultural narratives in order to make meaning of social events (Haste, 1993). In the process of conversation, where multiple narratives collide, participants negotiate with each other the meaning and trustworthiness of the different accounts. Thus, a key task in the analysis of the social dynamics of learning is to reconstruct the larger social narratives invoked by participants, in which their thinking and arguing are embedded. This analysis provides insight into why different elements of a controversial issue have more or less significance for different participants, and how certain connections between elements are established, broken or mitigated.

Positioning—Narratives make certain identity categories available that allow participants to position themselves and others as being this or that kind of person (Harré & van Langenhove, 1999). In conversation, individuals engage in a variety of "discursive activities" through which they negotiate the implications that historical accounts and knowledge have for their personal and collective identities, as well as for their interpersonal and social relationships. Harré's concept of "positioning" is helpful to analyze the involvement of the self in the process of argumentation. As Harré and Moghaddam (2003) claim, the self that participates in dialogue is reconstructed in the process. While the individual brings a sense of self to

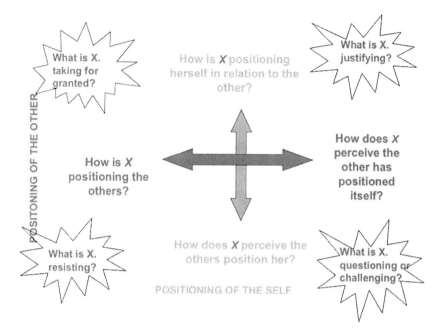

FIGURE 1. Discursive Rhetorical Analytic Model

the conversation, it is constantly redefined with others through the process of arguing. Consequently, another key task in the analysis of the social dynamics is to examine how the participants in the controversy relate to one another through the content, meaning and purpose of their arguments.

Figure 1 illustrates the analytic model used for the subsequent analysis.

DATA ANALYSIS

The following analysis focuses on the later portion of the discussion thread in which students argue about when and how it is appropriate to bring the past to explain current events. The analysis of rhetorical stances showed that prior to that, the controversy had divided pretty strongly into two different discourses. One sustained that racism is a sore *reality* that has its roots in a long history of oppression of the African American population, and other minorities (Latinos and Native Americans). These participants argued that racism is still alive in current social inequalities, stereotypes and discrimination that mark the life of these minorities. The other discourse sustained that racism is a self-perpetuating *fiction*, resulting from black's (and other minorities') resentment against white people. According to these students, racism remains alive in the racial tension created by the attitude of African Americans who blame their problems on white people.

NARRATIVES AS THE LARGER CONTEXT OF MEANING

In the following excerpt of the online discussion students begin an argument about how to locate the incidents of 1991–1992 in relation to the past. As we see, students invoked very different narratives about the role and significance of the past in the present, which led to a heated controversy.

Right Winger[5]
In a nutshell, the riots were minority groups protesting white men doing their job and defending their lives against a black felon. That's what I think.

Kit Koi
One thing to remember is that the Rodney King Verdict was not the entire reason for people to react the way they did; it was also from oppression they had felt for quite some time then. This incident may just have been the breaking point.

The contrast between these two postings highlights how the students organize the time framing. RightWinger attributes the L.A riots to the action of "minority groups" who protest "white men doing their job." His explanation is thus bound to the present. It is the clash between the responsibility of white men (who do their job in spite of the risks it brings) and the felony of blacks what gave rise to the riots. Kit Koi provides a very different account. "People" were reacting to something larger that the verdict. The L.A. events were "the breaking point." Drawing upon this metaphor, he portrays the uprisings as one fragment of an ongoing process, but a fragment with a special potential to change the state of affairs. The distinctive features of these two accounts continue to build up in following interaction.

Jessie
In case you didn't know the Rodney King incident was an opportunity. Many people came out of their shells to fight for what they believed in. […] Did you know that the Mexican-Americans had to suffer through stereotyping of being trouble makers during the zoot-suit riots?

Jfoxx
Zoot Suit Riots had nothing to do with the King beating.

---

[5] All names used are the alias names that the students chose to use in the Forum.

Jessie

For your information it wasn't just the blacks that were involved in the riots. it was everyone in LA and the Zoot Suit Riots did have something to do with it. the hispanic community has been through a lot. the Zoot Suit Riots were a root of why the hispanics jumped in.

Jfoxx

I really don't care what you say about Zoot Suit Riots. How long ago was that?!? How many people that lived in the 90s were in it?!?!? Please let me know.

Jessie

So what if the Zoot Suit Riots were a long time ago? the woman's rights to vote were also along time ago, and that's still a motivation for women to come out and do what they have too.

Jfoxx

When you say, "The Zoot Suit Riots are the reason why the hispanics jumped in," are you saying that the riots were a good thing???

Jessie builds over the images of continuity suggested by Kit Koi. His notion of "opportunity" extends the idea that the L.A events were a "breaking point," a moment of change in a long historical process, and provides a concrete image for this abstract idea: Hispanics "came out of their shells." He also explains how the experience of people in the past *motivates* the action of people in the present, no matter how long ago, and offers an example of this relationship: the suffering of Hispanics at the time of the Zoot Suit Riots were at the root of why they jumped in during the L.A riots.

JFoxx challenges Jessie's temporal connection. He implies that the events that happened long ago cannot motivate people in the present that did not live through them. In this way, JFoxx supports RightWinger's claim that the events of the present are to be explained within the present, and explicitly states a discontinuity between this and the past. The last posting by JFoxx reveals what is at stake: making a causal (or motivational) connection between past and present seems to justify the riots and the actions taken by minorities. Therefore, proposing causal explanations is "morally inappropriate."

In contrast, Jessie and Kit Koi articulate a different form of this relationship between past and present. Similar experiences occur across time, past events are the root, cause or motivation of actions taken in the present, and present events are the culmination of long-term processes. Therefore, according to this narrative it is appropriate and necessary to bring up the past in order to understand the present and to guide your action in it.

TABLE 1.   Contrast Between Narratives of Past and Present

Narrative of Continuity	Narrative of Discontinuity
• Current events are rooted in the past	• Current events result from relationships bound to the present
• Current events are a breaking point in a long-term process	• Current events are to be explained within the present
• Past causes and motivates the present	
• Causal connections with the past are necessary to understand the present	• Causal connections with the past justify current events
• References to the past are necessary and appropriate	• References to the past are unnecessary and inappropriate

NARRATIVE, VALUES AND EMOTIONS IN HISTORICAL UNDERSTANDING

The analysis of narratives is fundamental to the understanding of the social dynamics of conversation and learning because it reveals the larger context of meaning of any particular topic, and of the distinct positions espoused by participants. As Gee (1999) points out, the positions expressed by individuals in a controversy draw upon and contribute to an ongoing social conversation, and the meaning of any individual position has to be appreciated within the context of these larger debates. In the Twilight L.A. Forum, the discussion between students invokes a larger controversy at the heart of American culture. On the one hand, the narrative that highlights *continuity and fluidity between past and present* resembles the Black Heritage discourse. On the other hand, the narrative that highlights discontinuity between past and present, and a present-future orientation, resembles the American Dream discourse.

The point is that individuals don't construct meaning as the result of lonesome reflection, but drawing upon and transforming existing social themes and motifs. Since these cultural narratives reflect larger social and moral values that provide the language to think, feel and talk about particular issues, they "prescribe" and "proscribe" how individuals make sense of and speak of controversial issues (Haste, 1993). However, as the Twilight Forum evidences, participants invoke different or competing narratives that enter into conflict and become the object of discursive negotiation in which individuals play an active and creative role. As Billig (1987) argues, discourse serves precisely the rhetorical function of allowing individuals to dispute established accounts of an event or experience and to expose the two sidedness of a phenomenon.

This kind of analysis recognizes a relationship between knowledge and power while capturing the active role of the individual in constructing and negotiating meaning. Importantly, it implies a departure from the notion of a unitary discourse or "episteme" put forward by Foucault (1972), according to which discourse operates in an unarguable manner. While for Foucault discourses operate to obliterate argument in the interest of domination, Billig (1987) proposes that discourse involves "endless ideological dilemmas" that manifest in themes and counter-themes (or what he labels as "*logos and anti-logos*"), and afford the possibility of criticism, "finding the gaps in orthodoxies" (1987).

POSITIONING: BUILDING ON NARRATIVES TO NEGOTIATE IDENTITIES

The different narratives about past and present create identity categories that students mobilize to position themselves and each other, and thereby, achieve different constructions of self and other identities. As the following excerpts show, the continuous and discontinuous images of past and present implicate very different identity definitions, in particular, of how they define the boundaries and qualities of "I," "We," and "They."

NubiaQueen

2 Jfoxx: You have no idea what AFRICANS AMERICAN go through in your day 2 day lives. your ancestors brought us over here to do your dirty work they raped our women and killed our men. they would burn us inside of our own houses and the would hang our men right in front of our children. (…). African American men are always being followed by police officers or we are always accused for something that we never did. (…) the white man took this land away from the NATIVE americans and from MEXICANS. (…) Look into your ancestor background and you'll probably find out that you ancestors killed mine.

NubiaQueen blends the historic and the contemporary self. In describing what African Americans go through in their daily lives, Nubia moves with fluidity between present and past. She stresses the continuity between instances of violence and oppression in the past, and instances of discrimination and stereotype in the present. A continuous "we" is victimized over time. In her account, the past is something that lives with you.

Nubia also blends the individual and collective self. The boundaries between I/We are fluid. The experience of her ancestors is her own experience. The inclusive pronouns "we/us" blend her with her ancestors. She is part of a "collective actor" that was "brought over here" and "raped." Likewise, using the same collective voice, she positions JFoxx as one of the "whites" that in the past enslaved and harmed her people. In both cases, her ancestors and JFoxx's ancestors are collective agents defined by race, rather than by individual features. Above all, NubiaQueen positions her self as "African American" and JFoxx as a "white-men."

Now lets see what Nubia's discourse provokes in JFoxx, and how he manages identities in a very different way.

Jfoxx

Slow down there Queen Latifa. My ancestors had nothing to do with anything. Before you start making assumptions about my heritage, can you guess where my heritage starts?? My grandpa came from England. He was born and raised there until he was about 10 years old. He then moved to Hawaii and then into the states. There he had my dad and my dad had me. So what was that about me doing stuff to your ancestors? Assumption is the mother of all screw ups, and you just proved it.

Wow, I never knew you are in slavery. ... I'm sorry you feel that I had blacks do my "dirty work," and that I "raped" the black women and "killed" the black men. I have no recollection of myself ever doing that. I laugh when I hear people like you talk about what you go through because of slavery. You have never been through it. If you have, then you would be how old?? rrriiiiggghhttt.

JFoxx resists how NubiaQueen positions him. He responds with detailed facts about his ancestors, to prove that they were not involved in slavery and thus, he cannot be blamed for it. In this way, highlighting their individuality, JFoxx makes a clear distinction between his ancestors and the general category of "white men."

He then turns to challenge NubiaQueen's definition of herself. With irony he questions Nubia's use of the collective voice, and her adoption of the experience of slavery and victimization of her ancestors as her own experience. And by pointing to the chronological impossibility of her account, he positions NubiaQueen as ignorant or confused: "You have never been through slavery—If you had, then you would be how old??"

Lets add another voice in the discussion to get a sharper vision.

Holiday

Nubien queen: you need to grow up and face the facts. slavery is over!!! you can make your life whatever you want but it is going to go nowhere if you blame everything on slavery and the white man doing all these things to your ancestors ...you will amount to nothing in your life if you cant let the past go. it's good to know the past, but don't live in it.

Holiday positions NubiaQueen as a childish person that does not want to accept reality. "You need to grow up and face the facts," says Holiday, and reinterprets Nubia's account of the past as a strategy of "blaming everything on slavery" instead of taking charge of her own life and moving forward. Echoing Jfoxx, Holiday establishes a sharp discontinuity between the memory of a collective experience in the past (slavery) and the advancement of the individual in the future. There is a distinctive effort to connect the

TABLE 2. Contrast Between Constructed Identities

Fluid Identities	Discrete Identities
• Blends individual self (I) and collective self (We)	• Sharp distinction between individual self (I) and collective self (We)
• Blends historic and contemporary self	• Distinguishes historic and contemporary self
• Identity defined by collective categories such as race	• Identity categories defined by individuality
• Past is an indelible heritage that lives with you.	• Past is a burden that you must let go of.

idea of "not letting go of the past" with the idea of "not making anything of yourself in the future."

Taken together, these excerpts depict how the different narratives about past and present implicate very different definitions of self and other identities. While some students were criticized for being "too stuck in the present," others were criticized for being "too obsessed with the past." To some, the past is an indelible heritage that lives in you; to others it is something you must let go of. The following table synthesizes the contrasting features of two different constructions of identity that result from the discursive process of positioning.

Considering this larger context of social meaning, it is evident that the opposing discourses made some students more inclined to situate the LA Riots within a long-term process of social and race relations, and others more inclined to focus on the weight of individual's actions and choices in the present. This difference does not necessarily suggest a more developed capacity for systemic thinking or understanding of historical causality on the part of some students, or the lack of such capacity on the part of other students, but rather, a rhetorical use of whatever capacities students have.

Similar instances manifested throughout the Forum, in which the limits to students' performance in the historical analysis did not seem to result from an actual lack of capacity. This becomes evident when student performance is analyzed across topics or across audiences. Students displayed certain capacities, more or less developed, when analyzing one topic or conversing with some participants. Yet, these capacities seemed to "disappear" when discussing other topics or when the conversation involved different participants. It appears that the discursive context of conversation informed how students *made use* of their cognitive tools for historical inquiry. Consider the following extracts as an example.

Holiday

If people feel so mad and angry about the whites taking over land that belonged to the "Native Americans" or angry at whites because "we" brought the "african americans" over then why don't you people do something about it. (…) if you feel so mad about these occurrences that happened hundreds of years ago, then why don't you live in africa?!?!? people like you need to pack up your stuff and get out of wonderful america and move to africa. after a few days of hunger, desease, war, death, i can just about guarentee that you will want to come back

Jfoxx

Holiday: Exactly!! Many people fail to realize that if it wasn't for the taking over of the land, we would not be here right now. And Queen over here is mad at the fact that she is alive. None of anything would be here if the rebel English hadn't come over. Queen wouldn't be here if they didn't bring over slaves. Therefore, she is mad that she is alive. Go figure. I agree with you that if she is so mad at America and that it's a "white man's world" then yea, pack up your things and get out. America, to me, is the best place in the world, and she is complaining about it. I wonder if she thinks September 11th was okay? Apparently so if she thinks what she speaks.

NubiaQueen's criticism of the past offended Jfoxx and Holiday. Their sense of national (collective) identity (as American-whites) was touched: Both Holiday and Jfoxx challenge Nubia to be "consistent." If she hates America and its progress, if she is so stuck in the past, she might as well go to Africa! Responding to her offense, JFoxx positions NubiaQueen as ungrateful, loosing sight of what she has today: being alive, and living right here and now in "wonderful America." JFoxx uses the force of an extreme formulation, "I wonder if she thinks September 11th was okay?" to augment what is at stake in the discussion.

These prior postings do not necessarily display sophisticated historical thinking, but what is interesting is the shift in argumentative strategy that happens here. In JFoxx's view, Nubia owes her existence and place to the hard work of the "English rebels" who took over this land and brought over slaves. In this instance, Nubia is questioned for "failing to realize" the connections between present and past, and both JFoxx and Holiday switch to a discourse that establishes such continuity: they owe what they have today to what others did in the past. This switch appears to be motivated by the discursive function it serves. While the narrative of discontinuity served to undermine the validity of Nubia's claims about white racism, the narrative of continuity serves to position her as ungrateful and unpatriotic and thus undermine the morality of her stance. The changing discursive context calls for, or inhibits, different levels of sophistication in students' historical thinking.

POSITIONING, VALUES AND EMOTIONS IN HISTORICAL UNDERSTANDING

As we see in these excerpts, the discourses that students invoke imply assumptions and values to which their identity is deeply connected. These constitute social referents that become objects of discursive negotiation through which the individuals define their sense of the social world (what is normal and good, what is wrong or abnormal, what is desirable, what is relevant, and what is irrelevant). Further, in arguing for or against a position, participants define who they are, who is the other, and how they want or not want to be interpreted. Davis & Harré denominate this process "the discursive production of selves" (1990). Their claim is that individual's subjectivity (the persons' understanding and experience of their social identity, the social world, and their place in it) is generated through discursive practices. As the data show, the discursive production of selves is achieved through positioning and repositioning oneself and the other in ways that claim or attribute values, beliefs, intentions, needs, and boundaries. The variety of positions also allows contracting different sorts of relationships with each other. These claims and attributions, as well as the relationships established and broken, spark complicated emotional responses. Much of what goes on in the social dynamic of learning history is, inevitably, what Gee (1999) calls "recognition work", or the task of getting our selves, our relationships and our realities recognized in particular ways.

DISCUSSION AND CONCLUSION

The online discussion excerpts analyzed in this paper evidence the presence of values and emotions in historical understanding. Called on stage in the processes of narrative meaning making and discursive production of selves (which are inevitably intertwined with the process of learning history), values and emotions operate as referents, filters, and signifiers of what students encounter "anew" in the classroom. Yet, values and emotions get mobilized in a variety of ways, depending on the particular context of conversation, on the audience, and on the discursive functions that participants try to achieve through the discussion of a specific historical topic.

The claim advanced in this paper is that simultaneous with the intellectual dynamic of analyzing and generating disciplined understanding of a historical topic, there is a social dynamic at play in which participants negotiate narratives, meaning, and identities. This social dynamic modulates the intellectual dynamic of the group, and the particular ways in which participants make use of their thinking capacities. The management of causality by Jfoxx and Holiday in order to achieve specific discursive functions is only one illustration of this phenomenon. In this case we can not conclude that students lack the cognitive capacity to perform more complex thinking, but rather that the engagement in critical-thinking-with-others raises a conflict in terms of identity and social standing that they need to manage. In other words, learning and understanding history is situated in social and inter-personal relationships that motivate thinking, and bear its consequences.

This paper also shows that considering both the intellectual and the so-cial dynamics involved in learning about the past sheds new light over the role of values and emotions in historical understanding. Methodologically, this highlights the importance of drawing upon two different theoretical lenses and analytic models. The constructive-developmental model, which has been widely used in the field, is necessary to shed light on the intellec-tual dynamic of historical thinking. In turn, a discursive-rhetorical model, along the lines of the one presented in this paper, is necessary to shed light on the social dynamic of narrative meaning making and negotiation of identities. Used in conjunction, these two models afford the possibility of better understanding how these two dynamics intertwine, and thus, how disciplined thinking, values and emotions interplay with each other. The following table proposes what each approach could contribute to a more comprehensive understanding of the process of learning history.

Finally, a consideration for further research is due. In the examples ana-lyzed in this paper, values and emotions developed into obstacles that held

TABLE 3. Comparison of Theoretical Lens

		Discursive Rhetorical Approach	Constructive-Developmental Approach
Object of Analysis	⇨	Intellectual dynamic: Process of reflexive inquiry to construct reasonable explanations	Social dynamic: Process of construction & negotiation of narratives, meaning, identity, and social positions
Focus	⇨	Thinker as a developing individual	Thinker-in-relationship-to-others
Location of meaning Construction	⇨	Individual's reflection	Dialog & negotiation
Source of Structure of Arguments	⇨	Individual's cognitive operations/Internal structures of the mind	External structures of dialog/purpose and consequences of talk
Illuminates	⇨	Logical structure/intellectual tools underlying to participants understanding analytic complexity & explanatory quality	Larger context of conversation and meaning needs & vulnerabilities of thinking-about-the-past-with-others-in-the-present
Overlooks	⇨	Social-relational context that embeds thinking and learning	Development and quality in reflection used to advance augmentation

back the analytic potential of the historical thinking tools and capacities that students had, and hindered the intellectual quality of the conversation. This was the result of the particular way in which the intellectual and social dynamics fed each other. Yet, in further research, it is necessary to examine other ways in which the two dynamics may interact with each other, such that values and emotions can be harnessed to support the development of deep, relevant and purposeful historical understanding.

REFERENCES

Alridge, D. (2006). The limits of master narratives in history textbooks: An analysis of representations of Martin Luther King, Jr. *Teachers College Record, 108*(4), 662–686.

Barton, K. C., & Levstik, L. S. (1998). "It wasn't a good part of history": National identity and students' explanations of historical significance. *Teachers College Record, 99*(3), 478–513.

Barton, K. C., & Levstik, L. S. (2001). *Doing history. Investigating with children in elementary and middle school.* Mahwah, NJ: Lawrence Erlbaum Associates.

Barton, K., & Levstik, L. (Ed.). (2004). *Teaching history for the common good.* Mahwah, NJ: Lawrence Erlbaum Associates, Inc.

Barton, K. C., & McCully, A. W. (2010). "You can form your own point of view": Internally persuasive discourse in northern Ireland students' encounters with history. *Teachers College Record, 112*(1), 142–181.

Billig, M. (1987). *Arguing and thinking: A rhetorical approach to social psychology.* Cambridge, UK: Cambridge University Press—Editions de la Maison des sciences de l'Homme (2nd. Ed. 1996).

Bermudez, A., & Stoskopf, A. (2012). *Values and emotions: Cultural tools for deep and purposeful learning of history.* Manuscript in preparation.

Carretero, M. (2011). *Constructing patriotism. Teaching history and memories in global worlds.* Charlotte, N.C.: Information Age Publishing.

Davies, B., & Harré, R. (1990). 'Positioning: The discursive production of selves.' *Journal for the Theory of Social Behaviour, 20,* 44–63.

Dickinson, A. K., Gordon, P., & Lee, P.J. (Eds.) (2001). *Raising standards in history instruction. International review of history education, 3.* London: Woburn Press.

Dickinson, A. K., Lee, P. J., & Rogers, P. J. (Eds.). (1984). *Learning history.* London: Heinemann Educational Books.

Ferro, M. (1984). *The use and abuse of history: or How the past is taught to children.* London: Routledge. French Edition, *Comment on raconte l'Histoire aux enfants à travers le monde entier.* Paris: Payot, 1983.

Foucault, M. (1972). *The archaeology of knowledge.* London: Tavistock Publications.

Gee, J. P. (1999). *An introduction to discourse analysis theory and method.* New York: Routledge.

Hahn, C. (1994). Controversial issues in history instruction. In M. Carretero & J. F. Voss (Eds.), *Cognitive and instructional processes in history and social sciences,* (pp. 201–220). Hillsdale: Erlbaum.

Hall, S. (1997). *Representation: Cultural representations and signifying practices.* London: Sage Publications.

Hammack, P. L. (2010). Youth, historical narrative, and the legacy of political conflict. *Human Development, 53,* 173–201.

Harré, R., & Moghaddam, F. M. (2003). *The self and others: Positioning individuals and groups in personal, political, and cultural contexts.* Westport, CT: Praeger.

Harré, R., & Van Langenhove, L. (1999). *Positioning theory: Moral contexts of intentional action.* Oxford: Blackwell Publishers.

Haste, H. (1993). Morality, self and sociohistorical context: The role of lay social theory. In G. G. Noam & T. Wren (Eds.), *The moral self* (pp. 175–208). Cambridge, MA: The MIT Press.

Lee, P. J. (1984). Why learn history? In: A. Dickinson, P. J. Lee, & P. Rogers (Eds.), *Learning history* (pp. 1–19). London: Heinemann Educational Books.

Leinhardt, G., Beck, I. L., & Stainton, C. (Eds.). (1994). *Teaching and learning history.* Hillsdale, N.J: Lawrence Erlbaum Associates.

Luczynski, J. (1997). The multivoicedness of historical representations in a changing sociocultural context: Young Polish adults' representations of World War II, *Culture & Psychology, 31,* 21–40.

Portal, C. (Ed.). (1987). *The history curriculum for teachers.* London: The Falmer Press.

Shemilt, D. (1980). *History 13–16 evaluation study.* Homes McDougal.

Stearns, P. N., Seixas, P., & Wineburg, S. (2000). *Knowing, teaching, and learning history: National and international perspectives.* New York: New York University Press.

Von Borries, B. (1994). Moral judgment: On relationships between interpretations of the past and perceptions of the present. In M. Carretero & J. F. Voss (Eds.), *Cognitive and instructional processes in history and social sciences,* (pp. 339–356). Hillsdale, N.J.: Erlbaum.

Voss, J. F., & Carretero, M. (Eds.). (1998). *Learning and reasoning in history. International review of history education, 2.* London: Woburn Press.

Wertsch, J. W. (1997). Narrative tools of history and identity. *Culture and Psychology, 3,* 5–20.

Wineburg, S. (2001). *Historical thinking and other unnatural acts.* Philadelphia: Temple University Press.

CHAPTER 15

COMMENTARY

Student Identities in the Present and Their Historical Understanding of the Past: Complications and Implications for Future Research

Alan Stoskopf

In this chapter I argue for greater collaboration among educational practitioners and researchers in defining and actualizing what constitutes the powerful teaching and learning of history in a transnational world. I make this case by first reprising some of the key themes and issues raised in six papers presented in this volume. I then situate this discussion within an international context of ongoing research and scholarly discourse as it pertains to how factors in students' present day lives shape their understanding of the past. After highlighting some of the current trends in this research I suggest another type of research agenda that speaks more directly to issues facing educators attempting to incorporate the disciplinary tools of historical analysis into their pedagogical practices.

All papers reviewed underscore how student ideas of the past are influenced by their notions of how they position themselves in the present. As

History Education and the Construction of National Identities, pages 221–235

alluded to in each of the papers, these ideas need to be reckoned with if students are to develop a more nuanced and complicated understanding of how they evaluate choices and events by historical actors. The formal accounts represented in text book narratives and nationalistic images, discussed respectively in Foster (2012) and Carretero et al. (2012), speak to the remarkable persistence of certain story lines explaining the birth of a nation or the justification of entry into war. Grever (2012) and Bermudez (2012) underscore how informal and social affiliations serve as sources for strong emotional and value laden attachments to narratives about the past. Finally, Reisman and Wineburg (2012) and Bellino and Selman (2012) challenge researchers and practitioners in history education to think if it is desirable or even possible for students to "transcend" their "subjective" selves in order to gain a deeper and more complex understanding of the past.

Stuart Foster describes the persistence of master narratives in textbooks around the world. With the exceptions of the United Kingdom and Sweden, Foster maintains that the notion of the "best story... [serves] as propaganda attempting both to reinforce ideologically constructed national identities and to appease social and political agendas in the present" (p. 49). As a counterpoint to these official story lines, Foster calls for individual teachers to provide alternative accounts to complicate the thinking of their students and encourage the kind of disciplinary inquiry that is now built into the textbooks and the national curriculum of the U.K. While acknowledging the varying political contexts history/social studies teachers operate in, no clear picture emerges on how this can realistically occur given the restrictions imposed by state mandated standards and accountability tests so prevalent in many countries around the world.

Mario Carretero and colleagues adopt a similar focus on how an official narrative or, what is referred to as "romantic history," is represented through iconic images from Argentine's past. His interview study of 80 adolescent and adult, middle class subjects reveal a common theme of transcendent and ontological conceptions of "Argentineness" that run counter to the actual historical record of nation formation in Argentina. There is recognition that strong popular and a-historical influences are at work here, which begs the unanswered question; to what extent can disciplinary approaches to the study of history provide a more accurate and sophisticated understanding of the construct of nationhood?

From the formal accounts here examined the focus shifts to the examination of informal factors that influence how students make meaning of the past for their lived identities today. Maria Grever emphasizes the challenges present in the new multicultural realties that make up urban classrooms in the United Kingdom, Netherlands, and France. In her survey study of 678 secondary school students from 12 schools in urban districts she stresses the importance of striving for the plurality of meaning and the shared under-standing of commonality when students study history in multicultural class-rooms. She maintains that the foreground knowledge students bring into the classroom about history derives from family, ethnic, and religious ties, and these often run counter to a disciplined understanding of the past. For example, she points out the differences among immigrant, Islamic students and native born Dutch students when they engage in discourses about how they understand watershed moments in European history. Grever argues that civil society requires some kind of shared understanding when explor-ing the past, and this can best come about by acknowledging different nar-ratives, as well as students learning and employing the disciplinary tools of historical investigation. One wonders if this reasonable assertion is enough to create the sense of commonality through plurality she considers essential for civil society in the 21st century.

Angela Bermudez goes even farther in exploring the social context of learning history. Her analysis of an online discussion forum among 120 American high school students discussing the racially charged Rodney King case of 1992 brings into sharp relief the role values and emotions play in how students understand and express themselves about the case and their own racial/cultural identities in relation to it. Her analysis of the transcripts reveals how many white and African American students talked past each other, relying on their respective folk understandings of social mobility and equality of opportunity over the course of American history to present their opinions about what that case meant to them today. Little evidence of measured and nuanced reasoning among the students took place, and the emotional responses and value laden comments about fairness were never deeply explored by the teachers facilitating the discussion. Bermudez makes a strong case for the reality of students' emotional and ethical selves influencing their views about the past and its relationship to students' per-sonal and social identities, but it is clear that much more research needs to take place before educators can better understand how these two domains might not just hinder historical understanding but also enhance it.

Reisman and Wineburg argue that good history instruction should en-courage students to hold in abeyance their own values and emotions when they attempt to understand events and choices made by historical actors. They assert that students need to "develop the consciousness of their own historical subjectivity, and transcend it in an effort to understand others" (p. 172). The authors believe this consciousness is best achieved through practicing the skills of disciplinary historical reading.

In their quasi experimental study of the Reading Like a Historian (RLH) curriculum the authors examined the RLH approach to historical investiga-tion, which emphasized a sequence of activities for examining and discuss-ing historical, document based questions. Their study sought to find out if the RLH curriculum intervention would promote greater self-awareness of students' own subjectivity during whole class discussions of historical documents. While the study's participating 11th grade RLH classrooms yielded statistically significant improvements in overall reading comprehension, factual recall, and historical thinking compared to traditional classrooms, only three of the 100 lessons videotaped in RLH classrooms revealed a heightened student awareness of their subjectivity.

The authors conclude that this finding highlights the need to move students beyond a binary mode of thinking about the past, where they either perceive it as a strange place obscured by arcane facts or a familiar past that mirrors issues similar to their own lives today. The authors believe this latter tendency is often encouraged by many social studies teachers in their zeal to make the past relevant enough so their students engage in historical inquiry. Reisman and Wineburg argue that this approach undermines the need to correct students' misconceptions of the past and "create classroom conditions where students acknowledged their historical subjectivity" (p. 184). The authors contend that creating classrooms where students engage in this kind of self-reflection would not just improve their historical understanding but also cultivate "humility, caution, and reason" (p. 185) essential for informed, democratic participation.

Bellino and Selman on the other hand emphasize the potential of student ethical and emotional selves to coincide with and/or enhance disciplined historical inquiry. Rather than view these dimensions as liabilities of presentist thought that need to be overcome by students, the authors suggest that for early adolescents they are important elements in their learning process. The authors ask, "what educational opportunities do we lose if we insist that adolescents learn to think on strictly differentiated disciplinary terms before they are naturally disposed to do so" (p. 194)?

Bellino and Selman explored this question through a qualitative analysis of 9th and 10th grade student responses to a question about the choice a Bosnian Serb teenager who betrayed her best friend, a Bosnian Muslim, to an extremist para military group during the inter ethnic conflict that engulfed the former Yugoslavia in the early 1990s. (The study was part of a secondary analysis of data from a larger experimental evaluation of the Facing History and Ourselves educational program). The authors analyzed 621 student responses to the question: "How would you explain what she [Bosnian Serb girl] did" (p. 195)? They discovered three kinds of moral responses to the question: valenced (positive or negative judgments of the girl's actions), neutral (non response to the question based on lack of information), and unresolved (some acknowledgment of both positive and negative aspects of the girl's actions). One of the key findings in the study was that on average, student responses were nearly two times more likely to offer an explanation based on historical understanding when they exhibited an unresolved moral judgment compared to a more valenced position.

The authors conclude that this kind of ethical reflection on choices made in the past does not "necessarily preclude historical thinking" (p. 196). While they acknowledge the dangers of either over simplifying or distancing human experiences in the past based upon on unreflective value judgments and emotional responses, they also believe that ethical reflection can have a vital place in students' historical understanding. This is especially true for early adolescents who developmentally "are struggling to find a moral voice" (p. 198). They argue there is an intersection between students' personal and social identities and the choices they make in the present with their examination of choices made in the past. How this intersection is negotiated by teachers can be done well or badly, but it cannot be ignored for history to matter for students. Indeed, this begs the question if the study of history by people of all ages must acknowledge the emotional and ethical lenses humans use to comprehend a more familiar world of the present and a stranger world of the past.

These papers echo some of the ongoing and emerging research trends in the field of student ideas and identities and historical inquiry. In the last 15 years there has been a considerable amount of research on how representations of the past influence and our influenced by students' personal and civic identities in the present. A theme that runs through this research is the recognition that in a rapidly changing, intercultural world it is necessary for students to become more self-reflective and open to investigating and evaluating competing historical narratives. There is a strong consensus among researchers that good, disciplined historical investigation is an antidote to nationalistic or binary narratives still commonplace in many classrooms. And, this "antidote" also serves as a building block for students to construct a civic identity more in keeping with an enlightened democratic impulse for a multicultural and transnational world.

Much of this research has focused on narratives presented in officially sanctioned textbooks. Sirkka Ahonen's (2001) study of history textbook narratives in Germany and Estonia before and after the fall of communism reflects this trend. Her research explored to what degree the inclusion of minorities in the narratives of a country's history altered when political regimes changed. In the case of Estonia she found that the pre-1990 Marxist-Leninist master narrative ignored the historical agency of ordinary men and women in favor of the power of impersonal forces at work. This conception of historical agency changed with the advent of democratic governments in Estonia, and the new textbooks emphasized the role of individuals "as the active agents of history" (p. 182). What did not change was the lack of inclusion of minority groups in the shaping of historical events. Instead, Ahonen maintained "the conversion of history took place as one master narrative replaced another and not as a conversion from one mode of knowledge to another, e.g. from mono-perspectivity to multi-perspectivity" (p. 183).

In the case of the absorption of the former German Democratic Republic (GDR) into the Federal Republic of Germany Ahonen notes there was a reframing of the historical narratives in the portrayal of key historical actors and groups from reactionary in the GDR era to democratic heroes in the newly westernized version of the narratives. So, Martin Luther was portrayed as a "lackey of the princes" in the GDR texts and then became a "liberator of German minds" in the post-communist era textbooks (p. 186). In both instances Ahonen argues that historical inquiry was not problematized for students; events too often were seen as black and white in both versions. Based on the German and Estonian cases Ahonen recommends a curriculum that fosters a critical community that includes alternative narratives, "where the past is both shared and multi-faceted, discussion can occur in an open space, and the future can consist of options" (p. 190). Ahonen acknowledges this direction might threaten those in power who make decisions about official textbooks and curricula, but there is no further discussion of this issue in his study.

Jan Germen Janmaat's (2006) examination of the Great Famine in Irish and Ukrainian history textbooks raises a similar issue around the need for a diversity of voices and critical views in the writing and interpreting of historical narratives. Janmaat traces evolving trajectories of the representations of these famines in Irish and Ukrainian textbooks and curricula. The Great Famine, as it has been characterized in both nations' history, has played a pivotal role in promoting a certain kind of national identity for Irish and Ukrainian citizens. In the case of Ireland Janmaat's analysis of textbook representations of the Great Famine from the 1960s onward reveals a more nuanced and complicated portrayal of the British government's role in the catastrophic events of the 1840s. Before the 1960s a predominant nationalist narrative emphasized the culpability of the British government and landlord classes in creating conditions for the famine and in their near criminal responses to it. It was a sort of "morality tale" of the victimization of the good Irish peasant by the bad British overlord. Since the 1960s accounts have become much more balanced, and contemporary writing emphasizes a more ambivalent stance toward the British government's role in the disaster, aimed at stimulating "student creativity rather than to inculcate an anti-English outlook and encourage the rote-learning of taken for granted knowledge" (p. 359).

To a more limited extent Janmaat describes a similar process in how the Ukrainian famine was depicted in textbooks during the Soviet and post Soviet eras. While there were nationalistic overtones condemning Stalin's role in targeting Ukrainian peasantry for resisting collectivization, the post Soviet era textbooks were more varied than one might expect. While none of the Ukrainian texts go so far as mentioning the collaboration of ethnic Ukrainians in the pillaging of grain depositories, they desist from stereotyping Soviet officialdom as ethnic Russians or Jews responsible for the plight. Janmaat stresses that positive developments in complicating the narratives of the famine are due in part to the greater co-operation between Ukrainian historians and teachers with their western European counterparts through such organizations as Euroclio. This is also the case in Ireland where for a longer period of time and through more involved contacts with the European Association of Teachers Irish teachers were able to deepen and diversify their approaches to the teaching of history. These international contacts and exchanges of ideas have encouraged the publishers of Irish history textbooks to provide more balanced accounts of the famine.

Janmaat's study of the textbook representations of the Great Famine in Ireland and Ukraine has an important sub-text. While not the ostensible purpose of the comparative study, there is a strong linkage between the call to problematize narratives through an informed trans-national discourse and the creation and sustainability of a democratic society. As Janmaat puts it, one needs a "conviction that diverging historical views are part of a democratic society and therefore deserve respect" (p. 368). While these two studies have been highlighted as examples of inquiry into the roles textbooks play in promoting master narratives and identity formation, numerous other studies have had a similar focus. In the United States research has been conducted focusing on the triumphalist arc of American history books (Lowenthal, 1998; VanSledright, 2008; Zimmerman, 2003) and the tendency to transform historical actors into celebrated heroes (Alridge, 2006). Nor, has romanticizing the past been confined to the United States. Other studies around the world have also discussed this common phenomenon (Akinoglu, 2005; Carretero, Jacott, & Lopez-Manjon, 2002). Almost all of this scholarship asserts that alternative narratives, inclusion of underrepresented groups in these narratives, and a general stance of interrogating narratives through critical historical inquiry will promote a democratic sensibility among learners (Barton & McCully, 2005; Phillips, Goalen, McCully, & Wood, 1999).

Along with the examination of the narratives of formal accounts there have also been investigations into the informal means by which students construct narratives about the past to inform their identity today. These informal accounts often times provide a type of resistance to the official textbooks and school curricula. Studies (Epstein, 2000; Fordham, 1996) in the United States have revealed considerable alienation among African American students to standard representations of the "march to freedom" in American history textbooks. Sources for these alternative narratives have come from family, relatives, and indigenous social affiliations within church and community groups, rather than textbooks and formal school curricula (VanSledright, 2008).

Barton and McCully's (2005) interview study of 253 students in Northern Ireland reveals fascinating patterns in how students draw upon multiple sources to attach significance and meaning to pivotal moments in Ireland's past. While there were numerous differences between ages, region, gender, and religion in how students identified with images from various periods of Irish history, one recurring feature among most students was their predilection to analogize periods of conflict in the national past to situations of community conflict today. This presents an opportunity for deeper inquiry by teachers, but Barton and McCully's interviews indicate this does not occur for most students. The authors maintain, "...students have little opportunity to engage directly the relationship between past and present. Our interviews suggest that students do make such connections on their own; without teacher mediation those connections are likely to be highly selective and uncritical" (p. 108). The authors believe that teachers' fears on how to handle the emotional responses of students prevent them from probing students' beliefs.

The importance of emotional attachments to narratives of the past is particularly highlighted in a survey and interview study conducted by Kay Traille (2007) of 124 British students aged 13–17 from urban classrooms. For students of African-Caribbean descent there was a marked emphasis on their emotional connection to historical topics pertaining to their own ancestral heritage. Yet, in responses to survey questions and in interviews many students stated their teachers were afraid of tackling issues that might pertain to issues of inequality and racism in history. Hence, students relied on their own folk references from family and community to supply counter narratives from the official text and curriculum. These narratives spoke to their needs for self-affirmation, however historically accurate or inaccurate these conceptions were. As Traille suggests, there needs to be "a better understanding of the informal versions of history that students may bring into the classroom" (p. 6) in order for teachers to be able to successfully employ disciplinary tools of historical investigation. One cannot ignore the students "cognitive and emotional conceptions about what these students think history is for" (p. 6) because if that occurs than disenfranchised students will "create historical narratives that clash with the ideals of a democratic society" (p. 8). How these conceptions can be channeled effectively in a multicultural, urban classroom intent on disciplined historical inquiry is not discussed in this study.

In a qualitative study of 70 urban, Latino high school students in an AP history class Sevan Terzian and Elizabeth Yeager (2007) also recognized the importance of informal sources as being instrumental in shaping students' conceptions of American history. However, in this study the students' views converged with the master narrative presented in their American history textbook accounts. Again, it was a narrative of the United States serving as a land of opportunity, defender of democratic freedoms, and a beacon of progress for the rest of the world throughout its history. Almost all of the Latino students were of Cuban origin. The Cuban American students' informal sources of information for history converged with the official narratives they learned in their text and from their teacher. These sources derived principally from family members, newspapers, and local media. They tended to confirm the narrative of progress and freedom and downplay controversies and issues of inequality. Their teacher also discouraged them from "dwell[ing] on episodes or issues that are morally ambiguous, controversial, or unflattering to the nation" (p. 74).

This situation yielded an opposite set of responses compared to the Traille's study. In Terzian's and Yeager's study informal sources provided the cognitive and emotional affiliations for students to identify with the master narrative on national identity rather than contest it or disengage from it. The fact that these students were from a particular ethnic community in Miami that had a unique immigrant experience is cited by Terzian and Yeager as a contributing factor in their consistent acceptance of the master narrative as an organizer for their own personal and civic identities. At the same time both Terzian's analysis of Cuban American students and Traille's study of British students of African Caribbean descent demonstrated that informal and formal accounts of a nation's history were not problematized within the curriculum or instructional practices for either group of students. Both groups did not engage in questioning the narratives they accepted. There was no active interrogation of sources that followed established protocols for historical source analysis (Donovan & Bransford, 2005; Howell & Previnier, 2001).

In all of the above cited research there have been at least tentative suggestions on how to help students develop a more sophisticated process for interrogating competing narratives of the past. Barton and McCully (2005) note in their study of Irish schoolchildren's identification with historical images that children did not just passively absorb "established historical narratives but actively construct their historical identification from a range of sources" (p. 107). This provides opportunities for teachers to engage students in these sources and begin the rudiments of historical analysis by comparing and contrasting the purposes, audiences, and contexts for the children's sources. In other words the authors seem to suggest the need to take advantage of what the students are telling them about where they get information and then build upon that, rather than discount or ignore their informal ways of "knowing" the past. Barton and McCully link this activity to the development of critical thinking skills necessary for a democratically informed citizenry.

Other studies not explicitly focused on identity formation through historical narratives also have linked specific disciplinary and pedagogical practices needed to create informed citizens for the 21st century. Keith Barton's (2001) research on American and Northern Irish students' use of "cultural tools" to shape their representations of the past is instructive. Overall, he asserts that American students rely upon chronological narratives to structure their thinking about history while the Northern Irish students focus much more on the "social and material life rather than narratives of event" (p. 901) to gain an understanding of their past. Barton acknowledges the different political and social contexts for these choices, but he stresses in the study's conclusion the need for greater research on how students in various countries appropriate culturally situated tools from their surroundings and in turn how to help students evaluate the respective strengths and limitations of these tools. According to the authors if students engaged in this kind of activity, the quality of history teaching and learning would improve far more than simply decreeing edicts from policy makers on what needs to be done in history classrooms.

Other researchers have focused on the pedagogical and content knowledge teachers need to know before effective history teaching can take hold. Kaya Yilmaz (2008, 2009) places great stress on teachers needing a deeper understanding of what historians actually do before they can model investigate practices for their students. In particular his research has revealed that most history teachers do not reflect on their own assumptions or theoretical propositions about the nature of the discipline, resulting in unexamined practices in the classroom. Yilmaz believes if teachers "become familiar with the nature of history and multiplicity of historical explanations, they can help students not only avoid accepting any claim at face value but also construct a deeper and more nuanced understanding of the past" (2008, p. 171).

In a similar vein Chauncey Monte-Sano's (2008) case study of student performance on evidence based, history essays highlighted the importance of teachers' disciplinary understanding of history. The study focused on the contrasting teaching approaches of two history teachers, where one reflected a more disciplinary approach to history and the other more of a standard school history approach. In the former case there was an emphasis on understanding history as more of an interpretive process rather than as a set story line that needed to be rehearsed. This teacher believed students should be apprenticed in "how to read and write and practice with guidance and feedback" (p. 1072). Her students showed the greatest improvement on essays that called for interpretation of historical documents using multiple forms of evidence.

This attenuated review of current research in the field of historical understanding pertaining to student conceptions of the past and disciplined historical inquiry complements many of the themes raised in the six chapters. Both the chapters and the above mentioned studies emphasize the problematic situation of having formal and informal accounts of historical narratives go uninterrogated by students. Virtually all the chapters and studies call for more disciplined intervention by teachers to rectify this process, especially given the changing transnational and intercultural environment students around the world are experiencing. Yet, I would argue there needs to be a fresh approach in how research and practice in history education moves forward to address these issues.

New partnerships of researchers and practitioners need to be formed if we are to move beyond playing the same song again and again about the lack of effective disciplinary tools employed by instructors in classrooms around the world. There now is an opportunity and critical need to bridge this researcher and practitioner "divide" by initiating new forms of collaborative inquiry that could potentially yield insights into the teaching and learning of history. I would argue that this collaborative research agenda should encompass the exploration of three essential questions germane to student identities and their ideas of the past. They are:

- To what extent are the psychological and social needs for collective identity formation compatible with the critical stance of disciplined historical inquiry?
- How can a better use be made of digital media to enhance a more self-reflective use of the cultural tools students rely on to make meaning of historical narratives?
- What are the political, economic, and cultural factors that need to be considered if a more critical stance toward historical narrative can be practiced by teachers and students around the world today?

Each of these questions will be briefly taken up within the framework of collaborative partnerships between researchers and practitioners.

The need for a sense of identity larger than oneself is one of those basic attributes that has been a signifier of our humanity throughout time. The role collective memory has played in this process has been well documented by historians and other scholars from antiquity through today (Breisach, 1994; Lemon, 2003, Munslow, 2004; Wertsch, 2002). How this need gets negotiated through history education has been fraught with tension and ambivalence. On the one hand most researchers have called for a more questioning stance of historical narratives through the practice of developing student ability in such historical concepts as evidence, causality, agency, and significance (Ashby, Gordon, & Lee, 2005; Stearns, Seixas, & Wineburg, 2001). On the other hand there is a call for teachers to help their students intellectually and emotionally identify with popular and master narratives of their nation's history in order to cement national or ethnic allegiances today (Conway, 2005). History teachers know this tension in a way that is immediate and palpable. As some of the papers referenced in this essay suggest, students bring their emotional and social selves into discussions of the past. How are those domains channeled in a way that allows for a purposeful exploration of history while acknowledging a need for students to have a sense of identification with some of the narratives or "stories" of the past? This is a formidable challenge for history/social studies teachers, one that other K–12 subject areas do not face in the same way.

This question needs to be vigorously explored by researchers in history education in the immediate future. An agenda that involves the close participation of classroom teachers in the research process is imperative. Whether qualitative and/or quantitative designs are employed in this endeavor is not so much the point as is the need for more sustained and deeper conversations to take place between teachers "on the ground" and university based researchers. These "conversations" can lay the foundation for a range of research designs. Through formal venues, as in conferences and symposia or through informal on ground or virtual meetings via social media, a richer and more textured sense of the realities of teachers' and students' lives would emerge. These, in turn, would better inform the research questions and methodological approaches designed to explore the roles personal and collective identity formation play in the ways students learn history.

The second question posed for a new research partnership with practitioners is timely on several levels. K–12 teachers encounter students every day who communicate through digital social media such as Facebook, Twitter, and a host of social networking sites on lap tops and wireless handheld devices. Today, students have more contact with each other, both face to face and virtually, and this reality should be factored into history education. The potential for a more powerful and purposeful use of this media in teaching and learning has already begun to be demonstrated across different subject areas (Doering & Veletsianos, 2008; Ketelhut, Nelson, Clarke, & Dede, 2010; Veletsianos, 2010). Students now can access primary sources through digital archives, engage in cross cultural conversations about those documents, and blog about their reflections that can be open to their teachers, classmates, and participating researchers. Exciting and interesting research agendas can be co-constructed with practitioners and researchers on how new media can aid in the building of both collaborative and self-reflective forms of inquiry by students exploring competing narratives of the past.

Finally, the very real political and economic pressures on educators who teach history in K–12 settings cannot be ignored. For reasons already stated the teaching and learning of history has high stakes attached to it that go beyond state testing mandates. The creation stories and narratives of a nation's past engage a range of stakeholders from policy makers and business leaders to school committees and community groups. Depending upon the particular country and school setting often times this means different versions of a "romantic historical narrative." In the very least the research community in history education needs to take seriously the challenges teachers face in implementing what has been termed the pedagogical content knowledge appropriate to historical inquiry. Once again close conversations with practitioners on the types of restrictions they face and the "free spaces" they have negotiated within these restrictions to provide alternative accounts for their students would inform researchers in a way that has not frequently occurred up until this point. In the very least it would create a sense of common purpose among researchers and practitioners that would benefit all who care about encouraging the powerful teaching and learning of history for today and tomorrow.

REFERENCES

Ahonen, S. (2001). Politics of identity through history curriculum: Narratives of the past for social exclusion- or inclusion? *Journal of Curriculum Studies, 33*(2), 179–194.

Akinoglu, O. (2005). History education and identity. *International Journal of Historical Learning, Teaching and Research, 5*(1), 71–81.

Alridge, D. A. (2006). The limits of master narratives in history textbooks: An analysis of representations of Martin Luther King, Jr. *Teachers College Record, 108*(4), 662–686.

Ashby, R., Gordon, P., & Lee, P. (Eds.). (2005). *Understanding history: Recent research in history education.* New York, New York: Routledge Falmer.

Barton, K. C. (2001). A sociocultural perspective on children's understanding of historical change: Comparative findings from Northern Ireland and the United States. *American Educational Research Journal, 38*(4), 881–913.

Barton. K. C., & McCully, A. W. (2005). History, identity, and the school curriculum in Northern Ireland: An empirical study of secondary students' ideas and perspectives. *Journal of Curriculum Studies, 37*(1), 85–116.

Bellino, M. J. & Selman, R. L. (2012). The intersection of historical understanding and ethical reflection during early adolescence: A place where time is squared. In M. Carretero, M. Asensio, & M. Rodríguez-Moneo (Eds.) *History education and the construction of national identities* (pp. 189–202). Charlotte, NC: Information Age Publishing.

Bermudez, A. (2012). The discursive negotiation of cultural narratives and social identities in learning history. In M. Carretero, M. Asensio, & M. Rodríguez-Moneo (Eds.) *History education and the construction of national identities* (pp. 203–219). Charlotte, NC: Information Age Publishing.

Breisach, E. (1994). *Historiography: Ancient, medieval, & modern* (2nd ed). Chicago: The University of Chicago Press.

Carretero, M., Jacott, L., & Lopez-Manjon, A. (2002). Learning history textbooks: Are Mexican and Spanish students taught the same story? *Learning and Instruction, 12*, 651–665.

Carretero, M., Lopez, C., González, M. F., & Rodríguez-Moneo, M. (2012). Students historical narratives and concepts about the nation. In M. Carretero, M. Asensio, & M. Rodríguez-Moneo (Eds.) *History education and the construction of national identities* (pp. 153–170). Charlotte, NC: Information Age Publishing.

Conway, D. (2005). Why history remains the best form of citizenship education. *Civitas Review, 2*(2), 1–10.

Doering, A., & Veltsianos, G. (2008). Hybrid online education: Identifying integration models using adventure learning. *Journal of Research on Technology in Education. 41*(1), 23–41.

Donovan, M. S., & Bransford, J. D. (Eds.) (2005). *How students learn: History in the classroom.* Washington, DC: National Research Council.

Epstein, T. (2000). Adolescents' perspectives on racial diversity in U.S. history: Case studies from an urban classroom. *American Education Research Journal, 37,* 185–214.

Fordham, S. (1996). *Blacked out: Dilemmas of race, identity, and success at Capitol High.* Chicago: University of Chicago Press.

Foster, S. (2012). Re-thinking history textbooks in a globalised world. In M. Carretero, M. Asensio, & M. Rodríguez-Moneo (Eds.) *History education and the construction of national identities* (pp. 49–62). Charlotte, NC: Information Age Publishing.

Grever, M. (2012). Dilemma's of common and plural history. Reflections on history education and heritage in a globalizing world. In M. Carretero, M. Asensio, & M. Rodríguez-Moneo (Eds.) *History education and the construction of national identities* (pp. 75–91). Charlotte, NC: Information Age Publishing.

Howell, M. & Prevenier, W. (2001). *From reliable sources: An introduction to historical methods.* Ithaca, NY: Cornell University Press.

Ketelhut, D.J., Nelson, B.C., Clarke, J., & Dede, C. (2010). A multi-user virtual environment for building and assessing higher order inquiry skills in science. *British Journal of Educational Technology, 41*(1), 56–68.

Janmaat, J. (2006). History and national identity construction: The great famine in Irish and Ukrainian history textbooks. *History of Education, 35*(3), 345–368.

Lemon, M. C. (2003). *Philosophy of history: A guide for students.* New York: Routledge Taylor & Francis Group.

Lowenthal, D. (1998). *The heritage crusade and the spoils of history.* Cambridge: UK Cambridge University Press.

Monte-Sano, C. (2008). Qualities of historical writing instruction: A comparative case study of two teachers' practices. *American Educational Research Journal. 45* (4), 1045–1079.

Munslow, A. (2004). *The Routledge companion to historical studies.* New York: Routledge.

Phillips, R., Goalen, P., McCully, A., & Wood, S. (1999). Four histories, one nation?: History teaching, nationhood and a British identity. *Compare, 29*(2), 153–169.

Reisman, A., & Wineburg, S. (2012). Ways of knowing and the history classroom: Supporting disciplinary discussion and reasoning about texts. In M. Carretero, M. Asensio, & M. Rodríguez-Moneo (Eds.) *History education and the construction of national identities* (pp. 171–188). Charlotte, NC: Information Age Publishing.

Stearns, P., Seixas, P., & Wineburg, S. (Eds.). (2000). *Knowing, teaching, and learning history: National and international perspectives.* New York: Basic Books.

Terzian, S. G. & Yeager, E. A. (2007). "That's when we became a nation": Urban Latino adolescents and the designation of historical significance. *Urban Education, 42*(1), 52–81.

Traille, K. (2007). Teaching history hurts. *Teaching History. 127*(June), 1–7.

VanSledright, B. (2008). Narratives of nation-state, historical knowledge, and school history education. In Kelly, G.K., Luke, A., & Green, J., (Eds.). *What counts as knowledge in educational settings: Disciplinary knowledge, assessment, and curriculum* (pp. 109–146). *Review of Research in Education.* Thousand Oaks: SAGE Publications.

Veletsianos, G. (Ed.) (2010). *Emerging technologies in distance education.* Athabasca, AB: AU Press.

Wertsch, J.V. (2002). *Voices of collective memory.* New York: Cambridge University Press.

Yilmaz, K. (2008). Social studies teachers' conceptions of history: Calling on historiography. *The Journal of Educational Research, 101*(3), 158–175.

Yilmaz, K. (2008–2009). A vision of history teaching and learning: Thoughts on history education in secondary schools. *The High School Journal,* (December/January), 37–46.

Zimmerman, J. (2005). *Whose America?: Culture wars in the public schools.* Cambridge: Harvard University Press.

SECTION 4

MUSEUMS AND IDENTITIES

CHAPTER 16

HISTORICAL NARRATIVES IN THE COLONIAL, NATIONAL AND ETHNIC MUSEUMS OF ARGENTINA, PARAGUAY AND SPAIN

Marisa González de Oleaga

> Trend is not destiny.
> *René Dubos*

THE NATION RETREATS

As institutions, history museums have made significant contributions to creating and expanding nation-states and legitimizing neocolonial expansion. In the sphere of museums, narratives about a supposed shared past allow a new reality to be shaped: one based on the values and interests of an imagined community. Yet at the same time, these narratives enlarged the im-

History Education and the Construction of National Identities, pages 239–256

age of the metropolis through cultural pillage and economic exploitation (Coombes, 2004; Duncan, 1991; Earle, 2006; González de Oleaga & Monge, 2008; Kaplan, 2010; Macdonald, 2003; Preziosi, 2004). The museum's artifice consisted in passing off one version of history as history itself and in presenting the aspirations of rising social sectors as common values (Cohen & Toland, 1988). Within these new "temples of knowledge," narratives and objects mutually supported each other to show that what was on display was the product of true and unquestionable scientific knowledge (Giebelhausen, 2011; Hillier & Tzortzi, 2010). Within this strategy of domination, great efforts were made to associate the nation-state with the images and ideas of authority and culture, and to compare what could not be integrated within this logic with anarchy, strangeness and otherness (Arnold, 1969; Said, 1983). The national history museum has been among the institutions that have made a major contribution to promoting, spreading and legitimizing the state's homogenizing discourses while silencing—or deliberately covering up—other experiences. In Latin America, repeated visits to the national history museum have played an important role in the "emotional education" of school children for generations. These visits, along with lessons on the country's history and commemorative dates (Carretero, 2011; Carretero & Castorina, 2010; Escudé, 1990), were part of the collective experience of the past century.

The crisis of the state and the devaluation of national identities that the world has experience over the past decades (Clifford, 1988; Dubin; 2010; Heartney, 2004; Mitchell, 2004; Simpson, 2001; Walsh, 1992) has brought up a new question: how can history be taught in these new times of globalism and multiculturalism? Ethnic narratives have been presented as alternatives which in many cases have replaced grand national narratives. However, unidimensional representation might not be the main issue. In museums things from the past are not merely represented, but justifications are made, hierarchies are constructed and actions are defended from a contemporary viewpoint. In fact, realities or ways of perceiving, understanding and experiencing reality are created (Austin, 1962; Butler, 1990, 1993, 1997; Derrida, 1992).

Because of the potential transcendence of historical narratives, the discourses that circulate within museums must be critically analyzed from the point of view of the relevant disciplines. But more importantly, they must also be reviewed from a political/ideological perspective (Todorov, 1993). Museums are spaces for socialization, education and for the creation of identities. Just as the question of what to include and how to organize school curricula in history is discussed—along with the question of how to deal with certain prickly subjects like colonization and colonial looting—the same debate could be taken to the museum. Given the current international political scene, one in which the traditional—national identities—coexist with the new—ethnic and supranational identities—or one in which major challenges must be confronted, it is useful to ask what the purpose would be of promoting national loyalties through the teaching and circulation of historical narratives in schools and museums. What other type of identities could history museums represent or encourage?

On the one hand, there is the option of promoting the construction of ethno-nationalist identities. This has been a popular idea in Latin America of late, even in countries marked by European immigration such as Argentina and Uruguay. The nation-state, as it was conceived of and constructed in the middle and end of the 19th century—and maintained until the 1990s—worked to eradicate ethnic and cultural difference or at the very least, to relegate such difference to the private sphere. Hasn't the "nation" been a social and ideological prosthesis of the elites, one used to try to crush other identifications such as ethnic identities that now reappear in a sort of "return of the repressed" (Smith, 1995), as soon as the state's protection begins to flag? Since the state began its retreat, the least-favored members of the community have found reasons to justify their claims and protests through these other forms of identification. Yet the instrumentation or the strategic use of these identities does not necessarily make them the best or the most functional options for global citizenship. In the case of museums, ethnicity has flowered and institutions related to the indigenous world (and other minorities) have proliferated.

Ethnic identities could be one way out of this national dilemma: a way to construct new citizen identities in a global world. The other alternative could involve creating and spreading supranational identities. The history of Latin America could serve as an example. In spite of the fact that supranational appears to be a trend that began in the last century and grew particularly strong over the past few decades, the colonial world was a supranational reality conceived of in Europe, a fact that deserves attention. To what extent could this type of identification—which appeals to a new community based on its common history and language—substitute national identity? What are the consequences of constructing this global citizenship? Could the transition from national history to regional history benefit citizens or would it merely represent a minor modification in what it represents while leaving the foundations of this representation intact?

With my analysis, I would like to show that at issue is not only what is represented but also the way in which it is represented. Because it is not the nation but its representation that is at stake, I will analyze the Museo Histórico Nacional de Buenos Aires, whose permanent exhibit attempts to provide a contemporary version as an alternative to more conservative or traditional historical narratives of national life. Since national identities apparently coexist with ethnic ones, I will then analyze an ethnic museum, el Museo Jacob Unger of the Fernheim Mennonite colony in Paraguay's

Chaco Region. Finally, I will examine the narratives that circulate in a co-lonial and colonialist museum, el Museo de América in Madrid. I propose that these museums share a common view and an organized imaginary structure, based on the description provided by Timothy Mitchell (1988, pp. 18–23). In spite of their differences in scale, they all share a common perspective, that of an "external observer." This is a sort of eye of God. With-in this structure, all of the exhibits mentioned above conceive of identity (national, ethnic or colonial identity) as a palpable, visible entity. Yet this "divine perspective"—as well as the essentialist conception of identity—is not presented as a way of understanding reality or identification, but as the only "true" way of doing so. It is this misunderstanding, in which the part is taken as the whole, which goes against a more democratic version of global citizenship. If I am successful in this analysis and I manage to explain the similarities of the historical narratives of the different museums (national, ethnic, and colonial), I will then make some suggestions on how historical narratives can contribute to this global citizenship. Yet the problems that are created by national history museums never end: how can we preserve their documentary role as the product of a period while reducing their place as monuments in society? (Lord, 2007). In Buenos Aires, the bicen-tennial exhibition room at the MHN reveals a potential strategy.

SAME GAMES

Museo Histórico Nacional, Buenos Aires, Argentina: New heroes and old tombs

The Museo Histórico Nacional (MHN) has also been a school pilgrim-age for generations of Argentines. Since 1897, it has been housed in an Italian-style building located on one of the slopes of Parque Lezama, where Pedro de Mendoza supposedly founded Buenos Aires in 1536. The prop-erty is known as the "British Estate" because it belonged to a British fam-ily until 1857. Both the building and its garden have a clearly European air, which is quite surprising given that it is a national history museum (Di Liscia et al., 2010).

For nearly a century, only minor changes were made in terms of the museum's organization and collections. The exhibition had a strict chron-ological order and a predictable theme-based organization: the Colonial Room, the Room of the British Invasions, the Room of Independence, San Martín's Bedroom, the Rosas Anteroom, and the Room of Rosas and his Times. The MHN took on a nationalist role, constructing the country's past from the colonies through national organization and summarizing the his-tory of the nation without interruptions or conflicts. Until just a few years ago, a nationalist vision of Argentine history predominated, with its quota of heroes and tombs. Even in 1997, the museum's objective was stated as follows: "to recover the mythic space where the cultural awareness of our people is consolidated," (Faillace, 1997) in clear allusion to the divisions of the past. In 2004, museum director Juan José Cresto again demanded that the museum select exhibition objects that would represent and defend "the national being." (Di Liscia et al., 2010).

It appears that much has changed since 2005 when an archeologist with a PhD in history, José Pérez Gollán, took over as museum director. He had been exiled in Mexico during the country's last military dictatorship. The museum is now organized around the issue of violence and it has a clear objective: stable, inclusive democracy. The permanent exhibition is located in a small yellow room. San Martín's chamber and the replica of the door into his home in France can be found at the entrance. The room notes that Argentine history started with the indigenous population (10,000 years ago) and ended with the return to democracy (1983). A series of "altarpieces" separated from one another by large, transparent screens present different historical periods, allowing the visitor to view the entire historical process in layers. The screens generally show anonymous individuals who symbolize the abstract national community: locals playing the card game *truco*, Peronists showing their loyalty to the general on Día de la Lealtad, immigrants arriving to the port of Buenos Aires, a terrorist attack in the 1970s. The only individuals who can be recognized in the oversized figures are José de San Martín and Jorge Rafael Videla.

Visitors to the museum can choose between two itineraries. In the visit that begins to the right of the entrance, there is an overview of Argentine history from 1810 to 1976, focusing on the country's development and expansion, but particularly on its moments of crisis. The itinerary that starts to the left of the entrance leads visitors down a path from the colony to the armed groups of the 1960s and 70s. Groups ignored by politics are included here: indigenous people, women, workers, immigrants, and students. Their interventions are legitimized—even when violent—as just causes. The fact that this part of the museum is off to the left is undoubtedly intentional, and this path ends with a confrontation between the guerrilla forces and the military. In the center of the museum, at the end of the exhibition, no matter which itinerary is chosen—that which begins to the left or right—the visitor finds herself before the last picture (which can be viewed throughout the exhibit) in which a vibrant multitude celebrates the return to democracy in 1983. The glass case displays a head scarf of the Madres de Plaza de Mayo, an issue of the magazine *Humor*, a copy of the human rights report *Nunca más*, pins with the insignia of human rights organizations and ballots for the Justicialist and Radical parties.

If nationality, in the traditional historical accounts, was a political event with a moral tone, here is the result of a social, economic, cultural and ideological process with a lengthy history, one that goes back to the first inhabitants, as if nationality demanded a revision of all of these stories in order to come to terms with its legacy. Individual subjects do not have a very important role in national construction, but so do workers, immigrants, indigenous people, women, and all of those traditionally excluded from this construction. Although San Martín, the "saint with a sword" appears, the heroes of yesteryear must now coexist with these majorities. Political violence is acknowledged as an endemic illness of modern Argentina, but different types of violence are distinguished: the violence exercised by the authorities versus that of the militants. This violence of the excluded is also part of the country's national history and thus deserves a place in the museum's exhibits. The European legacy of the country's elites is presented in a cultural mosaic with the local and the indigenous. This emphasis on the value of the country's own contribution becomes particularly clear in the ironic way in which the material related to Peronism is organized.

The permanent exhibition of the MHN today marks a profound change in the contents of the exhibition. However, there is something in these narratives suspiciously similar to the previous ones, like the tendency towards maniquaeism and moral judgment. It is as if the museum were required to indoctrinate visitors one way or another, instead of circulating multiple narratives and incorporating other ways of organizing them.

Museo Jacob Unger. Filadelfia, Paraguay: Nature and Culture

The Museo mennonita Jacob Unger (MJU) of the Fernheim colony in Paraguay is a community museum and a good example of the kind of ethnic museums that have been so popular in the past few decades. It was founded in May 1957 by a teacher who believed it was necessary to "gather and preserve objects" and use them as an educational resource.[1] The museum is organized in two different disconnected floors of the "Colony House," one of the first four buildings of the community.

The ground floor houses the pioneer room. The exhibit has two guiding principles. One is technological and depicts the way in which the tools of Mennonite technology evolved, from butter churns to the colony press, from candles and kerosene lamps to the electrical installations. The other guiding principle, that of daily life, involves everyday objects: clothing, personal belongings, clocks, and pictures of the colony leaders throughout its history. Daily life has its own particular rules, which follow a peculiar grammar: from porcelain to tin and from tin to steel. In the first glass display cases, porcelain dishware is exhibited under lock and key, along with other objects. The Mennonites brought the porcelain to remember where they came from but they

---

[1] An article in the daily Mennoblatt, May 1957, reproduced in the brochure of the Jacob Unger Museum.

had no trouble substituting it for tin plates, the modest equipment that the Colonization Society provided for each Mennonite family. Since they were able to accept their new conditions and work hard, they managed to notably improve their lifestyle, as seen by the press, the electricity, the hospital alarm and the books published in the colony. No reference is made to life in the colony today; instead, the exhibition ends without a clear temporal marker, as if there were no need to show the current-day community or its success. The prosperity of Fernheim is clear as soon as one steps foot in the colony.

The first room in the upper floor has remains from the Chaco War (1932–1935). Grenades, different types of ammunition and wood cross-es carried by the troops all point to war as the only context in which the Paraguayans can be defined. Bearing in mind that the Mennonites are a pacific group, this association seems significant and far-reaching. It is not surprising, then, that in the drawings of indigenous children, Paraguayans always appear as soldiers while the Mennonites are sketched as merchants (Redekop, 1980: Appendix A). The indigenous population is represented by objects such as axes, baskets, ceramics, textiles, and in the case of the Ayoreos, by arms and trinkets. The predominant criterion for the selection of the handicrafts on display seems to be how eye-catching each item is. There are no texts explaining the indigenous world. Few differences are established among the different indigenous communities. As was the case in the world's first natural science museums, here the texts that accompany the ceramic works provide only the name of the person who donated the piece or the place where it was found (Classen & Howes, 2006; Macdonald, 1998). The Ayoreos deserve special mention because they were the most belligerent group in the region since the founding of the colony (Zanar-dini & Biederman, 2006). A small sign details the murder of a Mennonite family, the Stahls, by the Ayoreo Indians (1947). The ages of the murdered children and husband are listed. Ethnographic materials are classified in a similar way as the local fauna. The glass display cases that show birds, mammals and reptiles simply list the name of the animal shown. Materials are organized according to a formal logic: all of the feather headpieces are grouped together, as are the hats and the fiber bags, regardless of whether any of these objects had everyday use or were sacred. Nothing is said about the conflict over the land between the indigenous people who had lived here long before the colonizers arrived; no mention is made of the fact that the colonists believed that they were purchasing empty lands. Nor is mention made of the threat that the colonists represented for traditional Ayoreo life and for their hunting traditions.

As I mentioned earlier ethnic identities could be an alternative to the increasingly obsolete national identities. However, there are no major changes or novel aspects in the representation of ethnic identities, only minor modifications. The Mennonite ethno-nationality is a stable identity over time because it is based on inalienable values: faith, work and unity. The Mennonites define their identity as a performative one: we are who we are thanks to what we do. For this reason, identity is more associated with a process than with a specific event, although the diaspora—the act of leaving Russia, in the case of the ethnic groups represented in the Jacob Unger Museum—is what sets off the narrative. The subjects that can be identified in the exhibit are not individuals but families, pioneers in a hostile ecosystem who construct their historical epic. Just as there is a Mennonite identity, there are other apparently stable identities that result from activity: the Paraguayans and war, the amalgamated indigenous people and nature. In fact, these other identities so roughly sketched allow the Mennonites to distinguish themselves as a pacifist group (unlike the Paraguayans) and with technical capabilities (unlike the wild indigenous people).

Museo de América de Madrid (MAM), Spain: Imperial Nostalgia

Madrid's Museo de América was created by decree in 1941, two years after the end of the Spanish Civil War. Until then, the rich collections of the New World wandered from one national museum to the next. The museum is situated in an emblematic area of the city, at the intersections of the Avenida de los Reyes Católicos and Arco de la Victoria. The museum entrance is kitty-corner from this building, which commemorates the triumph of those who rose up, setting off the Civil War. The spatial layout gives us an idea of the museum's initial orientation: it served the purposes of a state that wanted to use its historic relations with Latin America to highlight its status as a neocolonial metropolis (González de Oleaga, 2001). The museum opened in 1965 in a building reminiscent of a baroque convent; it was closed for reforms in 1981 and was not officially inaugurated until 1994, when the current collection went on display. The Museo de América, opened during democracy, is a heir to Franquismo. Yet the new national government and the regional and municipal administrations have expressed no interest in resignifying this unpleasant legacy, which clearly extolled Spain's contribution of language and religion to the colonies. In fact, the 1994 inauguration of the museum was accompanied by a 92-meter watchtower that commemorated the discovery, conquest and colonization of the continent. This Faro de Moncloa "sheds light on the buildings beneath it,"[2] that is, on Museo de América, further emphasizing its colonial bias (González de Oleaga & Monge, 2008).

The museum has five central themes: knowledge of America, the reality of America, society, religion and communication. It is clear that the museum attempts to present a vision of unity, an almost natural one, in spite

---

[2] This is the comment included on the Faro's website, www.farodemoncloa.com, which is sponsored by the Madrid municipal government. Accessed on September 15, 2010.

of the evident diversity, which is nonetheless a visual feature that visitors cannot overlook. The entire exhibit is traversed by two guiding principles: one extols the Spaniards' technical progress, which pushed the metropolis to the top of the imperial power, while the other defends unity within diversity as part of the conquest and colonization (González de Oleaga et al., 2011a,b). In the first case, it is about moving from the myth—the first fantasy-filled representation of America[3]—towards Logos—the satellite map reproductions of the planet. Thanks to science and technology, Spain conquered America and the museum allows us to "truly" understand these realities. In the second case, it is the move from Babel, from the geographical, cultural and ethnic variety and diversity, to the unity that was provided by the Spanish language, a tool for progress in the world today. In this two-fold itinerary, the Spaniards are always represented by language; they have a voice, one that describes, tells and narrates. In contrast, the indigenous people are represented by objects, generally different types of clay pots.

Different human groups participated in the work towards continental unity, and these demographic contributions appear in the room entitled "Mankind." There, Africans, Asians and Europeans are integrated within Latin America without any trouble, with the natural ease of an organized trip. Not a word is said about violence, power, submission, domination or resistance (Price & Price, 1995). In terms of slavery, which is represented by objects in a glass case, reference is made to "African emigration," and the rest of the panels in this room are a clear attempt to show that the demographic debacle in Latin America was the result not of the conquest but of the wars of independence. Maps and charts point out that the conquest of North America was more traumatic in demographical terms than that of Latin America.

Throughout the exhibit, there is a visible tension between the acknowledgment of diversity—ethnic, cultural and religious—and the emphasis on how these differences are merely a question of appearances because deep down, we all belong to the same species. In the room with the "society" exhibit, which is divided according to the "vital cycles" as if it were a natural history museum, different rites are all treated the same: a Catholic communion, an indigenous initiation rite, a Jewish bar mitzvah and a fight among punk groups. In the religion room a documentary explicity states that "(...) Regardless of their ethnic or cultural background or the place where they live, men have always looked to religion for solutions to problems that are and have always been universal." At the end of the exhibition, there is a room on communication where two documentaries are shown. One is about indigenous languages and shows indigenous peoples talking about of their myths of origin. The speakers are framed in a shot

---

[3] The museum always makes reference to "America," competing for hegemony in the naming of the continent.

with scrolls in the background. In contrast, the documentary on castellano (Spanish, according to the museum) is a procession of writers who speak of the advantages of the language, with images brimming with rhythm and modernity (González de Oleaga, Bohoslawsky, & DiLiscia, 2011).

The relationship between Spain and America is historical. There is no reference to the current ties between the country and the continent, and the fact that the museum does not mention the national construction of these countries (which could suggest the end of Spanish domination) is noteworthy. The museum seeks to represent Hispanic America but it does so on the terms of the colonizers, using the language of the old metropolis. Hispanic Americans from the past and future are not represented. Everything related to the indigenous world, a world that is alive in many countries of the continent today, is portrayed in black-and-white photographs. In contrast, everything related to Spain, Europe or Western society appears in brightly colored pictures.

There is mention of (or to put it another way, there is no way to ignore) linguistic, ethnic and religious diversity, which is then transformed into formal features that are superimposed on the shared essence, that of human-kind. This exercise, which is repeated constantly throughout the museum, responds to the need to make Spain into the mediator or translator of the "others." It can take this privileged role for two reasons. First, because the others, the Hispanic Americans, are different in some way, though not in terms of their essence. Secondly because Spain, thanks to its common language and culture as well as its scientific knowledge can play this role of mediator within the international community. According to the museum, cultures are different responses to the same human need (Sahlins, 2008). Yet these responses can be classified according to a standard of development. The most evolved responses, the technically most sophisticated ones, are better. If there is one thing that characterizes the Museo de América it is its colonial bias, but it also shares the idea of a stable identity over time. Neither the post national nor the transnational seems to have a chance in this sphere.

We have seen the cases of a historical representation of a continent, of a nation, and of an ethnic group, and all have more similarities than differences. In the case of the MHN, we saw how the heroes of yesteryear were substituted for new ones, thus inverting (but not subverting) the official discourse. We could say, then, that new cards have been added to the game, or that some have been taken out and replaced with others but the game itself remains the same. We shall now see the rules of this game and evaluate how to subvert these rules in order to allow for new possibilities.

OTHER GAMES

The three museums analyzed have many things in common in spite of their differences. In all cases, reality is conceived of as a coherent, organized entity that is waiting to be re-presented by the historical narratives. There is no mediator between the observer and the observed; the interpretation that is essential to all historical texts is never shown to visitors and the narrative is not historicized. The MHN, which clarifies that its exhibit offers only part of the story, a single perspective or point of view. In spite of this clarification, however, the exhibit is organized based on a supposed criterion of scientific truth. There is one reality and one true story that must be adapted to what is real. In addition, in all of these museums, identity is a stable, limited, coherent entity. As if there were no question as to the existence of beings known as Paraguayans, Argentines, Mennonites, indigenous or Spaniards. These are presented as closed identities, without acknowledging the fact that it is the museum that is recreating them by naming, representing and signifying them. At the Museo Histórico Nacional, nationality is the natural and almost obligatory result of the action of different social subjects throughout history: an amalgamation of collective subjects who have traditionally been left aside. Something similar occurs at the Mennonite Museum and at Museo de América. In the first, "being a Mennonite" is also the result of the heroic efforts of the pioneers whose work, faith and unity consolidated this "way of being" for future generations. In an exercise that is less transparent but just as evident, Museo de América defines being Spanish as the sum of the actions taken to civilize the inhabitants of the New World over the past few centuries. The emphasis is on the colonial period, but at the end of the museum, the communications room presents today's apotheosis of the common language and culture. In all of the examples, identity is represented as something natural and inherited, as a way to distinguish oneself from the "others." These identities are the natural, unique and necessary result of a historical process excluding any other alternative.

In each of these representations, identity as a stable entity is part of a legacy, passed on from the previous generations. Yet within this transfer, the relationship that must be maintained is implicit. There is a demand to remain loyal to this inheritance: inclusive and determinately democratic in Argentina; heroic and hard-working in the case of the Mennonites and finally, supposedly maternal and civilizing in the Spanish case. I would like to point out the importance of this essentialist way of configuring identities, which appear as a product of the past that delineate and mandate behaviors in the present. Inheritance is not conceived of as something the subjects must resignify, incorporate or respond to, but as something to which they must be faithful, something that must be maintained (Hassoun, 2006)

In terms of the role of the others, identities are defined by the rule of opposites in all of the cases presented here: "we are what they are not" or to put it another way, the others must be redefined and minimized in order to be able to define one's own identity. We are democratic and egalitarian, says the Museo Histórico in Buenos Aires, and despise the oligarchic republic that buried the country's true history. We are pacific, hard-working believers, say the Mennonites in their museum, not like the Paraguayans or the warring indigenous peoples. We are (because we were) the avant-garde of Europe; we possess the science and technology that allowed us to incorporate a new world to the one we already knew (not like the indigenous people of these lands, enveloped in their internal skirmishes) and we are a nation that took our spiritual legacy to America (to establish a contrast with the materialism of the Anglo-Saxons). In all cases, the definition of identity is threatened by "the other," who must be plotted against, segregated and reduced to a mere caricature.

Now, how can the identities or identifications required for collective actions be presented without falling into the temptation of essentialized identities? By historicizing the historical narratives of museums and denaturalizing the supposed essence of identity. How can this be done without falling into the duality of the MHN, which clarifies that the knowledge of the museum is only temporary but then constructs narratives based on (supposedly) unquestionable affirmations? By doing exactly the opposite of what is done in the permanent exhibition. Instead of presenting a finished version of knowledge, we can show the seams and the stitches of the narrative, its biases and partialities, starting with the conditioned but instrumental role of the museum itself. Unquestionably, this would mean submitting the historical narratives of museums to a *mise en abyme* (Basu, 2007, p. 54), i.e. the acknowledgement that it is only one of many perspectives of knowledge. This does not mean showing that national, colonial or ethnic identities are false, only that they are constructed. This way, identities are not true or false: they are only appropriated or inopportune for the stated purposes. Hints of this can be found in the temporary exhibit on the bicentennial of Argentina's independence at the Museo Histórico Nacional de Buenos Aires. The exhibit shows how the images of the nation are a creation of the museum's first director Adolfo Carranza. The portraits of two of the most important *próceres*, José de San Martín and Mariano Moreno, were painted by the Chilean Pedro Subercasseaux following Carranza's detailed instructions. The "reality effect" (Barthes, 1967) stems from complex lighting and from important artistic details that made the country's founding fathers into the secular saints of the nation. Similarly, in order to present the process of nationalistic construction, the museum selected two large paintings: "El Cabildo Abierto del 22 de Mayo de 1810" ["The Open Cabildo of May 22, 1810"] and "El Himno Nacional" ["The National Anthem"] which are reprinted time and again on sheets, books and magazines. The effectivist staging of these works was better serve the national education agenda of the elites, for teaching the masses of school children and immigrants. The museum's ironic twist on the narratives inherited from the past involves a dramatization whose objective, as indicated by Hayden White (1992) in a reference to N. Frye, is to undermine "the normal expectations regarding the type of resolutions provided by organized history in other modes" (the romance with heroic archetypes, in the case of museums).

There is another way to break or alter the representation of museum identities that does not involve depriving visitors of that place for recognition and difference that is so essential for collective action (Appiah, 1991; Bennett, 2007; Spivak, 1988): work based on flows and connections. This would involve organizing exhibits around connections instead of national or ethnic entities. If there is no essence, there can be no objective position from which to discern it, only perspectives that vary according to the observer's position. This would mean presenting connections, but not connections that actually exist: connections that the viewer can establish and which can be acknowledged by the museum (Hetherington, 1997). These are flows that encourage reflection and establish the museum as a "contact zone" (Clifford, 1999; Pratt, 1992). For example, instead of speaking of Mennonites and indigenous people, the types of communities and community ideals of the El Chaco population could be presented as a museum topic. On the one hand, some inhabitants have individualist practices such as private property, while others take action based on a communal perspective, i.e. extending ownership of the land to the entire community. A division of this kind would reveal what subjects such as Mennonites and indigenous people, previously represented as different, irreconcilable groups, have in common. A different division that allows other aspects of reality to emerge, to enter into dialogue and establish connections.

Another possibility is presented by Ayse Caglar (1997; Macdonald, 2003), who states that "person-object relations as these exist in space and time" (Caglar, 1997, p. 180) and applies these to the networks of relations that have been created through these objects. This means not having to present communities as established entities, but instead showing fluid, malleable and rich connections that could favor global citizenship. One of the problems of letting the objects tell micro-stories is that the destruction of all grand narratives could destroy all signs of power and domination (Lord, 2007).

The museum not only imposes a way of organizing and understanding reality; it is also based on a specific sensory economy (Alpers, 1991; Bennet, 1999, 2010; Classen & Howes, 2006; Foucault, 1970; Mitchell, 1988). It is evident that the museums referred to here prioritize seeing as the superior sense. All of the exhibits concentrate on "seeing" the past, observing history. There is no mention of other ways of approaching what is real. A critical assessment of the narratives of history museums must necessarily address this, not to establish the superiority of a different sensorial order but to discover how its viewpoint was naturalized, i.e. to clarify that way of seeing the world as an exhibit. This is the only way to access other perceptual orders (Classen & Howes, 2006, p. 219).

The level of success in implementing these novel approaches has varied (Macdonald & Basu, 2007), but all attempts have broken with the traditional ways of organizing narratives in museum exhibitions. This has worried historians such as Tony Bennet, who wonders whether these "perpetual perceptual revolutions" (Bennett, 2007, p. 54) will end up turning museums into spaces for the educated elite, that is, for those with a symbolic capital sophisticated enough to allow them to understand the museums. However, Bennett indicates in reference to Bourdieu (Basu, 2007, p. 68; Bennett, 2007, p. 66), that repetitive practices (not ideas) are what change behaviors. A museum that opts for new activities and practices, one that moves visitors and surprises them, will contribute to changing or questioning these deep-rooted conceptions about "us" and "them." It is highly likely that a museum or exhibitions of this kind will meet with initial resistance (just as the codes of modernity met with opposition) but predictably, over time, new subjectivities will be created.

In such a museum, history would no longer be the representation of what has occurred. Instead, it would be an enactment that favors dialogue, communication and openness to difference, a sort of "shared incompetence," (Macdonald & Basú, 2007, p. 16), or of different competences whose common aspects are revealed. This enactment historicizes legacy and perceives reality as a sort of appropriation that depends on the viewer's experiences. It thus moves from a notion of truth to one of uncertainty and invites another kind of subject, one who is less assertive and more responsible. These new subjects are responsible because they know that what they say has political ramifications; what is said can affect others, and the one who speaks must answer for this. Their version is not a product of truth but a choice of a perspective or position. These responsible subjects base their actions on the belief that it is impossible to establish definitive knowledge, impossible to translate difference or take this part for the whole. They are, then, subjects who know that all knowledge involves invoking the other, the one who is different, in order to problematize that distance. It would involve not invoking truth as a way of adapting an underlying order of what is real but instead utilizing an operative truth, a vocabulary that serves human activities. Truth is more of an attitude towards others than a position in terms of the non-human (Rorty, 1997). What should perhaps motivate us now is not the interest in deciphering reality itself but the desire to find better ways of relating to the world—and this includes the numerous cultural universes of the planet.

REFERENCES

Alpers, S. (1991). The muşeum as a way of seeing. In I. Karp & S. D. Lavine, *Exhibiting cultures. The poetics and politics of museum display* (pp. 25–32). Washington-London: Smithsonian Institution Press.

Appiah, K. A. (1991). Tolerable falsehoods: Agency and the interests of theory. In J. Arac & B. Johnson (Eds.), *The consequence of theory* (pp. 74–83). Baltimore: John Hopkins University Press.

Arnold, M. (1969). *Culture and anarchy.* Cambridge: Cambridge University Press.

Austin, J. L. (1962). *How to do things with words.* London: Routledge.

Barthes, R. (1967). The discourse of history. *Comparative Criticism, 3,* 7–20.

Basu, P. (2007). The labyrinthine aesthetic in contemporary museum design. In S. Macdonald & P. Basu (Eds.), *Exhibition experiments* (pp. 47–70). London: Blackwell.

Bennett, T. (1999). Speaking to the eyes: Museums, legibility and the social order. In S. Macdonald, *The politics of display. Museums, science, culture,* (pp. 25–35). London: Routledge.

Bennett, T. (2007). Exhibition, difference and the logic of culture. In I. Karp, C. A. Kratz, L. Szwaja & T. Ybarra-Fausto (Eds.), *Museum frictions. Public cultures/global transformations,* (pp. 46–69). Durham and London: Duke University Press.

Bennett, T. (2010). Civic seeing: Museums and the organization of vision. In S. Macdonald (Ed.), *A companion to museum studies* (pp. 263–281). Oxford: Wiley-Blackwell.

Butler, J. (1990). *Gender trouble: Feminism and the subversion of identity.* New York: Routledge.

Butler, J. (1993). *Bodies that matter: On the discursive limits of 'sex.'* New York: Routledge.

Butler, J. (1997). *Excitable speech. A politics of the performative.* London: Routledge.

Caglar, A. (1997). Hyphenated identities and the limits of 'culture.' In T. Modood & P. Werbner (Eds.), *The politics of multiculturalism in the new Europe: Racism, identity and community,* (pp. 169–185). London and New York: Zed Books.

Carretero, M. (2011). *Documentos de identidad. La construcción de la memoria histórica en un mundo global* [*Identity documentes. The construction of historical memory in a global world.*]. Buenos Aires: Paidós.

Carretero, M., & Castorina, J. A. (2010). *La construcción del conocimiento histórico. Enseñanza, narración e identidades* [*The construction of historical knowledge. Teaching, narration and identities*]. Buenos Aires: Paidós.

Cohen, R. & Toland, J. (Eds.) (1988). *State formation and political legitimacy.* New Jersey: Transaction Books.

Coombes, A. (2004). Museums and the formation of nacional and cultural identities. In B. Carbonell (Ed.). *Museum studies,* (pp. 231–246). London: Blackwell.

Classen, C., & Howes, D. (2006). The Museum as sensescape: Western sensibilities and indigenous artifacts. In E. Edwards, C. Gosden, & R. B. Phillips, *Sensible objects. Colonialism, museums and material culture,* (pp. 199–222). Oxford-New York: Berg.

Clifford, J. (1999). Los museos como zonas de contacto [Museums like contact zones]. In J. Clifford *Itinerarios transculturales* (pp. 233–270). Barcelona: Gedisa.

Clifford, J. (1988). *The predicament of culture. Twentieth-century ethnography, literature and art.* Cambridge: Harvard University Press.

Derrida, J. (1992). *Acts of literature.* New York: Routledge.

Di Liscia, M. S., Bohoslavsky, E., & González de Oleaga, M. (2010). Del Centenario al Bicentenario. Memorias (y desmemorias) en el Museo Histórico Nacional. *A contracorriente. A journal on social history and literature in Latin America, 7*(3), 100–125.

Dubin, S. C. (2010). Incivilities in civil(-ized) Places: 'culture wars' in comparative perspective. In S. Macdonald, *A companion to museum studies,* (pp. 477–493). Oxford: Wiley-Blackwell.

Duncan, C. (1991). Art museums and the ritual of citizenship. In I. Karp & S. D. Lavine (Eds.), *Exhibiting cultures. The poetics and politics of museum display,* (pp. 88–103). Washington: Smithsonian Institution Press.

Earle, R. (2006). Monumentos y museos: la nacionalización del pasado precolombino durante el siglo XIX [Monuments and museums: the nationalization of the pre-Columbian past during the 19th century]. In B. González Stephan & J. Andermann (Eds.), *Galería del progreso. Museos, exposiciones y cultura visual en América Latina* [The gallery of progress. Museums, expositions and visual culture in Latin America] (pp. 27–64). Rosario: Beatriz Viterbo editora.

Escudé, C. (1990). *El fracaso del proyecto argentino* [The fiasco of the Argentine project]. Buenos Aires: Thesis.

Faillace, M. (1997). La memoria sustento dela identidad [Memory feeding identity]. In *Museo histórico nacional.* Buenos Aires: Mannique Zago ediciones.

Foucault, M. (1970). *The order of things: An archaelogy of the human sciencies.* London: Tavistock.

Giebelhausen, M. (2011). Museum architecture: A brief history. In S. Macdonald (Ed.), *A companion to museum studies,* (pp. 223–246). London: Blackwell.

González de Oleaga, M. (2001). *El doble juego de la Hispanidad [The double game of hispanicity].* Madrid: UNED.

González de Oleaga, M., Bohoslavsky, E., & Di Liscia, M. S. (2011). Entre el desafío y el signo. *Alteridades, [Between challenge and sign. Identity and difference in the Museo de América in Madrid], Alteridades, 41,* 37–59.

González de Oleaga, M., Di Liscia, M. S., & Bohoslavsky, E. (2011a). Ironía y literalidad. Los museos históricos en Paraguay y la Argentina [Irony and the literal. Historical museums in Paraguay and Argentina]. In T. Fernández García, *América Latina, dos siglos de Independencia. Fracturas sociales, políticas y culturales* [*Latin America, two centuries of independence. Social, political and cltural ruptures*] (pp. 307–320). Varsovia: Biblioteka Iberyjska.

González de Oleaga, M., Di Liscia, M. S., & Bohoslavsky, E. (2011b). Looking from above: Saying and doing in the history museums of Latin America. *Museum and Society, 9*(1), 49–76.

González de Oleaga, M., & Monge, F. (2007). El Museo de América: modelo para armar [Museo de América: a model to erect]. *Historia y Política 18,* 273–293.

González de Oleaga, M., & Monge, F. (2008). Museum & museo de America. In P. Y. Saunier, & A. Iriye, *The Palgrave dictionary of transnacional history,* (pp. 729–732). London: Palgrave.

Hassoun, J. (2006). *Los contrabandistas de la memoria* [*The contrabandists of memory*]. Buenos Aires: Ed. de la Flor.

Heartney, E. (2004). Fracturing the imperial mind. In B. Messias Carbonell, *Museum studies. An anthology of contexts* (pp. 247–251). London: Blackwell.

Hetherington, K. (1997). Museum topology and the will to connect. *The Journal of Material Culture, 2*(2), 199–220.

Hillier, B., & Tzortzi, K. (2010). Space syntax. The language of museum space. In S. Macdonald (Ed.), *A companion to museum studies* (pp. 282–301). London: Blackwell.

Kaplan, F. E. S. (2010). Making and remaking national identities. In S. Macdonald, (Ed.), *A companion to museum studies* (pp. 152–169). Oxford: Wiley-Blackwell.

Lord, B. (2007). From the document to the monument: museums and the philosophy of history. In S. Knell, S. MacLeod, & S. Watson, *Museums revolutions. How museums change and are changed* (pp. 355–366). London: Routledge.

Macdonald, S. (1998). Exhibitions of power and powers of exhibition: An introduction to the politics of display. In S. Macdonald (Ed.), *The politics of display. Museums, science, culture*. London: Routledge.

Macdonald, S. (2003). Museums, national, postnational and transcultural identities. *Museum and Society 1*(1), 1–16.

Macdonald, S. & Basu, P. (Eds.). (2007). *Exhibition experiments. New interventions in art history*. London: Blackwell.

Mitchell, T. (1988). *Colonizing Egypt*. Cambridge: Cambridge University Press.

Mitchell, T. (2004). Orientalism and the exhibitionary order. In D. Preziosi & C. Farrago, *Grasping the world. The idea of the museum* (pp. 442–460). Aldershot: Ashgate.

Pratt, M. L. (1992). *Imperial eyes. Travel writing and transculturation*. London: Routledge.

Preziosi, D. (2004). Brain of the earth's body: Museums and the framing of modernity. In B. M. Carbonell, *Museum studies. An anthology of contexts* (pp. 71–84). Oxford: Blackwell.

Price, R., & Price, S. (1995). Executing culture. Museé, museo, museum. *American Anthropology, 97*, 97–109.

Redekop, C. (1980). *Strangers become neighbors. Mennonite and indigenous relations in the Paraguayan chaco*. Ontario: Herald Press.

Rorty, R. (1997). *Truth, politics and post-modernism*. Amsterdam: Universiteit van Amsterdam.

Said, E. (1983). *The world, the text, and the critic*. Cambridge: Harvard University Press.

Sahlins, M. (2008). *The western illusion of human nature*. Chicago: Prickly Paradigm Press.

Simpson, M. (2001). *Making representations. Museums in the post-colonial era*. London: Routledge.

Smith, A. (1995). *Nations and nationalism in global era*. Cambridge: Polity Press.

Spivak, G. (1988). Can the subaltern speak?. In C. Nelson & L. Grossberg, *Marxism and the interpretation of culture* (pp. 271–313). Hampshire: MacMillan.

Todorov, T. (1993). Las ciencias morales y políticas [Moral and political sciences]. *Las morales de la historia* (pp. 9–22). Barcelona: Paidós.

White, H. (1992). *Metahistoria. La imaginación histórica en la Europa del siglo XIX* [*Metahistory. The Historical Imagination in Nineteenth-Century Europe*]. Buenos Aires: Fondo de Cultura Económica.

Walsh, K. (1992). *The representation of the past. Museum and heritage in the post-modern world.* London: Routledge.

Zanardini, J., & Biedermann, W. (2006). *Los indígenas del Paraguay* [*The indigenous of Paraguay*]. Asunción: Zamphirópolos.

CHAPTER 17

FROM IDENTITY MUSEUMS TO MENTALITY MUSEUMS

Theoretical Basis for History Museums

Mikel Asensio and Elena Pol

In this chapter new frameworks for history museums will be presented in comparison with traditional history museums. In particular we will focus on museum development in Spain. The frameworks of Identity and Mentality museums will be introduced, illustrated and related to historiography as proposed by the *Annales* School. It is proposed that heritage is better taken care of in these new frameworks, fostering better engagement with the public not only on a regional but also on a local level.

A BACKGROUND FOR MUSEUM DEVELOPMENT IN SPAIN

In the early 1990's most Spanish museums, whether archaeological, ethnological, historical, artistic or scientific, shared a vision that was very traditional and conservative. The fundamental idea was that visitors went to museums to view objects, that they were very passive and had no role in participation and interpretation. Especially in the case of museums devoted to history this implied a general message about history, political events, facts,

History Education and the Construction of National Identities, pages 257–268
Copyright © 2012 by Information Age Publishing
257

dates and heroes, that averts an active role and excludes people from interpretation (MacRainey & Russick, 2010). Most of these museums were based on either a general and universal treatment of messages, away from any explanation of the territory, based on their own idiosyncratic perspective, or a localism overly personal, instead focusing on characters and the collections, which did not reflect the historical, cultural and social development of the region (Jennings, 2007).

It was obvious that the type and, especially, treatment of the collections, that the messages and resources of these museums were more a reflection of nineteenth-century collecting than cultural projects connecting the communities in which they were based. Exhibitions were mostly unrelated to their local visitors and designed for the outside public (Asensio & Pol, 2002). The distance between the local and regional visitors within the museological discourse was huge, although some museums had begun to make efforts to change the situation.

Focusing on the last twenty years in Extremadura, a wide and representative region of Spain as to the problems and characteristics of museum development and cultural heritage (Caldera, 2005), five developments were to mark and change the development of history museums.

First of all, political leaders and institutions realized that history museums could serve political interests as a media resource and as a source of ideological discourse.

Secondly, two lines of action started being developed. One of them was to order the museum policy in the region, increasing significantly public resources, without forgetting the maintenance and improvement of existing museums. The other consisted of adapting museums to the interests of local authorities who were asking for museum infrastructures, equipment and resources.

Third, a territorial reorganization, related to the geographical distribution, required that new cultural resources should strengthen disadvantaged areas in articulating a cultural offer distributed throughout the whole territory of this region.

Fourth, a chance of economic viability and opportunity was given, mainly by the European Union, for all kinds of cultural infrastructures, including museums. The extent of these heritage investments is unparalleled in history. Most were dedicated to the archaeological and architectural resources, including museum buildings. However, a minimum proportion of this budget was dedicated to museological projects and developments (Asensio et al., 2006).

And fifth, a sense of regional pride started to be a significant cultural factor (Nettles & Balter, 2011). Citizens began to become aware of the quantity and quality of their heritage (cultural, but also natural, productive, economic, and untouchable). This process of regional identity has been, and still is, complex. Migrants have played important roles, very different from what had been acknowledged in national museums (Knell et al., 2011). It was clear that museums should participate in this process of identity formation.

The nineties started out with strong political and social demands for new museums in Spanish regions, far away from the cultural offer in the main cities. Museums became a central element in the cultural tourism offer (Asensio & Mortari, 2010; Dumont & Asensio, in press; Dumont, Asensio, & Mortari, 2010; Fernández & Asensio, 2012; Ibáñez et al., 2012). During the last twenty years, in Spain, we had a period of strong heritage recuperation and investment in new museums. The consequence of those years of recovering heritage, especially ethnographic, historical and archaeological, was the creation of interpretive centers and museums in many regions and localities. However, most of these projects lacked a previous study to ensure their viability. There was not museologic project but not even a "museistic" project (see Asensio, Pol, & Gomis, 2001 for a clarification between the three levels, "museistic," "museologic" and "museographic").

Most projects had a very partial presence of material culture. In some cases, the museum started from a total absence of collections, which forced an uptake plan, or started from a small collection that had needed to be completed. Something similar happened with the incorporation of the intangible heritage in the museum discourse, as well as in the museum management. In most cases, this knowledge was not accessible because it wasn't recovered or developed by previous anthropological studies. Even where this knowledge existed, it wasn't of great help, usually because it was excessively general, far from the concrete reality in which it was implicated. New museum frameworks were needed and encountered in the wake of the *Annales* School historiography.

THE FRAMEWORK OF IDENTITY MUSEUMS

The Museums of Identity framework is a global approach that aims at:

1. Coordinating all museum development planning in the region, establishing and maintaining connections between museums and communities (Chittenden et al., 2004);
2. Updating and improving the coordination of existing museums, including plans for dissemination (for example in a single coordinated webpage) and also training plans and developments of public and educational programs (Johnson et al., 2009);
3. A specific plan for the creation of new museums in a coordinated way (Anderson, 2006).

The framework of Identity Museums is supposed to invert the traditional patrimonial mechanism. The classic traditional museum is created or re-created from collections and actions that in any case revolve around the protagonist role of material culture (Anderson, 2004). In this sense museums are institutions that look to the past, trying to rebuild an existing knowledge. In fact, they supposedly re-interpret. But to do that, they are supposed to be based on a relativist epistemological paradigm and, on the contrary, they usually are based on a positivist one. Thus, many exhibitions are based on a museographical project that is a mere aesthetic illustration of the collections. The predominance of the collections and the decontextualized discourse are the keys of the traditional museum (Weil, 1990).

This is not always easy to detect. Many traditional museums had a disciplinary (geographical and historical) connection with the place where they are located. This is because the collections have a relationship with the regional cultures. However, this connection is very often very superficial and not very well developed. Usually, the traditional museum discourses arise from a rather superficial analysis based on general theories rather than on a close analysis of the local facts and circumstances of the region. The ultimate consequence is that, in most of the traditional museums, the local people do not feel identified with the collections, messages, or discourses (Silverman, 2010). Also, traditional museum discourse has a very elitist view of the culture. The discourse is mostly descriptive and explanatory. It attempts to present a taxonomical knowledge associated with the collections almost solely from a structural point of view, in a very superficial typological way, usually formal or iconographic. These descriptive discourses remain far from the interests of possible audiences. In most cases, they stay also far away from their visitors' comprehensive capabilities, which often leads to their abandonment behavior.

By contrast, Museums of Identity arise looking towards the future instead of the past. They start from a patrimonial situation towards an unfinished construction of knowledge. Sometimes, they do not have enough material culture or the intangible heritage was not systematically collected, but their starting point is the interest in socio-cultural processes that generate knowledge from industrial archeology, ethnology, science or art productions. Their main goal is to build a cultural project to ensure conservation in the future, as otherwise these memories will probably rapidly disappear in the whirlwind of the global post-industrial society (Fiemberg & Leinhardt, 2002).

Finally, the vehicular language of the museum's identity should be a narrative language that drives the story in an attractive way, close to the receptor. It includes issues of dialogue, emotion and multiculturalism, that are often left out of the traditional encyclopedic taxonomies. Of course, the descriptive and explanatory languages to complement the stories, the collections, and the messages of the museum can also be used.

The framework of identity museums was developed in a project in close cooperation with the local institutions, responding to requests from the towns and small cities themselves. For example, the mayor of a town would ask the regional government the help build a local museum about some cultural event or demonstration of the village. Also, the size, the shape and the exhibition design of the museum had to be directly related to the number of people needed to keep the museum alive and functioning. Identity museums were framed as modest institutions, in comparison to bigger cultural projects belonging to corporations or regional consortiums.

The identity museums have the explicit intention to contribute to the regional process of cultural revitalization. This way, projects could link with a very wide range of contents and proposals, open to many different aspects of cultural life as tourism, formal education, and others (Asensio, Asenjo, & Etxeberria 2009; Asensio, Asenjo, & Ibáñez, 2011; Fernandez, Kommers, & Asensio, 2004; Ibáñez, Asensio, & Correa, 2011; Packer, 2008). Identity museums have two main objectives in terms of their cultural offer. One is related to the region, reflecting the explicit relationship between the local development. The other is to maintain quality control and rigor for the museum contents.

Finally, the identity museums involve a very clear standard about visitor experience. They attempt to be immersive, generating an emotional and intellectual experience. Visitors are invited to participate in the stories through contextualized scenes and dioramas, "hands on" proposals and "living history" programs. Also, identity museums take very special care of intangible heritage, trying to show it and to favor its possible interpretation at the same time. On the other hand, they include a clear commitment to multiculturalism and in relation to this issue, they are as open as possible to different values and interpretations. At the same time, identity museums try to develop a narrative approach and try to take care of the value of the collections and material culture.

The Museum of "Empalao" provides an example of the identity museums described above. It is based on a local cultural and religious tradition. This tradition consists of a kind of religious march. During Holy Week several locals (usually men) take some agricultural object similar the cross, tie themselves up, put a crown of thorns and old clothes on, and walk barefoot around the city at night, praying and performing a dangerous and very complicated ceremony. Designing the museum, we met with local groups having two different approaches to this tradition. On one hand, we took into consideration the proposals of a religious interpretation. On the other hand, we also considered the agnostic interpretation of this ritual, which consists of a rite of passage, incorporating some religious syncretism, stemming probably from a Celtic period much earlier than its supposed Christian origins. The texts of this museum were literally negotiated with all parties so that everyone could see his opinion reflected and recognize and respect the other perspectives. Identity museums should incorporate from the beginning the testimonies, the memories and life stories of people by enforcing the old maxim from Trevor Pierce by the World Congress of ICOM in Melbourne, in 1998, that "people are more important than objects." Identity museums should collect the identity signs of a town or city, the differentiating feelings of the residents of a region, seeking and giving priority to those they feel most proud of and they consider are the most identity for them, so that will provide recovery and the assumption of its own historical development and favoring the involvement in their individual and collective responsibilities in the construction of their culture.

The proposed project of identity has some particular aspects and problems (Caldera, Asensio, & Pol, 2010). Firstly, from the point of view of museology, we need study profoundly the consideration about museums as tools for action and not only as tools of representation. Secondly, from a theoretical perspective, it is necessary to merge American anthropology, the traditional ethnography and the new French ethnology. And thirdly, the basic theory on social individuality should be taken into account, characterizing the audience not as a visitors but as a participants, including new technologies (Asensio & Asenjo, 2011). That conception demands of exhibit discourse that it goes beyond the contents, affecting their syntax and pragmatics, and should exploit what we know about the construction of historical memory and personal and collective identity (see a review of the international state of the art on Carter, 2007). Borrowing the metaphors, museums of identity and mentality would be the "mirrors and windows" that permit to reflect us and pass through our identity and otherness (Carretero, 2011), museums like scenarios of "imagined communities" (Anderson, 2006) that respond to the last representations that allow us to interpret our reality.

THE FRAMEWORK OF
MUSEUMS OF THE MENTALITIES

The Museums of Mentalities mark a new phase, initiated in 2007. Their most distinctive feature is recovering the memory of the community in relation to specific stories which had a significant impact on its past (Babuts, 2009), including compelling stories (Tsybulskaya & Camhi, 2009), and a significant presence of emotions and values. The difference between the framework of identity museums and mentality museums is a matter of emphasis. In the museums of identity the greater emphasis has been on production environments, closely related to local traditions and lifestyles, including also their implications for cultural performances (rituals, beliefs and customs, for example) (Heimlich & Falk, 2009).

These new museums are supposed to preserve, research and disseminate cultural heritage (tangible and intangible) through the analysis of specific past matters related to the region. That is, traits that characterize persons, a group of people, a generation, etc. These museums aim at restoring the heritage of not very well known people or communities, in contrast with traditional and positivist historiography. Therefore, the framework of mentality museum involves a social analysis of individuals and groups involved. Also it includes their popular beliefs, their collective imagination, artistic trends and rituals.

From the museologic point of view, the framework of mentality museums emphasizes narrative language in contrast with the descriptive and explanatory language of the traditional museums. For the public the narrative is one of the most potent tools to elicit curiosity and interest in the presented contents (Bruner, 1990). Disciplinarily speaking, it is the creation of new facilities based on new inherited historiography conceptions from the Annales School. That is, all the museums would arise as history museums, but as museums of a certain historiographical concept, linked to the epistemological basis of the "History of Mentalities," and of the "Cultural History," and of the "Microhistory." Below, we will consider a couple of prototypes of these new museums.

THE HIDDEN LIBRARY:
THE MUSEUM OF THE "TRAVELING SCHOOLS"

A construction remodeling undertaken in a primary school, in the small village of Navas del Madroño, Cáceres, uncovered a hidden library, revealing an intimate history. It were school supplies from the Educational Mission of the Spanish Second Republic. This "Traveling Schools" educational initiative had, at the beginning of the 30´s, brought many little Spanish villages a bit of poetry, literature, music, film criticism and social commitment. But all these experiences ended with the victory, at the end of the Civil War, of the Franco regime. All was hidden away by some of the teachers in between two walls more than 70 years ago, probably in the first days of the Civil War. One of the teachers was killed by the fascist troops and the other two were "depurated" of their liberal ideas, within the systematic ideological cleansing carried out by the fascism during and after the Civil War. The library hid about a hundred objects, like a jukebox, a movie projector, slate records, and books by committed writers and intellectuals of that period. Also there were educational materials, all of them considered "revolutionary" by Franco´s officials, simply because they were distributed by republican educators. The objects of the library were not very valuable, but they had a very particular political connotation, apart from their emotional component. The recuperated library has enabled a recovery of lost memory. The museum tells and restores a dignity of historical local actors. Several generations, mostly elder people, still remember the visit of these educational missions. But the younger citizens also remember, having received the story from their parents and relatives.

THE ETERNAL RETURN OF EXILED CULTURE:
THE MUSEUM OF THE MOORISH CULTURE

It is very fascinating that for centuries Catholic institutions in Spain have been systematically defending a strict censorship of all remembering of the Islam and Islamic cultural productions and performances. At the same time, interestingly enough, from landscapes to architecture, from language to agriculture, from water distribution to the place names, we are reminded that an important part of the peninsula has been Muslim longer than it has been Christian.

The new museum of Hornachos is a project of recovery of historical memory trough tangible and intangible culture associated with this small southern town of Badajoz's province, occupying a central role in the Moorish history. The finding of an Islamic prayer book and a book of Arabic calligraphy using Koranic texts, jewels of Moorish culture, allowed for a historical and anthropological discourse, forming a recovery of the Islamic past of the town. Today it is possible to trace descendants of the "hornachegos" as far as Rabat (Morocco), where in 1627 the Independent Republic of Salé was founded (England, Holland, France and Germany recognized it and named ambassadors), engaging in trade and piracy. Many families of Salé still retain their original lineage and surname and, until 1934, the governors of Rabat were of Moorish's Hornachos origin.

The mentality museums should have a close relationship with everyday life. This relation should also be meaningful and close to the receiver of the exhibition. Delving into Moorish legacy of the territory is no less than understanding the past and the present, from gastronomy to music, from technology to language, from beliefs to values.

THEORETICAL BASES OF THE
MUSEUMS OF IDENTITY AND MENTALITY

The general objective of these museums of history would be to promote interdisciplinary studies, which would include the study of very different historical experiences of certain regions. This project of local museums, in which the interest in research and documentation of the content has prevailed above the importance of collections themselves, is having surprising results, including the location, recovery and documentation of tangible and intangible heritage of the first order that had been "ignored" for decades, even centuries. That is, the mission of taking care of the heritage of any museum is being met far more even than in many traditional museums which just take care of the collections.

An important part of this research is modeled on the history of mentalities inherited from the Annales School. The constant concern of Marc Bloch and Lucien Febvre, the founders of the journal *Annales d'histoire économique et social* (in 1929), was to write a synthetic history, which led them to study the economic and psychological and cultural basis of historical facts. Their clearly anti-positivist position attacks a history of philosophy that separated the ideas from time, space and social life. The School of Annales developed a historiography that joined social sciences such as geography, sociology, economics, social psychology and anthropology, advocating an extension of the topics studied and rejecting the predominant emphasis on politics, diplomacy and military events of the twentieth century. The result was, firstly, an economic and social history that gradually acquired a dominant position on the historiographical production in the decades after II World War, and secondly, the development of the history of mentalities.

The term "mentality" is used since the early twentieth century to define social structures like an expression of culture. Thus, the history of the mentalities faced the collective representations and mental structures of societies. The study encompasses all expressions of everyday life as a complement to the study of macro-history. Compared to the traditional history of ideas, which had focused on the reconstruction of the great systems of thought from the perspective of the elites, the history of mentalities claimed a very different position. It extended towards studies of the groups, popular beliefs, the worldview of a certain age, cultural or artistic sensibility of the masses, and technical and scientific knowledge of a society. Moreover, it tried to retrieve the unconscious aspects of culture and beliefs of a society. Therefore, sources are not just the works of great thinkers and artists, but also everyday texts, gestures, iconography, popular forms of representation of a society. There's a sensitivity to a more global concept of history, where the motives of the actors and communities are considered and grounded in broader social realities, in comparison to previous historiographical endeavors.

THE EXPANSION OF MUSEUMS OF MENTALITIES AND SOME TENTATIVE CONCLUSIONS

Some of the mentality museums are very close to the museums of identity, for example, the Wine Museum (Asensio, in press), but take a step further. In this case the wine, beyond being identified as a product, begins to raise a number of questions about our own history. For example, why did Muslims not uproot the grape plants if, in theory, they don't consume alcohol? The wine becomes a reason to analyze not only successive cultures and heritage, but also a cultural background incorporated into our current customs and traditions. The museum tracks minds, and sometimes recovers forgotten stories that are explanatory of the actual history of territories and the peoples of these territories. Projects of identity and mentality have led to reflection on the transmutation of the concept of museum. We have tried to reflect on the tangible and intangible culture, about the exhibition offer, their receivers and their management in order to respond comprehensively to new realities of space assets presentation. We conceive these spaces as true "culture factories" that are based on an unfinished project that should be enriched with the participation of citizens, integrating them into the territorial dynamics.

The traditional museum was designed from the point of view of maintaining the power of culture above all, along with a very traditional view of knowledge production. The alternative of museums of identity and mentality proposes that any contribution can be significant to the public and that the dialogue is the source of knowledge production. Moreover, the authority is not given by institutional position but must be earned reputation in the field, designing museums as places of enunciation and negotiation with the otherness.

Identity museums and mentality museums are looking for participants instead of just visitors. They seek both constructors of shared knowledge and accomplices in values, who can unravel the cultural discourse underlying all speech, including the implicit and silence as a substantial part of meaning making. The history and the stories of the identity and mentality museums are closer to people because they are more adapted to the expectations, motivations, feelings, and previous knowledge. In this way we need a very clever planning of varied and repeated evaluation (Asensio & Pol, 2008; Diamond et al., 2009; Fernandez & Asensio, 2008).

From our point of view, developed in this paper, heritage is nothing less than building a symbolic language, based on shared thinking and signs. If identity and mentality do not reify the heritage, it will not even exist as an ontological reality. If we do not build these signs that allow us to develop our own symbols, the heritage will get lost.

REFERENCES

Anderson, B. (2006). *Imagined communities*. London: Verso.

Anderson, G. (Ed.). (2004). *Reinventing the museum. Historical and contemporary perspectives on the paradigm shift*. Lanham, MD: Altamira Press.

Asensio, M. (in press). Ruby glass boxes: How to develop a sciences and arts wine museum. In J. Blánquez & S. Celestino (Eds.), *Vine and wine cultural heritage—Patrimonio cultural de la vid y el Vino*. Mérida: Consejería de Hacienda de la Junta de Extremadura—Ayuntamiento de Almendralejo.

Asensio, M., & Asenjo, E. (2011). *Lazos de Luz Azul: Museos y Tecnologías 1, 2 y 3.0. [Connections of blue light: Museums and technologies 1, 2, and 3.0]*. Barcelona: UOC.

Asensio, M., Asenjo, E., & Ibáñez, A. (2009). Websites and museums: New informal learning applications. *Proceedings of ECEL; The 8th European Conference on e-Learning*. Held at the University of Bari, Italy.

Asensio, M., Asenjo, E., & Ibáñez, A. (2011). Sitos WEB y Museos. Nuevas aplicaciones para el aprendizaje informal [Websites and museums. New applications for informal learning]. In A. Ibáñez (Ed.), *Museos, redes sociales y tecnología 2.0 [Museums, social media & 2.0 technology]* (pp. 9–26). Zarautz: UPV-EHU Editorial.

Asensio, M., Colomer, L., Díaz, P., Fohn, M., Hachimi, T., Hupet, P., Lefert, S., León, C., Léotard, J. M., Luxen, J. L., Le Bouëtte, S., Nicolau, A., Martinet, F., Miles, D., Páll, L., Ruiz, J., Sanz, N., Sarkadi, E., Teller, J., Tinant, M., Zidda, G., Zwetkoff, C., Warnotte, A., & Wilson, V. (2006). *The APPEAR Method: A practical guide for the management of enhancement projects on urban archaeological sites.* European Commission Research Report n° 30/4. www.in-situ.be.

Asensio, M., & Pol, E. (2002). *Nuevos Escenarios en Educación. Aprendizaje informal sobre el patrimonio, los museos y la ciudad [New scenarios in education. Informal learning about patrimony, museums and the city].* Buenos Aires: Aique.

Asensio, M., & Pol, E. (2008). Conversations of informal learning in museums and heritage. In F. Fernandez (Ed.) *Tourism, heritage and informal learning: Museums as e-labs: emotion and education.* Electronic version available on: http://www.pasosonline.org/Publicados/pasosoedita/pasosrep1en.pdf

Asensio, M., Pol, E., & Gomis, M. (2001). *Planificación en Museología: el caso del Museu Marítim. [Planning and museology: the case of the Museu Marítim.]* Barcelona: Museu Marítim.

Babuts, N. (2009). *Memory, metaphors, and meaning.* New Brunswick, NJ: Transactions Publishers.

Bruner, J. (1990). *Acts of meaning.* Cambridge: Harvard University Press.

Caldera, P. (2005). La Red de Museos de Extremadura. [The network of museums of Extremadura]. *Revista de Museología, 32,* 13–19.

Caldera, P., Asensio, M., & Pol, E. (2010). De los Museos de Identidad a los Museos de Mentalidad: bases teóricas de la recuperación de la memoria de los Modernos Museos de Extremadura. [From identity museums to mentality museums: theoretical bases for the recuperation of memory of the modern museums of Extremadura.] *Museo, Revista de la Asociación Profesional de Museológos de España (APME), 15,* 49–82.

Carretero, M. (2011). *Constructing patriotism, teaching history and memories in global worlds.* Charlotte, NC: Information Age Publishing.

Chittenden, D., Farmelo, G., & Lewenstein, B.V. (Eds) (2004). *Creating connections, museums and the public understanding of current research.* Walnut Creek, CA: Altamira Press.

Diamond, J., Luke, J. J., & Uttal, D. H. (2009). *Practical evaluation guide.* Lonham: Altamira Press.

Dumont, E., & Asensio, M. (in press). From blind dating to matchmaking: learning from tourist to manage the cultural offer. *International Journal of Web Based Communities (IJWBC), 8*(2).

Dumont, E., Asensio, M., & Mortari, M. (2010). Image construction and representation in tourism promotion and heritage management. In P. Burns, C. Palmer, & J. Lester (Eds.), *Tourism and visual culture Vol.1: Theories and concepts.* London: University of Brighton Press.

Fernandez, H., & Asensio, M. (2008). Informal learning in museums: An example using natural marine heritage. In F. Fernandez (Ed.), *Tourism, heritage and*

informal learning: museums as e-labs: Emotion and education. Available in: http://
www.pasosonline.org/Publicados/pasosoedita/pasosrep1en.pdf

Fernández, H., & Asensio, M. (2012). e-Heritage and e-museums: Technological
resources for tourism planning. *International Journal of Web Based Communities
(IJWBC), 8*(1), 5–23.

Fernandez, H., Kommers, P. A. M., & Asensio, M. (2004). Conceptual representations for in-depth learning. IOS Press (Eds.), *Cognitive support for learning* (pp.
229–240). Amsterdam: IOS Press.

Fiemberg, J., & Leinhardt, G. (2002). Looking through the glasses: Reflections of
identity in conversations at a history museum. In G. Leinhardt, K. Crowley, &
K. Knutson (Eds.), *Learning conversations in museums* (pp. 167–212). Mahwah,
NJ: LEA.

Ibáñez, A., Asensio, M., & Correa, J. (2011). 'Mobile Learning' y Patrimonio. Apre-
ndiendo historia con mi teléfono, mi GPS y mi PDA [Mobile learning and
patrimony. Learning histiry with my telephone, GPS and PDA]. In A. Ibáñez
(Ed.), *Museos, redes sociales y tecnología 2.0 [Museums, social media & 2.0 technol-
ogy]* (pp. 59–88). Zarautz: UPV-EHU Editorial.

Ibáñez, A., Asensio, M., Vivent, N., & Cuenca, J. M. (2012). Mobile Devices: A tool
for Tourism and Learning at archaeological sites. *International Journal of Web
Based Communities (IJWBC), 8*(1), 57–72.

Heimlich, J. E., & Falk, J. H. (2009). Free choice learning and the environment. In
J. H. Falk, J. E. Heimlich, & S. Foutz (Eds.), *Free choice learning and the environment.* New York: Altamira Press.

Johnson, A., Huber, K. A., Cutler, N., Bingmann, M., & Grove, T. (2009). *The museum
educator's manual.* Logham: Altamira Press.

Knell, S. J., Aronsson, P., Amundsen, A. B., Barnes, A. J., Burch, S., Carter, J., Gosselin, V., Hughes, S. A., & Kirwan, A. (Eds.). (2011). *National museums, new
studies from around the world.* New York: Routledge.

McRainey, D. L,. & Russick J. (Eds.). (2010). *Connecting kids to history with museum
exhibitions.* Walnut Creek, CA: Left Coast Press.

Nettles, R., & Balter, R. (2011). *Multiple minority identities.* NY: Springer Pub. Co.

Packer, J. (2008). Beyond learning: Exploring visitors' perceptions of the value and
benefits of museum experiences. *Curator. The Museum Journal, 51*(1), 33–54.

Silverman, L. H. (2010). *The social work of museums.* New York: Routledge Press.

Tsybulskaya, D., & Camhi, J. (2009). Accessing and incorporating visitor's entrance
narratives in guided museum tours. *Curator. The Museum Journal, 52*(1), 81–
100.

Weil, S. (1990). *Rethinking the museum and other meditations.* Washington: The Smithsonian Institution Press.

CHAPTER 18

COMMENTARY

What is the Purpose of a History Museum in the Early 21st Century?

Veronica Boix-Mansilla

The case is compelling. In two thought-provoking chapters in this volume, Marisa González de Oleaga, Mikel Asensio and Elena Pol argue that history museums—nineteenth century hallmarks of civilization and national collective memory—are unfit to help us make sense of our world. Contemporary societies, characterized by the accelerated traffic of people, capital, ideas and products the world over, call for a serious reconceptualization of museums as places of inquiry, reflection, learning, enjoyment and identity construction. Through their elaborate critique, analysis and illustrations, we learn that "traditional history museums" are limited on three grounds: (a) the choices about how the past is represented; (b) the epistemological assumptions on which exhibits are based, and (c) the expectations held by museums about the constitution and experience of their audience. In what follows, I review the main critiques and interesting alternatives proposed by these authors, considering what they reveal *vis a vis* the purpose of history museum institutions in the early 21st century.

History Education and the Construction of National Identities, pages 269–277
Copyright © 2012 by Information Age Publishing
All rights of reproduction in any form reserved.

THE CRITIQUE OF TRADITIONAL MUSEUMS

Problematic Representations of the Past

"Traditional museums," Asensio and Pol argue, prioritize two contrasting takes on the past. On one end of the spectrum, the past is presented as national or global histories that appear as universal and disconnected from the particular locations in which the museums stand. These narratives, tend to be densely populated by political events, facts, dates, and heroes that remain only superficially connected to the local realities of their communities. As a result, they fail genuinely to engage museum visitors. In sharp contrast, community museums have tended to confine history to very local and overly personal views of the past. They have focused on characters, material culture and collections, without reflecting on the broader historical, cultural and social development of the region or revealing the meanings attributed to objects by actors in the past, thus failing to engage visitors as well.

González de Oleaga, contributes to the critique by describing how change over time and geopolitical perspectives have shaped traditional museums' representations of the past and their concomitant collective identity construction agendas. Through vivid descriptions of museums in Latin America and Spain, she helps us understand how national histories are revised and expanded to serve new identiary purposes. For example, in the Museo de Historia Nacional of Buenos Aires, newer national narratives are juxtaposed to old ones to propose a modified national identity. In the Museo Jacob Unger in Paraguay, national histories are challenged by novel ethnic ones, designed to recruit feelings of belonging among members of particular ethnic groups such as the Fernheim Mennonite colony. Still in other cases, as in the Museo de America in Madrid, museum exhibits take a region [e.g., Spanish Speaking America] as their unit of analysis, obscuring local sub-regional differences with the aim of reinforcing, in this case, a Spanish sense of colonial Metropolis. González de Oleaga concludes that the accounts of the past and units of analysis prioritized by traditional museums—bounded notions of nation, ethnic group, or region that highlight internal homogeneity to distinguish its members from and imagined "other"—are, by necessity, exclusionary.

The authors of both chapters challenge representations of history that admit few alternative accounts in the name of preserving group identity, and they do well. The early 21st century finds us inhabiting societies of increasing cultural, ethnical and ideological complexity. Historical accounts that consider individual and group identity in more complex and dialogical ways are likely to prepare us better to understand our world (Suárez Orozco, & Baolian Qin, 2004; Suárez Orozco, Darbes, Dias, & Sutin, 2011). A more nuanced understanding of identity may help us see the multiplicity of coexisting commitments,—cultural, gender, religious, generational, technological, national,—that shaped lives passed. A clearer purpose for 21st century history museums emerges —not the creation of a compacted group identity but the contribution to a more nuanced and inclusive understanding of the past. Such understanding will not enable us to predict the future, but certainly to meet the complexities of our increasingly diverse world better informed (Appleby, Hunt, & Jacob, 1994).

Epistemological Stance

Even more important than inviting multiple historical narratives is considering how such narratives are construed. The epistemological stance of traditional history museums comes under attack in the work of Asensio & Pol and González de Oleaga. The authors denounce the positivist perspective permeating exhibits. In such exhibits, narratives and objects are displayed in ways suggesting that what is on display is the product of true and unquestionable scientific knowledge. Static discourse conveys information about the collections, prioritizing form and taxonomy over meaning. Exhibitions "illustrate" what is presented as a certified version of the past. History, in turn, is narrated by a purportedly dis-interested external observer who holds the "eye of God." Interpretation, an essential component of all narratives and curatorial decisions, is invisible.

Pointing to the political implication of this epistemic stance, González de Oleaga alerts us to the museums artifice of passing off a given version of history as history itself, while presenting the aspirations of rising social sectors as broadly shared common values. She views the positivist discourse as a strategy of domination. In it, the museum seeks to associate the nation-state with ideas of authority and culture, relegating perspectives of the past that are not approved within this logic to strangeness and otherness. Left outside of the symbolic world of the national museum are not only the voices that do not easily fit the grand narrative proposed, but also the interests of the museums local audiences and visitors. In the traditional museum as here portrayed, the collections are presented as self-evident representations of the past—one past, one reality, one authoritative story to be told. There is no mediator between the observer and the observed, leaving the visitor blind to the constructed and contestable nature of historical narratives.

The authors offer a strong epistemological critique of the positivist assumptions of the traditional museum and, in González de Oleaga's case, forcefully denounce its political agenda. What they do not address is how powerfully the epistemological assumptions of the traditional museum described speak to the unschooled mind (Gardner, 1999, 2007). Shorn of careful instruction in history, visitors are likely to think of the past as a stable reality to be "discovered" by historians and represented in ways that are "accurate" and "complete." Lacking an opportunity to revise intuitive beliefs, visitors might hold inductivist or empiricist orientations. They may be inclined to believe, that "seeing" the past directly would enable them to "know it." They may be inclined to experience photographs or sources as unproblematic and uncontestable windows into a palpable past. Understanding the constructed nature of historical accounts is paramount to deepening our understanding of the past through history (Boix Mansilla, 2004; Lee & Ashby, 2000; Lee & Shemilt, 2007; Wineburg, 2001). At a time in which unprecedented amounts of information of varying degrees of reliability are available to us at a mouse click, museums offer unique opportunities for detained analysis of claims about the past. Also they can involve participants in reflective curatorial processes, or engage them in accessible and intelligently presented historiographic debates. The goal is to make historical knowledge construction visible and nurture healthy skepticism that characterizes an educated public—another candidate purpose of the 21st century museum.

Assumptions About Audience

A positivist historical outlook reveals a particular conception of museum audience and targeted museum experience. The authors point out that the traditional museum operates with an abstract idea of a visitor: ready to admire and absorb authoritative stories of the past as part of her national, ethnic, or regional identity. The idealized visitor, Asensio and Pol claim, is viewed as lacking expertise about her region, her past or the museums surrounding community. Engagement is contemplative and purely intellectual without local identitary valence. Because museums do not problematize what it means to understand ones local context, community, and past, the local public fails to identify with collections or messages that remain distant from their institution and actions. A new conception of museum actors, purpose, and experience is needed.

How should a contemporary museum of history think about its audience? Any general or static claim about history museum audiences is bound to prove problematic. The old olive farmer rooted in his Spanish village for generations, seems to bear little resemblance with the British college student roaming around Spain in search of self. Yet, it is important to note that both individuals are actors in the broader matrix of uneven processes of globalization that shape their lives. In thinking about their audience, history museums of the 21st century cannot forget this reality. In fact they would do well in capitalizing on it. In other words, in times of rapid globalization and localized dynamics the history museum can help the public deliberate about local impact of global transitions in the past, reflect about the role local communities played in shifting geopolitical dynamics and learn from close study of analogous processes of change in the past. This approach sidesteps the problem of presentism (Seixas, 1997). It accepts asking new questions about the past that that stem from present concern, but stays vigilant about the risk of projecting present sensibilities onto past actors in the construction of accounts.

In sum, the vibrant critique of the traditional museum (national, regional, local, ethnic) invites us to re-think the monolithic ways in which the past is represented, the epistemological assumptions on which history museums stand, and the conception of audience that mobilizes their efforts. How can the schemas dominating the traditional museum be reframed to respond to the demands of the early 21st century? To address this question let us turn to what the authors of these chapters propose. González de Oleaga builds on her review of history museums in Argentina, Paraguay and Spain to propose telling reconceptualizations. Asensio and Pol propose a strikingly novel approach to museum development. Drawing on a series of practical experimentations, they outlines how museums can be grounded on the symbolic and material capital of local towns and territories and the mentalities that inhabit them.

HISTORY MUSEUMS REFRAMED

Moving beyond distant, authoritative, and essentialized depictions of the bounded nation, ethnic group or region, demands that we historicize these categories, claims González de Oleaga. Museum exhibits would do well in presenting multiple narratives about the past positioning them as "perspectives" and thus, by necessity, partial, limited, unfinished. "Identities" (national, regional, ethnic) too, she argues, are to be presented not as fixed and given qualities, but as constructed categories that prove more or less helpful in organizing past experience. Museums will indeed, be better positioned to meet the demands of the 21st century when they are able to present identities in this light, recognizing the multiplicity of affiliations that individuals hold and can put into play depending on context, purpose and need.

Asensio and Pol take the argument a step further. They characterize a series of museum innovation initiatives, called "identity" and "mentality" museums, designed not merely to present a given narrative, but to co-construct it with those for whom such narrative matters. As a result the topical focus of these museums is not on grand, national histories but on cultural and productive practices, about which communities hold expertise. Exhibits, co-curated, are the result of collective efforts to recover the material and symbolic capital in the territory—artifacts and tools as well as testimonies, documents, and meanings. Not all topics are deemed acceptable. Most characteristically these museums have focused on themes such as the production of cherry, nougat, olives, pagan and religious rituals, and materials emerging by chance from excavations such as a "hidden library." Inspired by the Annales School, as well as micro- and cultural history, the identity and mentality museums focus, for instance, on agricultural products that mark the local economy and organize life. These products can be seen as shaping the landscape, and set holidays, dress, folklore, arts and crafts, events, beliefs and ceremonies, giving rise to a complex cultural mesh submitted to collective examination. Language and discourse remain accessible to museum users, and museum institutions serve as places for community recreation, education, reflection, memory preservation and knowledge construction. Mentality museums, Asensio and Pol, explain "should have a close relationship with everyday life. This relation should also be meaningful and close to the receiver of the exhibition" (p. 264).

How do these museums intersect with the accelerated global dynamics of the 21st century? They prioritize the preservation of cultural heritage that stands at risk when confronted with homogenizing forces. Museums do not only preserve but enrich the symbolic, and material cultural and capital of a community and the territory to which it belongs. Furthermore, Asensio and Pol call on these museums to revert traditional power relations and exclusions. They explain:

> The traditional museum was designed from the point of view of maintaining the power of culture above all, along with a very traditional view of knowledge production. The alternative of museums identity and mentality proposes that any contribution can be significant and that the dialogue is the source of knowledge production. Moreover, the authority is not given by institutional position but must be earned reputation in the field, designing museums as places of enunciation and negotiation with the otherness. (p. 266)

A number of qualities render the museum of identities and mentalities promising *vis a vis* the representation of the past they advance, the epistemological assumption on which they stand and the conception of audience that drives them. Transforming the notion of a museum into that of a popular cultural center charged with the construction of locally relevant knowledge, could render informed reflections about the past a shared community practice. Just as anyone can draw, make music, or dance from an early age, the principle goes, anyone might be empowered to tell stories about the past, reinterpret artifacts, decode marks on the landscape and preserve original sources. These museums break away from traditional museum epistemology: knowledge construction and curatorial deliberations are not only visible, they are participatory. Audiences are not abstracted, they are actors in the re-construction of the past. In fact, the power of mentality museums is that they promise to broaden and heighten *sensitivity* toward the past, placing memory and inquiry on an accessible center stage, deepening a community's historical consciousness. Predictably, Asensio and Pol as well as González de Oleaga view these features in a positive light.

However, the proposed museum design, principles and models, also raise important questions—especially once examined in the broader context of globalization shaping the early 21st century. Consider, for example, how the past is represented. Focusing on local and territorial practices that stand within the cultural repertoire of community members (the production of cherries, the making of wine) can reveal various takes on history. On the one hand, the past can be approached in the spirit of cultural retreat in the face of globalization. This approach would seek to reinforce local identities. The study of local traditions may produce boundaries that highlight local uniqueness with pride and to be defended from a "global other." On the other end of the spectrum, local practices are explored in connection with other societies, investigating mutual influences and interdependence across peoples and communities. I propose that the second approach, which may include tracking broader regional influences on local practices or comparing how other communities have come to conduct similar tasks, is more likely to prepare the communities mentioned by Asensio and Pol for contemporary life. By virtue of focusing on a more comprehensive explanation of local global interactions instead of on a commitment to reinforcing local belonging, this representation of the past can prepare participants to orient themselves in the present in informed ways. In sum, one could argue, to meet their purpose, museum institutions in the early-21st century may need to balance understanding of local-often at risk- cultural patrimony and the recognition of the global, trans-regional contexts that give them new meaning.

A related set of questions can be raised regarding the epistemological assumptions on which these museums stand. It is laudable to advance institutions committed to broadening participation in our collective reflection about the past, the preservation of heritage and its aesthetic communication. If well managed, participatory investigation offers ample opportunities for community members to deliberate on epistemological matters, even if only tacitly so. From topic choice to source gathering to curative measures, mentality museums invite participating communities to weigh matters of historical significance, causality, points of view, periodization and the construction of coherent accounts. Few history curricula in formal education hold the promise of authenticity that the mentality museum holds. And yet, the design principle of attributing equal weight to all perspectives (historians, farmers, artisans) calls for further clarification. What is the role of expert historians or anthropologists in the mentality museums? How are disciplinary and local knowledge and epistemologies integrated, if they are, in productive ways? Furthermore, how might a participatory museum of this kind address the challenge of historical reasoning?

In my view, the power of considering multiple voices of inquiry stems not so much from its attempt to contest forms of "scholarly empowerment," as from its capacity to yield deeper explanations and more inclusive understanding of the past. Both, the farmer and the historian may hold accounts of soil treatment among past inhabitants of the land. Their dialogue is trans-disciplinary in the sense that it is not contained in a disciplinary—nor an interdisciplinary—community. For this exchange to be productive, accounts need not be measured by *who* produces them but by *how well* they enable us to produce a cognitive advancement—i.e., a more textured story, a more revealing explanation, a more effective account. In other words, the relative weight assigned to the perspectives on the table will depend on the purpose that guide the museums' inquiry into the past. On matters of broad contextualization in time and space, historians are likely to contribute most, as they will on matters of explanation, evidence, and complex narrative structure. On matters of practice, contemporary meaning, and deep understanding of human environment dynamics the farmer might hold the upper hand. Yet a powerful transdisciplinary dialogue is not limited to a distribution of labor based on ontology but on the deliberative negotiation of expertise *vis a vis* the purposes of inquiry. And that includes a respectful dialogue about the question that holds most significance, the sources of evidence that prove most reliable, the explanatory factors worth considering and the communicative devises that will prove most compelling to engage the community in interpreting the past.

Predictably, epistemologies will clash and, at times, prove incommensurable in term of contents (Carretero & Kriger, 2011) and historiographical assumptions. For instance we now understand that individuals develop their understanding of historical causal explanations in ways that move from blending description and explanation, to attributing agency to individuals, objects and events, to understanding the dynamics between context and agency and ultimately reflect about the constructed nature of explanatory accounts (Lee & Shemilt, 2007). To the degree to which the kinds of deliberation within institutionalized democratic spheres like the ones proposed by the mentalities museums advance an informed interpretation of the past, the mentalities museum presents a viable path forward. In this deliberation, not all stories are equally relevant and authoritative accounts do not stand unquestioned. In this deliberation, the reconceived museum places its epistemological assumptions productively somewhere between the relative and the absolute.

To conclude: the early 21ˢᵗ century, calls for an aggiornamento of the history museum. To respond to the demands of an increasingly interrelated world, museums may need to do more than digitalizing their collections and experiences. They will need to rethink how the past is represented, the epistemological assumptions on which it I does so, and the conception of audience for which it designs its exhibits. In so doing, museums will need to find their unique productive balance across local, regional and global dynamics in representing the past; between relative and absolute epistemological impulses, and in their conception of audience and participation. While a pluralism of approaches will serve us well, one point is clear, museums like the ones proposed by González de Oleaga and Asensio & Pol that are geared to advancing their visitor's historical consciousness—will need to examine how such consciousness can embrace local/global dynamics, i.e. to advance a *global* historical consciousness of sorts. Few enterprises might be more exciting.

REFERENCES

Appleby, J., Hunt, L., & Jacob, M. (1994). *Telling the truth about history,* London: W.W. Norton & Company.

Boix Mansilla, V. (2004). Between reproducing and organizing the past: Students' beliefs about the standards of acceptability of historical knowledge. In (AU: EDITORS?), *International review of research history education.* London, Fran Cass.

Carretero M., & Kriger, M (2011). Historical representations and conflicts about indigenous people as national identities. *Culture & Psychology, 17*(2), 177–195.

Gardner, H. (1999). *The disciplined mind.* New York: Simon and Schuster.

Gardner, H. (2007). *Five minds for the future.* Cambridge: Harvard Business School Press.

Lee, P., & Ashby, R. (2000). Progression in historical understanding among students ages 7 to 14. In P. Seixas, P. Stearns, & S. Wineburg (Eds.), *Knowing, learning and teaching history* (pp. 192–222). San Francisco: Lawrence Erlbaum Associates.

Lee, P., & Shemilt, D. (2007). New alchemy or fatal attraction? History and citizenship. *Teaching History, 129,* 14–19.

Suárez-Orozco, M., & Baolian Qin, D. (2004). *Globalization: Culture and education for a new millenium.* Berkeley: University of California Press and Ross Institute.

Suárez Orozco, M., Darbes, T., Dias, S.I. , & Sutin, M. (2011). Migration and schooling. *Annual Review of Anthropology, 40*(1), 311–328.

Seixas, P. (1997). Mapping historical significance. *Social Education, 61,* 1.

Wineburg, S. (2001). *Historical thinking and other unnatural acts: Charting the future of teaching the past.* Philadelphia: Temple University Press.

SECTION 5

COLLECTIVE MEMORIES AND
REPRESENTATIONS OF PAST AND FUTURE

CHAPTER 19

ARE FAMILY RECOLLECTIONS AN OBSTACLE TO HISTORY EDUCATION?

How German Students Make Sense of the East German Dictatorship

Sabine Moller

Historical consciousness is based on different ways of knowing the past, and one of these is *family memory*. While many of our images of the past are shaped by the media, how we interpret them is strongly influenced by our everyday lives, including family recollections. This chapter looks at the relationship between family memory and German history from different angles, starting with a discussion of the terms *historical consciousness, family memory,* and *contemporary history,* followed by a snapshot of the current debate over the lack of historical consciousness in the former East Germany. An empirical perspective is used to discuss how students think about the German Democratic Republic (GDR). The chapter concludes by address-

History Education and the Construction of National Identities, pages 281–295
Copyright © 2012 by Information Age Publishing
281

ing a crucial debate that began twenty years after the Berlin Wall fell: Do family recollections prevent students from recognizing "real" German history?

In 2009, when Germany celebrated Remembrance Day, it incorporated several other celebrations. I wish to focus on the three most significant: the 70th anniversary of the German assault on Poland and the beginning of the Second World War; the 60th commemoration of the formation of the Federal Republic of Germany (FRG); and the 20th year after the fall of the Berlin Wall. Such highly important anniversaries falling so close together provide a clue to the complexities of contemporary history in modern-day Germany.

Even in the twenty-first century, Germany's state-mandated memory, objectified in monuments, museums, and textbooks, is based on negative connotations (Fulbrook, 1999; Reichel, 2007). From this perspective—one that evolved in West Germany during the 1980s—the Holocaust is regarded as the *singular* or *central crime* of the twentieth century. In the wake of the disbanding of the East German state, the German Democratic Republic (or GDR), in 1989 and the reunification of Germany the following year, any discussion of Germany's past has become even more difficult, given the burden of a *double dictatorship*—the National Socialist regime in the 30s and 40s, followed by the Socialist one in East Germany (Jarausch, 2002).

The relationships between the three contemporary German histories (the "Third Reich," the GDR, and the FRG) are exceedingly complex. Although there is consensus that Germany has tried to come to terms with its Communist past on a political and juridical level (Großbölting, 2010), any tendency to accept this process as exemplary has been vehemently criticized by some (Beattie, 2008). Historian Andrew Beattie has shown that following reunification, the multifaceted pasts of East and West were often simplistically reduced to a dichotomy, with horror stories about the East colliding with success stories about the West. Former East Germans were supposed "to accept this polarized bleak image of their former state" (Beattie, 2008, p. 9). As a result, nostalgic reminiscences about life in the GDR were seen as a reaction to the commonly presented picture of a society dominated by the *Stasi* (East German secret police) (Ahbe, 2005; Cooke, 2005). Although all forms of state-mandated memory now consider the GDR a second German dictatorship, such a consensus has not been shared by private and public memories of the history of the Communist German Democratic Republic (Sabrow, 2009).

The intent of this paper is to offer a glimpse into the debates surrounding German *history and memory* that culminated in 2009, when the level of young people's knowledge about the history of the GDR became public, and evidently misleading family reminiscences were blamed for the students' lack of historical consciousness.

Given the controversy this debate engendered, I wanted to explore the role of family memory from different angles.

Theoretically. I start by drawing on Jörn Rüsen's concept of historical consciousness and its significance to didactics and education regarding present-day German history. Secondarily, I clarify the terms family-, cultural-, and communicative memory and their interrelationship with contemporary history.

Empirically. The debate on historical consciousness in Germany in 2009 was based on a quantitative study that indicated East German students are influenced by family remembrances. Using an excerpt from a focus group of East and West German tenth graders, I will explore this phenomenon from the perspective of my own qualitative research.

Pragmatically. While the outcome of the public debate called for specific lessons and authoritative interpretation to inform teaching East Germany history, my own analysis recommends further disciplined orientation.

HISTORICAL CONSCIOUSNESS AND GERMAN HISTORY EDUCATION

History and memory are not the same, but neither are they opposites. "History is," Jörn Rüsen (2007) writes, "an elaborated form of memory" (pp. 169–170). While memory suggests an immediate relationship with the past, history reflects a temporal distinction between past, present, and future. History and the discourse on historical consciousness involve rational criteria and "truth claims" by drawing on specific historical understanding and methodology. This paper draws on a model redefining Rüsen's concept to claim that the goal of teaching history is a *reflective and self-reflexive historical consciousness.* This concept is helpful, because it makes certain aspects (already included in Rüsen's theory) explicit, and thus easier to transfer to an educational setting (Schreiber et al., 2006).

In this sense, historical consciousness is *reflective,* in that it accepts that past, present, and future all have different time horizons, while history is a present reconstruction related to specific expectations for the future. It is *reflexive,* in that it adheres to the fact that an individual approach to the past (the need for orientation) is based in the realm of practical life (*Lebenswelt*), including social and cultural frameworks such as family, religion, nationality, etc. This concept of historical consciousness combines a disciplined and moderately postmodern approach (Borries, 2008b).

FAMILY MEMORY AND CONTEMPORARY HISTORY

Family memory is a crucial point of origin for French sociologist Maurice Halbwachs and the work he did on *collective memory* in the 1920s. In his book on the social frameworks of memory, Halbwachs considered family memory exceptionally significant since, as he points out, a family is an indissoluble relationship. "Men may change their occupations or nationality, they may rise or fall on the ladder of social positions .... But a son does not become a father unless he builds another family—and even then he will always remain the son of his father" (Halbwachs, 1992, p. 69f.).

As studied and described by Halbwachs, family memory belongs to what we call *communicative memory*. This term was coined by Jan Assmann (1995, 2008) to describe the recent past; as witnessed by contemporaries, it represents a timeframe of 80–100 years, spanning three to four generations. One characteristic of communicative memory is its lack of organization, based as it is on everyday communications. No special training is needed in order to consolidate this kind of memory.

Halbwachs's approach has been quite influential, especially in the German discourse on memory, in helping to locate different levels of memory. Although Halbwachs followed a constructivist approach (which is well-suited to postmodern discourses), one must remember that he had a specific understanding of history which must be modified, i.e. Halbwachs regarded History as a monolithic discipline that had nothing to do with the reconstructive memories he explored (Moller, 2003, p. 36).

Contemporary academic history shares the same time horizon as communicative memory, functioning as a part of history witnessed by contemporaries (Caplan, 2007; Hockerts, 2001). Although contemporary historiography may be seen as a form of memory (Rüsen, 2007), it is organized quite differently, based as it is on the methodological inquiry of experts. This often presents difficulties in communicating findings to the public (Klessmann, 2002). Such circumstances can result in a precarious relationship between contemporary historiography and communicative memory, giving rise to the notion that contemporary witnesses are the natural enemies of contemporary historians (Hockerts, 2001).

Taken to an extreme, this problem is compounded by family memory. Relatives, who may possess only one perspective of an event, command loyalty ties that impact any reconstruction of the past. As Halbwachs put it almost a century ago, we cannot prevent our memory or imagination from being influenced, not only by ideas about our parents' moral nature, but by the event itself, even at the moment of reconstruction (1992, p. 61). To use an example from contemporary German history, the idea that "we are helpful members of our family" serves as a social lens for constructing the truth about our ancestors.

When the recent past perceived by a public- or state-mandated memory is negative, such a process can be particularly difficult. Given its legacy of double dictatorship, this was certainly the case with Germany, where survivors and descendants have had to integrate private photos and family memories with the official histories of a dictatorship institutionalized by memorials (Kaminsky, 2007, Sabrow et al., 2007).

Some of the crucial ideas of Halbwachs are reflected in the multigenerational interviews regarding National Socialism and the Holocaust (Moller, 2009b; Welzer, 2005; Welzer et al., 2002), in particular by the grandchildren of Third Reich contemporaries who, incredibly, tend to see their forebears' role during the war more positively than the grandparents themselves. These findings, published under the title "Grandpa Wasn't a Nazi," inevitably provoke the question of whether this process will repeat itself with East German recollections (i.e., "Daddy Wasn't a Member of the Stasi"). Of course, such a question ignores the fact that "Grandpa Wasn't a Nazi" has the paradoxical effect of being a "successful" public education campaign (or *Aufarbeitung,* after an educational unit on German war crimes in the extermination camps), generally unrelated to family recollections of the Third Reich.

THE DEBATE ABOUT EAST GERMAN NOSTALGIA

Over the past decade, the phenomenon of East German nostalgia, so-called *Ostalgia* (combining the German word for "east" with the notion of nostalgia), has attracted much attention (Ahbe, 2005; Banchelli, 2008). A *TIME Magazine* report on Germans "hankering for the bad old days" reported that East German teens seem to have "an extremely distorted view" of the former GDR (Kirchner, 2008).

The article stressed that according to an empirical investigation, misleading family recollections might be preventing students from recognizing the "true character" of the East German dictatorship (Deutz-Schroeder & Schroeder, 2008). The Schroeder study posited that parents and grandparents, in their role as contemporary witnesses of GDR history, not only stood in the way of students forming a critical perspective of East German history, but "impose[d] their own nostalgic view" (ibid., p. 604). The authors recommended visits to memorial sites and talking to victims of the East German regime as mandatory steps in breaking the grip of these family recollections. This method is generally considered a successful educational model, and had been previously used to moderate memories of the Third Reich in West Germany (Deutz-Schroeder & Schroeder, 2009).

The Schroeder study has resonated in Germany and abroad for many reasons, primarily the timing of the current commemoration of the fall of the Berlin Wall and German reunification. Another reason is the widespread assumption that "students have no clue about history," a lack of historical consciousness which is supposedly worse in former Communist states. Although the study was mainly based on quantitative data (i.e., a multiple-choice test)[1], the authors critique what they see as a problem with history education, and offer a specific formula for teaching history in the schools.

Before discussing these recommendations, I want to take a closer look at how students make sense of the East German past and respond to authoritative interpretation.

INTERVIEWING STUDENTS ABOUT THE GDR

In 2006 I conducted a research project looking at the transmission of East German history. My main goal was to study the cultural curriculum of the GDR past.

A *cultural curriculum* goes beyond the context of school; instead, it draws on a broad range of media, such as feature films, songs, objects, websites, even family albums, all things that people use to remember and make sense of the past (Wineburg et al., 2007). It was important that the reception of these sources served as the point of origin. Along with using textbooks, memorial sites, and other prominent *lieux de mémoire* as points of departure, I considered every source connected with the students' *communicative memory,* used either implicitly or explicitly to make sense of the past.

The leading research questions were: How do young people compose images and conceptions from such different sources as textbooks, movies, and own experiences? How do they mediate between lessons learned in school and family recollections? How is history appropriated by students and how do they make sense of the past overall?

I interviewed students from both eastern and western Germany from grades 1–12 at a variety of different schools (Moller, 2008). The students were randomly sampled from those who had received parental permission to participate in the investigation. The sample consisted of 46 group discussions with more than 200 students all told. Group discussions involved 4–8 participants and had a very open structure. The initial question was simply: "What comes to mind when you hear the term GDR?"

In the first phase, students were given the opportunity to talk spontaneously about their own associations, thoughts, and experiences. The main goal was to initiate a kind of self-directed discussion, as close to a normal, everyday school conversations as possible, given the artificial environment of the interview situation (Loos/Schäffer, 2001, p. 13). When the self-directed discussion was completed (or after 30 minutes, whichever came first), I would present the students with a visual stimulus, consisting of a matchbox-sized Trabant (East German car), an East German flag, and a photo of the fall of the Berlin Wall. During this phase of the interview I

---

[1] For a more detailed critique of the study, see von Borries, (2008a), and Moller, (2009a).

would ask questions about specific sources of information (i.e., literature, computer games, museums, etc.).

The following sequence was conducted with a group of five tenth-graders at a Gymnasium in the east part of Berlin in December 2006. This discussion, between three girls and a boy, took place during the initial, self-directed phase. All of the students were born after German reunification in 1990 and were between 15 –16 years of age. I have chosen this sequence because it embodies several important aspects of the debate about the effect of misleading family recollections on student knowledge.

The excerpt starts at a point after the students had been discussing ideas about the GDR for approximately 15 minutes. The student I call Bruno cites the importance of popular films as a form of historical consciousness. Whenever he pictures the GDR, he conjures up images from popular films (in the ongoing public debate over the GDR, these tragicomedies are commonly called *ostalgic*). But Bruno distances himself from this kind of memory since, as he puts it, *Ostalgia* minimizes the grim presence of the Berlin Wall and trivializes the general view of the GDR.

A classmate, "Julianne," simply considers most kinds of "Ostkult" (Eastcult, as she terms *Ostalgia*) embarrassing. Another student, "Alice," defends films she has never seen, claiming that "some things were actually like they are depicted," and that East Germans "felt and lived differently."

Bruno, however, finds this plea for diversity in the GDR unacceptable. He counters:

Bruno: We have to accept that the GDR was a regime of terror, the GDR was a state of terror.
           [The other students react excitedly, in unison: No, No—You can't—No—].
Julianne: It was a kind of hidden dictatorship, that's what you can call it.
Bruno: The first article of the GDR's constitution said that communism has to be protected, that the one-party system has to be protected.
Julianne: Yes, but it wasn't communism.
Bruno: That's not what I said, but it is stated clearly in the first article of the GDR's constitution.
Alice   I wouldn't call it a regime of terror at all. When you can say that everybody had a job in that state—except for a few, maybe some of them didn't even want to work—they got an education, and the best of them could go to university, and when you accepted it, like my family who lived happily—
Bruno: But people who had their own opinions, who had friends in other countries, who -
Alice: My grandparents had their own opinions.

Bruno: Yes, but it was like that pastor Brüsewitz[2] for example
Alice: We're not Christian.
Bruno: There was systematic repression of people who didn't fit into the system. And it was all arbitrary. When you crossed the border, a policeman who didn't like [the shape of] your nose could say: "No, you go back, you get checked again."
Alice: And how many people did that happen to? Do you know?
Julianne: But a regime of terror doesn't characterize any form of government, that's not possible.
Alice: Maybe there were some things that were rather cruel, but in general—
Bruno: It was the same thing people said about the Nazis—that everybody had a job.

This sequence exemplifies a common German theme in public discussions about adequate representation of the GDR past. During the students' discussion, the framework was articulated by Bruno, who was born in a reunified Germany, but whose parents grew up in West Germany. The well-founded perception that the GDR was a dictatorship was thoroughly accepted in the West. Thus, it was easy for Bruno to condemn the GDR using exaggerated rhetoric like "regime of terror."[3] In the East, however, it was a different matter.

His classmates appeared uncomfortable with Bruno's sweeping assessments. They tried to modify them and stress the diversity of life in the GDR, while rejecting Bruno's blanket condemnation of the East German state. Bruno's response echoes the public debate, discrediting considerations of daily life in East Germany by comparing the GDR to the Third Reich (for examples see Sabrow et al., 2007).

This discussion appeared to be governed by tacit rules that dictate what is acceptable to talk about—not based in any examination of East German history but rather adapted from the West German *Aufarbeitung*, and its effort to cope with Germany's National Socialist past. In a sense, then, the reconstruction of East German history appeared asymmetrical, with the Nazi past and its *Aufarbeitung* overshadowing any historical evidence the students were asked to discuss. So which sources of historical evidence were

---

[2] Oskar Brüsewitz was a Christian pastor who committed self-immolation (set fire to himself) in 1976 to protest repression in the GDR (Grashoff, 2006).

[3] Looking at this sequence more closely, it is important to remember that I was there as a West German researcher. In order to interpret these interviews, I applied Welzer's Hermeneutic Dialog Analysis which pays special attention to the question of who is speaking to whom, on the basis of which expectations (Welzer, 1993). Thus I assumed Bruno would address me in the same way he addressed his classmates.

significant for the students, and how did family recollections fit into these frameworks of historical consciousness?

FRAMEWORKS OF EAST GERMAN HISTORY

Alice started out defending the melodramas that depict the GDR past. She insisted that life in the GDR was similar to that shown in the movies—bright moments, along with stressful and even shattering events. Living in East Germany, her family had made the best of things. When she thinks about those years, she pictures her parents at a youth camp, an image that reflects an idea of organized youth, a community engaged in activities. For Alice, antifascism and the expropriation of wealth were a credit to the Socialist regime. Much conversation about the GDR apparently took place within her family, and Alice was not a blank slate. While she refused to condemn the GDR, she equated criticism of the Eastern State to a critique of her own family. Her view of the GDR was thus linked closely to her family's history. She rejected Bruno's concrete examples and challenged their relevance to an "average Joe" in the GDR—that is, her own family.

Julianne understood the GDR past in a critical but empathetic way. She distanced herself from the regime's paternalism. Her own parents had been targeted by the Stasi, and she had heard stories about East German surveillance. When she pictured the GDR, images of paintings she called "East-Art" (socialist realism) came to mind. She was also interested in books from that time, GDR thrillers she had found at a flea market, and East German punk music. Using these relics of the past, she was able to decipher the uniform and ideological character of socialism, alternatively portrayed favorably (in art and popular thrillers) or negatively (in the defiant lyrics of punk bands). Although her parents didn't hold a positive view of the GDR overall, they did speak about positive experiences or circumstances that were better back then, such as the fully staffed schools. Julianne rejected Bruno's condemnation of the GDR. Instead, the term she used was "hidden dictatorship," which seemed to echo her interest in locating signs of dictatorship in objects of everyday culture.

Bruno seemed certain in his condemnation of the GDR as a "regime of terror." Comparing and equating two German dictatorships were inherent in his use of the term, and they were implicitly and explicitly articulated in most of his statements. His argument was based on two concrete examples: he referred to a critical documentary about the GDR he had seen in school recounting the self-immolation of Pastor Brüsewitz, and he illustrated the socialist state's character by citing the arbitrary nature of East-West border controls.

Given that the experience of harassing border controls seems mostly a West German one (Schloegel, 2009), this last example exemplified Bruno's background. This was a part of his *family memory* since, as was mentioned during the discussion, his father was a journalist who sometimes traveled to East Germany and had to pass through the Berlin Wall. Bruno's view of the GDR was framed by a family memory linked to an official view of East German dictatorship.

CONCLUSION

The students' discussion cited here is not representative in a statistical sense. However, it demonstrates an aspect of historical consciousness that can be seen around the world: family recollections are generally stimulating and trusted sources to engage with the past (Conrad et al., 2009). The sequence cited above reveals a reality that, for methodological reasons, is often absent in quantitative examinations: *how* people relate to their families' histories and recollections, and how difficult it is to counteract something they "know for sure," given that it was the firsthand experience of a family member. It is hard to trump that kind of emotionally charged evidence using abstract dates and "facts."

While this example cannot pretend to offer conclusive results or a strict formula for teaching German history, it does make us wonder whether reinforcing authoritative interpretations is the best tool for enhancing students' historical consciousness.

Like the other interviews in my sample,[4] this last example shows that students with an eastern as well as western German background were influenced by different *family memories*. Whereas East German family memories included details of everyday life, West German families tended to hand down an outside perspective: remembrance of the Berlin Wall with barbed wire and border controls. In this respect, a historical consciousness that reflected one's own approach to East German history seemed to be a necessary one for both groups of students.

At the same time the sequence illustrated an important but often overlooked finding of the Schroeder study: Students in eastern Germany were extremely interested in their own history, with 70% reporting that they wanted to know more about life back then.[5] This connection to the past is likely related to how often the GDR would come up in conversation and in family stories. Despite the problematic implications of this finding—that students might equate criticism of the GDR to a critique of their own family—the students' interest should be recognized as a valuable steppingstone to enriching history education.

---

[4] For more examples of how the views of students with West German backgrounds are framed by family memory, see Moller (2008).

[5] The exact numbers of students interested in GDR history were 69.5% eastern German and 53.3% western German (Deutz-Schroeder & Schroeder, 2008).

Historical consciousness is a dynamic construct for making sense of the past. Our interpretations of the past are related to our present experiences and expectations for the future (Jeismann, 1997). Thus, gloomy conditions in the present (i.e., unemployment, downsized teaching staffs) tend to romanticize life as it was "back then." It is inappropriate to refute such contradictions by simply discrediting them as ostalgic or conflating Ostalgia with a Nazi past. History education must address the contradictions as well as the moral ambiguity in the classroom, and do so in an authentic way that characterizes a liberal, open society (Wineburg, 2001, p. 230). In this respect, any German discussion of the *Aufarbeitung* of the GDR past requires fresh thought. Recent studies of students' historical consciousness suggest caution when qualifying Holocaust education in Germany as exemplary (Meseth et al., 2004, Welzer et al., 2002; Zülsdorf-Kersting, 2008). The West German approach to dealing with the Nazi past has been neither an educational success story nor the only approach to thinking about the GDR.

History education in Germany is based on democratic values. Historical consciousness in our society serves as an orientation (*Orientierungswissen*). While it is important to recognize that the GDR was a dictatorship, in a democracy, process is as important as values. Educators must neither overwhelm nor indoctrinate students to check the "dictatorship" box on a multiple-choice test. Instead, they should find a way to teach history that is linked to the *cultural curriculum* of a society, one that embraces *cultural and communicative memory*. History teaching, as Roy Rosenzweig (2000) put it, should be "somehow simultaneously more local and intimate and more global and cosmopolitan, more shaped by popular concerns and more enriched by insights based on systematic and detailed study of the past" (p. 280).

In this respect, strengthening and rediscovering a disciplined approach to teaching history both inside and outside the context of school may be the best way to come to terms with Germany's difficult multiple pasts. Any canon of specific knowledge or authoritative interpretations will misconceive the nature of history (Lee & Howson, 2009). The demand that we teach students a "true" German history is not only unrealistic, it neglects thirty years of debate about the didactics of German history. In order to help students understand the historical accounts in their textbooks or their family's recollections, they must understand that these are constructions based on different epistemologies. In turn, educators must provide them with the ability to deal with competing stories about the past.[6]

When treated as distortions of the truth, *family memories* become an obstacle to history education. Instead, we should help students recognize they

---

[6] I don't think it is promising if students start interviewing their own families or analyze their own family recollections, because these sources are too closely related to their own identity (see Moller, 2009b).

are a very specific source in a universe of possible other sources. While such a source can have a powerful impact on our orientation in time, like all sources it can be integrated into the bigger picture, using responsible and systematic reasoning.

REFERENCES

Ahbe, T. (2005). *Ostalgie: zum Umgang mit der DDR-Vergangenheit in den 1990er Jahren* [*Ostalgia: about dealing with the GDR-past in the 1990s*]. Erfurt, Landeszentrale für Politische Bildung Thüringen.

Assmann, J. (1995). Collective memory and cultural identity. *New German Critique, 65*, 125–133.

Assmann, J. (2008). Communicative and cultural memory. In A. Erll & A. Nünning (Eds.), *Cultural memory studies: An international and interdisciplinary handbook* (pp. 109–125). Berlin/New York: Walter de Gruyter.

Banchelli, E. (2008). Ostalgie: eine vorläufige Bilanz [Ostalgia: A make-shift balance]. In F. Cambi (Ed.), *Gedächtnis und Identität. Die deutsche Literatur nach der Vereinigung* [*Remembrance and identity. German literature after the reunification*], (pp. 57–68). Würzburg: Königshausen & Neumann.

Beattie, A. (2007). Learning from the Germans? History and memory in German and European projects of integration. *PORTAL Journal of Multidisciplinary International Studies, 4*(2). Retrieved from http://epress.lib.uts.edu.au/research/handle/10453/1524 [14/04/2011].

Beattie, A. (2008). *Playing politics with history: The Bundestag inquiries into East Germany.* New York: Berghahn Books.

Borries, B. von (2008a). *Vergleichendes Gutachten zu zwei empirischen Studien über Kenntnisse und Einstellungen von Jugendlichen zur DDR-Geschichte.* [*A comparative report of two empirical studies about knowledge and attitudes of youth on the GDR history*]. Retrieved from http://www.berlin.de/imperia/md/content/sen-bildung/politische_bildung/kenntnisse_ddr_geschichte.pdf [14/04/2011].

Borries, B. von (2008b). *Historisch Denken Lernen—Welterschließung statt Epochenüberblick: Geschichte als Unterrichtsfach und Bildungsaufgabe* [*Learning historical thinking—opening up the world instead of an epoch overview: History as instructional profession and educational task*]. Opladen: Budrich.

Caplan, J. (2007). Contemporary history: Reflections from Britain and Germany. *History Workshop Journal, 1*, 230–238.

Conrad, M., Létourneau, J., & Northrup, D. (2009). Canadians and their pasts: An exploration in historical consciousness. *The Public Historian, 31*(1), 15–34.

Cooke, P. (2005). *Representing East Germany since unification: From colonization to nostalgia.* Oxford, UK: Berg Publishers.

Deutz-Schroeder, M., & Schroeder, K. (2008). *Soziales Paradies oder Stasi-Staat? Das DDR-Bild von Schülern—ein Ost-West-Vergleich.* [*Social paradise or Stasi-state? The image of the GDR in students—An east west comparison*]. Stamsried: Verlag Ernst Vögel.

Deutz-Schroeder, M., & Schroeder, K. (2009). Essay: Demokratie? Diktatur? Achselzucken... Wie Wissenschaftler weiterhin die DDR weichzeichnen und die Untätigkeit von Lehrern und das Nichtwissen von Schülern entschuldigen.

[Democracy? Dictatorship? To shrug. How scientists persistently blur the GDR and excuse the inaction of teachers and the ignorance of students]. *DIE WELT*, 09.02.2009. Retrieved from http://www.welt.de/welt_print/article3170710/Demokratie-Diktatur-Achselzucken.html, [14/04/2011].

Fulbrook, M. (1999). *German national identity after the Holocaust.* Cambridge, UK: Polity Press.

Grashoff, U. (2006). Wie ein Blitzschlag in der hochelektrisch geladenen Atmosphäre eines totalitären Systems? Zum 30. Jahrestag der Selbstverbrennung von Oskar Brüsewitz in Zeitz [Like a lightning bolt in the electrically charged atmosphere of a totalitarian system. At the 30th anniversary of the self-cremation of Oskar Brüsewitz in Zeitz]. *Deutschland Archiv, 4*, 619–628.

Großbölting, T. (2010). Die DDR im vereinten Deutschland [The GDR in a united Germany]. *Aus Politik und Zeitgeschichte* (25–26), 35–41.

Halbwachs, M. (1992). *On collective memory.* Chicago/London: University of Chicago Press.

Hockerts, H. G. (2001). Zugänge zur Zeitgeschichte: Primärerfahrung, Erinnerungskultur, Geschichtswissenschaft [Access to contemporary history: primary experience, memory culture and historical science]. *Aus Politik und Zeitgeschichte*, S. 17–30.

Jarausch, K. (2002). A double burden: The politics of the past and German identity. In J. Leonhard & L. Funk (Eds.), *Ten years of German unification: Transfer, transformation, incorporation* (pp. 98–114). Birmingham, UK: Birmingham University Press.

Jeismann, K. E. (1997). Geschichtsbewusstsein—Theorie [Historical consciousness—theory]. In Bergmann et al. (Eds.), *Handbuch der Geschichtsdidaktik* (pp. 42–44). Seelze-Velber: Kallmeyer.

Kaminsky, A. (2007). *Orte des Erinnerns: Gedenkzeichen, Gedenkstätten und Museen zur Diktatur in SBZ und DDR [Places of remembering: Memorials, monuments and museums about the dictatorship in the Soviet Occupied Zone and GDR].* Berlin: Ch. Links Verlag.

Kirchner, S. (2008, September 29). Postcard from Berlin: Raising a glass to East Germany. *TIME Magazine*, p. 11.

Klessmann, C. (2002). Zeitgeschichte als wissenschaftliche Aufklärung [Contemporary history as scientific enlightenment]. *Aus Politik und Zeitgeschichte, 51–52*, 3–12.

Lee, P., & Howson, J. (2009). 'Two out of five did not know that Henry VIII had six wives': History education, historical literacy and historical consciousness. In L. Symcox & A. Wilschut (Eds.), *National history standards: The problem of the canon and the future of teaching history* (pp. 211–261). Charlotte, NC: Information Age Publishing.

Loos, P., & Schäffer, B. (2001). *Das Gruppendiskussionsverfahren. Theoretische Grundlagen und empirische Anwendung [Dealing with group discussions. Theoretical fundaments and empirical application].* Opladen: Leske und Budrich.

Meseth, W. (Ed.). (2004). *Schule und Nationalsozialismus: Anspruch und Grenzen des Geschichtsunterrichts [Schools and national socialism: rights and boundaries of history education].* Frankfurt: Campus Verlag.

Moller, S. (2003). *Vielfache Vergangenheit. Öffentliche Erinnerungskulturen und Familienerinnerungen an die NS-Zeit in Ostdeutschland* [*Multiple pasts. Public memory cultures and family recollections of NS-times in eastern Germany*].Tübingen Edition Diskord.

Moller, S. (2008). Eine Fußnote des Geschichtsbewusstseins? Wie Schüler in Westdeutschland Sinn aus der DDR-Geschichte machen [A footnote for historical consciousness? How students in western Germany make sense of the GDR history]. In M. Barricelli & J. Hornig (Eds.), *Aufklärung, Bildung, "Histotainment"? Zeitgeschichte in Unterricht und Gesellschaft heute* (pp. 175–187). Frankfurt am Main: Peter Lang.

Moller, S. (2009a). Review of Deutz-Schroeder, M & Schroeder, K. Soziales Paradies oder Stasi Staat? Das DDR-Bild von Schülern—ein Ost-West-Vergleich, Stamsried 2008. *Zeitschrift für Geschichtsdidaktik,* 8, 264–266.

Moller, S. (2009b). Teaching a troubled past: Potential challenges and pitfalls of incorporating family recollections into history education. *Zeitschrift für Pädagogische Historiographie,* (2), 56–59.

Reichel, P. (2007). *Vergangenheitsbewältigung in Deutschland: die Auseinandersetzung mit der NS-Diktatur in Politik und Justiz* [Handling the past in Germany: the discussion with the NS-dictatorship in politics and justice]. München: CH Beck.

Rosenzweig, R. (2000). How Americans use and think about the past: Implications from a national survey for the teaching of history. In P.N. Stearns, P. Seixas, & S. Wineburg (Eds.), *Knowing, teaching, and learning history: National and international perspectives* (pp. 262–283). New York/London: New York University Press.

Rüsen, J. (2007). How to make sense of the past: salient issues of metahistory. *TD: The Journal for Transdisciplinary Research in Southern Africa,* 3(1), 169–221.

Sabrow, M. (Ed.). (2009). *Erinnerungsorte der DDR* [*Memorials of the GDR*]. München: C.H. Beck.

Sabrow, M., Eckert, R, Flacke, M., Henke, K.-D., Jahn, R, Klier, F., Krone, T., Maser, P., Poppe, U., & Rudolph, H. (Eds.) (2007). *Wohin treibt die DDR-Erinnerung? Dokumentation einer Debatte* [*Where to leads the GDR remembrance? Documentation of a debate*]. Göttingen: Vandenhoeck & Ruprecht.

Schloegel, K. (2009). Generation Marienborn. Essay. *Aus Politik und Zeitgeschichte 21–22,* 3–6.

Schreiber, W., Andreas, K., Borries, B. v., Krammer, R., Leutner-Ramme, S., Mebus, S., Schöner, A., Ziegler, B. (2006). *Historisches Denken. Ein Kompetenz Strukturmodell.* [*Historical thinking. A structural competence model*]. Neuried: ars una.

Welzer, H. (1993). *Transitionen: zur Sozialpsychologie biographischer Wandlungsprozesse* [*Transitions: About social psychological biographic processes of change*].Tübingen: edition diskord.

Welzer, H. (2005): *Grandpa wasn't a Nazi: The Holocaust in German family remembrance.* Hg. v. American Jewish Committee (International Perpectives, 54). Retrieved from http://www.memory-research.de/cms/download.php?id=2 [14/04/2011].

Welzer, H., Moller, S., & Tschuggnall, K. (2002): *Opa war kein Nazi. Nationalsozialismus und Holocaust im Familiengedächtnis* [*Grandpa wasn't a Nazi. National Socialism and Holocaust in family recollections*]. Frankfurt am Main: Fischer.

Wineburg, S. (2001). *Historical thinking and other unnatural acts: Charting the future of teaching the past.* Philadelphia: Temple University Press.

Wineburg, S., Mosborg, S., Porat, D., & Duncan, A. (2007). Common belief and the cultural curriculum: An intergenerational study of historical consciousness. *American Educational Research Journal, 1,* 40–76.

Zülsdorf-Kersting, M. (2008). *Sechzig Jahre danach: Jugendliche und Holocaust: Eine Studie zur geschichtskulturellen Sozialisation* [*Sixty years later: the youth and the Holocaust: A study on historicultural socialization*]. Berlin/Hamburg/Münster: Lit Verlag.

CHAPTER 20

HISTORY AS A DYNAMIC PROCESS

Reanalyzing a Case of Anglo-Japanese Reconciliation

Kyoko Murakami

INTRODUCTION

This chapter addresses how history unfolds in the practice of remembering and reconciliation and illustrates the dynamic process of collective memory shaping, and being shaped by the individual memory. Over the past decade, I've been interested in the practices of remembering and reconciliation. I have examined a case of Anglo Japanese reconciliation in the context of war, and in particular, the post-war experience of British veterans who were prisoners of war (POWs) in Japan during the Second World War.

In this chapter, rather than discussing war as a cause and effect term, I shall focus on discursive practices as to how war affected people's lives and how history comes to intersect with their lives. In doing so, I wish to illustrate the relationship between national (or collective) history and prac-

History Education and the Construction of National Identities, pages 297–310
Copyright © 2012 by Information Age Publishing

tices of reconciliation. I shall explore these issues by drawing on a relatively unknown case of the experiences of former British prisoners of war whilst in captivity under the Japanese in the Far East and their post-war reconciliation experiences, both in Japan and in Britain (Murakami, 2001; Murakami, in press). The overall aim of this exploration is to rethink an approach to history as a grand narrative of nation-state by plotting individual experiences. The focus is on the interrelations between the national history, collective memory and individual recollection of the war events and experiences. Lastly, I shall address the significance of the discussion for history teaching.

THE EVENT: THE RUPTURE

In late May of 1998, the Japanese Emperor and Empress made a state visit to the United Kingdom. During that visit, on May 27, former British POWs who had been held captive in the Far East during the Second World War protested as the Japanese dignitaries made their way up the Mall to the official reception being held at Buckingham Palace in London. The protesters opposed a state visit from a nation that, in their view, had not provided a satisfactory level of apology and compensation in relation to the Japanese military's treatment of Far Eastern POWs (FEPOWs) during the Second World War. A group of FEPOWs and family members turned their backs and whistled "Colonel Bogey" (the theme tune from David Lean's celebrated film The Bridge on the River Kwai [1957] and emblematic of the former prisoners' resistance to Japanese military authority). One FEPOW burned the Japanese flag as the state parade passed by. The protesters and anti-Japanese sentiment were widely reported in the news media during the period of this state visit. The photographed images of the flag burning and other acts of protest embellished the front pages of the following day's national newspapers, coupled with headlines portraying eye-witness accounts of atrocities in captivities and testimonies of the post-war trauma of the former POWs and their family members. One of the national newspapers' "Letter to the Editor" section assembled a diverse range of views and opinions on the staged FEPOWs' protest and the wider issues of reparation, apology, reconciliation and forgiveness (Murakami, 1999; Murakami & Middleton, 2002).

UNFINISHED BUSINESS

Reconciliation is a fraught issue here. The Second World War ended over half a century ago. Since then, Japan has built a high profile in the global economy and plays a significant role in promoting peace in international politics and diplomacy. However, the staged protest against the Japanese Emperor in 1998 illustrates that the experiences of veterans from the Second World War were a live issue. Clearly, there is a sense of unfinished business, which draws implications for the nature of remembering and reconciliation. In more recent years, this has re-ignited the question of whether or not a formal apology can be identified in statements made by figures such as the Japanese prime minister and Emperor Akihito. This contentious past, including events such as the Second World War, gave me an entry point into studying the interplay of remembering and reconciliation. My inquiry explores how and in which ways the wartime and post-war experiences of these veterans are bundled [assembled] in the practices of remembering and reconciliation, with a methodology influenced by discursive psychology (Edwards & Potter, 1992). As an alternative approach to cognitive science and experimental psychology, discursive psychology shares tenets of social constructionism as a critical movement to the positivist paradigmatic thinking which is prominent, for example, in social psychology (Edwards & Potter, 1992; Potter & Wetherell, 1987). Drawing upon discursive psychology and social constructionism (Burr 1995; Gergen, 1997, 1999), I set out to study the former British POWs' experiences of reconciliation and addressed the importance of studying remembering as "social action"—not as individual psychological/interior phenomena but as discursive phenomena (Edwards & Middleton, 1986; Middleton & Edwards, 1990). Rather than assuming the mind as being a container of representations of the past or as an object of "remembering" in a culturally de-contextualized, confined laboratory space, I examined language use, discourse, as to how social actions (e.g., justifying, defending, blaming) are achieved within everyday talk-in-interaction in the research interviews. Studies using discursive psychological perspective have reworked cognitivist conceptualisations and replaced them with an analysis of action situated within a discursive context (e.g., Neisser's study of John Dean's memory [1981]; Edwards & Potter [1992, pp. 30–53]). Rather than assuming Dean's testimony, as a pathway to the nature of memory processes, the testimony, along with the various reports, is analyzed for uncovering social action involving blame, responsibility and mitigation.

HISTORIES:
THE COLLECTIVE AND THE INDIVIDUAL

The research using a discursive psychological approach has produced an empirically grounded analysis to support a view that remembering is a socially constructive process (Murakami, 2001). Its main argument is that reconciliation is achieved moment-by-moment in interaction, such as in research interviews (Murakami, 2001). Following this research, as part of a methodological critique on the discursive approach, Murakami and Middleton (2006) produced an analysis in highlighting the enduring aspect of the very interplay between the personal and the collective—the grand narrative of history and the individual lived experiences—and explored the complexity and web of emerging (and withering) relations. The analysis focused on the discourses around a grave near a former POW camp in Japan. The grave was built for 13 British soldiers who died in the camp during the war. A few decades after the war, the discovery of a grave opened up communications between the Japanese camp workers and community members and the British veterans, who were interned in the camp. Some of the British veterans were reunited with the former camp workers and community members in Japan as the veterans and their family members took part in the first reconciliation trip to Japan in 1992 (for a fuller story, please see Murakami & Middleton, 2006). The analysis traced the history of the grave and plotted the relational nodes in which humans and materials are held up as part of on-going reconciliation practices.

To examine the complexity and dynamic interplay of the collective (history) and the personal (experiences and local engagements), there are basically two approaches to reconciliation as a social practice. One approach is to begin from historical givens and then explore how persons contextualise their own memories in relation to some grand narratives of events. In so doing, they can construct plausible personal identities and biographies corresponding to the collective/history (Neisser, 1982). This requires the study of how the patterning of history can be taken as a particular global benchmark and context for an individual's memory and identity. Such work explores the ways in which autobiographical memory and identity are patterned in relation to significant historical events, such as declarations of war and national commemorations (e.g. Conway, 1997). In this sense, history would serve as a reference point around which individual lives might be organised. However, as Maurice Halbwachs (1981 (1950)) discusses, the formal accounts of history are rarely stable enough to serve as clear anchoring points for individual memories to be constructed around. In telling the personal narrative and constructing an identity, history is refracted by the collective framework. On one hand, the collective memory of an event defines membership, yet on the other hand, the collective memory collapses as it is not clear what a given event means, or even that it has significance as an "event" for everyone. The death of Princess Diana in Paris in 1997 is a classic case, which might be considered as an instance of memory crisis in modernity. What might be seen as a global benchmark is defined as an event that individuals are able to spontaneously and vividly recall. In fact, over a decade or so later, this event seems rather faded and outdated, overtaken by some other globally momentous event such as 9/11 in 2001 and the subsequent conflicts in Afghanistan and Iraq.

These global events in our time render our relationship to history hardly stable and indeed, somewhat fleeting. The events invoke diverse emotional and moral responses such as mourning and blaming and produce a set of interpretations. Mainstream psychological research on flashbulb memory (Brown & Kulik, 1977), for instance, explores the way in which people anchor their responses to major historical events. Despite its claim about resistance to forgetting and consistency of memory characterised by affect and emotional responses, flashback memory only captures the exact moment of interplay between the collective and the individual, failing to see the emergence and unfolding of new meanings in the event triggering rupture. In any case, it is not sufficient to assume that a global benchmark or grand narrative (or history) is as singular and coherent as it may appear at first glance. Under this misplaced, misconstrued homogeneity of global benchmarks in a grand narrative of history, shards of histories continue to surface in encounters with the cultural other and produce social, political and moral consequences. The earlier example of the staged protest by the FEPOWs precisely illuminates the unfixed and unpredictable nature of how the historical event (such as the Second World War) continues to resonate in the present within the trajectories of the Anglo-Japanese political-economic relationship as well as its wider moral consequences as the question of national identity is reframed.

Alternatively, a discursive approach (Murakami, 2001) begins by localising experience within lived interaction and by examining how the past—as both an individual and collective concern—is made relevant within the local communication (Billig, 1999; Middleton & Edwards, 1990). Whilst local interactional accomplishment (as discourse analysis for a discursive reconciliation) is made visible, the broader forms of experience with the major event are made invisible in the local interactions (such as the media coverage of the staged protest against the Japanese Emperor or any anti-Japanese campaigns). Yet, these two aforementioned approaches seem to fall short. Beginning with the global, we necessarily turn away from the actual experience of the British veterans toward the range of grand narratives in various historical records and popular films. However, as we know, these narratives do not always sit together side by side. The narrative of the Japanese people's victimhood and Japan as a peaceful country is precisely that which the British veterans seek to dispute. This means that we cannot use historical time as a clear benchmark or a fixed reference point for individual lives. On the contrary, working from the other direction using the discursive approach, we soon find that the very essence of reconciliation seems to collapse. Reconciliation as an object seems to dissipate. The narration of individual experiences and the reconstruction of the past do not fit into the complex international demands of the present, manifested by the staged protest.

CONNECTING THE LOCAL AND THE GLOBAL

The discussion of the two approaches begs a methodological question of how to study the relationship between the personal experience and the broader historical narratives. Is it possible to resolve the tension between the local and the global? There are multiple positions oscillating between the empirical fields: on the one hand is the immediately produced local interaction in the personal setting; on the other is the global context of historically anchored remembering (the collective remembering).

As Jens Brockmeier (2002) suggests, one way forward is to start with a position in which there is no principal separation between the individual or personal memory and the social, collective or historical memory. We can then ask what mediates between the local and the global. For example, we can look at James Wertsch's work on collective remembering as the study of the dialectical relationship between active agents and cultural tools (Wertsch, 2002). This way, we can explore the dynamic of collective remembering without attending to dualisms (neither individual (personal narrative) vs. collective (historical narratives/accounts), nor local vs. global and interior/psychological vs. exterior/social). In other words, we focus on a dynamic process of movement that combines and relates the self and the other, the now and the then, the here and the there (Brockmeier, 2002, p. 9). The focus then is to investigate "mediational action," which extends and folds the local and the global into each other. In other words, we examine how the local and the global intersect in ways that continually transform the matter-topic and substance of remembering and reconciliation.

REMEMBERING AND RECONCILIATION IN NETWORKS OF ASSOCIATION

In resolving the conundrum and challenging the reductive approach to sociological and psychological analysis, the work of Actor Network Theory (e.g. Callon, 1986; Latour, 1999) was drawn upon (for a full argument and analysis, see Murakami & Middleton, 2006). According to Marilyn Strathern, "actor network imagery offers a vision of social analysis that will treat social and technological alike; any entity or material can qualify for attention" (1996, p. 521). Actor networks are made up of a web of heterogeneous elements (including humans and nonhumans, culture and nature, technology and society, for instance). In this view, social structure is considered as an emergent effect of on-going processes of ordering rather than as a bedrock of rules, procedures and norms which affect our behaviors. Such analysis is different from the idea that the "social" holds the subject and the object together. Rather, sociality is formed by mediation through material artefacts. John Law says that "if human beings form a social network it is not because of the interaction with other human beings, it is because they interact with human beings and...materials" (Law, 1992, p. 2). Clearly, this approach demands not only the discourse analysis but also tracing the history of relations amongst people, places, materials, talks and stories, histories and popular culture.

CIRCULATING REFERENCE AND EMERGENT NETWORKS

This third position allows us to examine how reconciliation is accomplished both locally and globally in multiple networks involving humans, practices, places, materials and discourses. I shall try conveying the analysis, which addresses the emergence of networks that hold people and places within the unfolding history.

The commemorative gravesite in Kiwa, formally known as Iruka, in central Japan became a point of passage in the British veterans' participation in their post-war reconciliation visit back to Japan. Tracing the history of this memorial, we come to see the dynamic process of remembering and reconciliation. Using Bruno Latour's notion of "circulating reference" we can view this memorial site as both a point of collection in a heterogeneous network of elements (both humans and otherwise) which draw together local and global components of remembering and reconciliation as well as dispersing nodes of the network, which circulate around the memorial.

FIGURE 1.   The Iruka Memorial

This gravesite is situated in the area where the 300 British POWs worked in a copper mine from 1944 till 1945. Yet, this is not the original gravesite. The current memorial site was created by local Japanese people who lived in the village, some of them having worked alongside the British POWs in the mine. The present gravesite is an entry point into the history of the gravesite and its transformation. The graves were moved to a new site and refurbished as a local regeneration project a few decades after the British POWs left. This memorial, as the circulating reference, is a key to understand the dynamics of remembering and reconciliation.

By circulating reference is meant that the memorial is inscribed in stories of discovery, subsequent development of reconciliation initiatives, and drew a huge national and international (at least British and Japanese) attention in the late 1980s and 90s. The substance of the memorial is continually being transformed and extended into networks of circulating reference. Via this memorial, a reunion of the Japanese student workers, who worked alongside British POWs, was held in 1990. The grave was virtually unknown to the outside world, but the refurbished memorial led to further networks of bringing people, places, materials, and discourses together. The first reconciliation trip to Kiwa was initiated by the joint international collaboration in 1992 and with the Iruka Boys present, a joint memorial service for the dead POWs was held at the memorial site. The memorial is not just a place to visit; it is a point of passage or a node in a whole network, which is continuously creating heterogeneous relations and transformations.

In borrowing Latour again, he says it is a mistake to treat phenomena (such as remembering/reconciliation) as "the meeting point between things in themselves and categories of human understanding... Phenomena are what circulate all along the reversible chain of transformation" (Latour, 1999, p. 71). The original grave "and the memorial) continually transformed itself, place, people, social relations and even history. New meanings and new projects emerged—reunion, regeneration, reconciliation—now being a heritage site, a mine museum was built as a part of the network of transformations.

The key point here is that we cannot treat history as a solid static object, as if we are able to ascertain the essence of memory or representation of the mind of an individual. Certainly history in this example is not singular. It is transforming itself in the interplay of the local and the global as well as the public and the private, and the collective and the personal/individual. It is in the relational dynamic between the two, acknowledging the importance of looking at remembering and reconciliation as a phenomenon in which the two parties mutually influence one another by drawing on the Actor Network Theory, steering away from assuming history as a benchmark to map out the individual memories.

Certainly, the actor network theory analysis propels me to depart from my own methodological camp of discursive psychology. Indeed, a discursive psychologically informed argument is still sustained in echoing the assumptions of actor network theory. Yet, it allows us to bridge the local phenomena. Reconciliation is a moment-by-moment discursive accomplishment in which the ex-POW research participants actively engage in interaction with cultural others, which in turn reconfigures the significance of the past. Furthermore, this discursive achievement can be seen in the light of this interplay of history (a grand narrative and personal lived experiences) and the individual lives and connections mediated by artefacts such as the grave and psychological tools including the language to inscribe the past history as narratives that people produce as their own sense making.

To sum up the discussion so far, I have addressed the question of consequences of the war and that it is manifested in disparate ways. Also I have developed a critique on discursive psychology's methodology. I've explored an approach using Actor Network Theory in examining the dynamic interplay between the collective memory and the personal. In the dynamic interplay individually formed sense making and its manifestations produce discourses around national and personal identities.

HISTORY TEACHING

In line with the book's main theme, I shall ponder on some implications for history teaching. There is much research and debate on what history to teach, how to teach it and what purpose it meets (Seixas, 2004; Stearns, Seixas, & Wineburg, 2000; Wineburg, 2001). Since I am not an expert, I am not going to replicate a discussion on the very question of history teaching itself, but rather to put the overwhelming sentiment for the essential value of history teaching into perspective.

Like many students in the post-war generation of peace education, which by policy and otherwise has obliterated controversial history from Japanese history textbooks (Bukh, 2007; Carretero, 2011; Hirano, 2008; McCormack, 2000), I have missed out on learning key historical facts of the period in question discussed in this chapter. My ignorance indeed has a lasting impact on subsequent dealings with intercultural encounters. As in the staged protest against the Japanese Emperor in 1998, I came across a number of similar incidents in various parts of the world and observed profound ruptures in terms of national and cultural identity and historical (rather a-historical) being (Zittoun, 2006). In retrospect, such ruptures fostered a critical reflective stance on the way in which policy and curriculum in history teaching have shaped the collective and personal sense of self (or identity). I became more aware of the perspectives of those others in the opposing side of the debate, and subsequently, even undertook a research that would help to understand the dynamic interplay between history and person as demonstrated in the aforementioned. I would not dispute the noble purpose and significance of history teaching, say, for seeking to establish common and shared identity for democratic participation and citizenship (e.g. Barton & Levstik, 2004). Like any other school subject, history teaching is not problem-free. It must be understood as a discursive practice, which is framed in a particular ideological, institutional policy and curriculum context and valorized as a moral imperative to society.

The discussion and analysis using Actor Network Theory help us see that history is a dynamic process in which people, places, stories, etc. are folded and assembled continuously. Under a seemingly stable, formal, authoritative, legitimated account of events as the collective past, stories around the circulating object are dispersed and new networks of social relations are emerging. History is open as the network of relations is formed and re-formed or configured in different ways. Seen in this light, history teaching can be about conveying an open, non-deterministic process of human practices. Teachers and students consider themselves to be co-producer and actor in the process of history. History teaching (and learning) may involve students' understanding of diverse ways in which the underlying rationale, criteria for certain historical events, gets included (and erased or diminished) as relevant to forging a coherent national (or an imagined community's) narrative.

HISTORY IN THE MAKING

In reflecting history according to the perspectives and approaches referred to in this chapter, I cannot help relating to the famous quote on history by Marx:

> Men make their own history, but they do not make it just as they please; they do not make it under circumstances chosen by themselves, but under circumstances directly encountered, given and transmitted from the past. The tradition of all the dead generations weighs like a nightmare on the brain of the living. (Marx, 2008/1852, p. 15)

If we were to accept history as not just a set of knowledge of facts and events which happened and see it as a somewhat more open, unfolding process in which traditions and conventions, values and beliefs are in the making, we may be able to shed some light into how forgetting works in the context of history teaching. Questions are raised such as whether and to what extent we teach the dark side of history for posterity and how educators and parents alike teach the dark side of humanity. Forgetting seems to be construed as undesirable and negative in history teaching as a practice of remembering. In contemporary society, the significance of forgetting is overlooked as an equal importance in the memory process (Connerton, 2008). Perhaps we need to reconstitute the problem of the memory crisis as a natural, organic process called forgetting. Paul Connerton's typology of forgetting is useful to further this view. Our constant desire to remember the past is symptomatic to the modernity. Technologies for memory (externalizing the memory capacity) as a technological mediation help us to see the extent to which the need to be remembered in the form of archive and virtual sites for remembering is constantly being pushed and escalated. This constitutes a fundamental rationale for history teaching—never forget.

NEVER FORGET!

Common-sense tells us that it is essential and necessary to remember history including the most heinous crimes of humanity. We do not need to go back in history to make this point. Here I cast a somewhat dissenting voice to this sense of remembering in order not to repeat history (the negative) as educational "policy" in order that we will not repeat the same crime again. The caveat for this position of teaching history is well rehearsed in the paper by Di Paolantonio, who wrote about an interesting museum in Guantanamo designed and curated by Alicia Framis (2008). Di Paolantonio calls it, curiously, a museum of forgetting. He says: "the ubiquitous rhetoric of needing to remember in order to prevent the recurrence of our worst atrocities" (2010, p. 1). The museum of forgetting frames the way in which we value and deploy learning and remembrance. The underlying premise in such a position of teaching history is that:

> [W]e work with the belief that we make people remember better and harder, if we expose them to facts, artefacts and even interactive role-playing experiences conveying what happened in a terrible past, we will somehow both avert the repetition of this past and honour of memory. (Di Paolantonio, p. 1)

However, this view assumes a certain calculation of memory and an untroubling faith in which the accumulation of more knowledge and experience will lead to predictable and favourable results (Di Paolantonio, 2010). Much of the core value of peace education is shaped around this view. We teach history as knowledge and experiential knowing to avert the course of humanity. History teaching or learning is a deterrent for human atrocities and destruction. It is certainly possible to entertain the view that history is a non-deterministic, constructive process. My question is to what extent this view drives the decision for core criteria for history curriculum and pedagogy?

CAVEAT FOR HISTORY TEACHING

Although we tend to believe that we ought to mobilize the memory of a terrible past in order to sensitize and inoculate people against the possible future temptation of becoming complicit in mass violence, Phillips notes that we should be wary of the bone conscience of the educator administering remembrance (Di Paoloantonio, 2010). "[O]ur desire to pedagogically manage memory" (Di Paolantonio, 2010, p. 1) is the mainstream thought for implications of memory research for education. Di Paolantonio alerts us with a message that by virtue of history teaching we become part of this administrative process of managing knowledge and remembrance.

Simply put, teaching history would not guarantee to deter future war, conflict and violence. If we were to accept history teaching as this very process of managing remembrance, as Philips states, "where memory might lead—both what we might do with it, and what it might do with us—is unpredictable" (Phillips, 2005, p. 3). In a way it goes back to the kind of argument I made earlier with the case of Anglo-Japanese reconciliation. Coupled with the fascinating example of a museum of forgetting, the Guantanamo Museum, history is a beast that is impossible to tame. History, whether the national/collective or the personal/individual, is an "open" process. It may have its likely trajectories, but they are unfolding beyond what we can know. Through dynamic relations between history (and collective memory) and individual (and personal) experience mediated by artefacts and stories, history, memory and identities, one can see history as being laden with future possibilities for being otherwise (see analysis and discussion on the veterans' experience of redemption in Murakami, 2007). Unlike the conventional thinking that history, remembering and reconciliation turns people's gaze to the past, we come to realise that history, remembering and reconciliation are discursive practices geared toward the future.

REFERENCES

Barton, K. C. & Levstik, L. S. (2004). *Teaching history for the common good*. Mahwah, NJ: Lawrence Erlbaum Associates.

Billig, M. (1999). *Freudian repression: conversation creating the unconscious*. Cambridge: Cambridge University Press.

Brockmeier, J. (2002). Introduction: Searching for cultural memory. *Culture & psychology, 8*, 5–14.

Brown, R., & Kulik, J. (1977). Flashbulb memories. *Cognition, 5*, 73–99.

Bukh, A. (2007). Japan's history textbooks debate: National identity in narratives of victimhood and victimization. *Asian Survey, 47*(5), 683–704.

Burr, V. (1995). *An introduction to social construction*. London and New York: Routledge.

Callon, M. (1986). Some elements of a sociology of translation: Documentation of the scallops and the fishermen of St Brieuc Bay. In J. Law (Ed.), *Power, action and belief: A new sociology of knowledge?* (pp. 196–223). London: Routledge & Kegan Paul.

Carretero, M. (2011). *Constructing patriotism: Teaching history and memories in global worlds*. Charlotte, NC: Information Age Publishing.

Connerton, P. (2008). Seven types of forgetting. *Memory Studies, 1*, 59–71.

Conway, M. A. (1997). The inventing of experience: Memory and identity. In J. W. Pennebaker, D. Paez, & B. Rimé (Eds.), *Collective memory and political events: Social psychological perpectives,* (pp. 21–46). Mahwah, NJ: Lawrence Erlbaum.

Di Paolantonio, M. (2010). *Beyond the rhetoric of 'Never Forget': Considering what a museum of forgetting could be a museum of....* the Annual Conference of the Philosophy of Education, Great Britain. New College, Oxford (27th March 2010).

Edwards, D., & Middleton, D. J. (1986). Joint remembering: Constructing an account of shared experience through conversational discourse. *Discourse processes, 9,* 423–459.

Edwards, D., & Potter, J. (1992). *Discursive psychology.* London: Sage.

Framis, A. (2008). *Guantanamo Museum.* Retrieved 20 October 2010 from http://www.aliciaframis.com/.

Gergen, K. J. (1999). *An invitation to social construction.* London: Sage.

Gergen, K. J. (1997). Social psychology as social construction: The emerging vision. In C. McGarty & A. S. Haslam (Eds.), *The message of social psychology: Perspectives on mind in society* (pp. 113–128). Cambridge, MA: Blackwell.

Halbwachs, M. (1981 (1950)). *The collective memory.* New York: Harper & Row.

Hirano, M. (2008). *History education and international relations: A case study of diplomatic disputes on Japanese textbooks.* Honolulu, HI: University of Hawaii Press.

Latour, B. (1999). *Pandora's hope: Essays on the reality of science studies.* Cambridge, MA: Harvard University Press.

Law, J. (1992). Notes on Theory of Actor-networks. *Systems Practice, 54,* 379–393.

Neisser, U. (1981). John Dean's memory: A case study. *Cognition, 9,* 1–22.

Marx, K. (2008 [1852]). *The Eighteenth Brumaire of Louis Bonaparte.* London: Standard Publications.

McCormack, G. (2000). The Japanese movement to "correct" history. In L. Hein & M. Selden (Eds.), *Censoring history* (pp. 53–73). New York, NY: East Gate.

Middleton, D., & Edwards, D. (Eds.). (1990). *Collective remembering. Inquiries in social construction.* London: Sage.

Murakami, K. (1999). *Identity-in-action: Discourse analysis of letters to the editor on POWs and emperor.* Narrative Conference: Discourse and Representation. Lexington, KY, USA.

Murakami, K. (2001). *Revisiting the past: Social organisation of remembering and reconciliation.* Unpublished PhD thesis. Department of Human Sciences. Loughborough, Loughborough University.

Murakami, K. (2007). Positioning in accounting for redemption and reconciliation. *Culture & Psychology, 13*(4), 431–452.

Murakami, K. (in press). *Psychology of remembering and reconciliation: A study of Anglo-Japanese post-WWII conflict.* Hauppauge, NY: USA Nova Science Publishers.

Murakami, K., & Middleton, D. (2002). Identity in action: Blame and apology in remembrance of war. In P. Linnel & K. Aronsson (Eds.), *Jagen och rösterna: Goffman, Viveka och samtalet [Selves and voices: Goffman, Viveka and Dialogue],* (pp. 193–206). Linköping, Sweden: Studies in Communication, Linköping University.

Murakami, K., & Middleton, D. (2006). Grave matters: Collectivity and agency as emergent effects. *Ethos, 34*(2), 273–296.

Neisser, U. (Ed.) (1982). *Memory observed: Remembering in natural contexts*. San Francisco: W. H. Freeman.

Phillips, A. (2005). The Forgetting Museum. *Index on Censorship, 2*.

Potter, J., & Wetherell, M. (1987). *Discourse and social psychology: beyond attitudes and behaviour*. London: Sage Publications.

Stearns, P. N., Seixas, P. C., & Wineburg, S. (2000). *Knowing, teaching, and learning history: national and international perspectives*. New York: NYU Press.

Seixas, P. C. (Ed.) (2004). *Theorizing historical consciousness*. Toronto, Ontario, Canada: University of Toronto Press.

Strathern, M. (1996). Cutting the network. *Journal of the Royal Anthropology Institute, 2*, 517–535.

Wertsch, J. V. (2002). *Voices of collective remembering*. New York: Cambridge University Press.

Wineburg, S. (2001). *Historical thinking and other unnatural acts: Charting the future of teaching the past*. Philadelphia, PA: Temple University Press.

Zittoun, T. (2006). *Transitions: Development through symbolic resources*. Charlotte, NC: Information Age Publishing.

CHAPTER 21

THE FUTURE SHAPES THE PRESENT

Scenarios, Metaphors and Civic Action

Helen Haste and Amy Hogan

Human beings make sense of their present and give meaning to the past in the way that they story the future. This poses two interesting questions for both social science and education. First, how does storying the future reflect the construction of social and political meaning of the present? Second, how do young people's stories of the future relate to their motivation for civic engagement and their identity as effective civic actors? If we understand these we can consider how to use future stories effectively in civic education.

Accounts of historical events are constructed to validate contemporary explanations and identities. There is extensive literature on how history is constructed to explain and legitimate the present, whether this is a worldview, a socio-political system or the parameters of between-group relationships (Carretero, 2011). Other chapters in this volume address how history is utilized and the implications of this for education. In this chapter we argue that the storied future serves similar discursive purposes; scenarios are

History Education and the Construction of National Identities, pages 311–326

best understood as stories of the present. Occasionally future projections are a banal glorification of the present—the Nazi dream of a "thousand year Reich" for example. However, in the main scenario-building is either about providing remedies for the ills of today, or it is about anticipating desirable developments that might be encouraged or undesirable ones that should be avoided if possible (Turney, 2010). In the hands of experts, or social engineers, these agendas are analyses designed for action. For the lay person, future scenarios are linked to optimism or pessimism about the present, one's own position within that future and its personal implications, and the extent to which one can feel that one has any agency about one's fate.

Future projections may be positive or negative. We may expect that the good aspects and structures of contemporary life will endure because we have successfully managed values and institutions. Or we may be pessimistic that our contemporary structures are disordered or short-sighted, unsustainable and leaving us vulnerable to malevolent threats from "others." Whatever the story, optimistic or pessimistic, the narrative rests on justifications of, or problems deriving from, the perceived current world. As several writers note, narratives (whether of the future or the past) legitimize the present, justifying or making it normative, but they also serve to affirm collective solidarity, through a common memorializing and shared meaning (Elcheroth, Doise, & Reicher, 2011; Hammack, 2011; Reicher & Hopkins, 2001). This does not only mean "common" as in "agreed"; as Elcheroth et al. point out, knowing what will upset or destabilize the salient "other" is part of common meaning. From the Bible onwards, the curses hurled at the enemy presume that the dire predictions will matter to them.

Second, cultural narratives provide coherence and identity. Who one is, to which group one feels allegiance, within which worldview does one feel comfortable, are part of what the individual absorbs through the available stories. This is the infrastructure of education for patriotic "national identity" as well the psychological underpinning for ingroup affiliation and subjective construction of selfhood. How do stories of the future locate oneself and one's descendants—in terms of status, efficacy, happiness, fulfilment of aspirations, freedom from threat, and what action obligations do these stories place on the self in order to facilitate these futures?

Thirdly, narratives sustain the status quo, and for social change to take place, new narratives that reframe beliefs, values, goals, explanations and justifications must emerge and become normative. Such narratives re-evaluate the past, challenge the dominant story, and are potentially a new story which often challenges some basic current premises about the issues. There are numerous examples. Prior to the nineteenth century, hygiene was regarded as an individual matter. With new medical and public health techniques (for example vaccination and improved organization of waste disposal) it became normative to see contagion and prevention of disease as the legitimate responsibility of government, supported by law. Individual citizens had a duty to conform to such laws for the greater public good—even though there still remain pockets of arguments for the "freedom" not to conform (Beck-Gernschein, 2000; Castro & Mouro, 2011; Harré, 1998; Moghaddam, 2008).

A similar development has taken place with sustainability in the twentieth century. The narrative that environmental disasters loomed in the near future was first seen as highly marginal and counter to the optimistic progressive and expansionist views of the time. The new dark future story gained a wider audience quite fast, and with it the discourses of "responsibility"—who would save us? At first capitalism and government were targeted as both cause and cure, implying that the individual citizen could campaign for policy changes. The interesting shift came as the narratives turned to the role of individuals and their potential efficacy to effect change through actions in their own daily lives. This accompanied the accelerated shift of the issue from the eccentric margins to the mainstream, rapidly becoming a central theme in education at all levels. The responsibility became individualized and moralized, even for primary school children; "WE can and must save the planet." This is a considerable shift in narrative; individualized responsibility for social change tends to accompany (and be propagandized vigorously during) war time or social crisis. Yet legal moves and policy changes (such as waste disposal, clean air, pollution control) largely followed rather than led public opinion. Even though such laws are not always obeyed by individuals, normatively their benefit became widely recognized (Castro & Batel, 2008; Castro & Mouro, 2011).

Another example of a new future story transforming the narratives of the present is "homeland security" and the "war on terrorism." Both these evocative metaphors and their policy outcomes arose from the prediction of a future dominated by the threat of alien incursion, accelerated following 9/11. Securitization, the closing of boundaries and exclusion of undesirables, is a present activity legitimated by the dark future story; it coexists with but is increasingly a challenge to, the future story of a harmonious multicultural state in an increasingly globalized world (Nesbitt-Larking & Kinnvall, 2010).

HOW TO MANAGE THE FUTURE?

Underlying perceptions of how the future might be managed are perhaps three dominant metaphors. One is that the future is already determined and the mystery for humans is to predict events in order to have some control at least of one's response to them. This underpins divination, horoscopes, astrology and some religious positions. Although in the rational contemporary world we like to believe that this is superstition and no longer salient, there is plenty of evidence that this is not the case, even amongst the most powerful—we continually hear of heads of state who employ astrologers.

The second metaphor is about causality and continuity; the future is a direct consequence of the past and therefore, present and past actions are implicated. This is equally true whether one is thinking about personal morality or macro-economic or political forces. However, central to this metaphor is continuity and *order*. The future is predictable insofar as it builds upon the past; responsible behavior in the present should be rewarded by a better future, and vice versa. Future stories therefore make sense as explanations or justifications of the present; the future is reassuringly continuous to the present even if the message is negative.

The third metaphor has long cultural roots in various religious traditions but has gained scientific status in recent decades; that systems are chaotic and therefore unpredictable. It is important to recognize that chaos theory does not deny causality; it recognizes that causal factors may be very minor, and that their consequences are not predictable by the usual rules. In one sense this can be a very depressing message, akin to Niels Bohr's quip[1] that "prediction is very difficult, especially if it is about the future." If there is no continuous causality, we have no chance to envisage the future nor to deflect or direct it. However a positive aspect of chaos theory is that very minor events can have major effects; if one can isolate the action or policy that can be that fulcrum, we may be able to influence the future. This metaphor underpins many discussions both of the explanations and proposed solutions to climate change—in both the fictional and real world.

Social science has in fact been remarkably ineffective in predicting the future. It is difficult to think of a single recent social movement or political upheaval that has been envisaged in advance by social scientists, though subsequent analyses of such events have been rich and fruitful. To explain why it is so difficult to predict the future, it is helpful to understand how change happens and also what might be our objectives in scenario-building (whether professional or lay). There are three categories: 1) things that will not change; 2) things that will not change fundamentally but the way they are practiced, or their form, will change; and 3) things that will change considerably as a consequence of technological, social, political or economic developments. The problem in each case is predicting both what might change, and what the consequences would be. As to our objectives, we may wish to predict in order to prepare for developments in which although we may have no agency, we can at least prepare to respond to adaptively. Alternatively, we may wish to predict successfully in order that we can steer the direction of developments more favorably—or even stem the tide, Fi-

---

[1] This is attributed to Bohr but there is some dispute as to whether he invented, or merely used, it.

nally, we may need an accurate future picture so that we can initiate new developments in a direction we cannot envisage until we think through the implications of current trends. (An example might be, rather than finding ways to modify petroleum's problems or limit people's use of their cars, we move to developing electric or other fuelled cars and obviate the need for petroleum).

Change is studied in all fields, but the field of technology gives us particularly clear (and humbling) insights both about the processes of change and the problems of prediction. Gosling (1994) identified three kinds of change in the field of technology which also apply to social and political change. The first is "more of the same"; things in the future will be similar to the present, with minor changes in technology, or institutions, or social structures. This is fairly easy to predict as it is mere projection from the present. It is also in fact the only area of prediction where we have any real skill. Further, when people are asked to make future predictions, they almost universally assume "more of the same," which is why prediction exercises are such an accurate reflection of the storied present. The flaw of "more of the same" is of course vividly exemplified in the example much loved by philosophers; on December 24th (or the eve of Thanksgiving) the turkey, well-fed for 1000 days, confidently predicts that this will continue indefinitely..... (Taleb, 2007)

The second kind of change is "quantity into quality," where increase results eventually in morphing into something new. The village that grows into a town then a city, through the accretion of houses, factories and services is an example. A city is qualitatively different from a village, not just bigger. Experts (and the wise) can make intelligent predictions about these kinds of change. For most people, the sheer scale of change defeats the imagination. It would have been impossible to imagine in 1990 that by 2010, nearly 100% of young people in the developed world would own a personal cellphone—or to imagine that by 2010 the house purchased in 1975 would be worth thirty five times its initial value. Even experts get it wrong; technology gurus like Bill Gates early on grossly underestimated the amount of file space people would routinely come to use.

The third kind of change is the most quixotic and the most difficult to predict even by experts. This is the "knight's move"—as in chess. In the world of technology, such events are the invention, or discovery, of a new core process (such as the microchip) that transform whole systems, drastically reduce their size and cost, and open up new forms of usage. Within the world in which the developments take place there are obvious massive changes in efficiency and performance. However these knight's moves become even more interesting when their impact reaches beyond the world for which they were crafted, for example affecting social practices and ways of thinking about our interaction with experience.

The development of computers is an obvious example. This impacted on all forms of communication, storage and retrieval of information, transformation of every kind of control and timing system. But it also transformed the core metaphors of mind that influence both scientist and layperson (Gigerenzer, 2000). It transformed the concepts that we have about access to knowledge, power and each other. Not only are new skills required (and quickly acquired) but who has those skills changes and whole areas of work burgeon or disappear—the shorthand typist is one example, now redundant at least in her original form, and everyone, even powerful males, needs to type in order to do their email.

Mobile phones altered the social patterns of telephone communication. The phone became a personal body prosthesis rather than a shared, place-bound device. Texting further transformed the nature of communication itself (Haste, 2004a). Increasingly, as internet accessible mobile phones become less expensive, everyone in the developed world and a growing proportion of the rest will be able to access every single piece of knowledge in entire human history in their handheld device. Yet we have barely begun to consider the huge educational implications of this (Haste, 2009). We are beginning to get the measure of the political—potentially democratic but also potentially demagogic—possibilities of these developments but we have not yet worked out how to use them properly (Digital Youth Project, 2010; Haste, 2010; Livingstone, 2009; Sherrod et al, 2010)

Knight's moves in technology are palpable but there are knight's moves also in social, political and economic contexts, and these are the developments that social scientists have been deficient in predicting. Their effects are equally transformative, not only of political order but of discourses, concepts and metaphors that frame identity and boundaries. The civil rights, women's and gay movements have profoundly altered not only self definitions but also definitions and valences of the "Other," and in doing so, have reframed how difference itself is to be managed. What once was a dominant group's ethic of "tolerance" of "them" and objection to discrimination has changed, at least in liberal societies, to a discourse that group boundaries are fuzzy and that diversity implies multiple identities. The very concept of "tolerance" implies a dominant group's perspective of an alien minority and takes no account of multiple and reciprocal perspectives of all involved. As Foucault argued, homosexuality was defined as an attribute of persons only late in the nineteenth century (Foucault, 1976). The discourses around a homosexual person became medicalized and pathologized in psychiatric assessment measures, then through the gay rights movement, *entitlement* to a sexual alternative lifestyle first became recognized. Later, evidence of possible biological underpinning of sexual orientation enhanced the discourse of injustice around discrimination.

In the macro-political context, some researchers have vividly demonstrated how social and political reconstructions depend upon the power of narratives to frame identities and moral infrastructures, in Israel, Germany, South Africa and the UK (Andrews, 2007; Bar-On, 2008; Bartal, 2000; Hammack, 2011). The deconstruction of the Soviet empire (again, not predicted by social science) led to the reconstruction, or re-emergence, of national identities and discourses that had been obscured by the Soviet regime. Wertsch (1998), for example, describes how the parallel narratives of Estonian culture, kept alive during the Soviet years, emerged flamboyantly with the new independence. In former Yugoslavia, the resurgent narratives and identities, and their consequences, were considerably more fraught. In all former Soviet countries, the construction of new democracy did not draw upon US or Western European models (perhaps much to their chagrin) but to periods in their own history when either national democracy flourished or a period of national freedom and construction followed the heroic rejection of an oppressive regime (Haste, 2004b, 2010; Torney-Purta et al., 1999). Reicher and Hopkins (2001) show how contemporary Scottish national identity is constructed around the mythologies of historical heroes, none of whom were actually Scottish.

Examples of futures that story the present are legion, and often greatly entertaining in the ways that they incorporate "more of the same" social practices and relations. In a 1950s picture of the distant future kitchen, full of hi-tech devices projected from then-contemporary mechanical technology, stands a pneumatic, plastic-clad, unliberated housewife beaming in her frilly apron. Two more extensive examples are particularly rich. In 1893 US "opinion leaders" were asked to foretell the world of 1992. Their efforts reflected the preoccupations of the time. They predicted greater longevity, temperance, birth control and women's suffrage. They were much engaged with the wonders of electricity and new forms of transport. The most time-bound and anomalous was their prediction of ways to solve "the servant problem" (Walter, 1992).

In 1928 the British newspaper the *Daily Mail* created a special facsimile issue projecting the date January 1st 2000, with news stories, editorials and advertisements. The stories foresaw that we would travel long distance in airships, but local travel would be in our own individual biplanes which we would park on top of buildings. In all areas of life, including government, gender roles would be reversed—a situation described as normative but in discourses charged with defensive stereotypes. All food would be in the form of vitamin-rich pellets, and culinary pleasure is a distant dream. The "servant problem" also loomed, still unsolved, and in the adverts, created by real advertisers of the time, uniformed maidservants cleaned and polished and chauffeurs managed the car. Perhaps one of the richest pictures portrayed a crowd in Trafalgar Square, clad in futuristic projections of art deco clothes. The audience watched the cricket Test Match being relayed on to a giant screen from Australia, listening on large headphones; the national metaphors of cricket and empire solidarity endure....

The same scenario-building tendencies pervade the future of science. We predict from our current epistemological paradigms and we are prone to believe that our current theories and methods will prevail in the future. We predict from within the mainstream, whereas in all fields, innovation happens on the margins (and so is difficult to anticipate). The authors have conducted, with colleagues, DELPHI projects amongst British psychologists (Haggard & Haste, 1986; Haste, Hogan, & Zachariou, 2001). Senior members of the profession were invited to predict the state of the discipline twenty-five years hence. In 1984, the predictions for 2010 included the rise of neuroscience, and the possibility of neuroscience separating as a distinct discipline from other areas of psychology. However there was no mention of evolutionary psychology. Increased use of information technology was predicted, but within expert systems and information processing rather than in communication in general. Little attention was paid to the social implications of technological changes. Current preoccupations of the time are especially evident where they rapidly became irrelevant, such as concerns about unemployment that were highly salient in 1984.

YOUNG PEOPLE AND THE FUTURE

Professionals' future scenarios reflect their perception of their field's present preoccupations and objectives, as well as their hopes, fears, and desires for the future. Their illusions of control are embedded at least within adult and institutional confidence. For young people, in the absence of such confidence and power, the future is a fantasy that reflects scenarios of hope, despair or resistance. Several studies have demonstrated a relationship between current social and civic beliefs and future scenarios. There remains a debate as to whether a positive future scenario breeds confidence and trust in the present, leading to active civic engagement, or whether a negative future scenario breeds despair or resistance, and therefore active, if unconventional, civic participation (Hutchinson, 1996). To explore these issues we conducted a study of young British people's images of the future.

A consensus of previous research is that there are four main future scenarios:

- **Business as usual:** the future will be very like the present, with the same issues and solutions, but slightly more hi-tech
- **The technological fix:** accelerated science and technology will solve engineering, medical, economic and social problems
- **Edge of disaster:** things will get worse, both in society and the natural environment

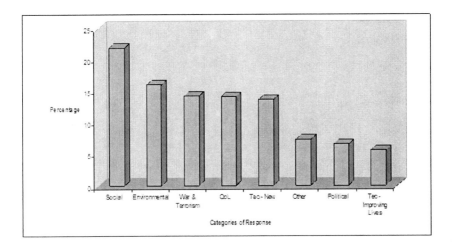

FIGURE 1.

• **Peaceful and sustainable society:** we will have found a way to work together for peace, sustainability and justice.

A questionnaire study[2] presented over 1000 British young people aged 11–21 with questions about the likelihood of these four scenarios, along with questions about their own recent and expected future civic action, their beliefs about what comprised a "good citizen," the social issues about which they would like to influence the government, how much they trusted the government, and the extent to which they felt upset by events in the news (Haste, 2005; Haste & Hogan 2006). In addition, the questionnaire included an open-ended item;

> Imagine you could meet someone who has travelled back in time from the year 2035. What TWO questions would you like to ask that person about the life they lead and the world they live in?

This study allowed us to explore the narratives they invoked to describe the future and the relationship between likely future scenarios and the constellations of attitudes and beliefs reflected in the questionnaire.

The open-ended item, the "visitor from the future," produced a range of narratives (See Figure 1). The most frequent overall category concerned the social conditions of the future; poverty, health, social unrest, crime. Because they were framed as questions it was not possible to identify whether these were seen as positive or negative. Second came environmental con-

---

[2] Funded by the Nestlé Trust, data collection by MORI

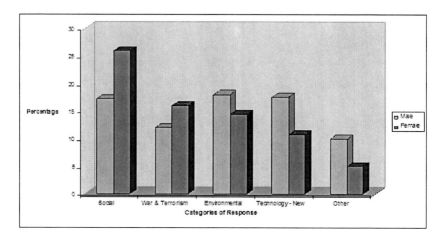

FIGURE 2.

cerns, closely followed by anxieties about war and terrorism, questions relating to their own lives ("Will I be rich? Will I still be alive then?") and
questions about the nature of new technology. Explicitly political questions
("Who is prime minister?") counted for less than 10% of the responses, as
did questions specifically linking new technology to improving life conditions.

There were quite striking gender differences (see Figure 2). Female respondents were significantly more concerned about both social issues and

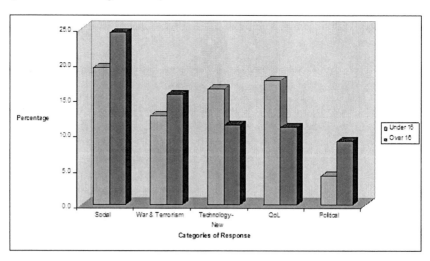

FIGURE 3.

war and terrorism, and male respondents about the environment and new technology.

There were also age differences (See Figure 3). Older respondents (over 16) were significantly more likely than younger to ask about social conditions, war and terrorism, and politics, and less likely to ask about new technology or their own personal futures.

The results from the analysis of the questionnaire scales revealed diverse patterns that suggest quite a strong relationship between future scenarios and civic action and beliefs. The exploratory factor analysis of current and future action and beliefs about the good citizen produced five factors:

- *Active monitoring:* valuing and being active in monitoring and discussing current affairs, but with little current involvement in civic action
- *Conventional participation:* expecting to vote in the future, signing petitions
- *Making one's voice heard:* protesting, boycotting, contacting one's political representative, signing petitions
- *Joining organizations:* including community groups and in the future, political parties
- *Helping in the community and the environment:* working actively to help people in the community, being concerned about the environment.

Endorsement of a likely "Business as usual" future scenario was associated significantly with the factor *Conventional participation* ($F = 5.19$: $p < .02$), and also with a high level of trust in the government ($F = 11.99$: $p < .001$).

Endorsement of a likely "Edge of disaster" future scenario was associated with the factor *Making one's voice heard* ($F = 8.46$: $p < .004$) with taking part in protest activities ($F = 5.55$: $p < .01$) and also with helping others ($F = 4.58$; $p < .03$). It was found more in older respondents. It was also associated with low trust in the government ($F = 41.92$: $p < .000$) and with often being upset by events in the news ($F = 18.65$: $p < .000$)[3].

Endorsement of a likely "Technological fix" future scenario was associated with the factors *Active monitoring* ($F = 25.52$: $p < .000$), *Conventional participation* ($F = 6.97$: $p < .008$) and *Joining organizations* ($F = 20.35$: $p < .000$) It was linked to believing that one's vote counts ($F = 24.33$: $p < .000$), trust in the government ($F = 38.21$: $p < .000$), signing petitions ($F = 25.37$: $p < .000$) and also with concern for many social issues including of health care, improving facilities for young people, and controlling both crime and immigration.

---

[3] It is also of interest that in both this study and another one conducted by the authors, there were gender differences, with girls more likely than boys to predict the "Edge of disaster" scenario (Haste et al,, 2008)

Endorsement of a likely "Peace and sustainability" future scenario was associated with the factors *Active monitoring* (F = 19.48: p < 00), *Conventional participation* (F = 14.52: p < .000) and *Joining organizations* (F = 13.95: p < .000) It was also associated with younger respondents (under 16) and trust the government (F = 104.33: p < .000). These respondents believe that votes make a difference (F = 26.33; p < .000) and that they can make their voice heard (F = 37.13: p < .000). They had tried to influence things in their school (F = 27.15: p < .000) and they had signed petitions (F = 24.35: p < .000). They expected to be active on civic issues in the future and they had been involved in the community and in helping others (F = 5.27: p < .02).

EDUCATIONAL IMPLICATIONS?

These findings are consistent with several studies concerning the profiles associated with civic action. The additional picture of predicted future scenarios enlarges these. First, the findings for the "Edge of disaster" scenario resonate with a considerable amount of research which shows that low trust in the government, being upset by events in the news (especially feeling angry) and feeling that one does have the resources to take action, are associated with unconventional civic action. The link between a negative future scenario and a proclivity towards becoming actively engaged, rather than responding with despair, suggests that there are a number of factors operating which may have implications for education as well as for understanding what promotes political resistance. This future scenario stories the present as heading for future problems; possible solutions may lie in taking action now to deflect these, to make active preparations to deal with them, or to sink into helplessness. A number of studies do indeed show that helplessness and despair can be one response to such a narrative. In research on peace movements in the 1980s, when the threat of nuclear war was seen as real, there was a distinction between young people who were fearful and impotent, and those who were angry and active (there were also those who either denied, or did not believe in the threat) (Haste, 1989; Thearle & Haste, 1986).

The "Technological fix" scenario is one positive future outcome of projected developments in the present. The focus is on technology and on assumptions about science as progressive. This scenario is considered more likely by males than by females, in this study and another one using the same materials (Haste et al., 2008). Our data support the view that optimistic future scenarios reflect a confident picture of the present which inspires engagement, with regard to conventional participation and trust in contemporary political institutions. This scenario is also associated with wanting to influence the government about several social issues such as racism, health and crime.

A second optimistic future scenario is "Peace and sustainability." It is even more hopeful about the trajectory of current developments towards a better world. It is associated with trust in the government and confidence that political and social institutions enable democratic engagement at all levels. Respondents who endorse this scenario actively take notice of current events. They join groups, fund raise and help others, they have been involved in school governance. Their participation is largely conventional but vigorous and they expect to continue this in adulthood. It would seem that they believe their own civic engagement contributes to the forces that move progress; they gain confidence from the belief that the future will be good. Some educators have argued that this perspective is a very good basis for building curricula to engage young people in peace-related, sustainability-related programs which give them both a constructive worldview and the skills and sense of agency to become active and effective citizens (Hicks & Holden, 2007; Hutchinson, 1996).

The "Business as usual" scenario reflects projection of "more of the same" and can be seen either as a safe future with few disruptions of the current comfort zone, or as a somewhat depressing projection of apathetic inertia. It would appear from our data that this scenario is associated neither with a strong current engagement with social issues nor with civic action. The association with conventional participation and with trust in the government suggests confidence in the status quo rather than desire for change, now or in the future.

The arguments and data presented in this paper have explored some intersections of future scenarios with present worldviews, and the role of metaphors of the future in making sense of, and giving value to, the present. We have also explored some data on the relationship between both these, and how they appear to contribute to the impetus towards civic action in young people.

However in considering educational implications we must be careful about causal relationships. One interpretation is that that young people who feel that they have efficacy and agency in relation to civic action, and trust current social and political institutions, latch on to positive future scenarios. In contrast those who feel equally efficacious but do not share that trust, envisage a negative future which they feel they must actively resist. Alternatively, absorbing a positive future scenario from one's cultural environment may inspire trust, hope and agency while a negative scenario creates the anger that provokes resistance and potential action. For the purposes of education, should we tailor education differently according to young people's preferred future scenario? And do we promote conventional civic activities and altruism for those who have an optimistic future scenario, and more challenging, less conventional activities for those who see a bleak future? In such an agenda young people's future fantasies could be used to facilitate their engagement, capitalizing on the agency and commitment that derives from the scenario to foster different potentials for engagement.

A second educational argument found in writings about young people's future scenarios, is that educating for particular scenarios provides empowerment as well as interest (e.g., Hutchinson, 1996). In this case the agenda is to decide the most appropriate scenario to achieve these goals and provide the materials to foster it, accompanied by opportunities for action whether through service learning or field work. It is consistent with the many programs throughout the world that engage very young students with the rainforest and other environmental concerns. The agenda is to help them engage with the future scenarios that enable them to gain commitment and the skills to enact it.

These are ways to utilize available contemporary stories about the future. There is also the option of constructing new scenarios which deliberatively reshape our interpretation of the present. At very least, an education program might draw attention to the relationship between future scenarios and explanations of the present, not just take them as given. Writers on the future whose scope is wider than education frequently argue that in order to shape a better future we must take responsibility in the present for the current trends, institutions and forces that can lead to a better (or worse) world. However, this responsibility also includes, they argue, the metaphors of the future themselves. A transformational metaphor needs be richer, more ethical, more encompassing as an essential prerequisite for breaking away from the trajectory towards disaster even while recognizing the obstacles inherent in what we have referred to as the "knight's move" in this paper (Adams & Groves, 2007). We might argue that there is a third educational implication of the material we have presented in this paper; to encourage young people to generate novel metaphors, to critically reflect on their implications for understanding the present and for shaping the future. In this way we might help them to appreciate how powerfully different stories can frame perception and policy.

REFERENCES

Adams, B., & Groves, C. (2007). *Future matters; Action, knowledge, ethics.* Boston: Brill.

Andrews, M. (2007). *Shaping history; Narratives of social change.* Cambridge, UK: Cambridge University Press.

Bar-On, D. (2008). *The others within us; Constructing Jewish-Israeli identity.* New York: Cambridge University Press.

Bartal, D. (2000). *Shared beliefs in a society.* London: Sage

Beck-Gernschein, E. (2000). "Health and responsibility." From social change to technological change and *vice versa.* In B. Adam, U. Beck, & J. van Loon (Eds.), *The risk society; Critical issues for social theory,* (pp. 123–135). London: Sage.

Carretero, M. (2011). *Constructing patriotism; Teaching history and memories in global worlds*. Charlotte, NC: Information Age Publishing.

Castro, P., & Batel, S. (2008). Social representation, change and resistance; On the difficulties of generalising new norms. *Culture & Psychology, 14*, 477–499.

Castro P., & Mouro, C. (2011). Psycho-social processes in dealing with legal innovation in the community: insights from biodiversity conservation. *American Journal of Community Psychology, 47*, 362–373.

Digital Youth Project (2010), *Hanging out, messing around and geeking out; Kids living and learning with new media*. Cambridge, MA: MIT Press.

Elcheroth, G., Doise, W., & Reicher, S. (2011). On the knowledge of politics and the politics of knowledge: How a social representations approach helps us rethink the subject of political psychology. *Political Psychology, 32(5)*, 725–758.

Foucault, M. [1976] (1998). *The history of sexuality Vol. 1: The will to knowledge*. London: Penguin.

Gigerenzer, G. (2000). *Adaptive thinking; Rationality in the real world*. Oxford: Oxford University Press.

Gosling, W. (1994). *Helmsmen and heroes*. London: Weidenfeld & Nicolson.

Haggard, M., & Haste, H. (1986). One generation after 1984: Psychology in the year 2010. *Bulletin of the British Psychological Society, 39*, 321–324.

Hammack, P. (2011). *Narrative and the politics of identity: The cultural psychology of Israeli and Palestinian youth*. New York: Oxford University Press.

Harré, R. (1998). The epistemology of social representations. In U. Flick (Ed) *The psychology of the social*, (pp. 129–137). Cambridge: Cambridge University Press.

Haste, H. (1989). Everybody's scared but life goes on; Coping, defence and action in the face of nuclear threat. *Journal of Adolescence, 12*, 11–26.

Haste, H. (2004a). *Joined up texting*. Croydon: Nestlé Trust, Nestlé Social Research Programme Report 3.

Haste, H. (2004b). Constructing the citizen. *Political Psychology, 25(3)* 413–440.

Haste, H. (2005). *My Voice, my vote, my community: A study of young people's action and inaction*. Croydon: Nestlé Trust, Nestlé Social Research Programme Report 4.

Haste, H. (2009). *Identity, community and citizenship*. Beyond Current Horizons, Bristol: Futurelab.

Haste, H. (2010). Citizenship education; A critical look at a contested field. In L. Sherrod, J. Torney-Purta, & C. Flanagan (Eds), *Handbook of Research on Civic Engagement in Youth*, (pp. 161–192). New York: John Wiley.

Haste, H., & Hogan, A. (2006). Beyond conventional civic participation, beyond the moral-political divide; Young people and contemporary debates about citizenship. *Journal of Moral Education, 35(4)*, 473—493.

Haste, H., Hogan, A., & Zachariou, Y. (2001). Back (again) to the future. *The Psychologist, 14(1)*, 30–33.

Haste H., Muldoon, C., Hogan, A., & Brosnan, M. (2008) *If girls like ethics in their science and boys like gadgets, can we get science education right?* British Science Festival, Liverpool, UK, September.

Hicks, D., & Holden, C. (2007). Remembering the future: what do children think? *Environmental Education Research, 13(4)*, 501–521.

Hutchinson, F. P. (1996). *Educating beyond violent futures*. London; Routledge.

Livingstone, S. (2009). *Children and the Internet*. Cambridge: Polity Press.

Moghaddam, F. M. (2008). The psychological citizen and the two concepts of the social contract; A preliminary analysis. *Political Psychology, 29,* 881–901.

Nesbitt-Larking, P., & Kinnvall, C. (2010). The political psychology of (de)securitization; Place-making strategies in Denmark, Sweden and Canada. *Society and Space, 28*(6), 1051–1070.

Reicher, S., & Hopkins, N. (2001). *Self and nation: Categorisation, contestation and mobilisation.* Thousand Oaks, CA: Sage Publications.

Sherrod, L., Torney-Purta, J., & Flanagan, C. (Eds.). (2010) *Handbook of research on civic engagement in youth.* New York: John Wiley.

Taleb, N.N. (2007). *The black swan; the impact of the highly improbable,* London: Penguin Books.

Thearle, L., & Haste, H. (1986). Ways of coping; Adolescents' response to nuclear threat. *International J. Mental Health, 15,* 126–142.

Torney-Purta, J., Schwille, J., & Amadeo, J. (1999). *Civic education across countries: Twenty-four national case studies from the IEA Civic Education project.* Amsterdam: International Association for the Evaluation of Educational Achievement (IEA).

Turney, J. (2010). *The Rough Guide to the future.* London: Rough Guides.

Walter, D. (Ed.) (1992). *Today then; America's best minds look 100 years into the future on the occasion of the 1893 World's Columbian exposition.* Helena, MT: American & World Geographic Publishing.

Wertsch, J. (1998). *Mind as action.* Oxford: Oxford University Press.

CHAPTER 22

MONUMENTS IN OUR MINDS

Historical Symbols as Cultural Tools

Jaan Valsiner

What happens in history is real—but what is written about it is not. Reflections upon history are non-existing objects[1] the *subsisting* of which is crucial for our social and personal lives. We—while living our lives—create stories *about* our lives, institutions create their stories *about* the bygone times and happenings. These stories become ephemeral monuments in our minds that we carry around—and use when circumstances make them needed.

[1] In the sense of Alexius Meinong and his students (1880s to early 20th century—(Albertazzi, Jacquette & Poli, 2001). The "Graz tradition" was unique in the history of psychology and philosophy in Europe by its focus on the contrast between existing and non-existing objects (Bozzi, 1996, Meinong, 1899, Modenato, 1996—for an overview—Rollinger, 2008). The non-existing objects are relevant as they subsist in our minds and constitute the main material for thinking and feeling. All mathematical objects—are non-existing objects—there are no geometric forms like triangles or squares in real life—even as there are myriads of triangular and quadratic objects that are real and from which these geometric notions could be abstracted. At the same time there are objects we can talk about—"a round triangle"—which cannot be imagined as existent. Yet as we can talk about such objects they are imaginable—even with the result of finding them to be impossible. We use such subsisting notions—love, justice, equality, freedom, etc.—in our everyday decisions—often with lethal consequences.

The human *psyche* needs narration about history—and the social institutions that need the collaboration and loyalties of the human beings have developed a sophisticated production system for such cultural products.

Stories told about history *look* real—while as stories they are of the same form that is characteristic of fiction writing (Eco, 2009, Valsiner, 2009). The one-time real persons who were part of historical events—Julius Caesar, Christopher Columbus, Winston Churchill, Iossif Stalin etc—are transferred into a status of completely fictional—yet believable—characters of novels, such as Anna Karenina, Harry Potter, or Karlsson (the one from the roof[2]). In their psychological functions for the living they are similar. They fill a need—for our *psyche*'s further living of the life, and for the social institutions to regulate their organizational order as they move further towards the future. The relevance of novels and history narratives is in their filling the space between the present and the yet-to-be-known future—albeit on the basis of stories of the past. Mario Vargas Llosa has captured that function well:

> When we read novels, we are not just ourselves but we are also those conjured-up characters into whose midst the novelist transports us. This transformation is a metamorphosis: the asphyxiating enclosure of our real life opens up and we leave it to become others, to live vicariously experiences that novels make our own. A lucid dream, a fantasy incarnate, fiction completes our mutilated beings that have had imposed on us the terrible dichotomy of having only one life and the desires and fantasies to have one thousand lives. *This space between our real life and the desires and fantasies that it be richer and more diverse in the terrain of fiction.*

> In the heart of all these fictions, protest is ablaze. The person who imagined them did so because he could not live them and whoever reads them (and creates them through reading) finds in their phantoms the faces and adventures that he needed to add to his life (Vargas Llosa, 1996, p. 324, added emphasis).

Narratives of history carry similar function. Yet the communicative intentions of their creation is that of "institutional authorship". Even if a text on history is directly authored by a particular person (an "I"), the whole genre of history text writing is governed by the directions of different—often contradictory—presentations (of different "we"-positions). History of censorship is evidence of the importance of the nature of particular presentations at a particular time—some dominant "we"-positions—exemplified by the

---

[2] As a fictional character in Astrid Lindgren's children's books, Karlsson is a very short, kind of fat, and humorously confident man who lives on the roof of a very ordinary apartment building, on a very ordinary street in Stockholm. When Karlsson pushes a button on his stomach it starts a clever little motor with a propeller on his back allowing him to fly. Karlsson is the best at everything, at least according to himself, and a good friend to children.

personal ("I-position") act of a censor—suppress or allow other "I→We" positions into the public domain.

HISTORY WRITING AS NEGOTIATION OF MEANING

Telling stories about history is an act of constructing cultural tools that enter the semiotic marketplace of negotiating our potential futures. Some of these are to be avoided (from some perspective)—others—maybe later to be described as "utopias"—elevated to the state of irresistible desire by many persons who make these stories their own. Revolutions and counter-revolutions and their constituents—peace and war—depend on the willing participants who re-frame their (and others') horrors of social and personal ruptures (Zittoun, 2006) through the feeling of awe. While school textbooks tell glory stories of social transformations due to wars of liberation and progressive revolutions, the disequilibria in the lives of the ordinary participants of such "historical events"—their misery of loss or relocation—is carefully kept out of the picture. The multi-faceted story telling about history that can range from the use of one extreme social representation to another. We are used to hear the story "*Napoleon as a hero*", in contrast to "*Napoleon as a war criminal*". If the latter were to be considered, the body of the hero might be taken from the Pantheon in Paris to the International War Crimes Tribunal in The Hague. Of course contemporary patriotic feelings of the French (and many others) would render such scenario impossible. Such contrasting social presentations are guided by the structured field of communication—the Semiotic Demand Setting (SDS). History writing is always the hostage to the goal-orientations of the writers—and of the institutions that guide their writing, or decide upon their fate after the texts are ready.

WHAT IS THE SEMIOTIC DEMAND SETTING (SDS)

Human psychological development proceeds through negotiation between the perception and action through the affordances that unite the actor and context, and the suggestions for feeling, thinking and acting that are proliferated through communication. For human beings, the world of objects is available immediately under limits upon action (e.g., need to act under time pressure, etc), yet otherwise the environment is mediated through meanings. These structured environments are Semiotic Demand Settings (SDS)—human-made structures of everyday life settings where the properties of the objects are co-determined by perceptual-actional and cultural-meanings' based possibilities and expectations (Valsiner, 2000, p. 125). It is based on the theoretical triplet of three interdependent "zones" that channel human development—the ZPA ("Zone of Promoted Action"), ZFM ("Zone of Freedom of Movement") and ZPD ("Zone of Proximal Develop-

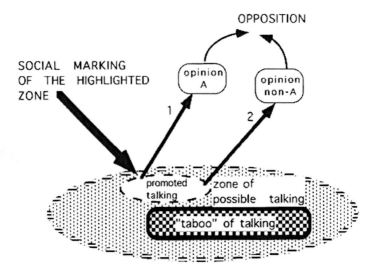

FIGURE 1. Semiotic Demand Setting (SDS)

ment")—transposed from their original context (Valsiner, 1987) to shed light upon the narrative practices in a society. All forms of semiotic presentations—not only verbal talk but iconic and indexical marking of social events in public—are covered by the SDS (Figure 1).

The SDS regulates human thinking, feeling, and doing (Valsiner, 2000). It organizes story-telling—a central feature of human lives—historically and ontogenetically. Yet many aspects of human experience are not turned into stories, and some are made into domains of purposeful silences (Ohnuki-Tierney, 1994; Orlandi, 1995).These domains are not merely closed for talking—they are vehemently maintained as such—through internalized affective regulators (Valsiner, 2001a, 2001b).

THREE ZONES OF COMMUNICATIVE ACCESS

Any domain of human personal experience can become culturally guided by some socio-institutional focusing of the person's attention to it in three ways. First, there is the realm of NO-TALK—the sub-field of personal experiences that are excluded from the realm of talk-based access (the "taboo of talking" in Figure 1). Some of that exclusion is guaranteed by social norms (e,g., no mentioning of private issues—sex, money, or religion—in public), other—specifically protected by their being of "zero signifiers" (Ohnuki-Tierney, 1994). The "zero signifiers" are powerful communicational tools by the absence of a sign. For instance, in different societies the name of a deity (e.g. "G_d") cannot be mentioned as it may evoke excessive symbolic powers. Likewise, the historical controversies about the iconic depiction of the images of deities—ranging from Byzantine 8th–9th century and European 16–17th centuries iconoclasms to 21st century Taliban dynamiting the Bamyian Buddha are examples of forcing some communicative domain to belong to the NO-TALK zone.

The rest of the field is the "zone of free movement" of talking—the MAYBE-TALK ("zone of possible talk" in Figure 1). Experiences within that field can be talked about—but ordinarily are not, as long as there is no special goal that makes that talking necessary. Most of human experiences belong to MAYBE-TALK—when we feel like it, or need to express ourselves, we can do so. Others, likewise, can ignore our doing so, or reciprocate—it is the most ordinary ways of interacting that has no consequences as to information exchange (e.g., a statement to somebody else- who is in the same situation—"the weather today is fine/bad"—carries no novelty function). Most of our interactions in the MAYBE-TALK field are of meta-communicative functions (Toda & Higuchi, 1994) or maintaining, establishing, or breaking relationships—rather than exchanging information.

The third domain of talking—the HYPER-TALK (zone of "promoted talking" in Figure 1)—is the socially (and personally) highlighted part of MAYBE-TALK that is turned from a state of talkability to that of obsessive and socially prescribed form of communication. Some people need to talk *ad nauseam*—and some outlets of mass media need to repeat obsessive political, economic, or health talk that already has reached its repetitive heights—over and over again. Our narrative environment is filled with repetitive flow of information of no novelty value. Social HYPER-TALK is a tactic to maintain the *focus of action directions on the act of talking itself*—and keep it separate from practical social actions. In human history, different political powers and religious institutions have used such prescribed talking for promoting persons' loyalty to their credos—prayers and pledges of allegiance all over the World are numerous examples. Contemporary democratic societies—aided by the commercial needs of the mass media—create the space for HYPER-TALK and preserve their own social stability.

How is the HYPER-TALK domain created? It starts from the social marking of the highlighted zone. The suggested focus (see Figure 1) can operate in two ways. First, it guides the person to reflect upon the focused experience—the zone of "promoted talking". Secondly, it provides the blueprint for talking in socially legitimized ways (Discourse ways marked by numbers 1 and 2 in Figure 1—leading to Opinion A and Opinion non-A, respectively). The acceptability (or non-acceptability) of opposition is thus enabled. Yet—as Gaston Bachelard has remarked—*opinions do not think!* When people are called upon to express *their own* opinions—in the never-ending flow of questionnaires, rating scales, and exit polls—they are disinvited to reflect upon the issues but make a choice between pre-packaged opposing ideas.

Encouragement of "*exchange* of opinions" between different ideological perspective-holders does not equal joint efforts to solve any problems—rather, it works to guarantee the survival of the given *status quo*. In a seeming inconsistency, one can observe moments where themes from the NO-TALK zone are brought over to the HYPER-TALK domain through media exposure. Since the opposites—kept separate—support each other (rather than undermine), such transfers only maintain the stable state of the SDS. Some previously unmentionable topic—vivid description of a sexual practice, or gossip about amorous relations of a president or prime minister—could be brought to the focus of enhanced talk. Yet such reversal is not an act of "being informed" or a positive feature of an "open society"—as the ways in which the new thematic material is brought to the HYPER-TALK zone have not changed. Previous "moral silence" about a theme becomes "moral outrage"—yet the latter's function is the same as the former's.

THE CLOSED NATURE OF OPENNESS: "HAVING A CHOICE"

We here arrive at a paradoxical result—a person or society that presents itself as if "open" might actually be the opposite[3]. The notion of such declared "openness" is presented as an axiomatic starting point—and is thus ruled out from being an object of any doubt. Yet all the parts of the "undoubtable whole" can be allowed to be disputed. The functions of bureaucracies (Herzfeld, 1992) in creating all kinds of forms to fill out is an example of distancing any doubt from the functions of such forms. There is always one more form to fill out—sometimes a form that pretends to explain the functioning of other forms, or even indicating that you may have the right—*if you sign this given form*—not to fill out *some* other forms. By making explicit the "doubtability" of some part of the whole, the "doubtability" of the whole itself is ruled out. By stating "*you now have the choice*" the social institution distances itself from the reality that it has given it to you, and has set up strict boundaries for the freedom of *making* choices (but not *creating* new choices). Our attention is directed towards discussion of a sub-part of the whole, while the practices of the whole remain secure. A social institution will survive when everybody in it is busy discussing some peripheral issue—designated as a "problem" by the institution—and thus keeping the talking by the participants away from other issues. Media talk shows can be seen as "vicarious pacifiers"—by creating a situated activity setting (talk-show) the participants in the setting (as well as its audiences in the comfort of

---

[3] Kurt Lewin's (1936) comparison of the interpersonal relationships in USA and in Germany demonstrates how the reality of "being open" or "being closed" is not a simple dichotomy. The theoretical scheme outlined here specifies that the opposition between these concepts is better replaced by their mutuality—so, persons and societies can be seen as "openly closed" or "closedly open" (see Valsiner, 1987, on *dependent independence*).

their own living rooms) become actively engaged in the issues ("serious" or "sensational", alike), do the talking about these issues—and leave the issues as those were in their reality. Previously, these topics could not be talked about—now they not only can be, but even should be.

Doing the talking can function in two ways—when it leads to acting, and when it does not. Social discourse can be institutionally channeled so that some previously "taboo" topics are not only turned into ones which can be spoken of, but which *must be* talked about. In other terms—one opposite (of enforced silence) becomes the other (enforces "talking through"). Whoever determines the transition from "may not" to "must be" has the fate control over the active inactivity of the doers—if it is made certain that the new openness (talk) does not threaten the existing social order. This latter method of social regulation of discourse is widely utilized in the so-called "open societies"—which, by showing off openness to the public talk about sensitive matters, actually close these matters from the domain of action.

The "field of talk" becomes defined as dis-united from the "field of action" by prescribing active exploration of a sub-part of the whole through talking—and moving the whole into the state of a given, axiomatically accepted, reality. The latter is crucial for any social institution that attempts to act in the social domain through the participation—voluntary or conscripted—by large numbers of individuals. The latter can do so if their semiotic self-regulation system includes the use of hyper-generalized sign fields within the personal culture.

THE CENTRAL ROLE OF HYPER-GENERALIZATION IN HUMAN LIFE

Phenomena of human affectivity are organized at different levels, from those closest to immediate physiological processes, to hyper-abstracted and over-generalized higher level feelings that guide our social and personal being (Beckstead, Cabell, & Valsiner, 2009; Valsiner, 2001b, 2007). A hypothetical depiction of these levels is given in Figure 2. The hierarchy of levels of semiotic mediation of affective processes that is depicted in Figure 2 sets up within the same scheme emotions and feelings of different generality. Level 0 is the universal—for all animal kingdom—physiological anticipation about the immediate next future event in life. Based on that level, the organisms can develop generalized, non-mediated "feeling tone" (or anticipatory affective state, kind of undifferentiated awareness of something—positive, negative, or ambivalent—that is about to happen). These Level 1 phenomena do not require semiotic mediation—they are pre-verbal generalizations. One can grant the reality of dog-lovers' reports about their favorite pets "feeling with" them at times of the owners' sadness or happiness—these phenomena (on the dogs' side) can belong to Level 1. Pre-verbal generalization allows for the organism to maintain previous

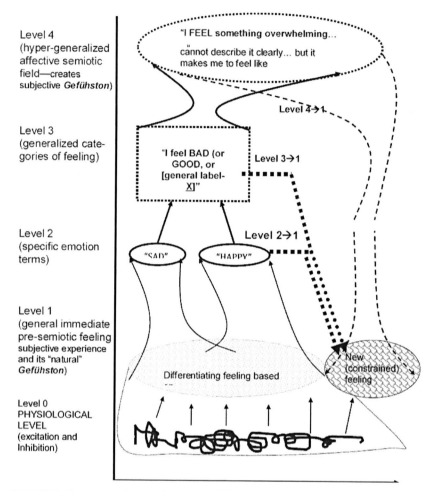

FIGURE 2. Processes of generalization and hyper-generalization in affective regulation of the flow of experience (from Valsiner, 2007, Figure 7.4)

experiences for further use, but does not require their encoding through signs.

Semiotically mediated (i.e., cultural) organization of the affective field begins at the move from Level 0 to Level 1. The person's primary affective field is already oriented by the person's previous experience. It becomes articulated at Level 2—where specific naming of emotions present "in" the experiencing person, by the person oneself, is taking place. The undifferentiated field of a particular directional quality (e.g., positive, negative, or ambivalent) becomes reflected upon through assigning the present state of the field a specifying name for the emotion felt. So, the person can say "I am sad", "I am disgusted", "I am happy" or talk about emotions like HAPPI-NESS, SADNESS, ANGER, SURPRISE, etc. as if those are permanent properties of human affective life.

Sign mediation creates the psychological distance of the thinker/talker from the differentiating affective field—discussing issues of human happiness does not mean that the discussing person oneself is happy. All the cognitive activity of persons that concentrates upon the de-contextualizing emotions—in terms of their specific categories or general prototypes—takes place at Level 2. That is the level of maximum articulation of the semiotic encoding of the affective field. Still it does not amount to maximal hierarchical integration. The latter—as will be shown later—can entail the development of a higher level de-differentiated field.

The mediational processes of Level 2 can become further generalized in ways that lead to higher-level (in terms of abstraction) de-differentiation of the affective field. Level 3 in Figure 2. depicts a situation where a person—after excessive use of emotion categories in one's internal self-dialogue—arrives at a new generalized—yet ill-defined—self-reflection. Thus, a statement "I feel bad" can result from generalization higher in abstractness than specification of emotion categories (sad, disgusted).

THE ESCALATION OF ABSTRACTION OF FEELING: HYPER-GENERALIZATION

Finally, the generalization of the sign-mediated field of feelings can reach the highest level of overgeneralization—that of a semiotically mediated state which is at the same time de-differentiated (Level 4). This entails emergence of feeling fields that overtake the person's psyche in its totality—yet these are not immediate (level 0→1) diffuse phenomena. The person "just feels" something—but cannot put that feeling into words. Examples of aesthetic feelings—catharsis experienced during a theatre performance, reading deeply moving poems or prose, or in an interpersonal situation of extreme beauty indicate that human affective field can become undifferentiated as a result of extensive abstraction of the emotions involved, and their overgeneralization to the person's general feelings about oneself or about the world. Theoretically, that process entails internalization and abbreviation (Lyra, 1999, Lyra & Souza, 2003).

It becomes important to emphasize that—contrary to Werner's and Kaplan's "orthogenetic principle" or Lev Vygotsky's emphasis on use of concepts—the highest levels of hierarchical integration do not entail increased articulation of the parts of the affective system, but just to the contrary—*the highest level of hierarchical integration is that of an hyper-generalized ("nebulous") semiotically mediated feeling ("higher feeling") subordinating all rational (Level 2) discourse about emotions to its ever-present (inarticulate) guidance.*

FIGURE 3. Ornament at the entrance to a church in Lecce, Italy

The entrance into a Baroque church in Lecce (Figure 3) includes a line ornament that for a post-World-War II Eurocentric viewer triggers the recognition of a swastika with all of the hyper-generalized affective load that immediately escalates and creates the context for the general feeling. Of course the church stands in its place by far longer than the socio-cultural history of the swastika was created in the context of Central European history[4]. Yet a person who has experienced the past century—and been under the influence of the post-WW-2 writings of history—may feel the need to accommodate one's immediate feelings to the historically older nature of the building. Symbols are not merely generalized but hyper-generalized—as they are guided by the semiotic fields we could label "values."

The example of the difficulty that psychology has had with the treatment of some higher-order affective phenomena—such as *values* (see Valsiner, Branco, & Melo Dantas, 1997)—is indicative of this process. Even as values can be posited—and traced—to be present in human conduct, bringing them out into the domain of explicit reflection by the carriers of values has been difficult. Values operate as affective-cultural tools for self-guidance for the person. They are constructively internalized, and externalized through all aspects. Yet as they have reached such hyper-generalized way of being, they are no longer easily accessible through verbally mediated processes. We can decisively act as directed by our values—but are ill at ease telling others what these values are. If we succeed, we have performed the Level 4à3 translation of a hyper-generalized semiotic field into general verbal statements (e.g., "I feel totally dedicated to science") that may refer to the direction of the values but cannot capture them in their entirety. Values are not entities—but dynamic semiotic fields. Superimposition of language onto such—nebulus-but-real —fields makes them into an entity.

DYNAMIC MOVEMENT IN THE SEMIOTIC FIELD

Human beings make meanings all the time—they cannot but be involved in this overwhelming activity. Like spiders at a lower level of biological organization who cannot but spin their webs—and may subsequently demolish them (Valsiner & Lescak, 2009), human beings are constantly creating fields of meaning/sense as they proceed in their life. This entails changes—slow or rapid—in the processes of generalization, hyper-generalization—as well as in concretization and pre-contextualization of the previously hyper-generalized meanings. Human beings make signs, use signs, abandon signs, and go on making more signs.

---

[4] The building of the church of San Giovanni Battista was finished in year 1691.

THE SWIB (SIGN WITH INFINITE BORDERS)

The crucial feature of sign mediation of the human *psyche* is not merely pre-sentation of the world via signs (that stand for something else)—which is the prevailing static view present in semiotics—but in the dynamic movement from one structure of signs to another. Affective tensions emerge—and find their resolution—in such movement. Some of these transformations of signs are rapid and directed toward complete takeover of the person's *psyche*. I call such rapidly expanding/constricting signs SWIB ("Signs With Infinite Bor-ders"). The phenomena of the sublime in aesthetic feelings are constructed through SWIBs—the emergent feelings of encountering a sunset, or enter-ing a Baroque church, a French garden (Carillo Canan, 2003), or the sound of church bells (Corbin, 1998). The role of SWIBs in the making (and un-making) of crowd feelings and group atmospheres is crucial in the field of social actions—hence the efforts by social institutions to either escalate the coordinated actions affect-driven mobs (create an act of demonstration, at-tack, or revolution), or calm them down by rules of social control.

We can think of explosive changes in the meaning-making in the form of sudden emergence of all-encompassing meaning fields—which strive to-wards specifying no boundaries for the field. The meaning construction is oriented towards infinity—yet such striving is in principle not possible to succeed. Each expanding perspective is limited by the horizon—an imaginary outer boundary of the exploring meaning-maker. That bound-ary can move together with the movement of the person (who changes one's position)—yet it can never be transcended. The movement towards such boundary is linked with a counter-process of moving away from such boundary. The exploding meaning field can equally dramatically enter into the opposite process of "collapse" or constriction of the field. The tension between the expansion and constriction can lead to an outburst of feeling (hyper-generalization caught moving towards infinity at Level 4) or its col-lapse into a point-like sign (at Level 2). The latter can lead to very specific action—crimes of passion are known both in life and through novels.

Yet there is a third option—the synthesis. Instead of acting out, the per-son under the SWIB may act inwards—and arrive at new field-like under-standing of the object. The realm of aesthetics is a result of such escalation. The whole rapid expansion of the sign from a point to a field to a SWIB is captured by constant tension of opposing feelings, well captured by Lev Vygotsky in his analysis of how the experiencing of art functions. According to him, the *general rule of aesthetic synthesis* is in that the given affect:

...which develops in two opposite directions, that in the culmination point, as if in the case of short circuit, finds its destruction (Vygotsky, 1987, p. 204[5])

SWIBS AT VARIOUS LEVELS OF SEMIOTIC PRESENTATION

How do the SWIBs function across the levels of generalizing◇un-generalizing semiotic fields (Figure 2)? All persuasion/propaganda and social efforts to *trigger actions* need to operate through creating SWIBs at Levels 3 or/and 4. All social efforts to *block actions* need to operate through creating SWIBs at Level 2– supported by fixed Level 3 and Level 4. Social regulation of human conduct involves negotiation of whether to let SWIBs proliferate (creating phenomena of communion, or a patriotic fervent). Such SWIB starting at Level 4 needs to be at the start of soldiers going into a battle—no words needed, complete guidance from the unmentionable total semiotic field. It is a state of personal full devotion to some unmentionable higher objective for which the outcome—survival or death—has become irrelevant for the person.

The SWIB at Level 3 can be viewed escalating at times of general changes of the affective context of living. Thus, with the move from peace to wartime—often implicitly feel-able—can be accompanied by increasing intensity of vague quasi- "philosophical" and highly moralistic flows of discussions about the war and its conditions. Patriotic discussions triggered by the move into wartime and appearing in any social context—from mass media to local taverns or family contexts—work for the making of the Level 4 background "rationally adequate." Yet there is no rationality in this SWIB-flow of vague, non-logically concatenated different ideas and practices. Burning books (or their authors) as acts of public displays in human history are activity contexts that are both made available by SWIBs at Level 3, and further fortify it. Political speeches and the presentations of patriotic or religious ideas in textbooks—without leaving the listener or reader any possibility for doubt—operate towards giving rise to SWIBs at this level[6].

SWIBs at Level 2 entail various "rational discussions" of human acting, thinking, and feeling. These are escalating disputes that are enacted as-if "logical"—yet they are based on the non-mentionable Level 4 sign-fields and may episodically reach Level 3 explicit sign complexes to feed forward

---

[5] "...*affekt, razvivajuchiessia v dvukh protivopoloznykh napravlenijakh, kotoryi v zavershitel'noi tochke, kak v korotkom zamykanii, nakhodit svoe unichtozenie*"

[6] It is interesting to add that the recipients of such "SWIB-boosting" communication messages often make themselves open to such messages, and *even seek them out on their own free will.* This dependency of course is the result of the practices of all forms of religious services over history—where the audience is provided with—and expects—communicative messages that are explicit at Level 3 and below (concrete action demands that follow)—all within the unmentioned context of Level 4

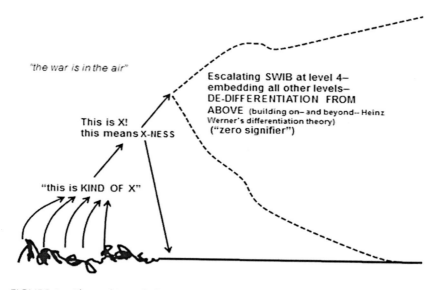

FIGURE 4. The making of silence through SWIB at the level of hyper-generalized meaning field (Level 4)

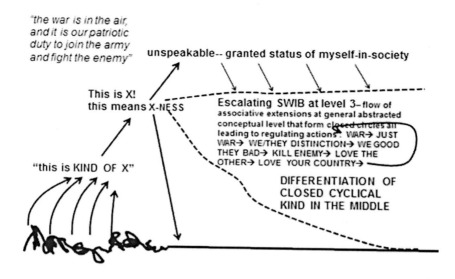

FIGURE 5. Escalating through SWIB at Level 3: flowing vague utterances

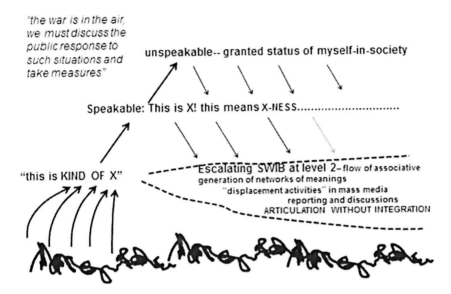

FIGURE 6. The function of SWIBs at Level 2 (socially expanding "rational" talk)

into the flow of Level 2 SWIB. Both internal and external dialogues of moral actions in society are enhanced by such SWIBs. Individuals are expected to "become involved" in such discussions, and their "participation" (a vague Level 3 notion) may be socially evaluated. The claimed-to-be-"logical" arguments are situated within the underlying assumptions of Level 3 complexes, which in their turn are guided by the non-mentionable Level 4.

IDENTITY UNDER SCRUTINY

History writing is aimed at the stabilization of identities. Yet identities—also a case of non-existing objects—subsist as constructed imaginary states that function as organizers of the self. The issue involved is a person's construction of versions of psychological substitutions of an imagined whole (e.g., nation, social group, family) for a part (self). Identity is constantly in a process of construction and maintenance, and it can never be presented as if its essence has a static form (Valsiner, 1997). There is no reason for describing identity in terms of object-like constructs (e.g., using terms like "having identity of X"), and guides him or her towards the description of the processes involved in the interpretive constructing of assumed identities.

From that standpoint the repeated actions of persons to make their identity declarations—ranging from participating in family's joint dinnertime activities or community religious services to recurrent salutes to national flag and uttering pledges of allegiance to a flag or to a political party—is crucial for guiding and maintaining the dynamic self-organization process. In terms introduced here, identity is produced by construction of affective bond through all four levels of semiotic mediation. Its core organizing unit is a hyper-generalized field-like identity sign at Level 4—hence identity as a topic of investigation is not addressable directly by verbal questioning. Instead, it can be studied by techniques that unleash its functioning in the form of a SWIB—triggering extreme affective escalations of "irrational" kinds by experimental "threats" to otherwise well-established (or dormant) relations with signs—iconic, indexical, or verbal. The overwhelming feeling of discomfort while seeing one's national flag being burnt, or a national monument defaced would tell the researcher more about the functioning of the person's identity processes than any questioning about one's identity. Direct questions about identity lead to its entification—which is a crystallized form of a process the role of which is to stay in a dynamic form. Identity needs to be studied as a process—not as a thing. The latter would amount to the "psychologist's fallacy" that William James alerted us to back in 1890[7].

CONCLUSION:
WHAT HAS ALL THIS TO DO WITH HISTORY TEACHING?

Everything! First of all—the notions of hyper-generalized sign fields and sign-field escalation (SWIBs) give us a new look at the phenomena that in everyday and political discourses is talked about as "freedom of speech". It follows from this theoretical exploration that such "freedom" is not without its constraints—both external (social) and internal (personal-cultural). Even more—in a seemingly paradoxical manner—exaggerated social demand for "narrative work" on history can become an act of the very reification of the target that is being investigated. Teaching of Columbus' "discovery of America" in Europe may close other possible perspectives upon the impact of the arrival of his flotilla in what is still called "West Indies."

Writing about history—as it functions as guidance for the future—entails the negotiation of the borders of the Semiotic Demand Setting. History as it was is never to be presented in its reality—but always turned into a pre-

---

[7] As he pointed to the misleading influence of speech:

"Empiricist writers are very fond of emphasizing one great set of delusions which language inflicts on the mind. Whenever we have made a word, they say, to denote a certain group of phenomena, we are prone to suppose a substantive entity existing beyond the phenomena, of which the word shall be the name. But the lack of a word quire as often leads to the directly opposite error. We are then prone to suppose that no entity can be there; and so we come to overlook phenomena whose existence would be patent to us all..." (James, 1890/1950, p.195)

sented object (*Gegenstand*). The borderlands of such object construction—as was shown in the case of SDS—are always contested. The reality in history is always ambiguous—the (presented) heroes act as (presentable) villains, the acts of "progressive" kind are "regressive" in relation to the previous social order that it undermines or demolishes. There are always multiple perspectives of persons in relation to historical events—starting from the basic question about changeability versus non-changeability of the current social order, and the desirability of such event. For instance, the role of the French Revolution in Europe was by far more relevant than the new rules, the guillotine, and Napoleonic conquests taken together. It changed the realm of what was possible—in action and in thinking:

> What made the revolution radical was the very idea of positing a moral community justified in terms of virtue rather than legitimated by custom, tradition, or religion (Fritzsche, 2004, p. 18)

Teaching history either enables the view of social innovation, or attempts to render it untenable. Hence it has a key role to play—and a responsibility the implications of which are probably too dramatic to outline. Our minds keep creating their monuments—in the depth of our subjective personal worlds—and those monuments guide us towards our own future.

Acknowledgments

The SWIB concept was introduced in previous presentations at PerSemSoc seminars in Paris (June, 15 and November, 17, 2009) organized by Jean Lassegue, Victor Rosenthal and Yves-Marie Visetti at CNRS.

REFERENCES

Albertazzi, L, Jacquette, D., & Poli, R (Eds.) (2001). *The school of Alexius Meinong.* Aldershot: Ashgate

Beckstead, Z., Cabell, K. R., & Valsiner, J. (2009). Generalizing through conditional analysis: Causality in the world of eternal becoming. *Humana Mente, 11,* 65–80. [http://www.humanamente.eu]

Bozzi, P. (1996). Higher-order objects. In L. Albertazzi, M. Libardi, & R. Poli (Eds.), *The school of Franz Brentano* (pp. 285–304). Dordrecht: Kluwer.

Carillo Canan, A. J. L. (2003). The gardens of Versailles and the sublime. In A.-T. Tymieniecka (Ed.), *Gardens and the passion for the infinite. Analecta Husserliana, 78,* 47–58. Dordrecht: Kluwer.

Corbin, A. (1998). *Village bells: Sound and meaning in the 19ᵗʰ Century French countryside.* New York: Columbia University Press.

Eco, U. (2009). On the ontology of fictional characters: A semiotic approach. *Sign Systems Studies* (Tartu University), *37*(½), 82–98.

Fritzsche, P (2004). *Stranded in the present: Modern time and the melancholy of history.* Cambridge, MA: Harvard University Press.

Herzfeld, M. (1992). *The social production of indifference: Exploring the symbolic roots of Western bureaucracy.* Chicago: University of Chicago Press.

James, W. (1950). *The principles of psychology* (Vol. 1). New York: Dover

Lewin, K. (1936). Some social-psychological differences between the United States and Germany. *Character & Personality, 4*(4), 265–293.

Lyra, M. C. (1999). Desenvolvimento de um sistema de relacoes historicamente construido: Contribucoes da comunicacao no inicio da vida. *Psicologia: Reflexao e critica, 13,* 2.

Lyra, M. C., & Souza, M. (2003). Dynamics of dialogue and emergence of self in early communication. In I. E. Josephs (Ed.), *Dialogicality in development.* Stamford, CT: Greenwood Publishing Group.

Meinong, A. (1899). Ueber Gegenstände höherer Ordnung und deren Verhältnis zur inneren Wahrnehmung. *Zeitschrift für Psychologie und Physiologie der Sinnesorgane, 21,* 182–272.

Modenato, F. (1996). Meinong's theory of objects: An attempt at overcoming psychologism. In R. Haller (Ed.), *Meinong und die Gegenstandstheorie* (pp. 87–122). Amsterdam: Rodopi.

Ohnuki-Tierney, E. (1994). The power of absence: Zero signifiers and their transgressions. *L'Homme, 34*(2, Whole No. 130), 59–76.

Orlandi, E. P. (1995). *As formas do silencio.* Campinas, SP: Editora da UNICAMP.

Rollinger, R. D. (2008). *Austrian phenomenology: Brentano, Husserl, Meinong and others on mind and object.* Frankfurt-am-Mail: Ontos Verlag.

Toda, M., & Higuchi, K. (1994). Common sense, emotion, and chatting—and their roles in interpersonal interaction. In J. Siegfried (Ed.), *The status of common sense in psychology* (pp. 208–244). Norwood, NJ: Ablex.

Valsiner, J. (1987). *Culture and the development of children's action.* Chichester: Wiley.

Valsiner, J. (1997). Constructing identity: A theoretical problem for social sciences. Paper presented at the Workshop *"Identitätsdiskussionenin der Psychologie",* in the framework of the Graduiertenkollegs "Identitätsforschung" of Martin-Luther-Universität, Halle-am-Saale, April 18.

Valsiner, J. (2000). *Culture and human development.* London: Sage

Valsiner, J. (2001a). Process structure of semiotic mediation in human development. *Human Development, 44,* 84–97.

Valsiner, J. (2001b). Cultural developmental psychology of affective processes. Paper presented at the 15. Tagung der Fachgruppe Entwicklungspsychologie der Deutschen Gesellschaft für Psychologie, Potsdam, September, 5.

Valsiner, J. (2007). *Culture in minds and societies.* New Delhi: Sage.

Valsiner, J. (2009). Between fiction and reality: Transforming the semiotic object. *Sign System Studies, 37*(1/2), 99–113.

Valsiner, J., Branco, A. U., & Melo Dantas, C. (1997). Co-construction of human development: Heterogeneity within parental belief orientations. In J. E. Grusec & L. Kuczynski (Eds.), *Handbook of parenting and the transmission of values* (pp. 283–304). New York: Wiley.

Valsiner, J., & Lescak, E. (2009). The wisdom of the web: learning from spiders. In R. Sokol Chang (Ed.), *Relating to environments* (pp. 45–65). Charlotte, NC: Information Age Publishing.

Vargas Llosa, M. (1996). The truth of lies. In M Vargas Llosa, *Making waves* (pp. 320–330). New York: Ferrar Straus and Giroux.

Vygotsky, L. S. (1987). *Psikhologia iskusstva*. Moscow: Pedagogika.

Zittoun, T. (2006). *Transitions*. Charlotte, NC: Info Age Publishing

CHAPTER 23

COMMENTARY

The Complex Construction of Identity Representations and the Future of History Education

Floor van Alphen and Mikel Asensio

Collective memory, as Maurice Halbwachs already noted, is everywhere (Halbwachs, 1992). The enormous diversity shaping our narratives and identities also characterizes the variety of approaches in the last section of this volume. History education forms only a small part of our consciousness of the past. Particularly when recent history is concerned, the transmission of beliefs from one generation to the next is beyond education. Nonetheless, school history "too often acts as if it is the only player" (Wineburg, Mosborg, Porat, & Duncan, 2007). Mainly the (distant) national past is being taught and typically other "voices of collective remembering" (Wertsch, 2002) are left out. However, the burgeoning research in the collective processes surrounding history education has opened up a field of interest impossible to ignore, vast in extension and complexity. Especially because "a common past [...is...] perhaps *the* crucial instrument—in the construction of collective identities in the present" (Seixas, 2004, p. 5).

History Education and the Construction of National Identities, pages 347–359

The four contributions in this section consider different aspects of the construction of representations as a complex process that is influenced by at least four major psychological and social factors: (a) family and social group considerations; (b) knowledge transmitted in the school environment, especially in the subjects of history, geography, religion and art; (c) the general media, especially the press and the audio-visual media of cinema and television; and (d) patrimony as the setting for the presentation of historic events that relate to identity. These social mechanisms make individuals aware of historical knowledge that influences the identity construction process. The four contributions in this section provide a critical reflection on the social and personal representation processes; the authors base their analyses on previous investigations and empirical studies on the construction of social and historical memory.

The contributions all highlight the complexity of the representation process and its less intuitive aspects, which will require further investigation in the near future. A clarification of these processes may elucidate mechanisms for analyzing social situations, which can facilitate plans for inclusive and multicultural education and governance. Simultaneously, these processes can reveal certain manipulations of social and cultural representations with ulterior motives, which is an important task.

The complexity of representation and identification might be illustrated by recent research among participants in the Nicaragua revolution (Asensio & Pol, in preparation). Some findings will be presented and discussed in the light of issues raised by Jaan Valsiner, Sabine Moller, Kyoko Murakami, Helen Haste and Amy Hogan. Similar to the research by Murakami and Moller, but also Wineburg et al. (2007) and Bietti (2010), recent history is involved. The interviewed were themselves part of the historical process under study. Note that in these cases identification processes are clear and immediate, however, they might differ from those relating to the distant past. Something to consider, particularly with respect to history education. The relevant question, in the context of this volume, as to what the complexities of collective memory and identity construction imply for history education will be discussed. School history is a mere fragment of vast collective memory and can impossibly account for all of it. But as history is taught in a developmental period crucial for the construction of representations and identities, shouldn't it at least be opened up for other possible accounts?

IDEAS REGARDING THE PERCEIVED CONSTRUCTION OF SOCIAL REPRESENTATIONS OF HISTORICAL KNOWLEDGE OF IDENTITY

The following excerpts come from recent anthropological interviews in Nicaragua, in the context of a request from the Universidad Nacional Autónoma de Nicaragua to evaluate the possible creation of a museum about the

(Sandinista) revolution.[1] Participants are Sandinista ex-guerrillas who are between 45–55 years old and were very young during the revolution (1979). The entire sample is of a peasant origin, including individuals from families with very low social and educational levels. The respondents have clear indigenous origins, although they do not belong to any of the country's indigenous minorities that are recognized as differentiated groups. Ideologically, they continue to be Sandinistas, although they hold various degrees of criticism about the revolutionary process. They are especially critical of the official Sandinista representatives, who recently won the general elections and the presidency of the country. The respondents are from León, which in 1979 was the first city to be liberated by the revolution after heavy periods of armed confrontation between the guerrillas and civilian population and the dictatorship. All of the respondents except one maintained various levels of political activity in left-wing parties, unions or associations. All of the respondents view themselves as Sandinista revolutionaries, and they consider their guerrilla past and their political activity to be the most important elements of their social identities (Asensio & Pol, in preparation).

> Our history has always been poorly told because newspapers and television channels were constantly lying ... Because they are in the hands of the landholding rightwing.... During the revolution, they told the poor peasants that we guerrillas used to eat their daughters and that we were going there to destroy the little that they had, and the poor people believed it. The "contras" (counter-revolutionary guerrillas) had a lot of money because they were paid by the United States, but it was never a real threat, they were in the mountains, but they served for those who were on the inside to put a brake on the revolution, to prepare a discourse ... the people did not know who we really were, what we wanted to do, because no newspaper or radio station was telling them. ... The children in school were not studying the revolution, they were studying what was then called "civil war," and it was not a civil war, everyone had risen up against the dictator, including now, today, in this city, the Front received more than 90% of the votes, everyone had voted Sandinista. Children ought to study with books that tell the truth. ... It is true that there are families that are not Sandinistas, the contras did a lot of damage, and they made mistakes. Right here we have a politician who is suspected of indiscriminate killing of indigenous people. ... We need a museum of the

---

[1] Referring to the process of overthrowing the dictatorship of the Somoza presidential family by the *Frente Sandinista de Liberación Nacional*, FSLN, or the Sandinista National Liberation Front. Work that can be consulted for more historical detail is:
—Cabezas, O. (1999) *La montaña es algo más que una gran estepa verde*. [The mountains are more than just vast green steppes.] Tafalla: Editorial Txalaparta.
—Ortega, H. (1980) *50 años de lucha sandinista*. [50 years of Sandinista struggle.] Managua: Editorial de Ciencias Sociales.
—Zimmerman, M. (2003) *Carlos Fonseca Amador y la revolución sandinista*. [Carlos Fonseca Amador and the Sandinista revolution.] Bluefields: Universidad de las Regiones de la Costa Caribe Nicaragüense.

revolution so that in the future they will know what we tried to do that will tell what happened, and that will recover the places where things happened, because León is the city of the revolution, and the museum ought to be here, and this is the right moment.

The social and historical reality discussed here illustrates, in the first person and in a radical and dramatic fashion, the central aspects of identity construction. First, when listening to these individuals, one observes an important difference in relation to other Latin American countries. The traditional European-indigenous dialectic continues to influence their reflections on personal and social identity. However, although indigenous cultural influences are very strong in Nicaragua, they are only mentioned as exclusion factors to refer to particular minorities; indigenous cultural influences are not mentioned when the respondents refer to themselves. A similar pattern emerges with reference to the cultural influence of the colonial past; the majority of the interviewees do not use a colonial history to define their identity.

Potentially as a result of the revolutionary and contra-revolutionary wars, the participants' social identities revolve around the definition of their need to self-identify, as a key aspect of daily survival. Interestingly, it is common to meet people who identify themselves as revolutionaries. However, it is rare to meet people who identify themselves as counter-revolutionaries. Instead, one finds that the revolutionary factor is relevant to the degree of the bitter critiques of the revolutionary process, including its excesses and leaders. Yet, one cannot distinguish an identity factor that is sufficiently agglutinating or explicitly recognized as being counter-revolutionary.

INTUITIVE FACTORS THAT INFLUENCE THE CONSTRUCTION OF IDENTITY

The phrases cited above combine some of the patterns that guide the process of personal identity in a significant way. All of the participants explicitly recognize that identity is a complex process that is influenced by internal and external aspects. The participants' implicit-intuitive theory is based on the idea that aspects of identity involve a personal attitude that depends on individual decisions but is strongly influenced by social context. For example, interviewees explain their identification with the revolutionary process in the context of two factors. They consider the socio-political context in which they lived during the war, which necessarily led to the conscientization of an unjust social situation. For example, they indicate that "it was the only thing that one could do in that situation" and that "anyone who had lived through it" would have done the same thing. They suggest that "it provided its own context" that determined their actions. However, they also mention their personal decision and commitment to change their situation, regardless of the personal cost, and to achieve a set of social improvements related to values of social solidarity. For example, they mention that "there were people who did not want to struggle" and that "some did not want to defend the interests of all but merely their own." Their theory includes a condition that applies to people who have lived through an experience that they consider to be definitive. For the respondents, phenomenal awareness is central for establishing an identity-based reality, whether as an inclusive factor ("if you lived it, then you would have a strong level of identification") or an exclusive factor ("if you did not live it, then it would be very difficult to have the same level of identification").

However, their implicit-intuitive theory also includes the prediction of what occurs in the absence of personal experience. When identity does not depend on personal experience, the factors of social transmission are fundamental, and those with experience suspect that there has been identity manipulation. The individual psychological factor is regarded as a predisposition that is related to family ("you belong to a family of revolutionaries or to a family of the right, or you have a family member who is relevant and significant in one direction or the other") or social group influence (especially environments for socialization) rather than a personal choice. In addition to this influence, much importance is placed on two determining social factors: education and media influence.

Education is considered to be a central factor in identity formation. Interviewees believe that school transmits certain biases that depend on the political choice of one's educational background, such as public, private or religious. The biases are explicitly transmitted in assignments in history, religion, geography, art and literature and the social sciences. To the same degree, interviewees insist that the media directly and decisively influenced the construction of identities that are related to the revolution. The newspapers and radio networks play an important role, whereas television plays a secondary role because of its lower level of development. Paradoxically, this understanding is currently being inverted in the process of re-reading identity, which is discussed below.

Finally, heritage is another determining factor for identity. The value of material and intangible cultural features, together with natural heritage, shape a central element of identity by converting heritage into the most important element of historical memory. Heritage appears in our conversations as the determinant of identity through a process of establishing benchmarks that guarantee the survival of identity values. This reference value makes heritage relevant for establishing identities. Thus, the conservation and enhancement of heritage is a priority for social groups that identify with a particular ideal. Respondents explicitly consider heritage to be laden with cultural and social meaning as well as self-identification. In addition, its reference value plays a determining role that other forms of social influence do not guarantee; heritage contains a greater projection of the future than a textbook or documentary, which are ephemeral. Most of the interviewed subjects explain the need to recover heritage sites that are related to the revolution. They consider the creation of a museum of the revolution as a priority for repairing and safeguarding their revolutionary identity. They also support the collection of personal material from homes, such as recordings of personal narratives. This attachment to the past represents a normal attitude in collectives that feel as though they are losing their material culture. Kyoko Murakami (2012) also provides a clear example.

THE CONSTRUCTION OF IDENTITY AS A PROCESS OF RE-INTERPRETING THE FUTURE

Representations of identity are often considered to be constructions from and for the past. This view exists in academic studies and can also be found in the intuitive views of the respondents. However, the construction of identity is for the individual in question, and it concerns the future. A person expects to identify with what that individual wishes to be. Identity always has a teleological component that, until now, has been seldom studied. Something also prioritized by Haste and Hogan (2012). Our interviewees are very clear about this "future" component. In a reiterative manner, they are concerned about two issues. First, they are directly concerned about promoting their future image. They are aware that the manipulation of the social environment, the media, their education and their heritage are central for ensuring that their identity is understood and preserved as an end in itself. Second, they are concerned about the process of construction, and an explicit recognition of this process exists at the intra-subject level (which is in evident danger of a historical manipulation of these representations). The implicit-intuitive theory is sensitive to processes of re-reading and re-writing, both internally and externally, the identity process. The affected persons are aware of these problems in terms of what they consider to be internal deviations or direct external constructions that come from various "aggressions" of the factors cited. The greatest influence comes from the media. It is easy to identify external aggressions from "the other" as having interests that are contrary to their own identity. All of the interviewees mention the re-writing of the revolutionary period that is occurring at present. This re-writing includes various factors, but it fundamentally involves the media, such as television, documentaries and historical re-creation series. These interesting re-writings provoke a re-reading of the individual identity processes. The most dangerous aspect of these changes is the lack of awareness of those affected because the mechanisms of influence are not transparent to the epistemological identity processes. For example, when referring to outside influences, respondents report that "It is incredible because people believe what the media tell them all over again."

These processes of re-interpretation produce an indirect relationship between influential factors and the construction of representations of identity. For the media and other social agents, a re-reading of the past does not always involve the same re-readings by people, but it provokes reactions that are difficult to foresee. Many people who are subjected to an intense re-reading do not change their positions, and the re-readings reinforce their identities and isolate them in an intense endogamic process. The process is often impenetrable from social or gregarious points of view because the processes of identity construction are not usually transparent. As becomes clear in the contributions of this final section. All agree that education is essential, especially given biased information in the media. Dealing with diversity in that context is, however, easier said than done.

COMPLICATIONS FOR HISTORY EDUCATION

How can education be organized given the complexity of identity construction processes? Or more concretely: should we take collective memories and identity construction into account in history education? Considering the case of Nicaragua we are inclined to say yes, as official and media accounts are limited and biased. Other perspectives, the history of the revolutionaries, should also be included. If a child cannot identify with the master narrative told at school, because her community was not represented in that historical account, we feel that a voice has been smothered and that human rights are violated. The issue of including indigenous histories is discussed in more detail by Seixas (2012). Yet on the other hand we have been warned about how collective memories can obscure a clear vision of the past, or rather, how the emphasis on identification in history education might limit a disciplinary understanding of the past (Carretero & Bermudez, 2012). To allow collective memories in the history classroom might actually set the stage for a limited and biased national history, excluding indigenous communities, to be taught. However, the question posed above is not a very good one: collective memory is the context framing history education and the latter is already intertwined with processes of identity construction.

Collective memory and history are often referred to interchangeably in the ongoing debate on education and identity construction. Particularly the school history aimed at fostering (national) identities can be seen as an elaborate form of memory (Rüsen, 2007, as quoted by Moller, 2012). More often than not collective memories are transmitted through history teaching in and out of school (Carretero, 2011). They are not the same as the teachings of disciplinary history. As Carretero, Rosa, and González (2006) have signaled school history is more but also less than historiography. It involves many more values and beliefs, not only the ones stressed by teachers, curricula or textbooks, but also those brought into the classroom by the students themselves (Grever, 2012; Tutiaux-Guillon, 2012). As it has been argued by Wineburg (2001) their often presentist psychological mindset can pose limits on complex historical understanding. This limitation is not essentially individual: children are very early on exposed to collective memories and national history, so the bias they present could be a consequence of the stories they were told and the way in which this happened. Carretero (2011) observes that participation in patriotic rituals, the acting out of national history, seems to significantly determine later historical narrative consumption, production and identification with that narrative. But then again, national history is more collective memory than disciplinary historiography.

History and memory both imply some consciousness of the past. And they do not merely involve passive reception of stories from the past in the present, but also active construction of narratives. Yet, what past we are aware of, and the way we are aware of it, differs when we are remembering or when we are historicizing, according to Rosa (2006). He distinguished between on the one hand an individual faculty that is practical and capable of imagining or forgetting what has happened in function of the present. Remembering, or not, can also happen collectively, and constitutes both a personal and a social identity. It establishes the continuity needed in the face of ambiguity. On the other hand there's the disciplined and contemplative practice of generating "true" knowledge, following the rational criteria conventionally agreed upon by experts (Rosa, 2006; see also Wertsch & Roediger, 2008). A historian remembers, but ideally does not forget what is less convenient or desirable: he confronts historical sources that might reveal particularly uncomfortable features of the past. Identification with that history is more likely to generate shame than to foster pride. Disciplinary history provides tools for national (self)critique, but would be equally critical of attempts by local minorities or ethnic communities to legitimize present interests. Thus, managing memory and history in the educational context is far from easy, particularly because education is concerned with both emancipation (of identities) and (disciplined) contemplation. Indeed, in practice memory and history can hardly be separated.

Yet conflicts emerge between collective memory and disciplinary history, as illustrated by Moller (2012). She investigated whether family recollections might hinder the learning of history. In the discussion between German students about the former GDR, it becomes pretty clear that the familiar variant of collective memory determines their view of the past. But instead of emphasizing authoritative history and its tools for enhancing historical literacy, Moller argues wisely: "When treated as distortions of the truth, *family memories* become an obstacle to history education. Instead, we should help students recognize they are a very specific source in a universe of possible other sources. While such a source can have a powerful impact on our orientation in time, like all sources it can be integrated into the bigger picture, using responsible and systematic reasoning" (pp. 291–292).

Emphasizing the authority of historians might actually generate the idea of limited historical understanding: I (agent of disciplined history) know more than you (often a novice or agent of collective memory). Instead of judging collective memories from a historical point of view, these memories might in their own terms provide the necessary checks and balances for avoiding one potentially dangerous all-encompassing narrative. For example, in the case of Nicaragua Sandinista-accounts strike a balance with an official history. Historians, we've seen for example in Berger (2012), haven't been perfectly neutral. Collective memory could serve the diversity of perspectives that so many working and researching in the field of history education are actually looking for.

In line with this argument, Murakami (2012) makes an interesting suggestion, be it rather on a methodological level. Starting from an historical event as organizing individual experiences, she writes, you arrive at different historical contents then when you start the other way around: plotting individual experiences and other historical actors. The narrative arising from this network, most likely chaotic and dynamic, might actually be closer to how things happened than the narrative organized around a historical criterion, often set in presentism anyway. In the same vein it would be interesting to look at the historical concepts social scientists themselves use, organizing their discourse and possibly that of students as well. Thus "nation" can become a tool or leitmotiv while constructing a narrative, without a student necessarily being a nationalist: he is just using the tool available to him.

Valsiner (2012) proposes a similar idea in terms of a Semiotic Demand Setting: a field of meaning making wherein we all operate, that determines what we can and cannot talk about. History writing he conceives of as a negotiation of meaning, and a construction of cultural tools with a certain objective: framing what is talked about. This establishes monuments in our minds, for example stable identities. Not only does this mean that the dynamic identity process goes unaccounted for, but also that talking about one thing is concealing another. Indeed, collective memory is vulnerable for forgetting, but in Valsiners view, so is history.

Murakami too warns against forgetfulness. Yet she is optimistic about discursive practices geared towards the future and stresses the openness needed for history education. For her history is laden with future possibilities of being otherwise. Valsiner, however, shows the paradoxical nature of talking about openness. "Having a choice" *determines* that you have choices, and what choices you have. And it's worse, talking prevents actual action.

He is not just optimistic and states that the reality in history is always ambiguous; progress for some is regress for others. History teaching has a very important role to play, as it can either enable the view of social innovation or attempt to render it untenable. Indeed, Sandinista accounts can be included in Nicaraguan history education. This can both be maintained from historiographic discipline, to counteract forgetfulness, as from collective memory, to include other voices. Or it can remain left out, from a disciplinary point of view because it´s tendentious, and from a collective memory point of view because it jeopardizes national unity. History thus has myriad ways towards the future.

Although, the idea of past determining present determining future is turned upside down by Haste and Hogan (2012). In their discussion of civic agency they maintain that one can be optimist or pessimist about the future, feeling agency or not, trusting institutions or not, and this can frame our narratives. Ideas about continuity or change connect future, present and past. Young people's stories about the future appear to relate to their motivation to civically engage and their identity as civic agents. "Human beings make sense of their present, and give meaning to the past in the way that they story the future" (p. 311). In Valsiner's terms we are still just talking here, whether future fantasies actually result in engagement is not certain. But here we might find a criterion for an educational agenda, other than the opposing objectives of history teaching that we are currently juggling with. History education is built on aiming at romantization or enlightenment of the past, on identification or on disciplinary criticism (Carretero, 2011; Carretero & Bermudez, 2012). Particularly when legitimizing our present practices with (biased) narratives about the past, we can hardly maintain to teach for the future. Shouldn´t we focus ahead of us instead?

The argument that we should educate for the future is often heard (Grever & Stuurman, 2008; Murakami, 2012). Not an easy task, when the future is hardly predictable. And, just as in turning to the past, there should be clarity about what future, and for whom? (Rosa, 2006, 2012). It seems that every time there's some major contemporary political or economical change school history curricula are adapted (Carretero, Rosa, & González, 2006; Foster, 2012). The teaching of history, unavoidably, happens every time from a different present. Thus education slugs behind contemporary developments. We cannot foresee new historical knowledge that might change historiographical content. We cannot foresee the society to which our students will have to be prepared. And can we really know what history, or even if history, matters for their future?

In the face of an uncertain future identities are constructed, that at the same time help to make sense of the past. Our identities are framed every time anew in the dynamics of collective memory, present experience and future interests. No one definition seems possible, complicating significantly research efforts and educational implications. If we learn one thing from this section, and even the whole book, it's that there are multiple perspectives on multiple subjects, and that there's a strong relation between what we look at, and how we look at it (see also Wertsch & Roediger, 2008). A cultural psychologist looks at an individual using tools available to him. A discursive psychologist looks at the discourse we engage in. A history educator looks at how conscious or literate of history we are. A civic educator looks at how well our agency as civilians is developed. The common denominator is collective memory as a dynamic process relating past, present and future in complex ways. Collective memories can be situated between (or behind) selves and others, between us and them, between recent and distant past, between what will be remembered and what will be forgotten. They are defined and redefined depending on what needs prevail. Making those explicit is not the easiest enterprise while one identity divides into many and many nations dissolve into one. Moreover, now that we live in a world faced with uncertainties, there´s a stronger revindication of the present through the past, making memory and history more vulnerable for conservatism and indoctrination. However, if education is in any way directed at future generations it should not be legitimizing the status quo but open up alternative possibilities. Whether it's trying to account for as many different identities as possible, or wanting to foster critical historical awareness. And ultimately the student will have to see for herself, so why not let her start investigating straight away?

It's an important task to clarify our multiplicity and this section gives us the necessary variety in directions for further exploration of how history, memory, identity and narrative are intertwined. Just as important is sharing the responsibility, and to consider what it really means to open up for future generations. Being otherwise also involves serious self-criticism. For social scientists and educators this means being critical of ourselves and our role in establishing semiotic settings. We should be weary of justifying our own discipline in the views that we propagate and concepts we continue to use, as this would mean participation in the very process so many of us are criticizing.

REFERENCES

Asensio, M., & Pol, E. (in preparation). *Una evaluación previa sobre el Museo de la Revolución en Nicaragua* [*A preliminary evaluation of the Museum of the Revolution in Nicaragua*]. León: Universidad Nacional Autónoma de Nicaragua.

Berger, S. (2012). De-nationalizing history teaching and nationalizing it differently! Some reflections on how to defuse the negative potential of national(ist) history teaching. In M. Carretero, M. Asensio, & M. Rodriguez-Moneo (Eds.), *History education and the construction of national identities* (pp. 33–47). Charlotte, NC: Information Age Publishing.

Bietti, L. M. (2010).The construction of the moral self in autobiographical memory: being an "ordinary" man within the experience of dictatorship in Argentina. In S. Salvatore, J. Valsiner, J. B. Travers Simon, A. Gennaro (Eds.), *YIS: Yearbook of idiographic science—Volume 3* (pp. 253–273). Rome: Firera & Liuzzo Publishing Group.

Bruner, J. (1990). *Acts of meaning.* Cambridge, MA: Harvard University Press.

Carretero, M. (2011). *Constructing patriotism. Teaching history and memories in global worlds.* Charlotte, NC: Information Age Publishing.

Carretero, M., & Bermudez, A. (2012). Constructing histories. In J. Valsiner (Ed.) *Oxford handbook of culture and psychology* (pp. 625–646). Oxford: Oxford University Press.

Carretero, M., Rosa, A., & González, M. F. (2006). Enseñar historia en tiempos de memoria [Teaching history in times of memory]. In M. Carretero, A. Rosa, & M. F. González (Eds.), *Enseñanza de la historia y memoria colectiva [History teaching and collective memory]* (pp. 13–38). Buenos Aires: Paidós.

Foster, S. (2012). Re-thinking history textbooks in a globalized world. In M. Carretero, M. Asensio, & M. Rodriguez-Moneo (Eds.), *History education and the construction of national identities* (pp. 49–62). Charlotte, NC: Information Age Publishing.

Grever, M. (2012). Dilemma's of common and plural history. Reflections on history education and heritage in a globalizing world. In M. Carretero, M. Asensio, & M. Rodriguez-Moneo (Eds.), *History education and the construction of national identities* (pp. 75–91). Charlotte, NC: Information Age Publishing.

Grever. M., & Stuurman, S. (Eds.) (2008). *Beyond the canon. History for the twenty-first century.* New York: Palgrave Macmillan.

Halbwachs, M. (1992). *On collective memory* (L. A. Loser, Ed.). Chicago: The University of Chicago Press.

Haste, H., & Hogan, A. (2012). The future shapes the present: Scenarios, metaphors and civic action. In M. Carretero, M. Asensio, & M. Rodriguez-Moneo (Eds.), *History education and the construction of national identities* (pp. 311–326). Charlotte, NC: Information Age Publishing.

Moller, S. (2012). Are family recollections an obstacle to history education? How German students make sense of the East German dictatorship. In M. Carretero, M. Asensio, & M. Rodriguez-Moneo (Eds.), *History education and the construction of national identities* (pp. 281–295). Charlotte, NC: Information Age Publishing.

Murakami, K. (2012). History as a dynamic process: Reanalyzing a case of Anglo-Japanese reconciliation. In M. Carretero, M. Asensio, & M. Rodriguez-Moneo (Eds.), *History education and the construction of national identities* (pp. 297–310). Charlotte, NC: Information Age Publishing.

Rosa, A. (2006). Recordar, describir y explicar el pasado, ¿Qué, cómo, y para el futuro de quién? [Remembering, describing and explaining the past: What, how and for the future of whom?] In M. Carretero, A. Rosa, & M. F. González (Eds.), *Enseñanza de la historia y memoria colectiva [History teaching and collective memory]* (pp. 41–51). Buenos Aires: Paidós.

Rosa, A. (2012). What history to teach? Whose history? In M. Carretero, M. Asensio, & M. Rodriguez-Moneo (Eds.), *History education and the construction of national identities* (pp. 63–72). Charlotte, NC: Information Age Publishing.

Seixas, P. (Ed.) (2004). *Theorizing historical consciousness*. Toronto: University of Toronto Press.

Seixas, P. (2012). Indigenous historical consciousness: An oxymoron or a dialogue? In M. Carretero, M. Asensio, & M. Rodriguez-Moneo (Eds.), *History education and the construction of national identities* (pp. 125–138). Charlotte, NC: Information Age Publishing.

Tutiaux-Guillon, N. (2012). A traditional frame for global history: The narrative of modernity in French secondary school. In M. Carretero, M. Asensio, & M. Rodriguez-Moneo (Eds.), *History education and the construction of national identities* (pp. 109–123). Charlotte, NC: Information Age Publishing.

Valsiner, J. (2012). Monuments in our minds: Historical symbols as cultural tools. In M. Carretero, M. Asensio, & M. Rodriguez-Moneo (Eds.), *History education and the construction of national identities* (pp. 327–345). Charlotte, NC: Information Age Publishing.

Wertsch, J. V. (2002). *Voices of collective remembering*. New York: Cambridge University Press.

Wertsch, J. V., & Roediger, H. L. (2008). Collective memory: Conceptual foundations and theoretical approaches, *Memory, 16*(3), 318–326.

Wineburg, S. (2001). *Historical thinking and other unnatural acts*. Philadelphia: Temple University Press.

Wineburg, S., Mosborg, S., Porat, D., & Duncan, A. (2007). Common belief and the cultural curriculum: An intergenerational study of historical consciousness. *American Education Research Journal, 44*, 40–76.

CPSIA information can be obtained at www.ICGtesting.com
Printed in the USA
LVOW071328021212

309698LV00001B/26/P